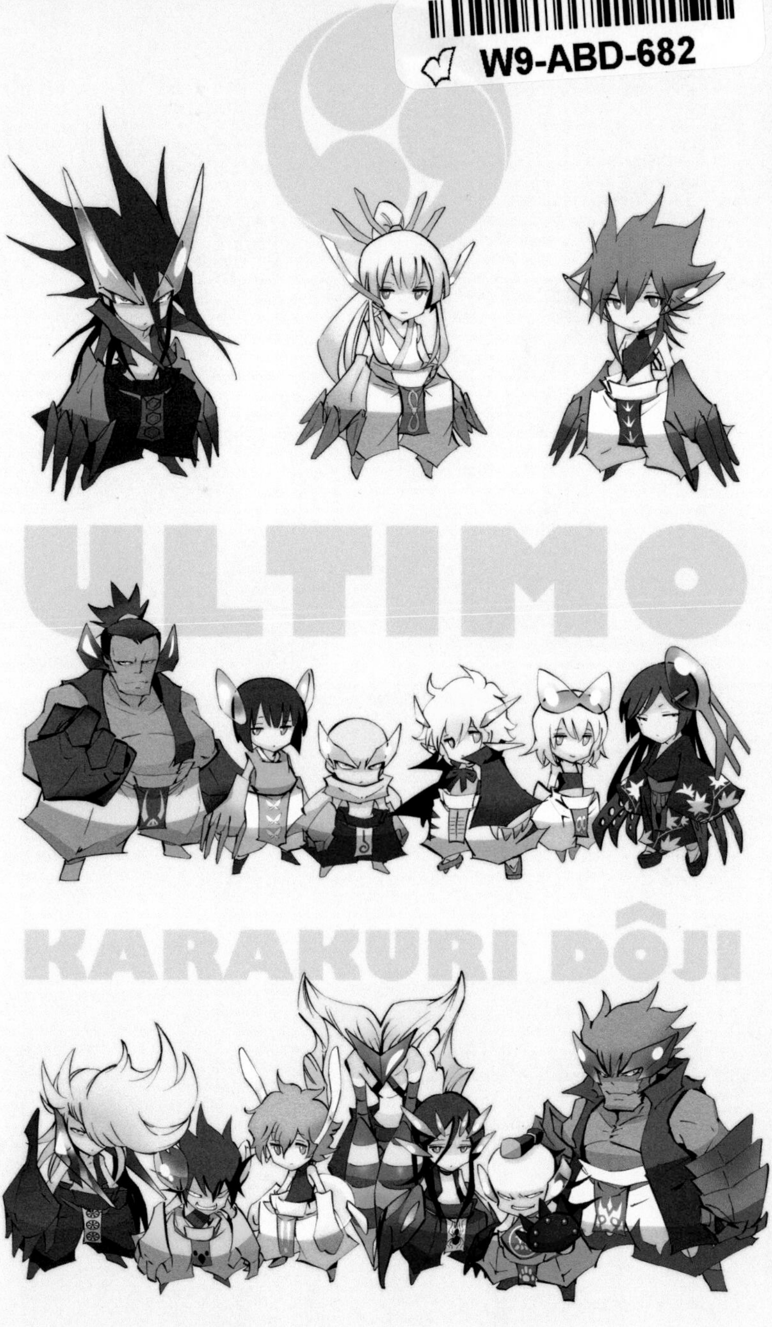
ULTIMO
KARAKURI DÔJI

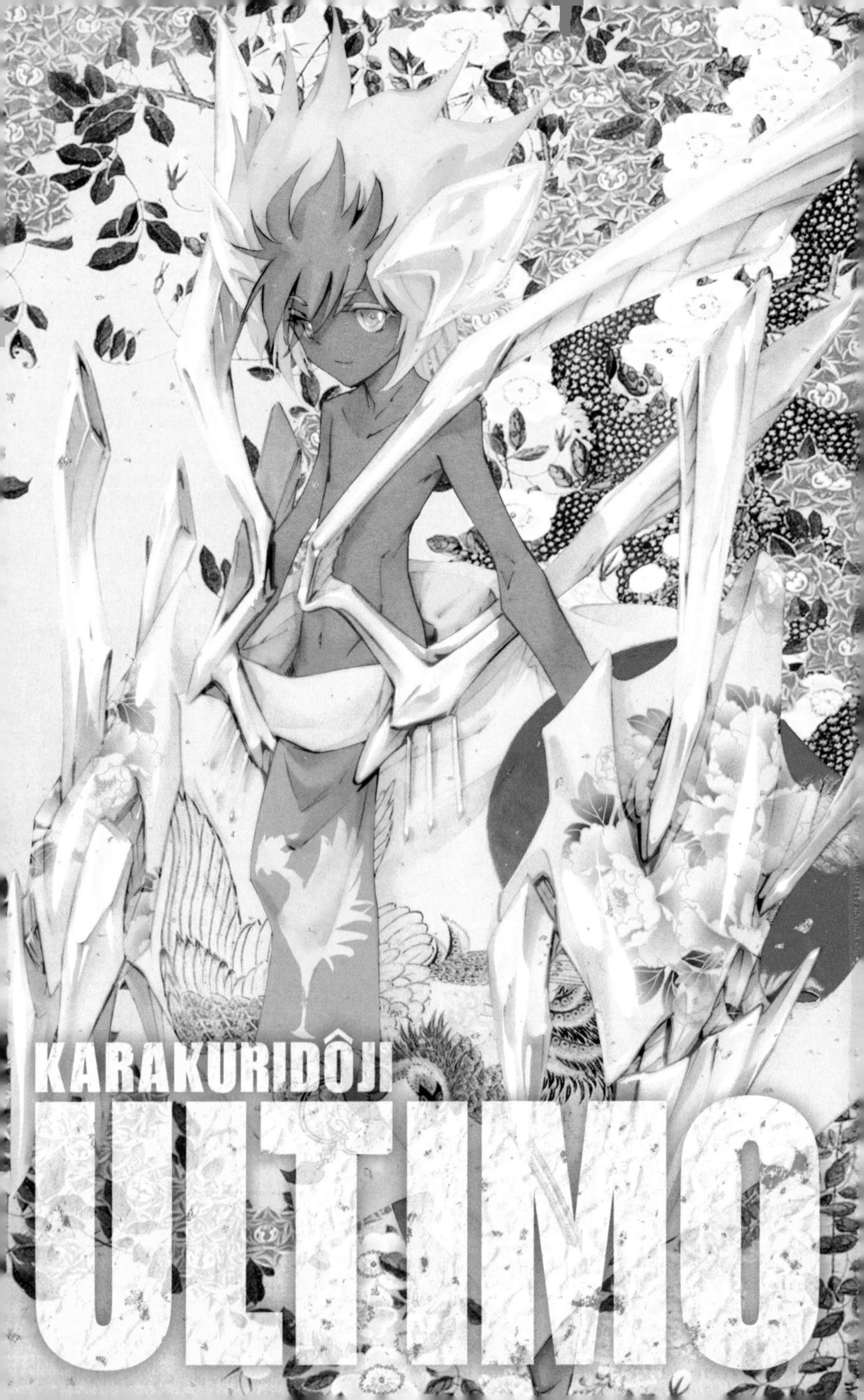
KARAKURIDÔJI
ULTIMO

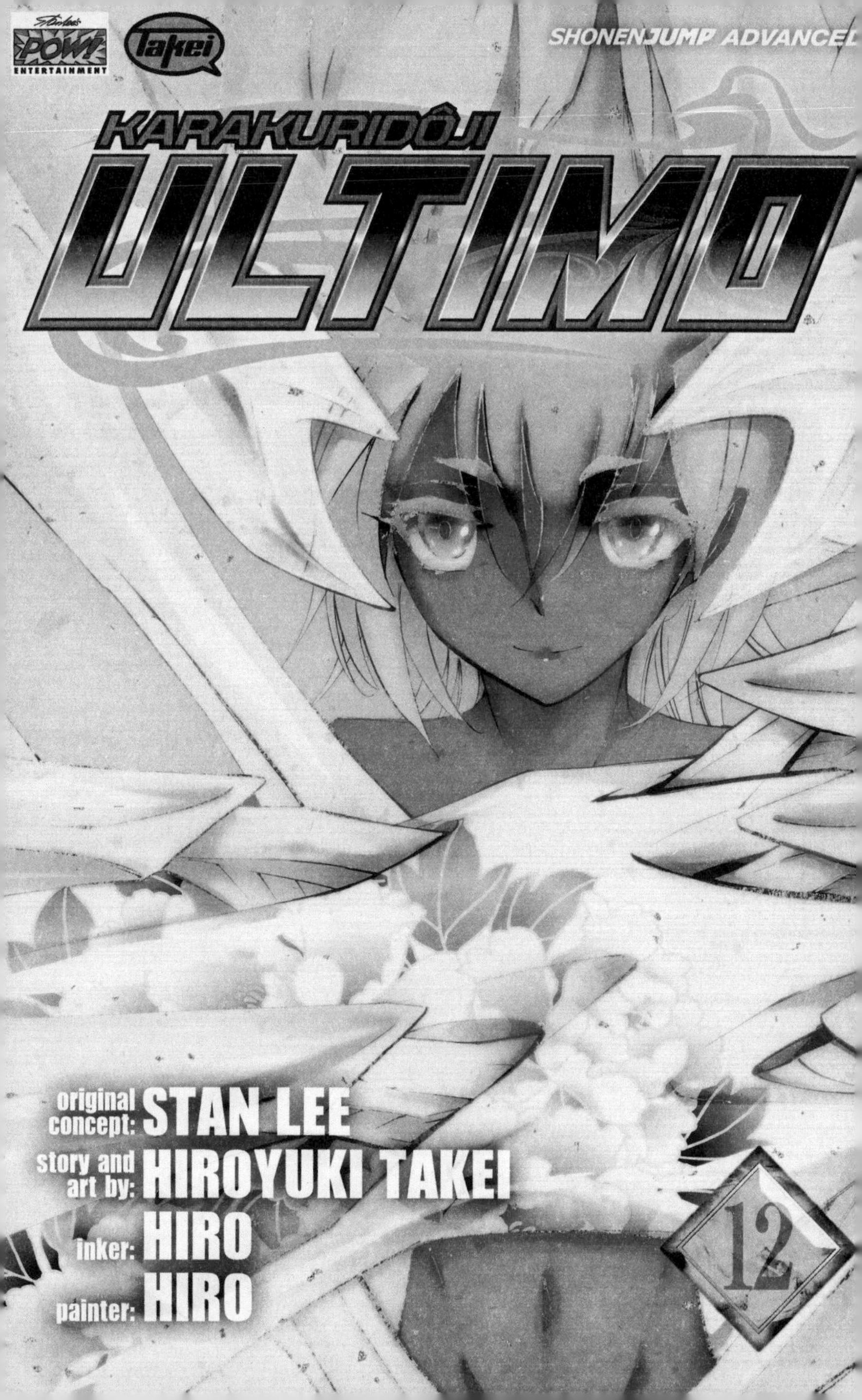
Stan Lee's POW! ENTERTAINMENT
Takei
SHONENJUMP ADVANCED
KARAKURIDÔJI
ULTIMO
original concept: STAN LEE
story and art by: HIROYUKI TAKEI
inker: HIRO
painter: HIRO
12

Karakuri Dôji Ultimo

Characters

Ultimo

Agari Yamato

Vice

K

The Story Thus Far

Kyoto in the 12th Century. A bandit named Yamato encounters a mysterious man named Dunstan and two Karakuri Dôji who embody ultimate good and evil.

West Tokyo in the 21st Century. Yamato is reborn and reencounters the good dôji Ultimo, leading to the Hundred Machine Funeral—the ultimate battle between good and evil that Dunstan has been plotting. At last, the true Hundred Machine Funeral begins. In place of fallen comrades, Sayama and the other three girls join the fight. Having learned of Sayama's true identity in the past, Yamato confronts Rune in an effort to bind together both good and evil. And now...the final battle!!!

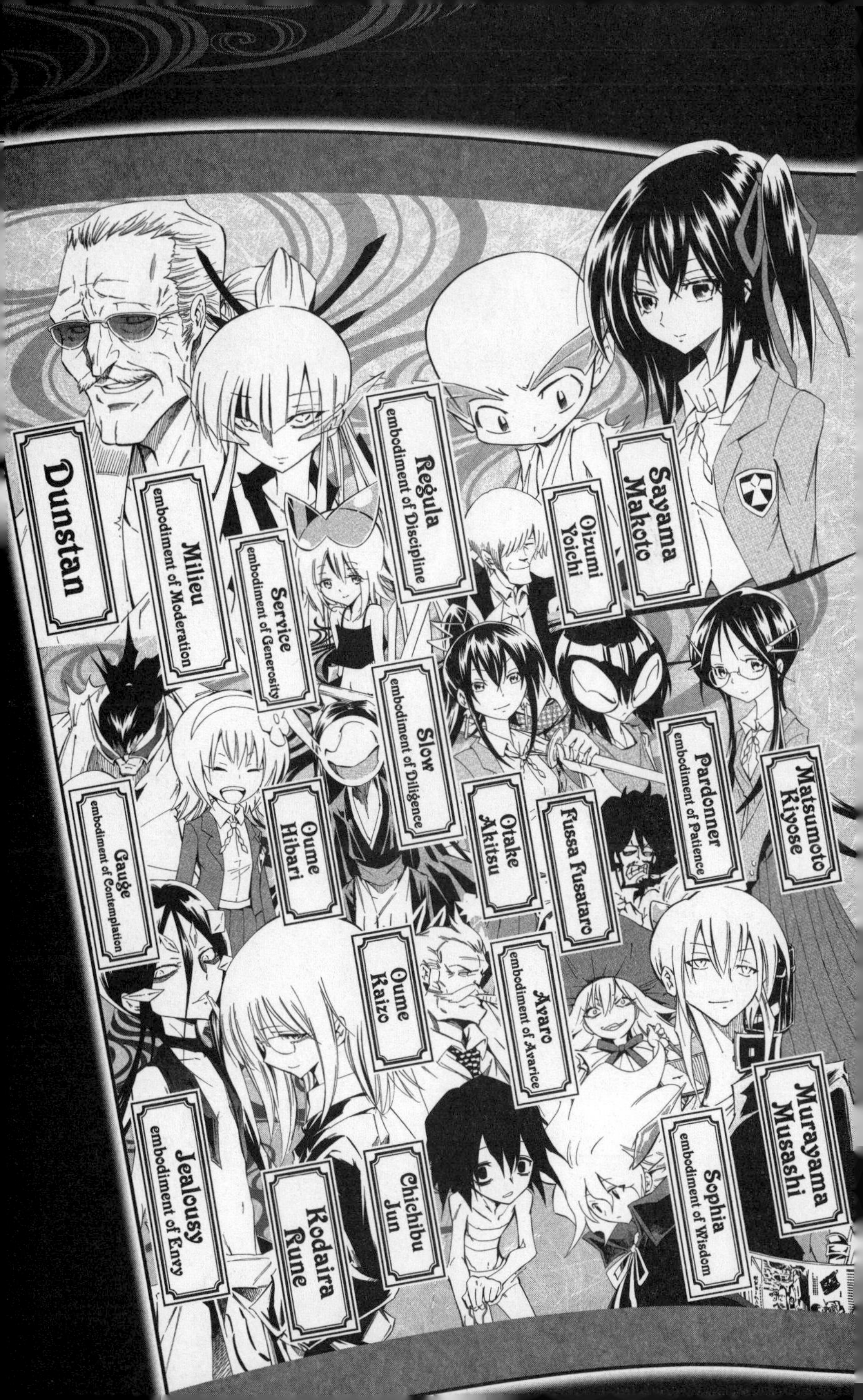
Sayama Makoto
Oizumi Yoichi
Regula embodiment of Discipline
Service embodiment of Generosity
Milieu embodiment of Moderation
Dunstan
Matsumoto Kiyose
Pardonner embodiment of Patience
Fussa Fusataro
Otake Akitsu
Slow embodiment of Diligence
Oume Hibari
Gauge embodiment of Contemplation
Avaro embodiment of Avarice
Oume Raizo
Murayama Musashi
Sophia embodiment of Wisdom
Chichibu Jun
Kodaira Rune
Jealousy embodiment of Envy

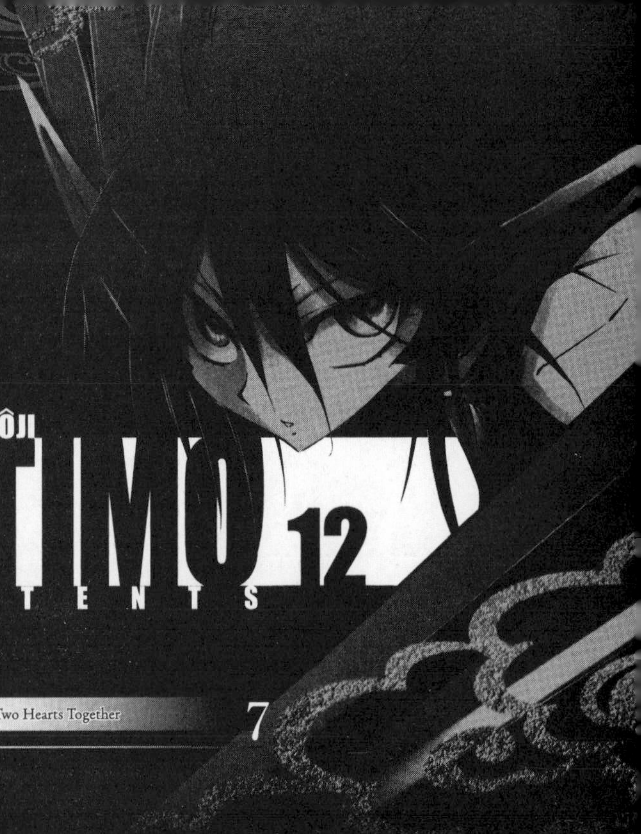

KARAKURIDÔJI

ULTIMO 12

CONTENTS

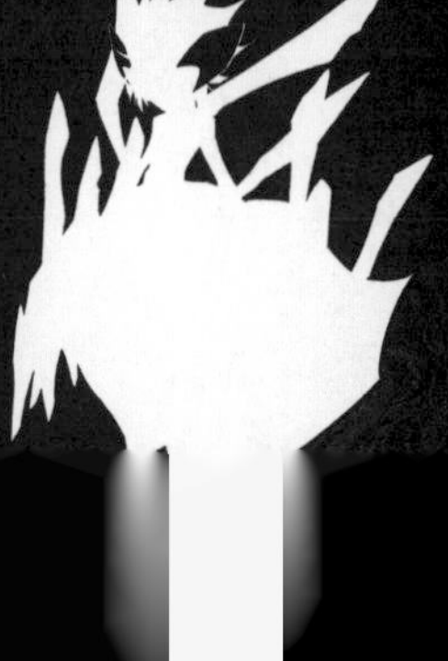

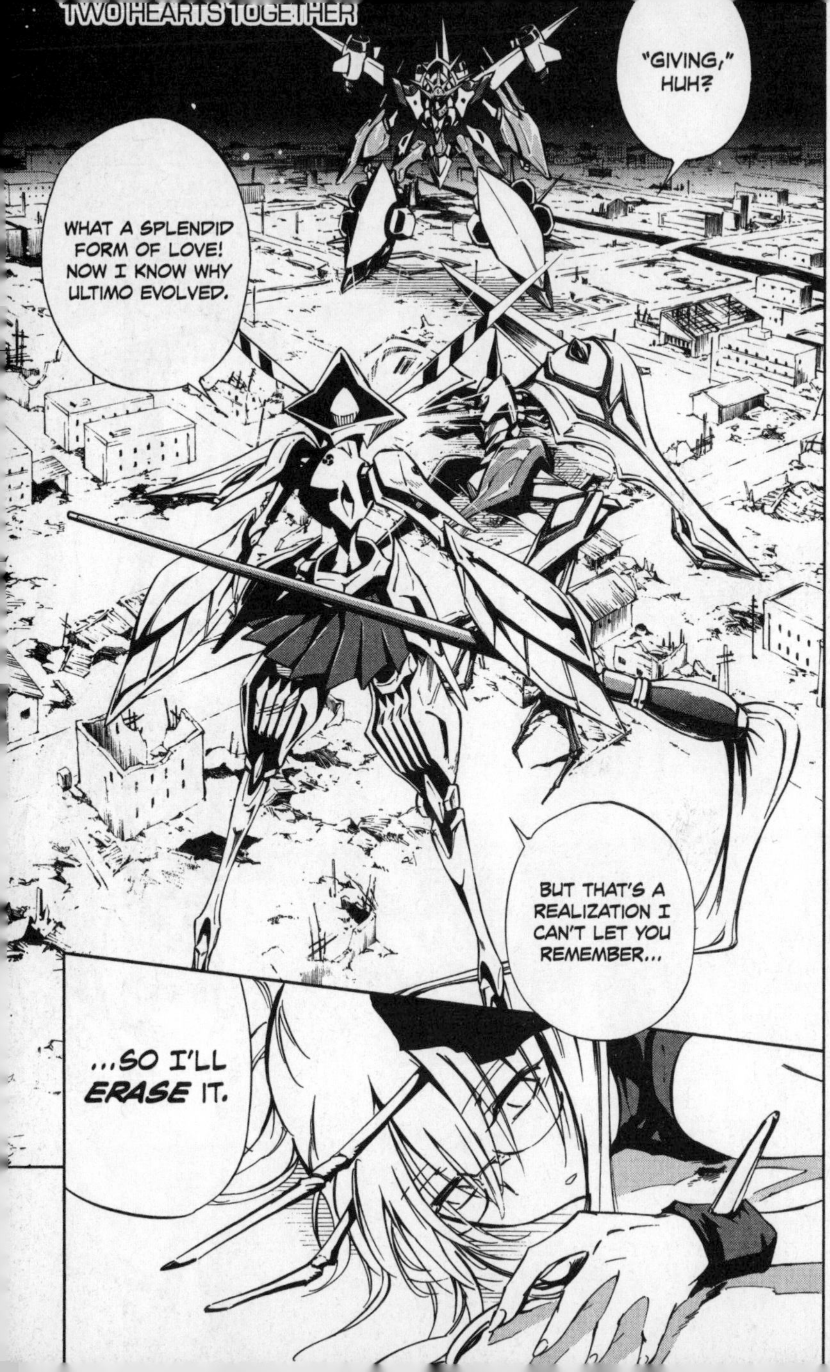
"GIVING," HUH?
WHAT A SPLENDID FORM OF LOVE! NOW I KNOW WHY ULTIMO EVOLVED.
BUT THAT'S A REALIZATION I CAN'T LET YOU REMEMBER...
...SO I'LL *ERASE* IT.

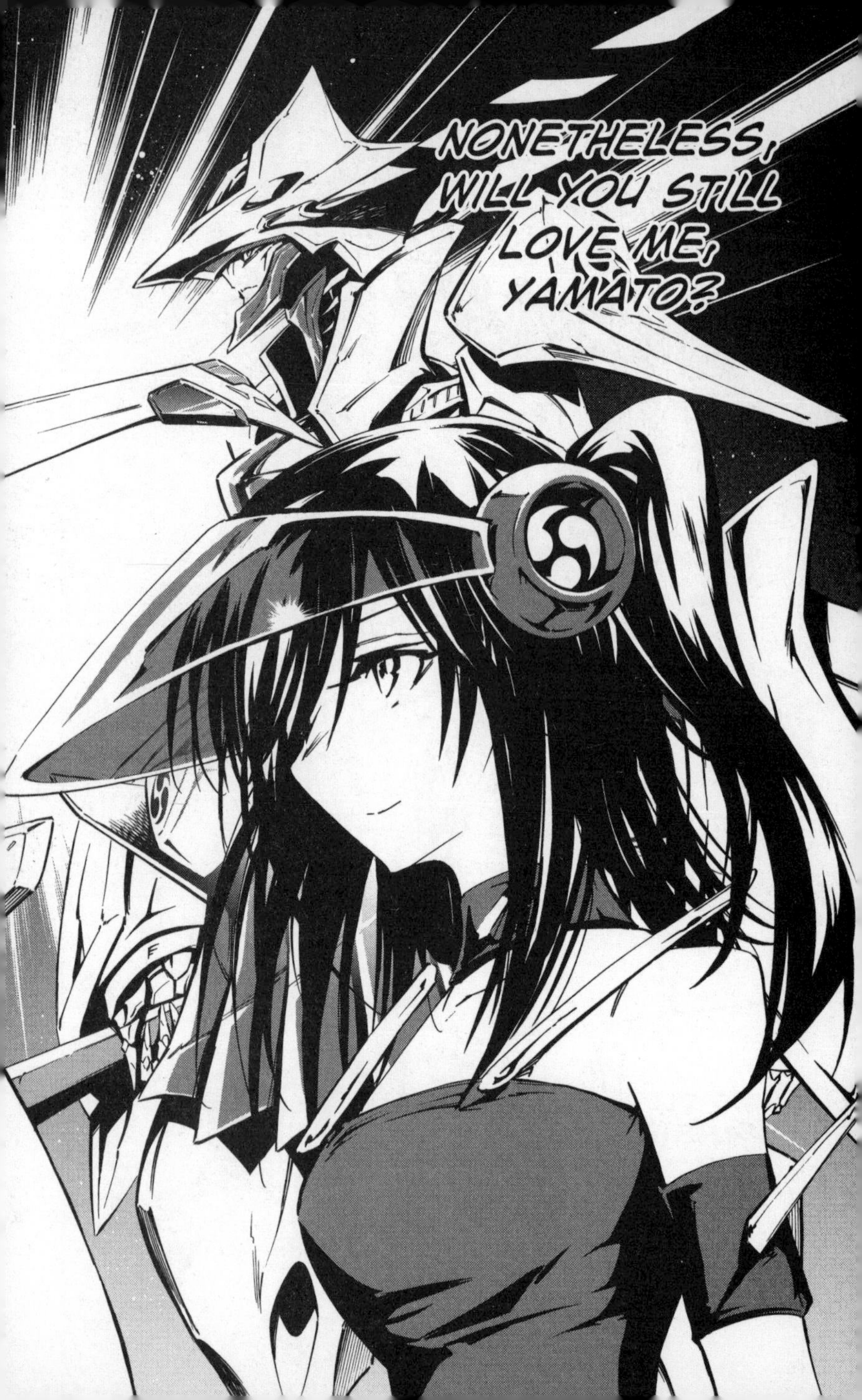
NONETHELESS, WILL YOU STILL LOVE ME, YAMATO?

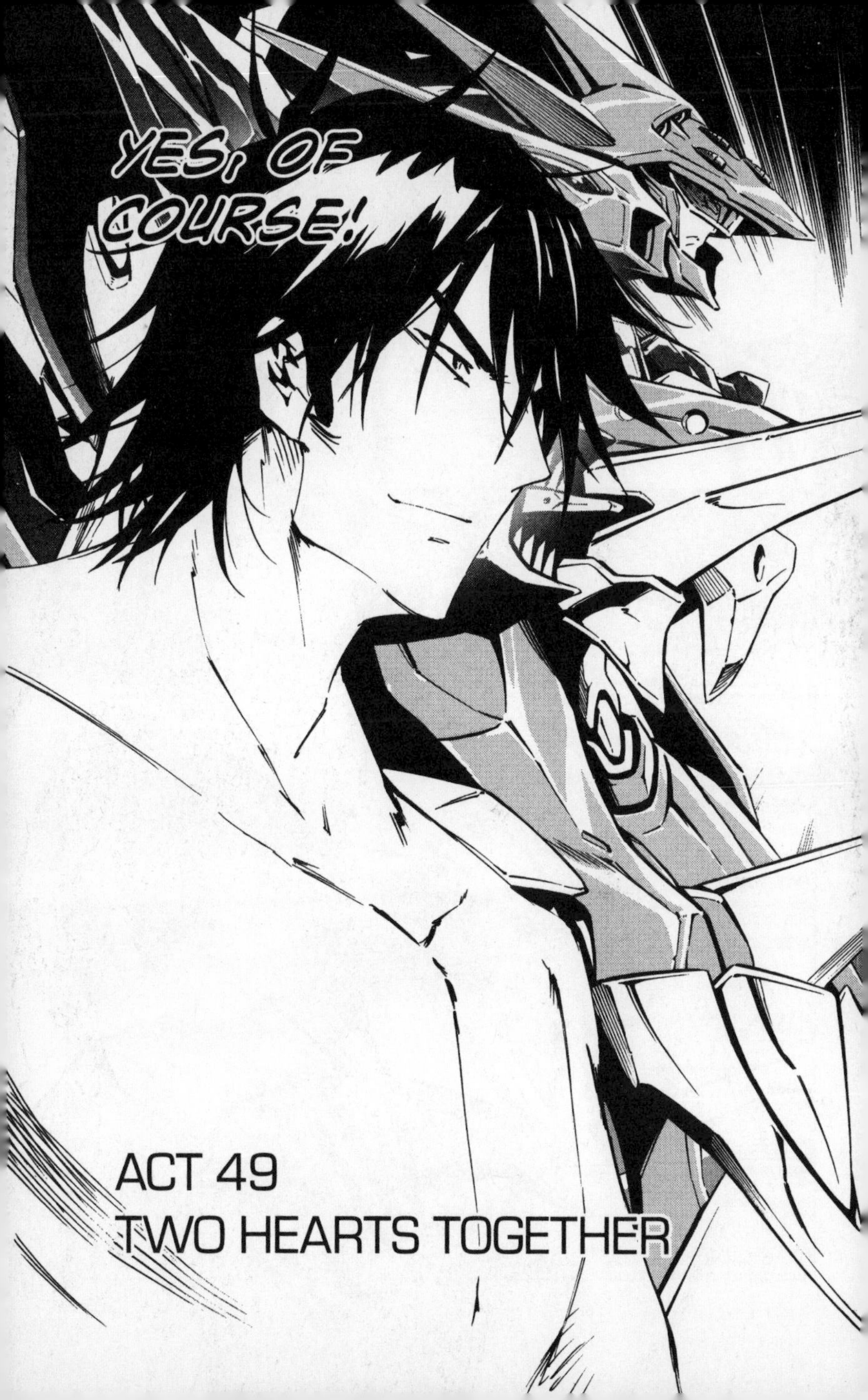
YES, OF COURSE!
ACT 49
TWO HEARTS TOGETHER

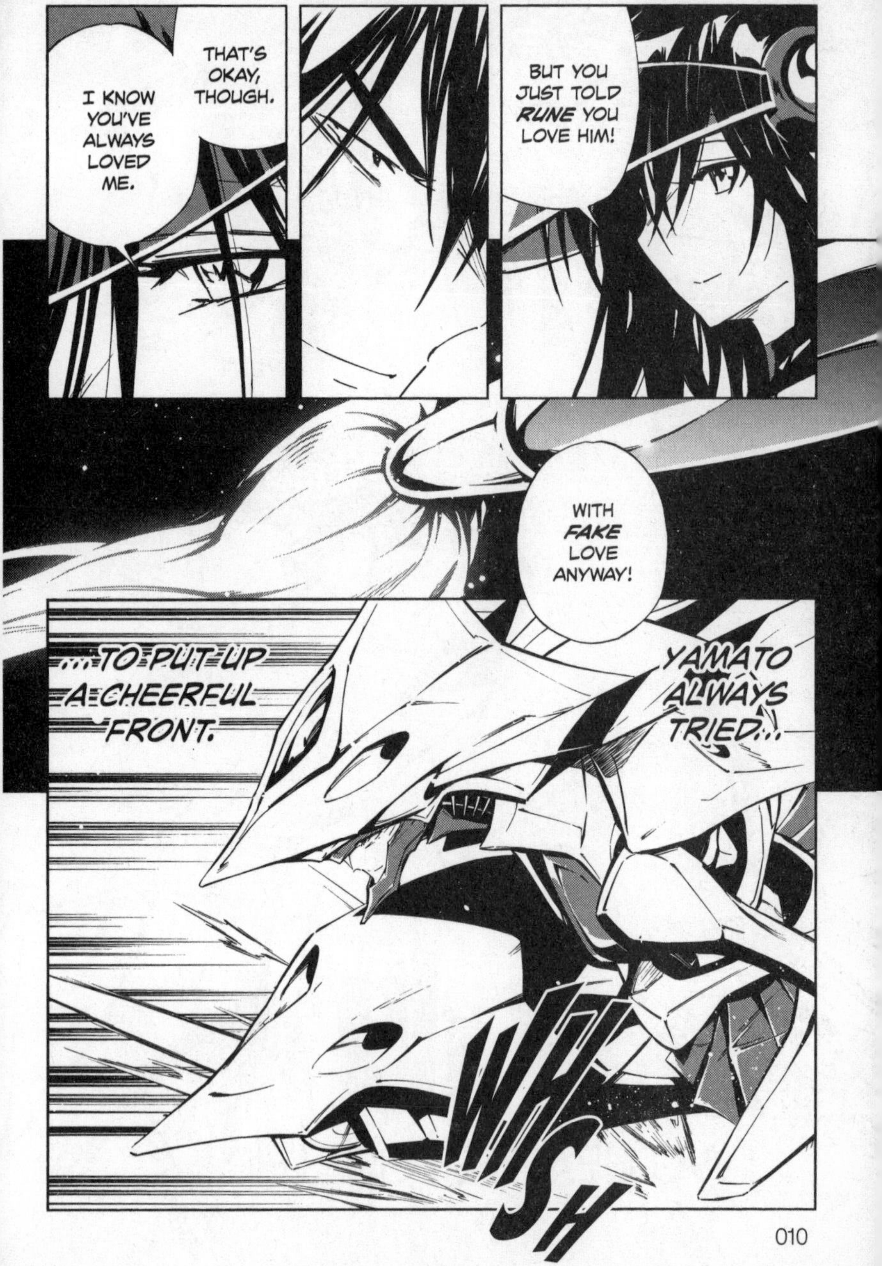
BUT YOU JUST TOLD *RUNE* YOU LOVE HIM!
THAT'S OKAY, THOUGH.
I KNOW YOU'VE ALWAYS LOVED ME.
WITH *FAKE* LOVE ANYWAY!
YAMATO ALWAYS TRIED...
...TO PUT UP A CHEERFUL FRONT.

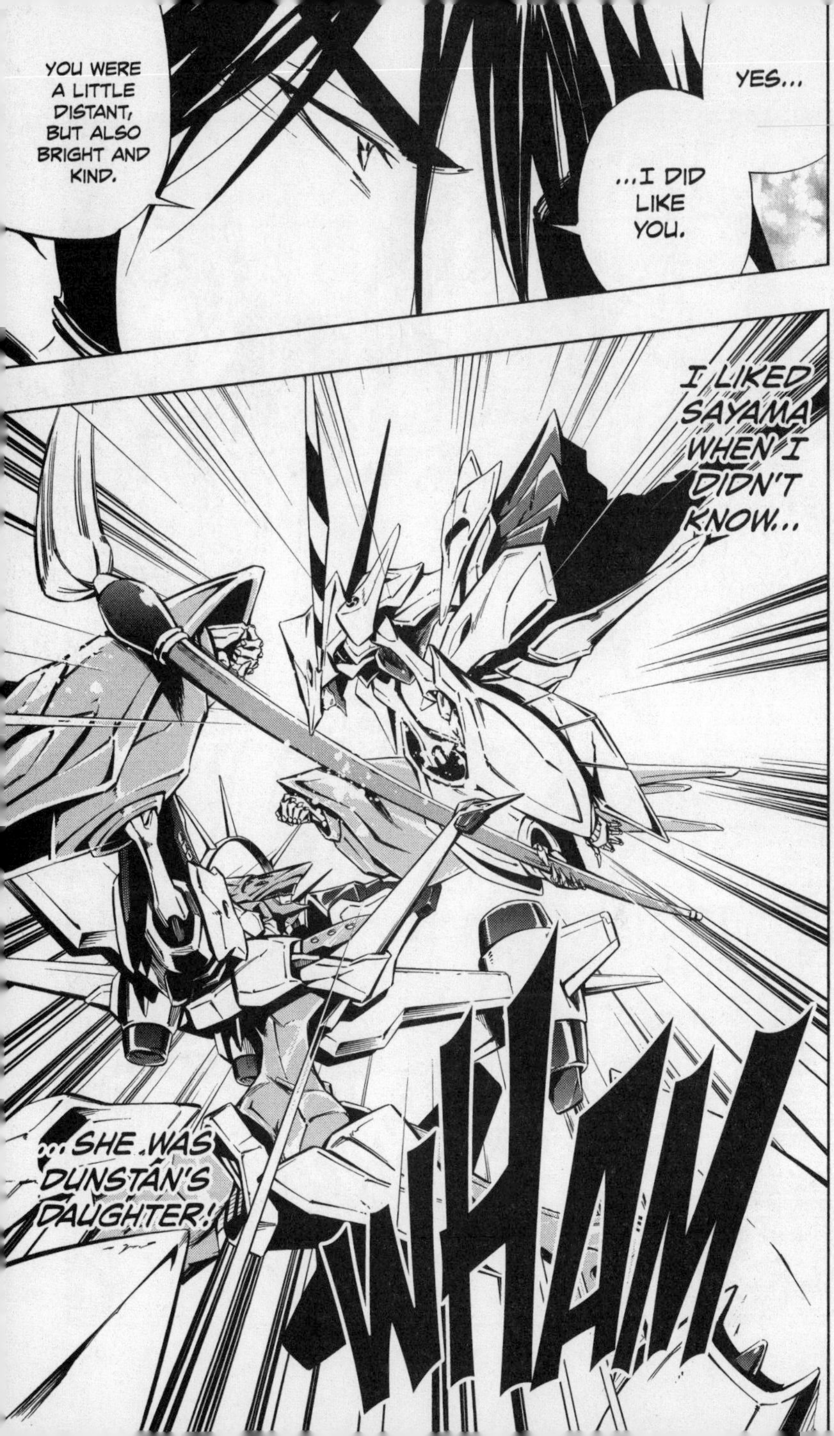
YES...
...I DID LIKE YOU.
YOU WERE A LITTLE DISTANT, BUT ALSO BRIGHT AND KIND.
I LIKED SAYAMA WHEN I DIDN'T KNOW...
...SHE WAS DUNSTAN'S DAUGHTER!
WHAM

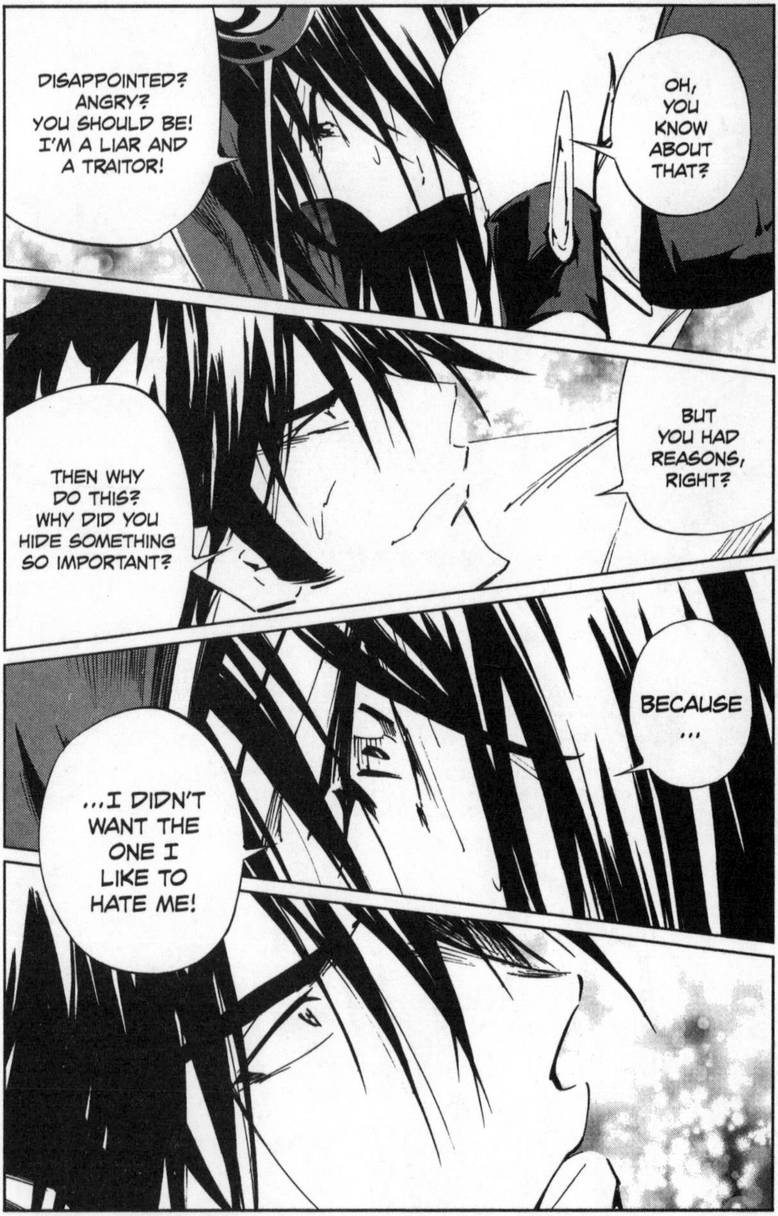
OH, YOU KNOW ABOUT THAT?
DISAPPOINTED? ANGRY? YOU SHOULD BE! I'M A LIAR AND A TRAITOR!
BUT YOU HAD REASONS, RIGHT?
THEN WHY DO THIS? WHY DID YOU HIDE SOMETHING SO IMPORTANT?
BECAUSE ...
...I DIDN'T WANT THE ONE I LIKE TO HATE ME!

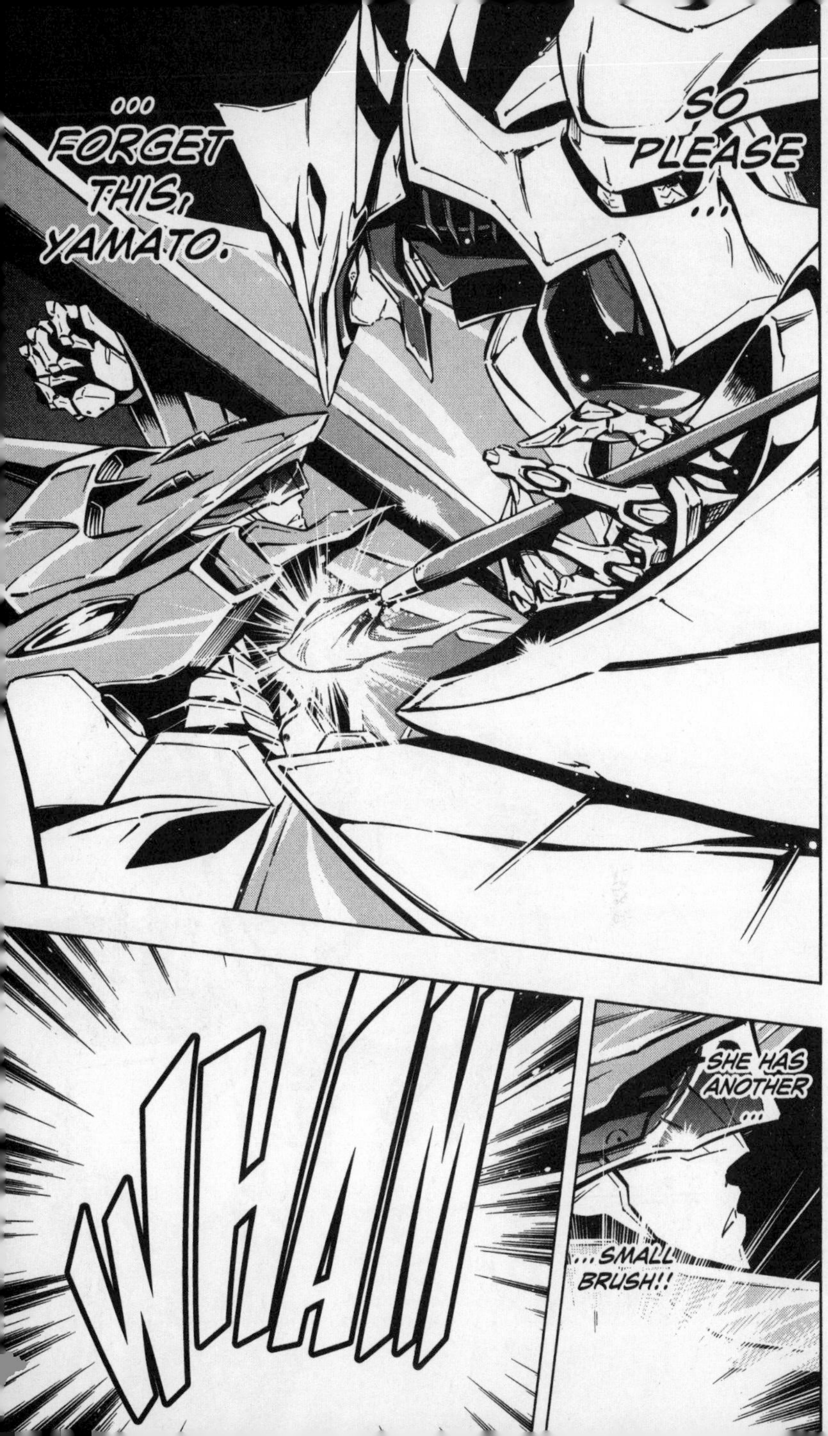
SO PLEASE ...
... FORGET THIS, YAMATO.
SHE HAS ANOTHER ...
...SMALL BRUSH!!
WHAM

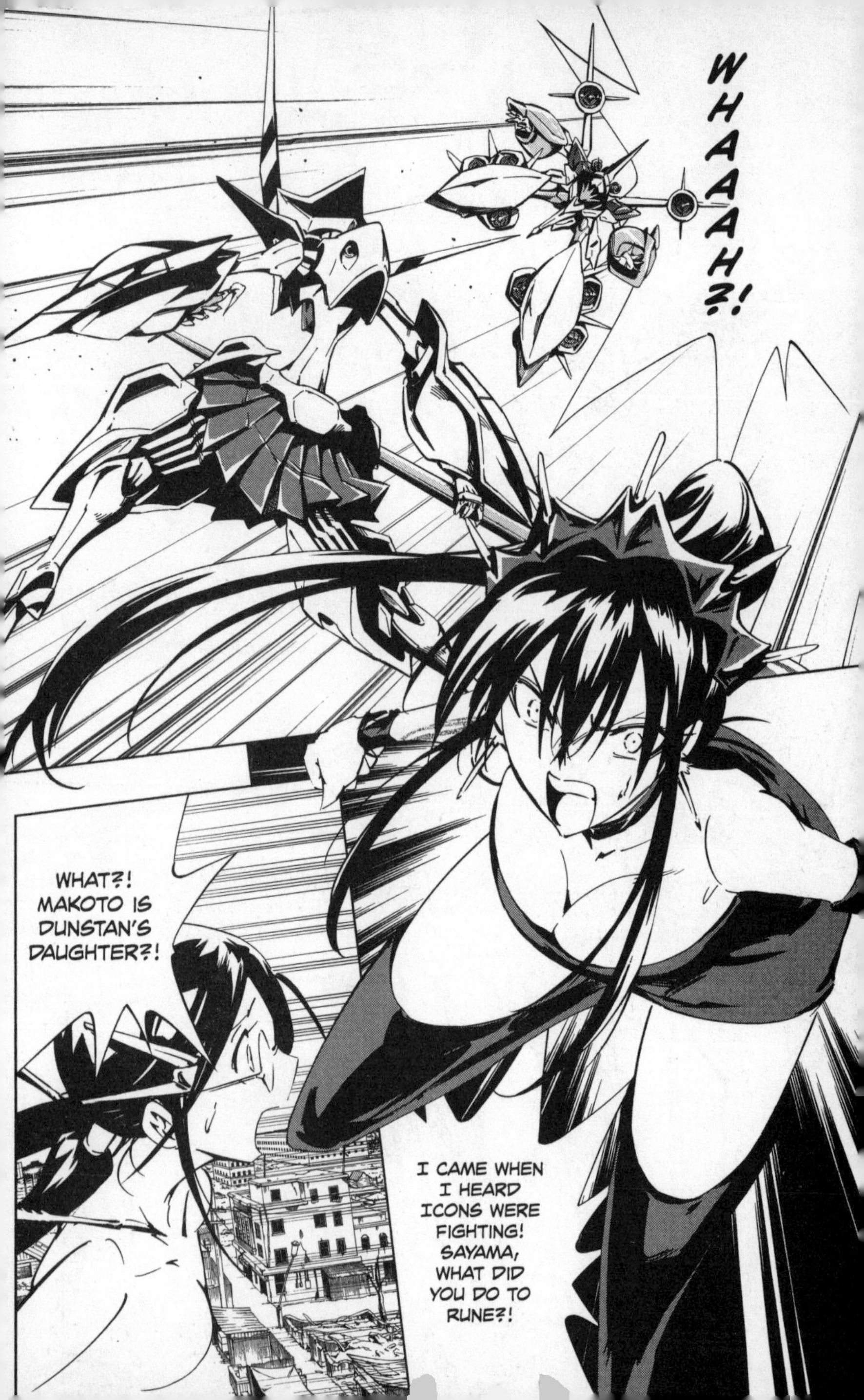
WHAAAAH?!
I CAME WHEN I HEARD ICONS WERE FIGHTING! SAYAMA, WHAT DID YOU DO TO RUNE?!
WHAT?! MAKOTO IS DUNSTAN'S DAUGHTER?!

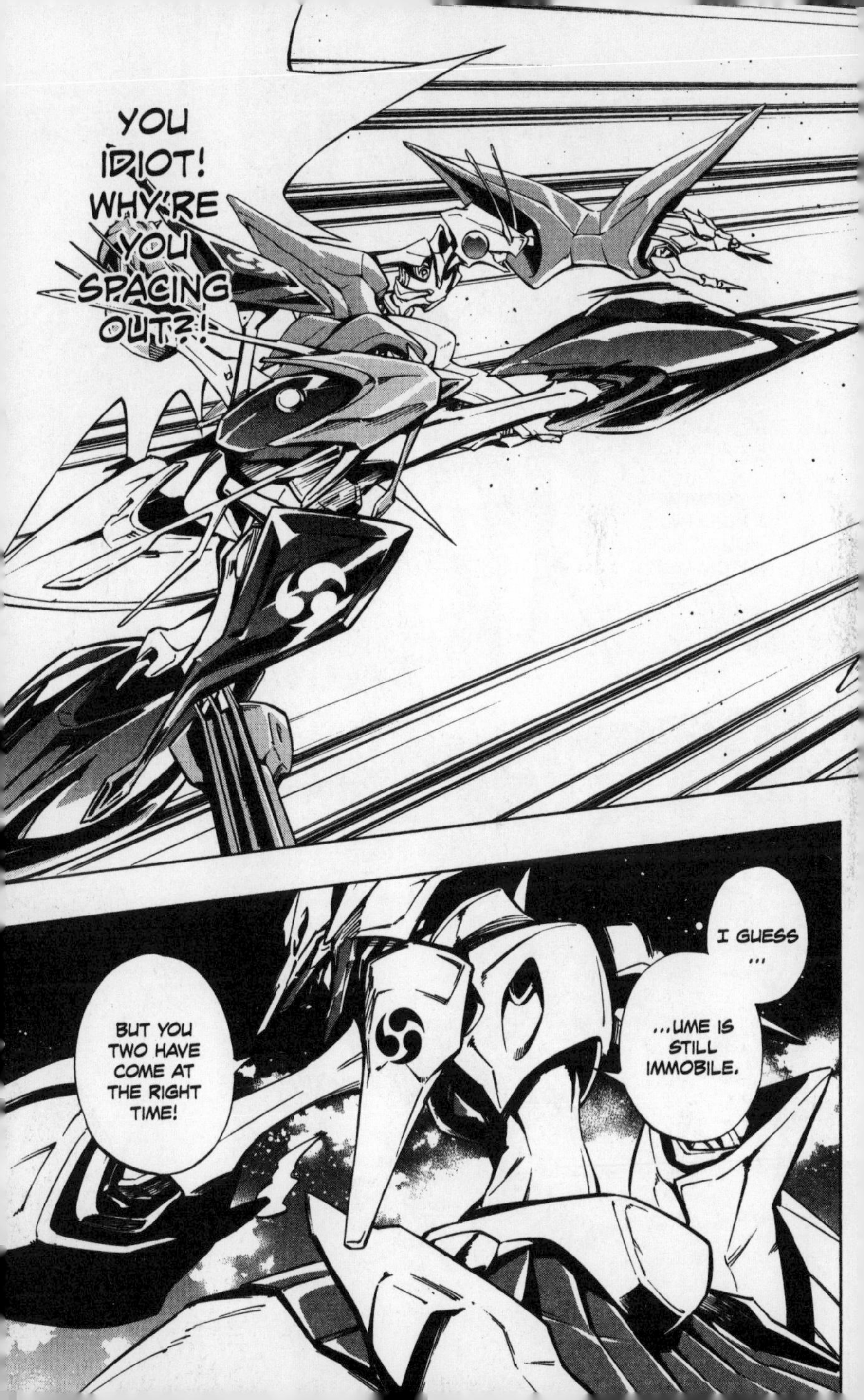
YOU IDIOT! WHY'RE YOU SPACING OUT?!
I GUESS ...
...UME IS STILL IMMOBILE.
BUT YOU TWO HAVE COME AT THE RIGHT TIME!

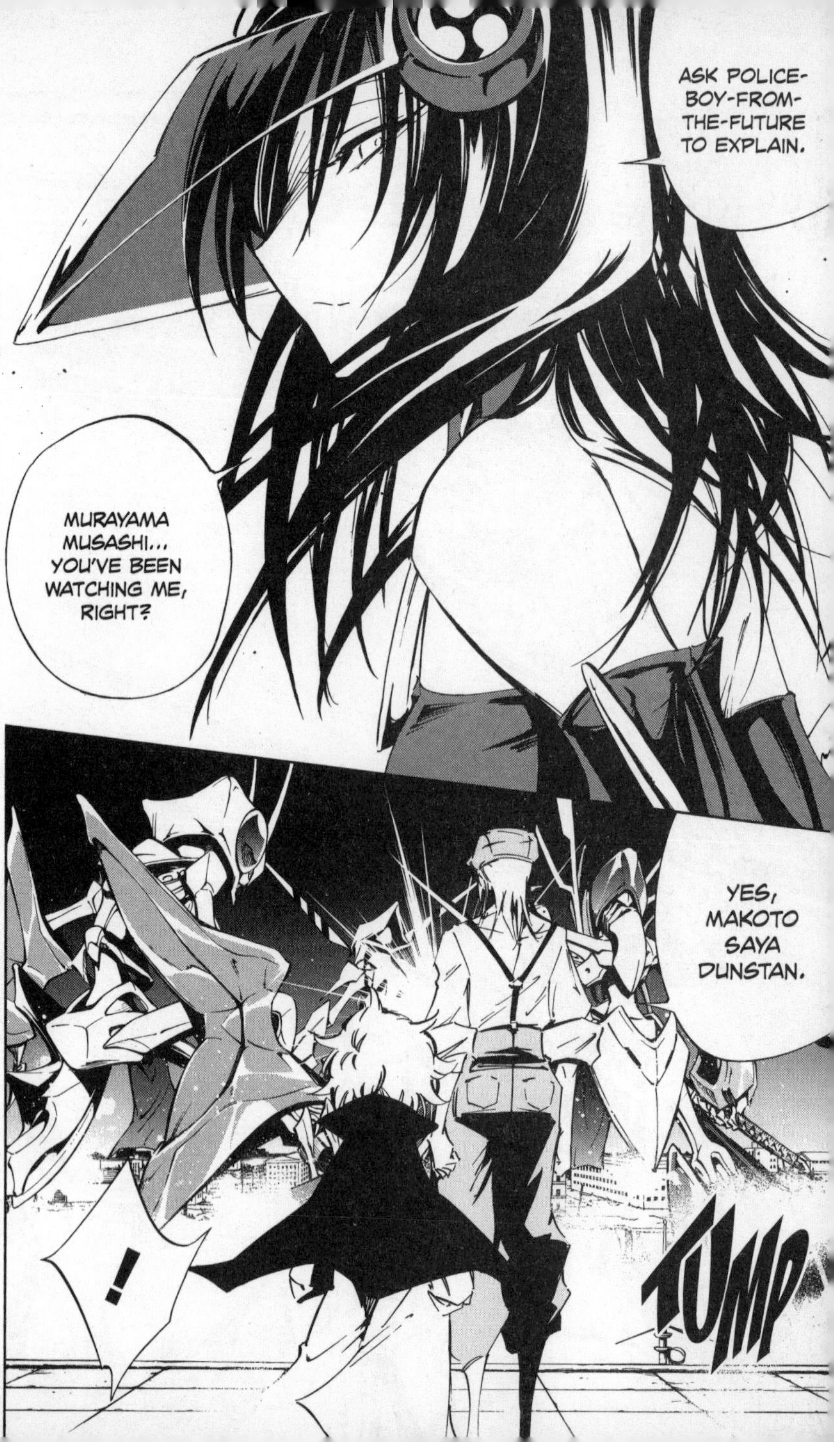
ASK POLICE-BOY-FROM-THE-FUTURE TO EXPLAIN.
MURAYAMA MUSASHI... YOU'VE BEEN WATCHING ME, RIGHT?
YES, MAKOTO SAYA DUNSTAN.
TUMP
!

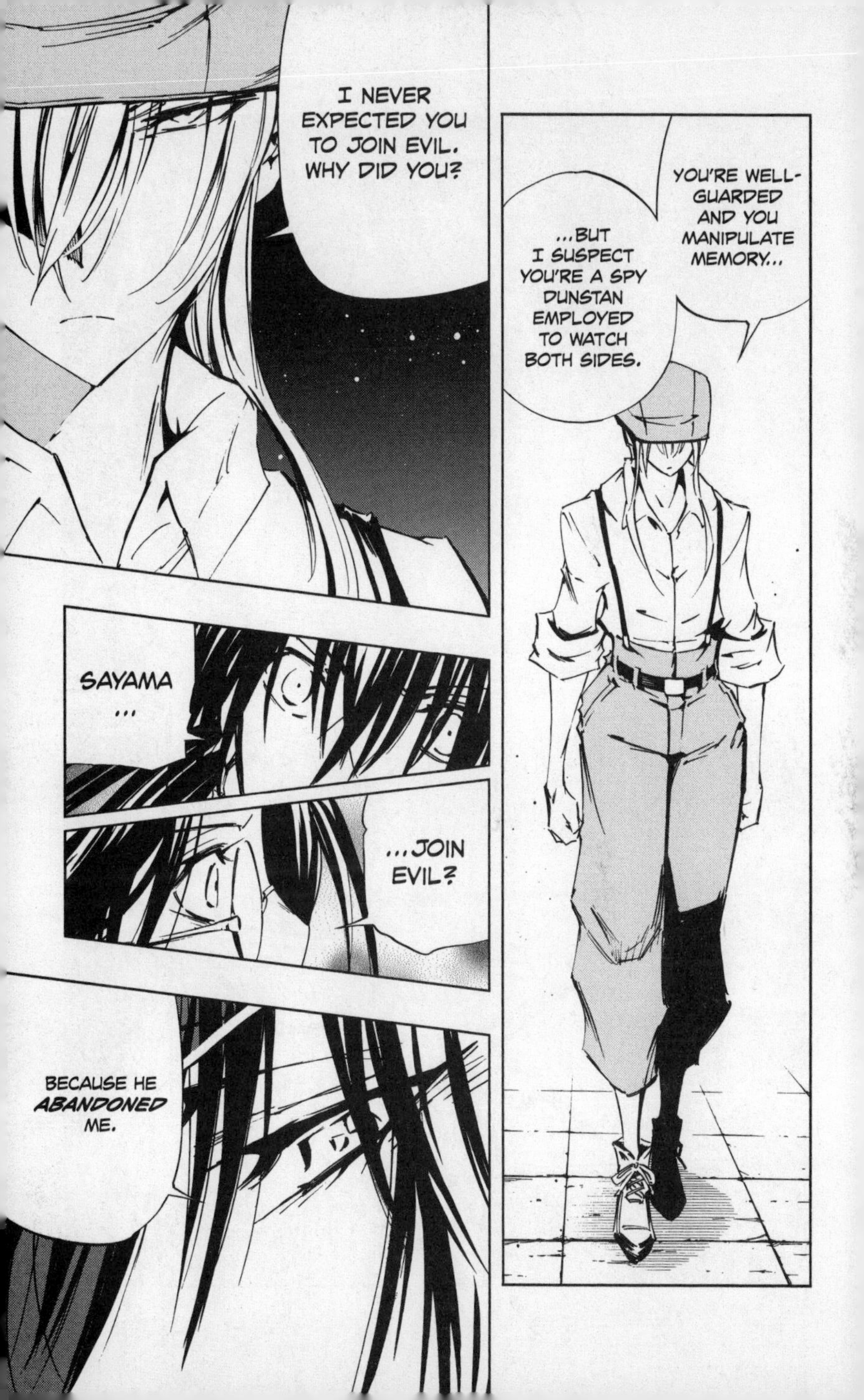
YOU'RE WELL-GUARDED AND YOU MANIPULATE MEMORY...
...BUT I SUSPECT YOU'RE A SPY DUNSTAN EMPLOYED TO WATCH BOTH SIDES.
I NEVER EXPECTED YOU TO JOIN EVIL. WHY DID YOU?
SAYAMA ...
...JOIN EVIL?
BECAUSE HE *ABANDONED* ME.

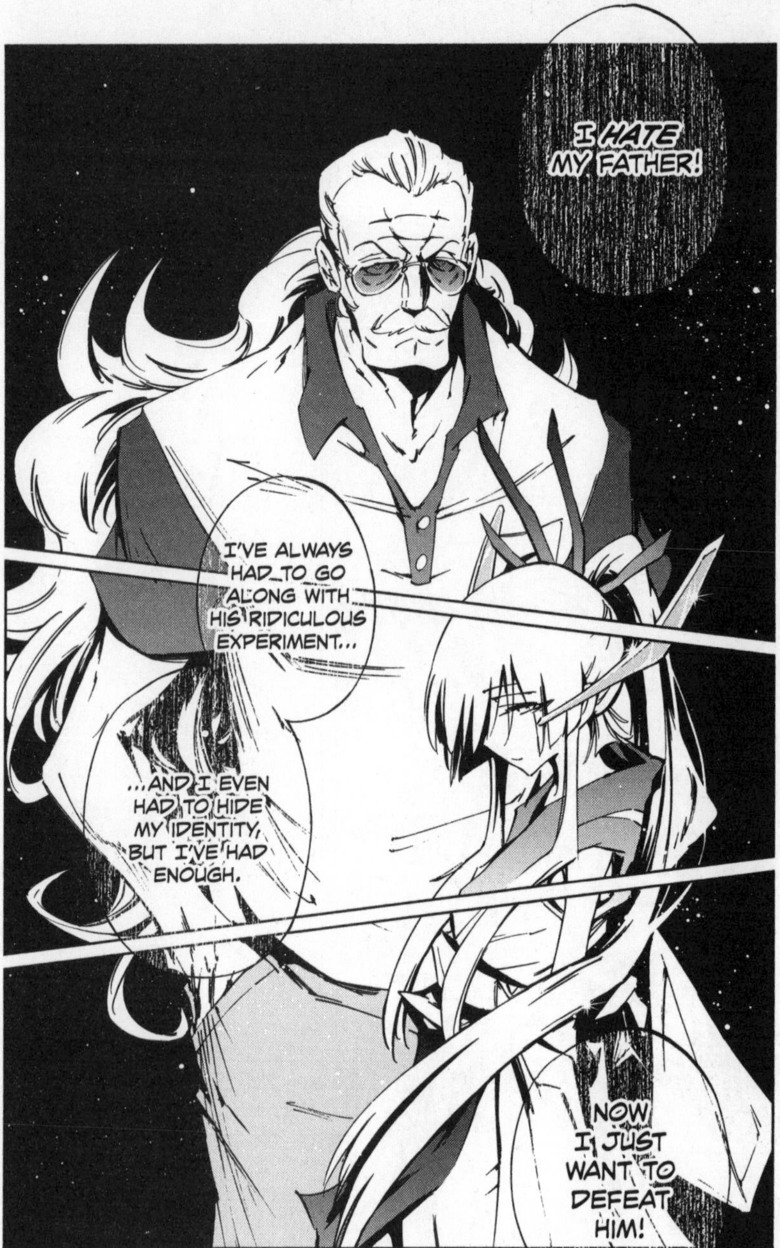
I HATE MY FATHER!
I'VE ALWAYS HAD TO GO ALONG WITH HIS RIDICULOUS EXPERIMENT...
...AND I EVEN HAD TO HIDE MY IDENTITY, BUT I'VE HAD ENOUGH.
NOW I JUST WANT TO DEFEAT HIM!

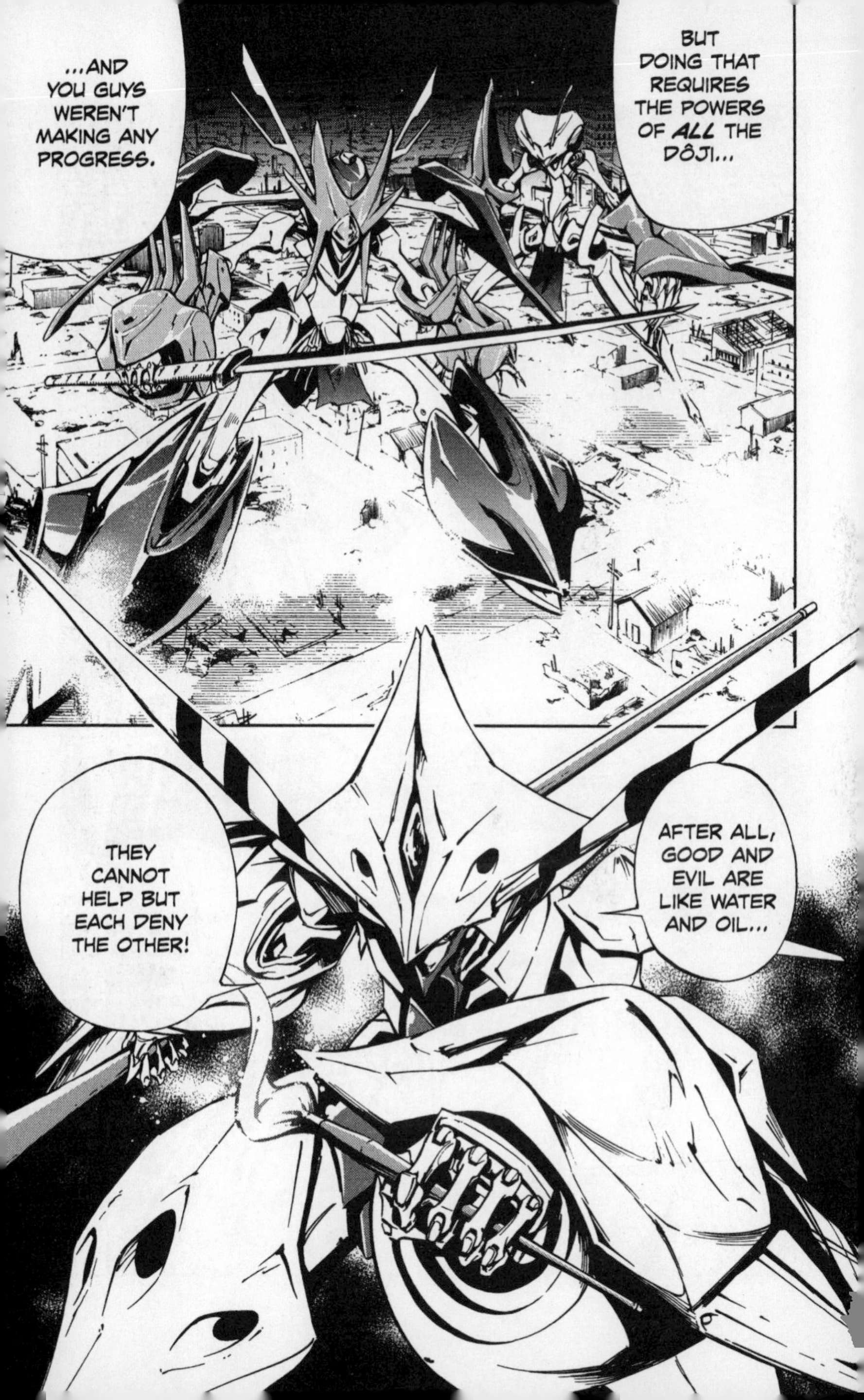
BUT DOING THAT REQUIRES THE POWERS OF ALL THE DÔJI...
...AND YOU GUYS WEREN'T MAKING ANY PROGRESS.
AFTER ALL, GOOD AND EVIL ARE LIKE WATER AND OIL...
THEY CANNOT HELP BUT EACH DENY THE OTHER!

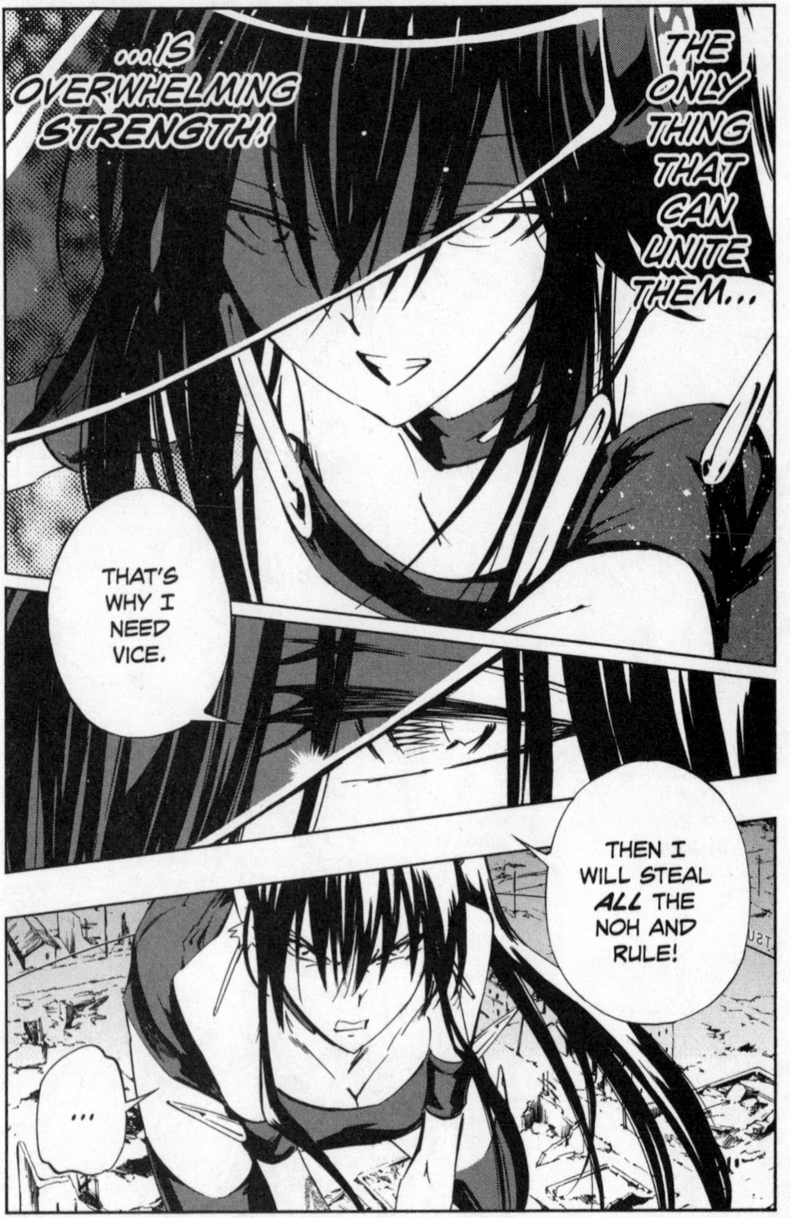
THE ONLY THING THAT CAN UNITE THEM...
...IS OVERWHELMING STRENGTH!
THAT'S WHY I NEED VICE.
THEN I WILL STEAL ALL THE NOH AND RULE!
...

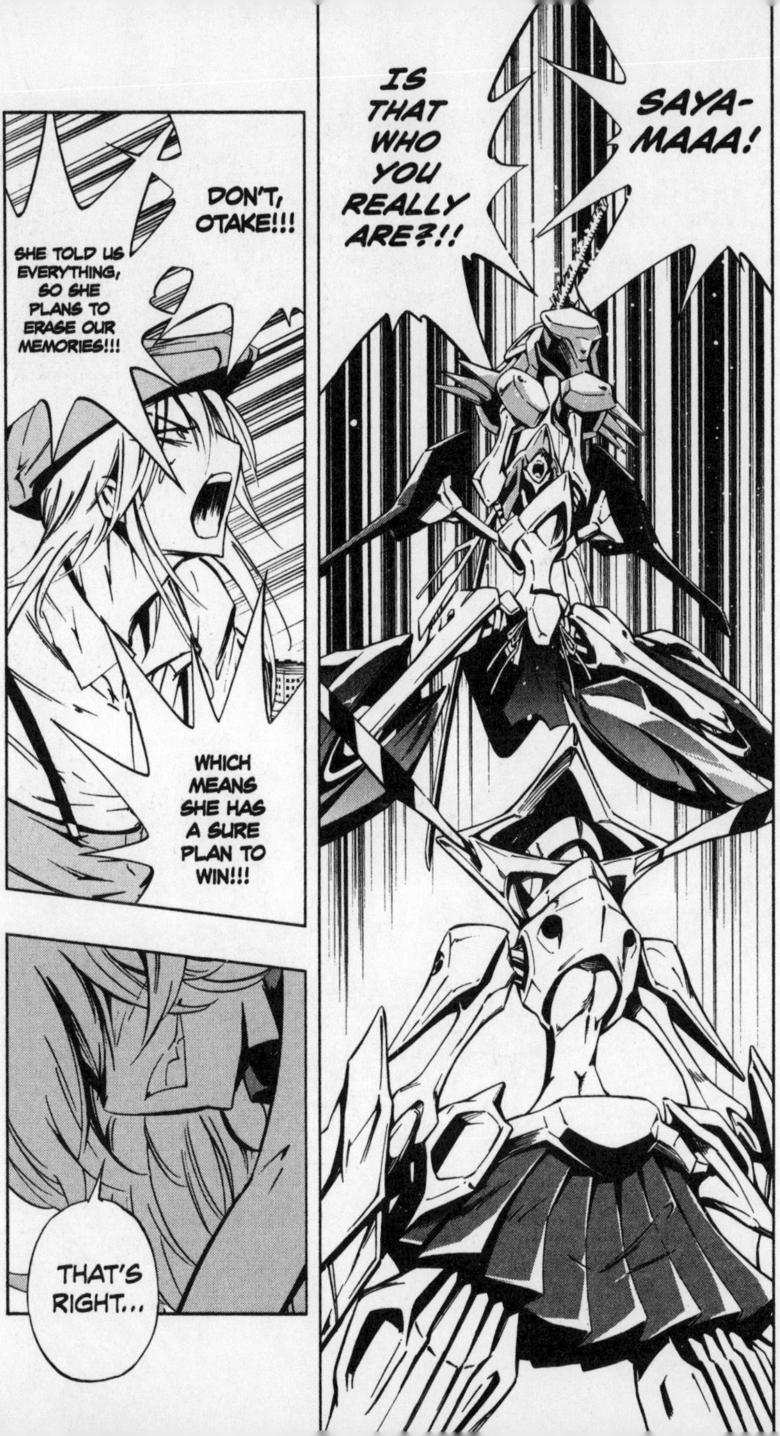
SAYA-MAAA!
IS THAT WHO YOU REALLY ARE?!!
DON'T, OTAKE!!!
SHE TOLD US EVERYTHING, SO SHE PLANS TO ERASE OUR MEMORIES!!!
WHICH MEANS SHE HAS A SURE PLAN TO WIN!!!
THAT'S RIGHT...

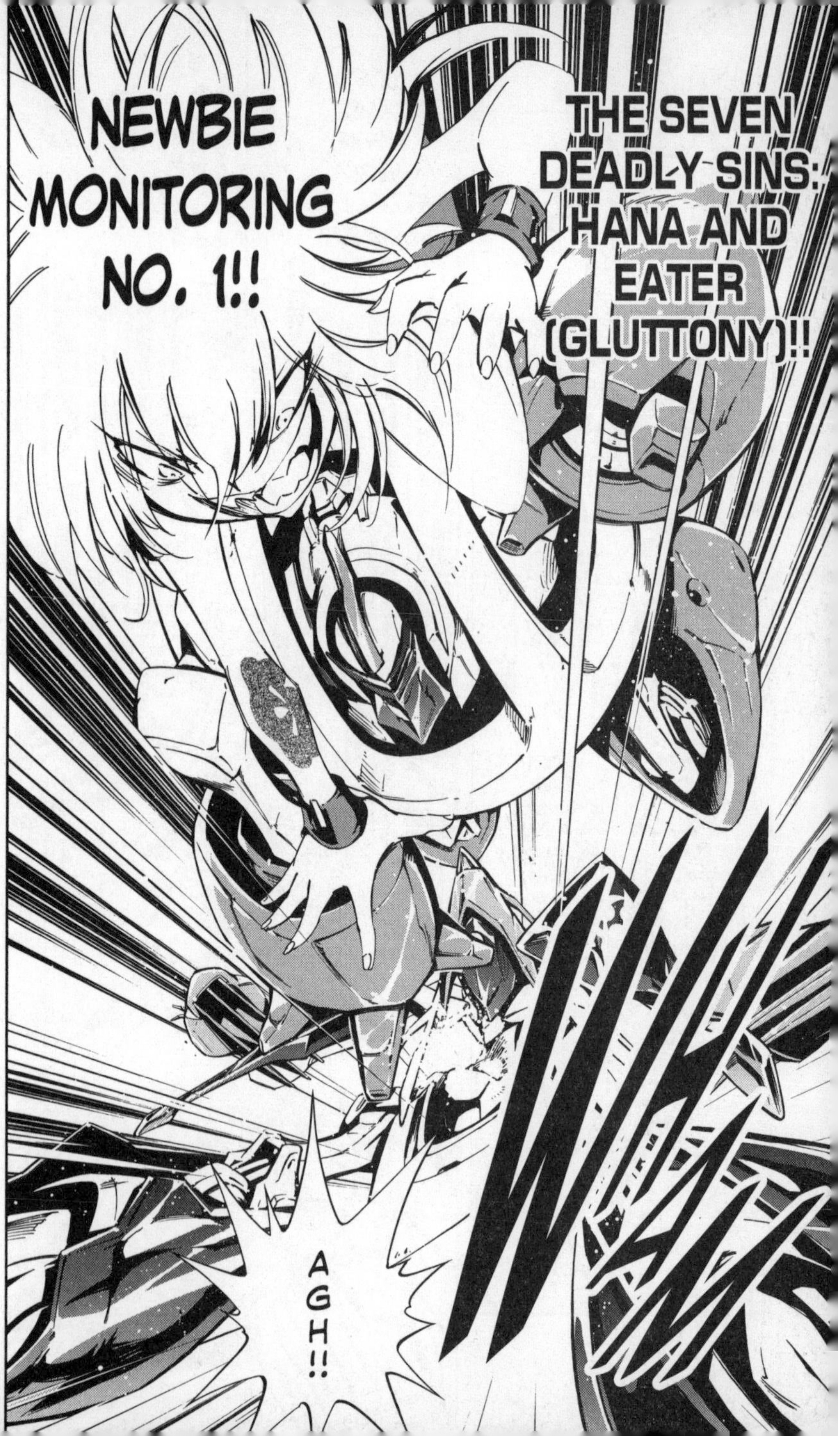
THE SEVEN DEADLY SINS: HANA AND EATER (GLUTTONY)!!
NEWBIE MONITORING NO. 1!!
AGH!!

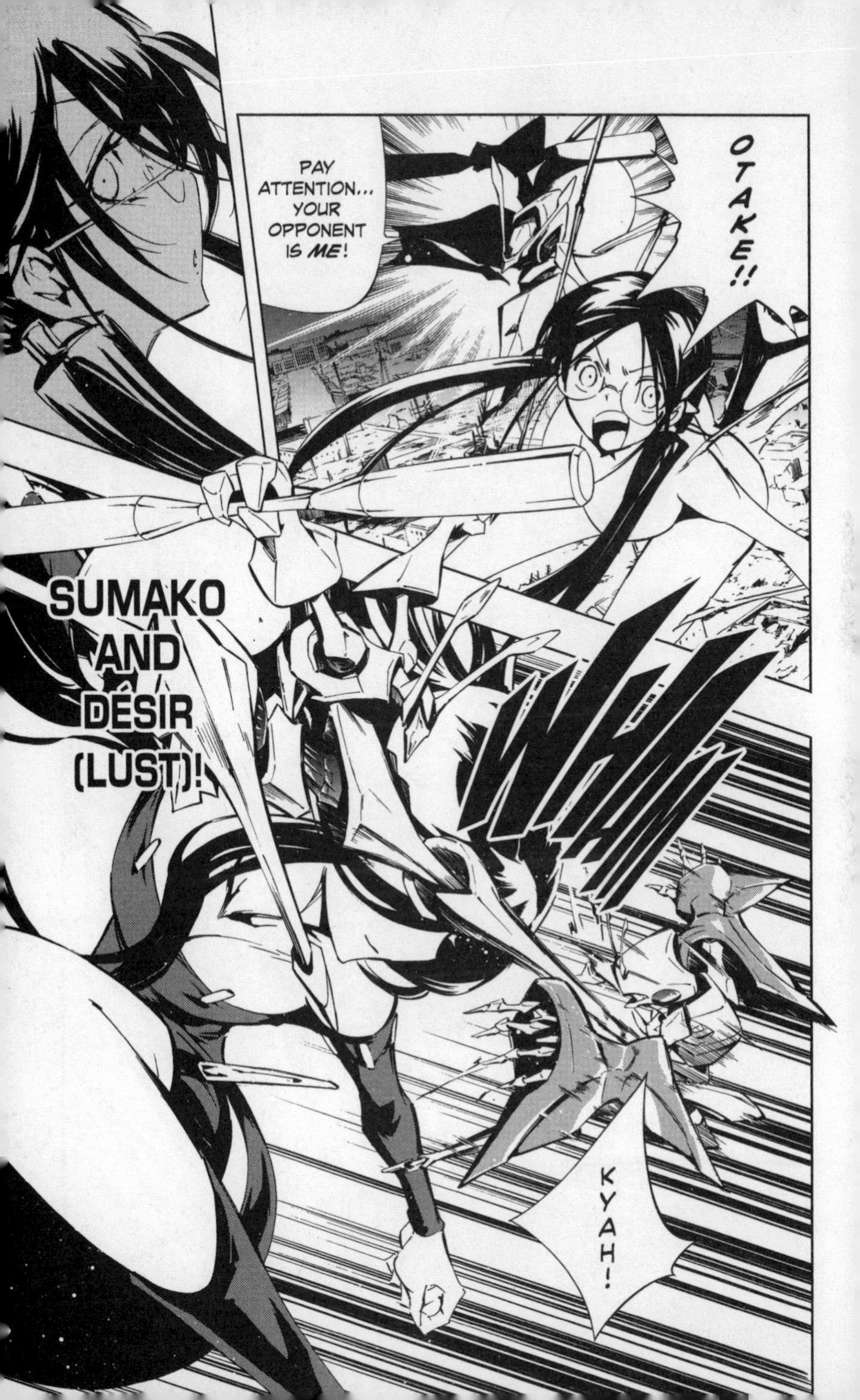
OTAKE!!
PAY ATTENTION... YOUR OPPONENT IS ME!
KYAH!
SUMAKO AND DÉSIR (LUST)!

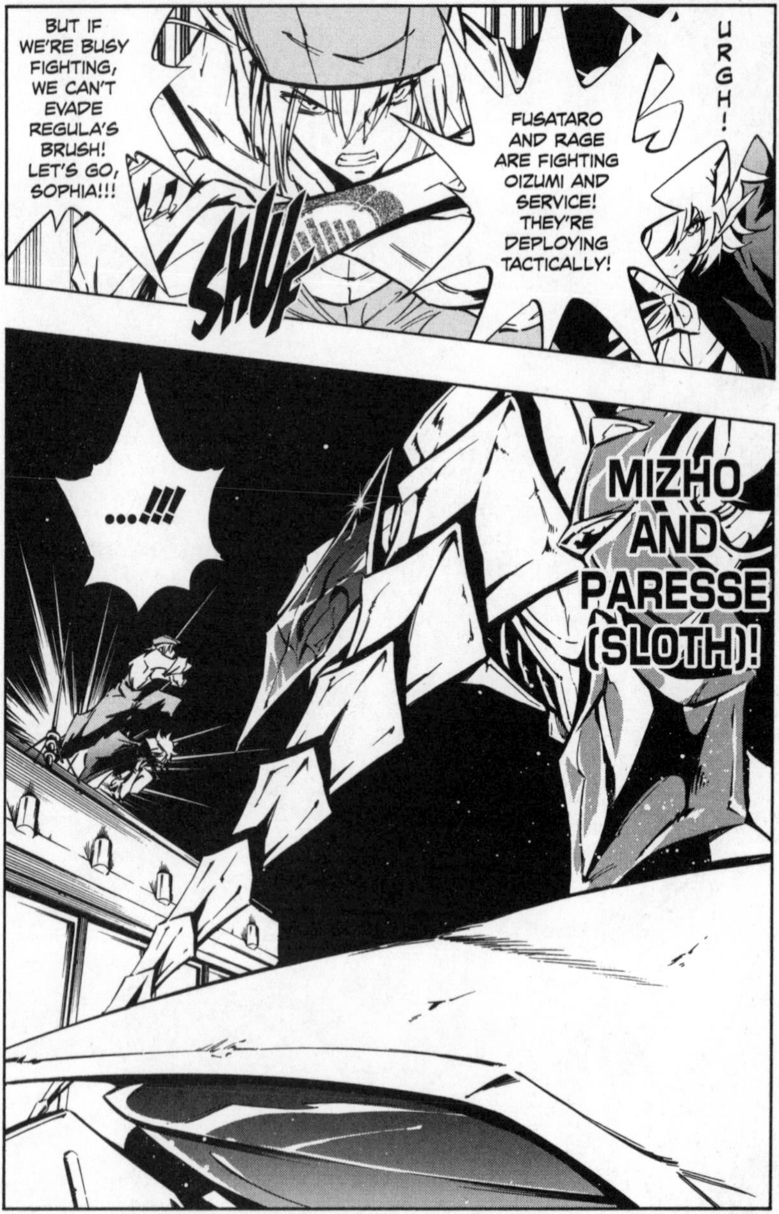
URGH!
FUSATARO AND RAGE ARE FIGHTING OIZUMI AND SERVICE! THEY'RE DEPLOYING TACTICALLY!
BUT IF WE'RE BUSY FIGHTING, WE CAN'T EVADE REGULA'S BRUSH! LET'S GO, SOPHIA!!!
SHUF
MIZHO AND PARESSE (SLOTH)!
...!!!

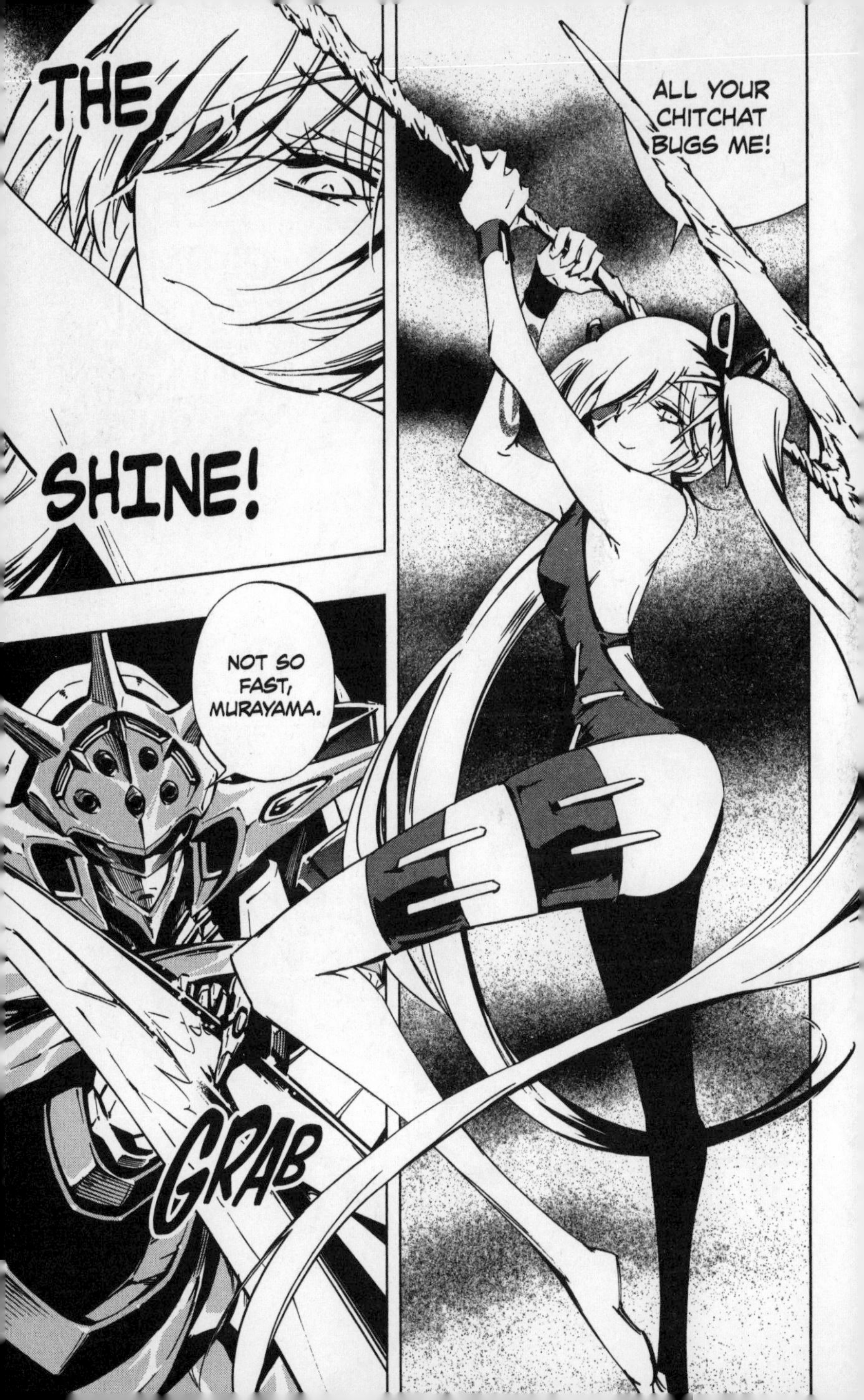
ALL YOUR CHITCHAT BUGS ME!
THE SHINE!
NOT SO FAST, MURAYAMA.
GRAB

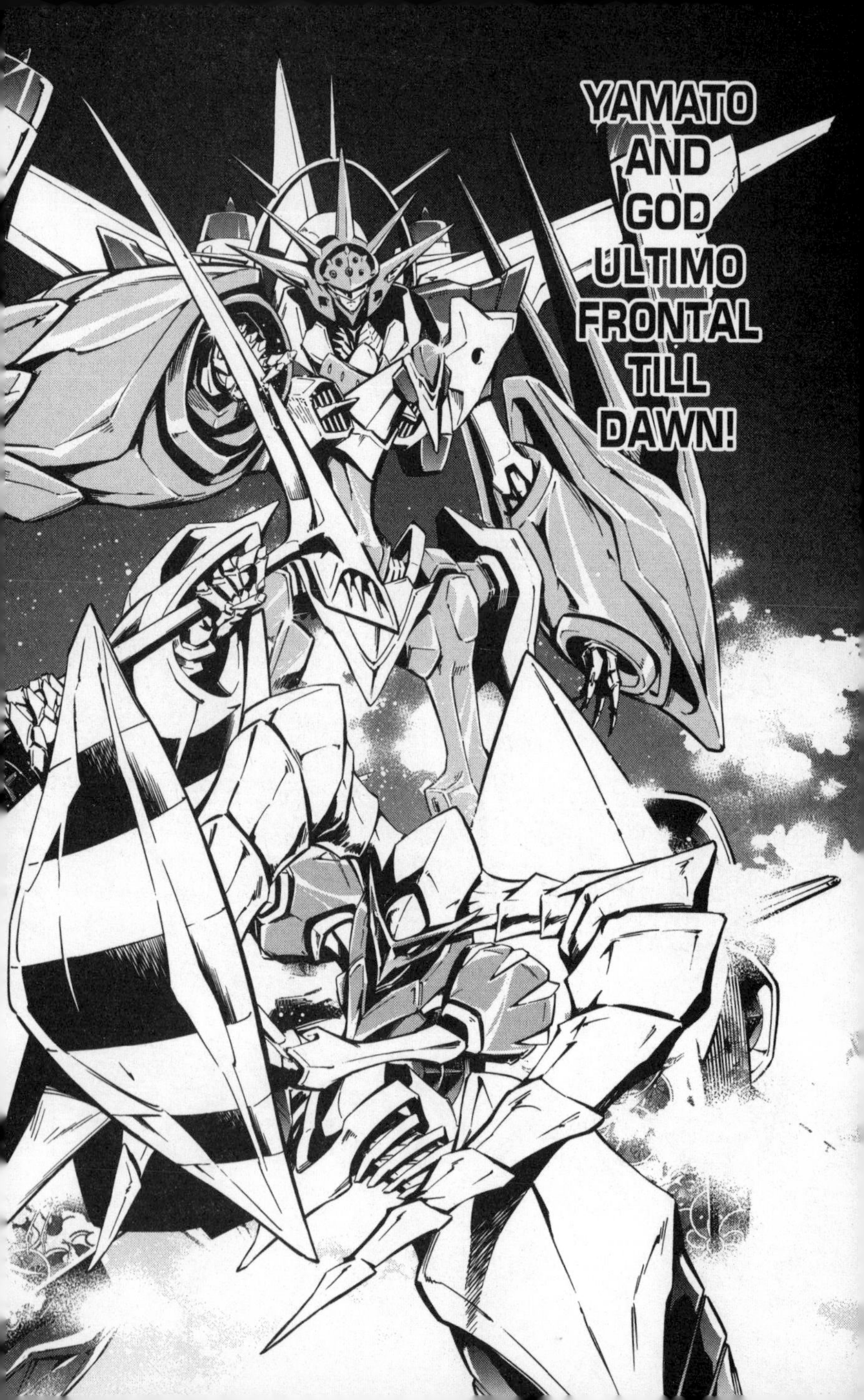
YAMATO AND GOD ULTIMO FRONTAL TILL DAWN!

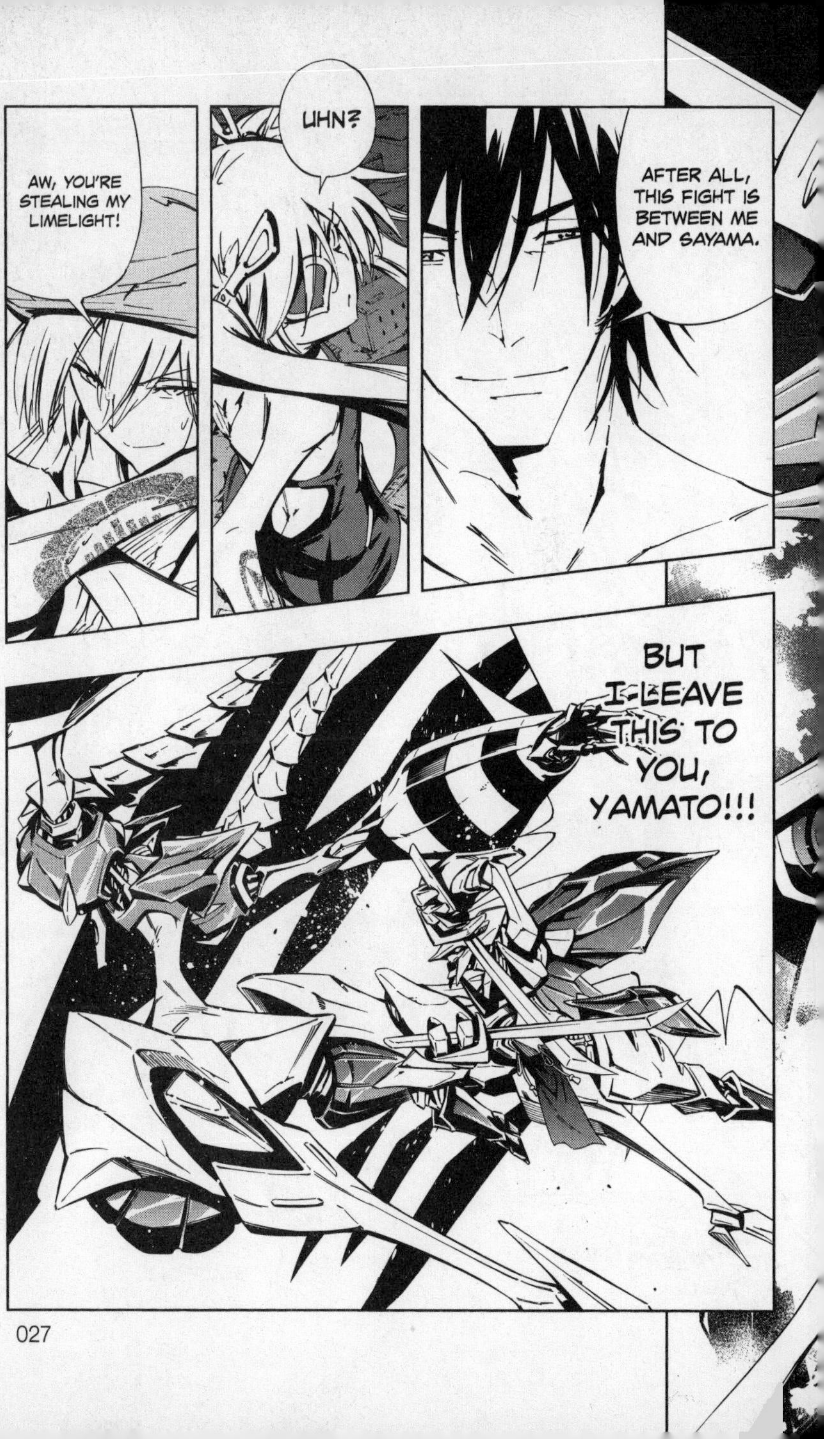
AFTER ALL, THIS FIGHT IS BETWEEN ME AND SAYAMA.
UHN?
AW, YOU'RE STEALING MY LIMELIGHT!
BUT I LEAVE THIS TO YOU, YAMATO!!!

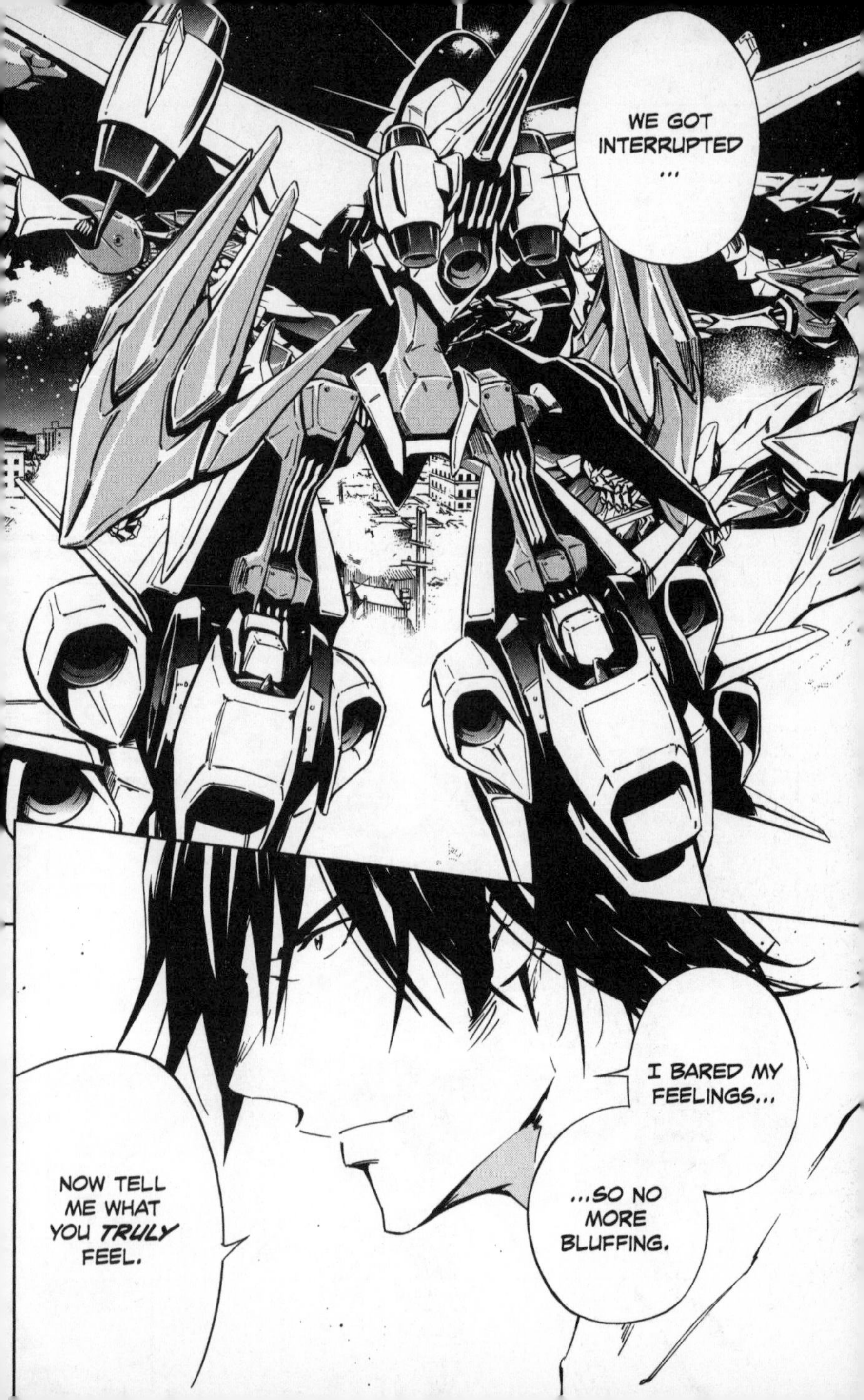
WE GOT INTERRUPTED ...
I BARED MY FEELINGS...
...SO NO MORE BLUFFING.
NOW TELL ME WHAT YOU *TRULY* FEEL.

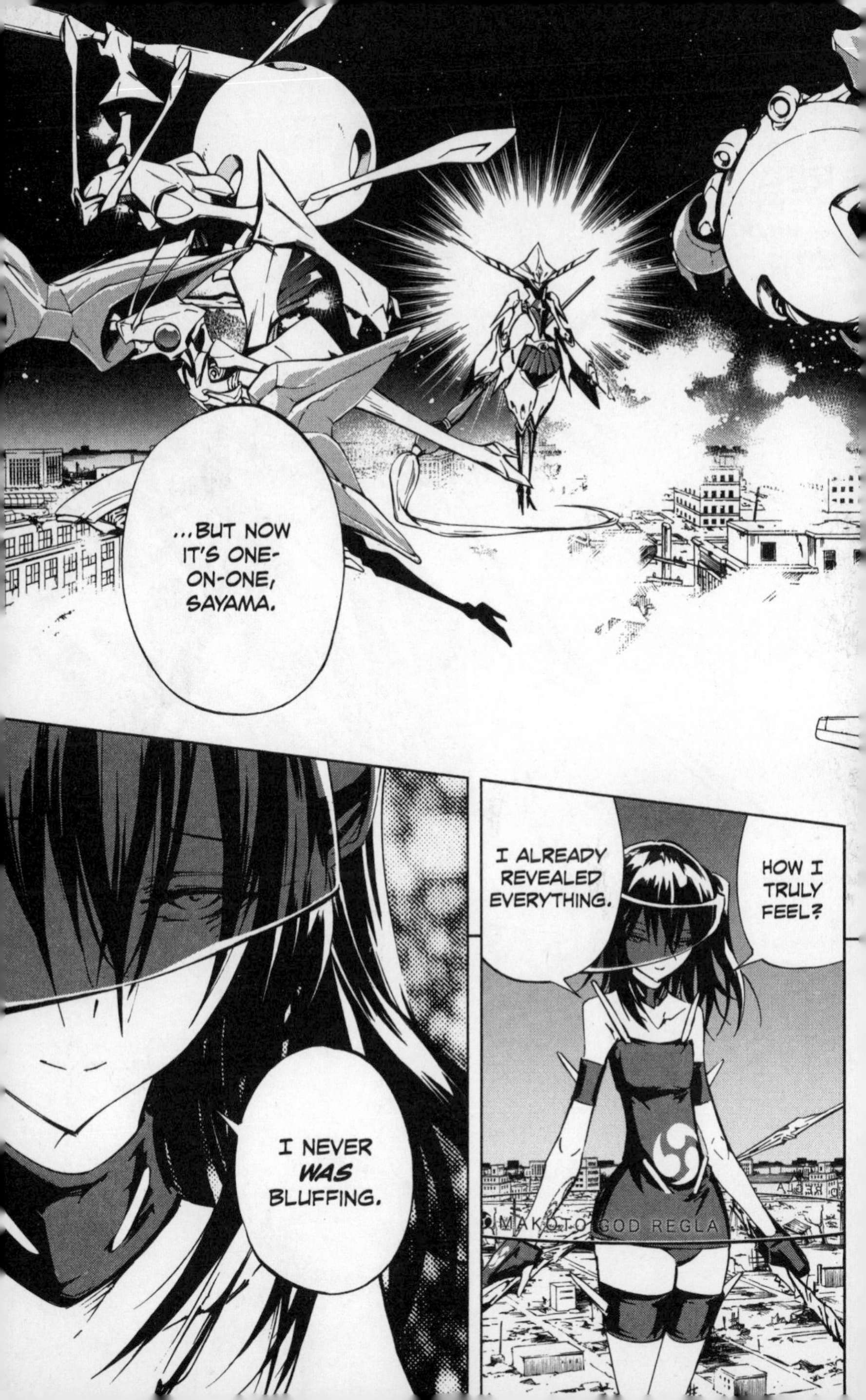
...BUT NOW IT'S ONE-ON-ONE, SAYAMA.
HOW I TRULY FEEL?
I ALREADY REVEALED EVERYTHING.
MAKOTO GOD REGLA
I NEVER *WAS* BLUFFING.

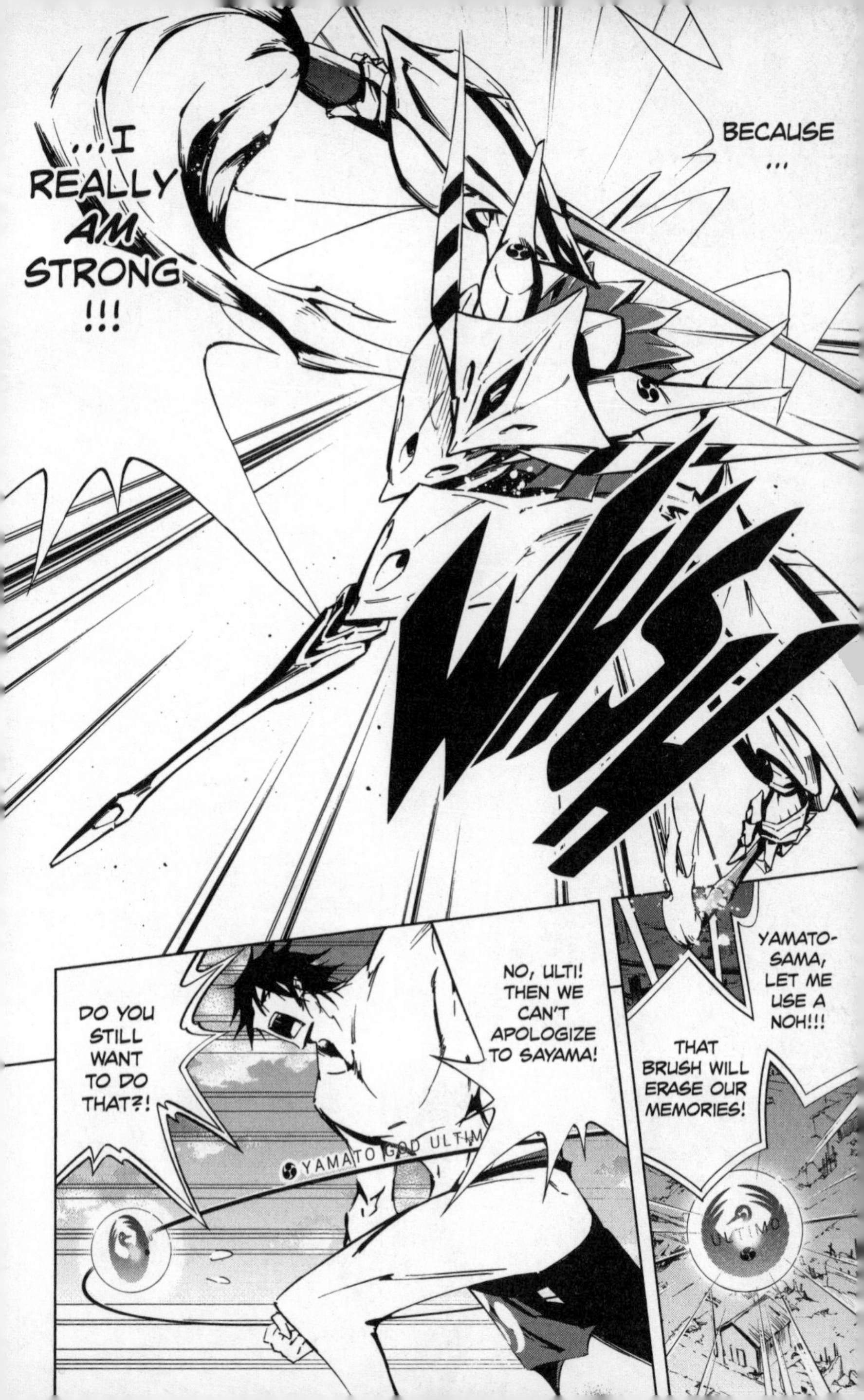
BECAUSE ...
...I REALLY AM STRONG!!!
WHSH
YAMATO-SAMA, LET ME USE A NOH!!!
THAT BRUSH WILL ERASE OUR MEMORIES!
ULTIMO
NO, ULTI! THEN WE CAN'T APOLOGIZE TO SAYAMA!
DO YOU STILL WANT TO DO THAT?!
YAMATO GOD ULTIM

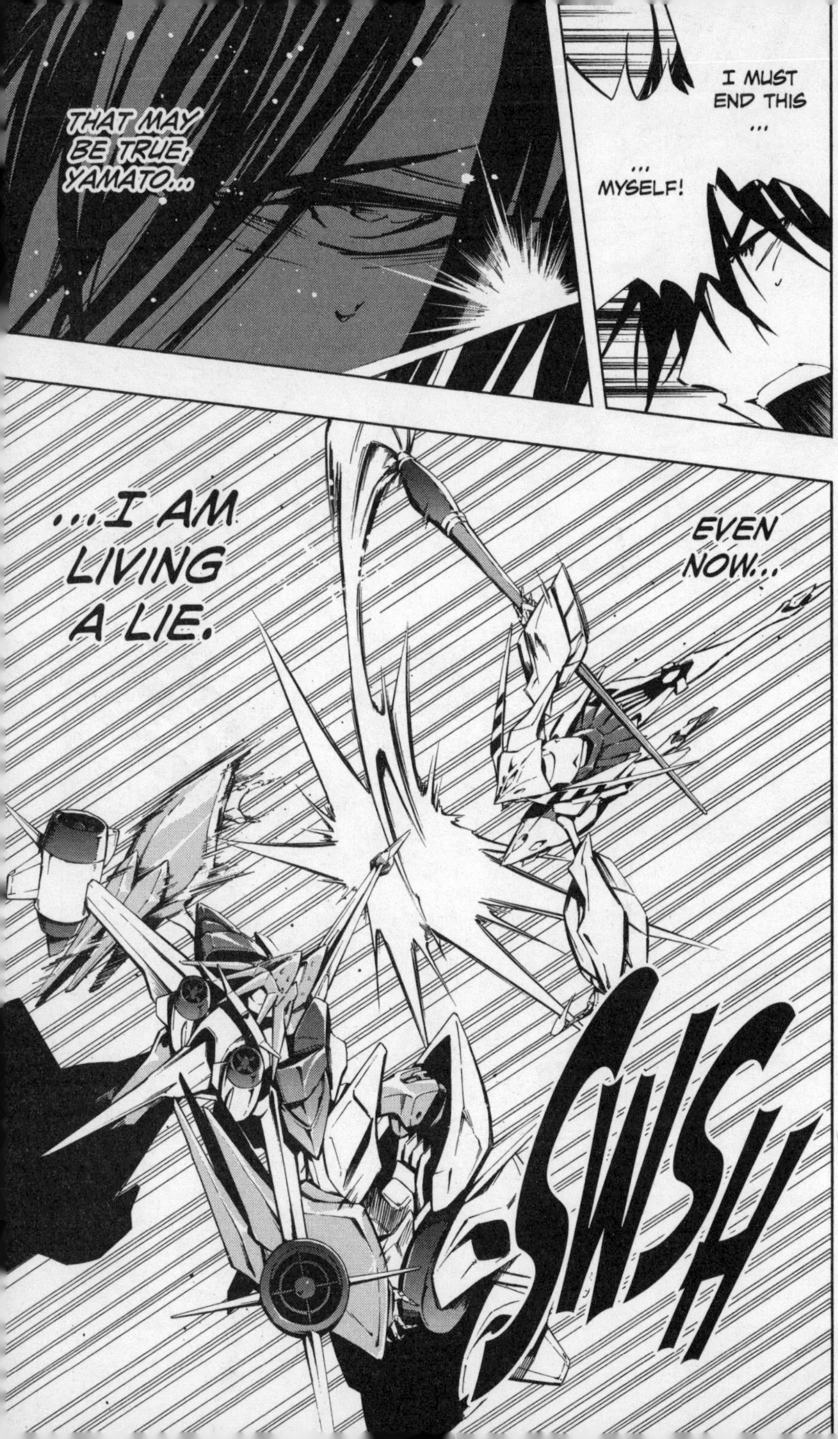

I MUST END THIS ...
... MYSELF!
THAT MAY BE TRUE, YAMATO...
EVEN NOW...
...I AM LIVING A LIE.
SWISH

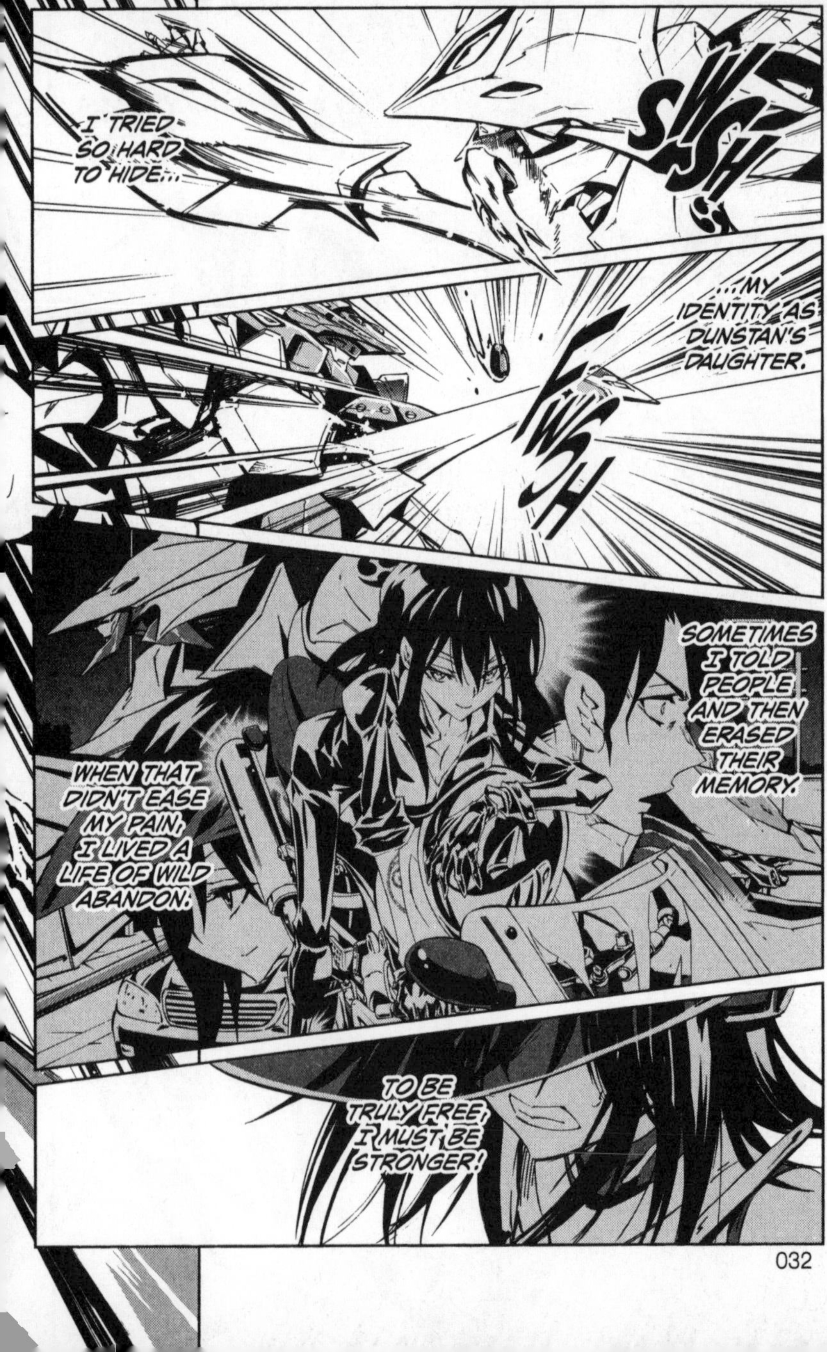
SWSH!
I TRIED SO HARD TO HIDE...
...MY IDENTITY AS DUNSTAN'S DAUGHTER.
FWSH
SOMETIMES I TOLD PEOPLE AND THEN ERASED THEIR MEMORY.
WHEN THAT DIDN'T EASE MY PAIN, I LIVED A LIFE OF WILD ABANDON.
TO BE TRULY FREE, I MUST BE STRONGER!

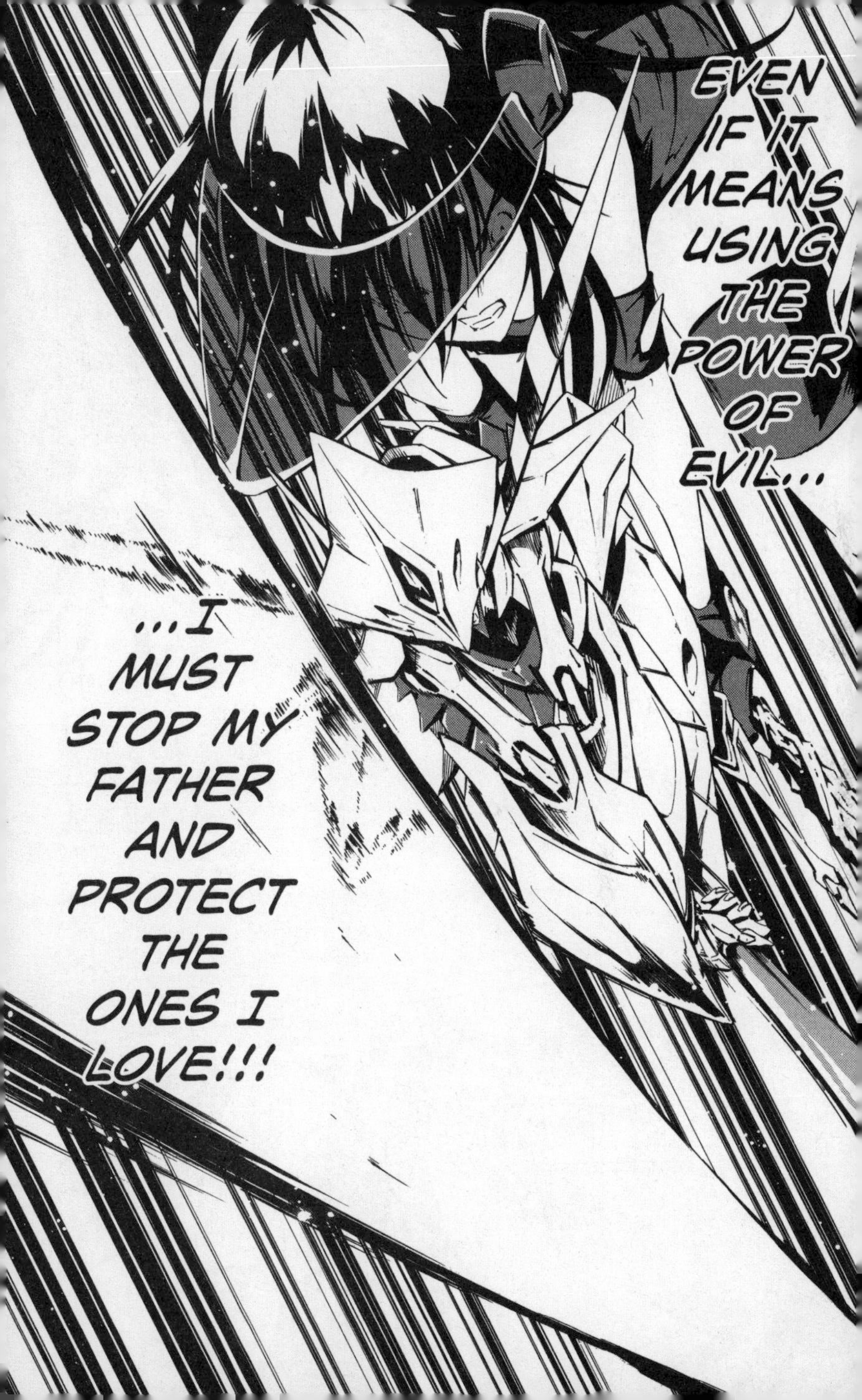
EVEN IF IT MEANS USING THE POWER OF EVIL...
...I MUST STOP MY FATHER AND PROTECT THE ONES I LOVE!!!

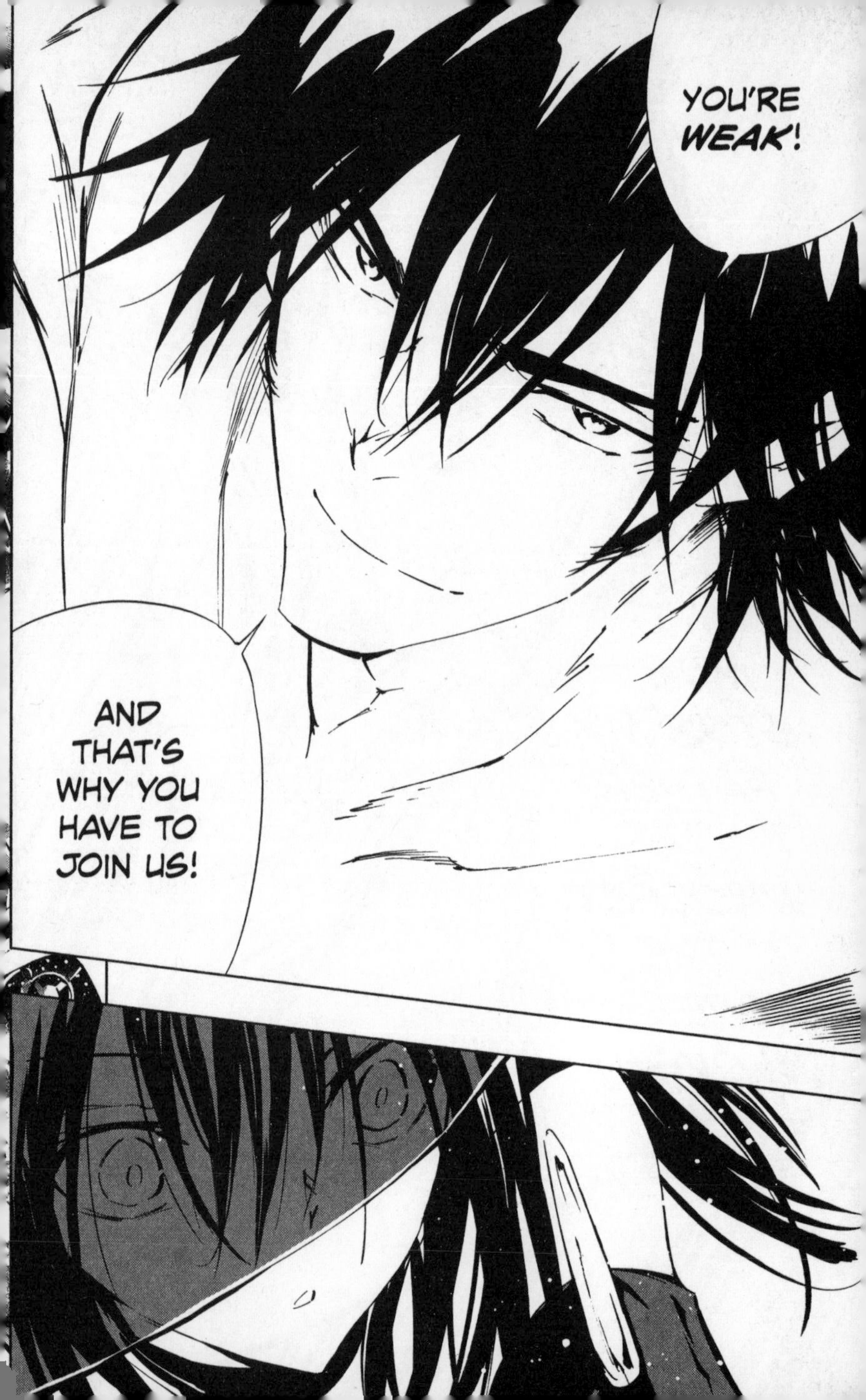
YOU'RE WEAK!
AND THAT'S WHY YOU HAVE TO JOIN US!

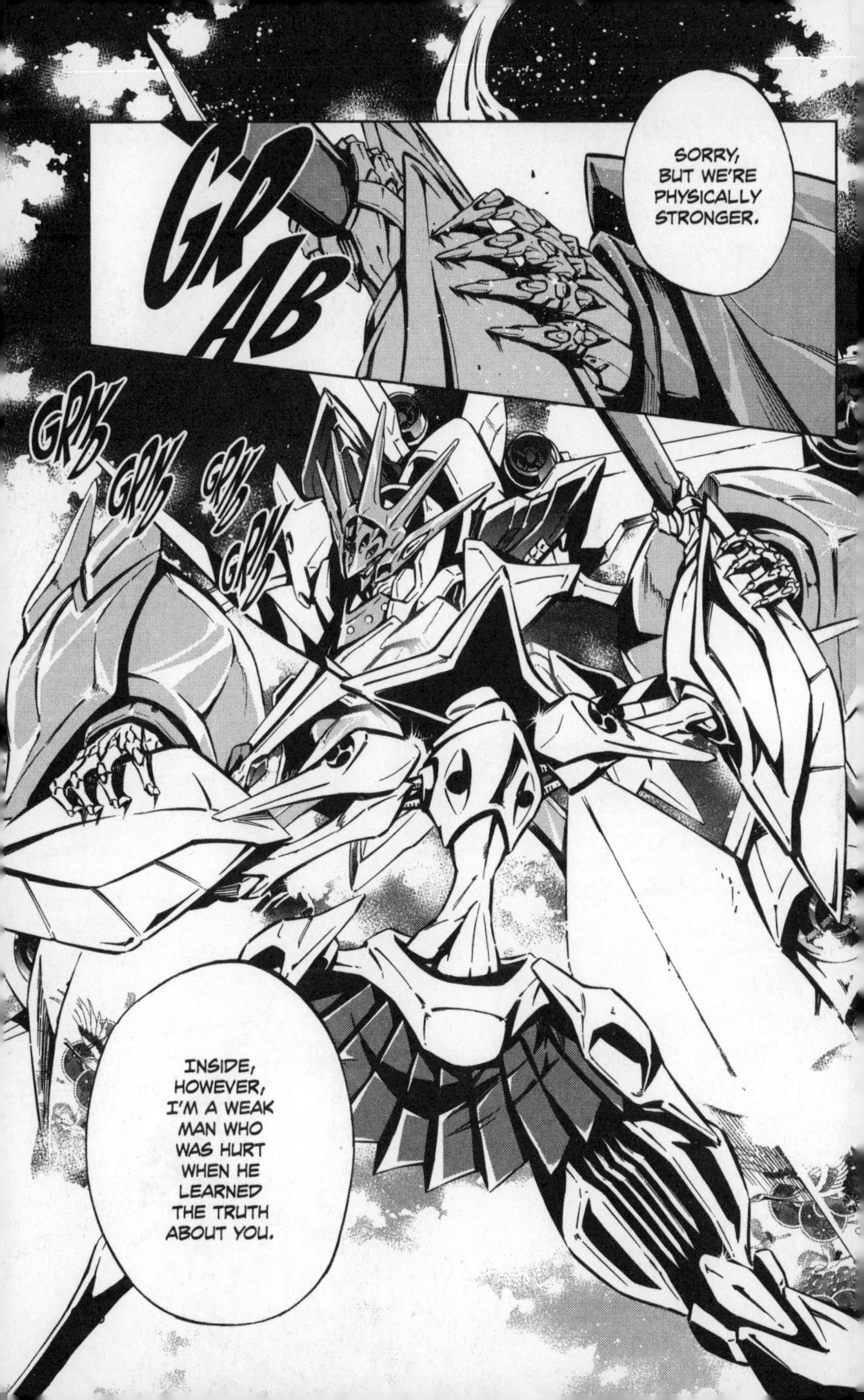
SORRY, BUT WE'RE PHYSICALLY STRONGER.
GRAB
GRK GRK GRK GRK GRK
INSIDE, HOWEVER, I'M A WEAK MAN WHO WAS HURT WHEN HE LEARNED THE TRUTH ABOUT YOU.

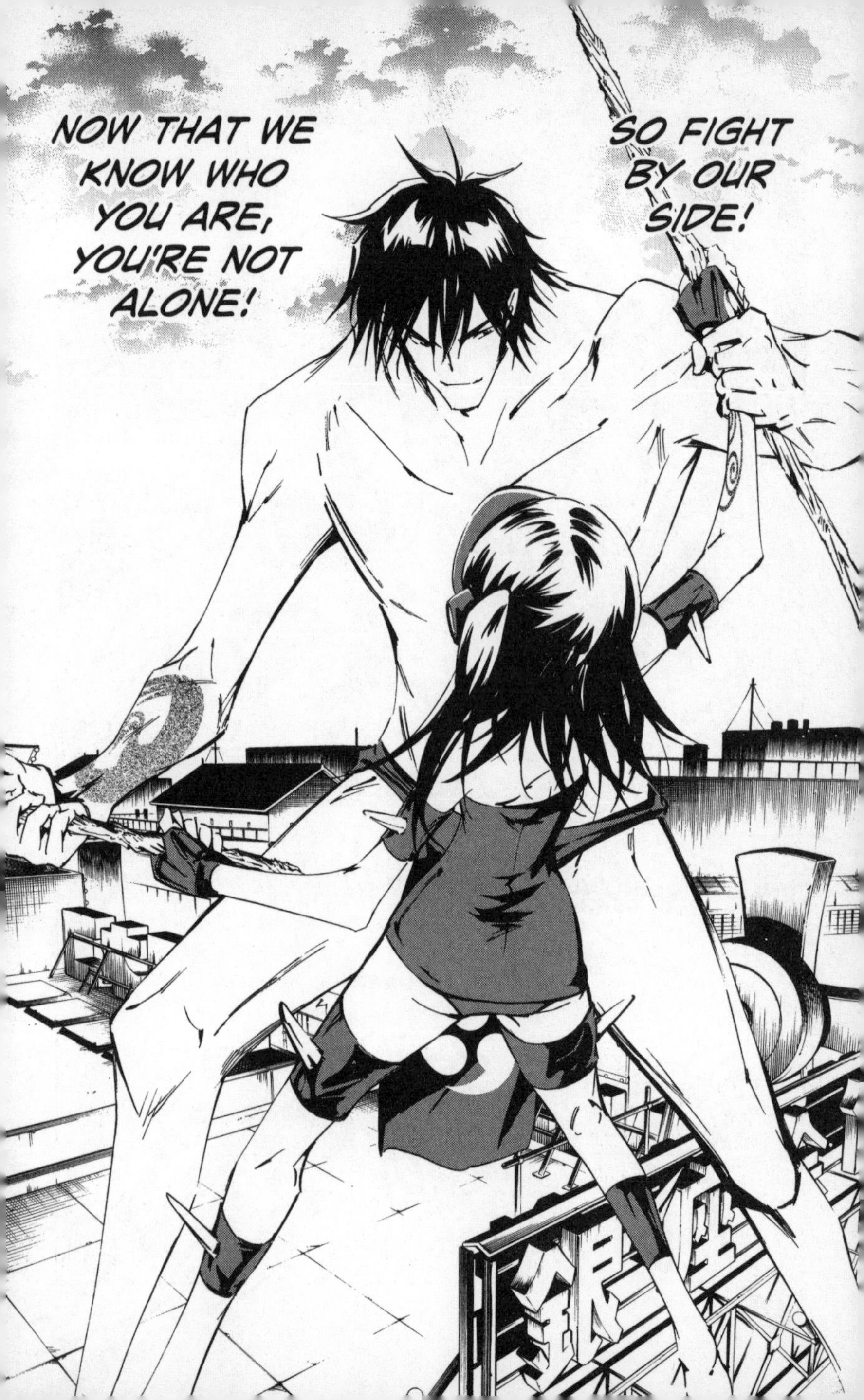
NOW THAT WE KNOW WHO YOU ARE, YOU'RE NOT ALONE!
SO FIGHT BY OUR SIDE!

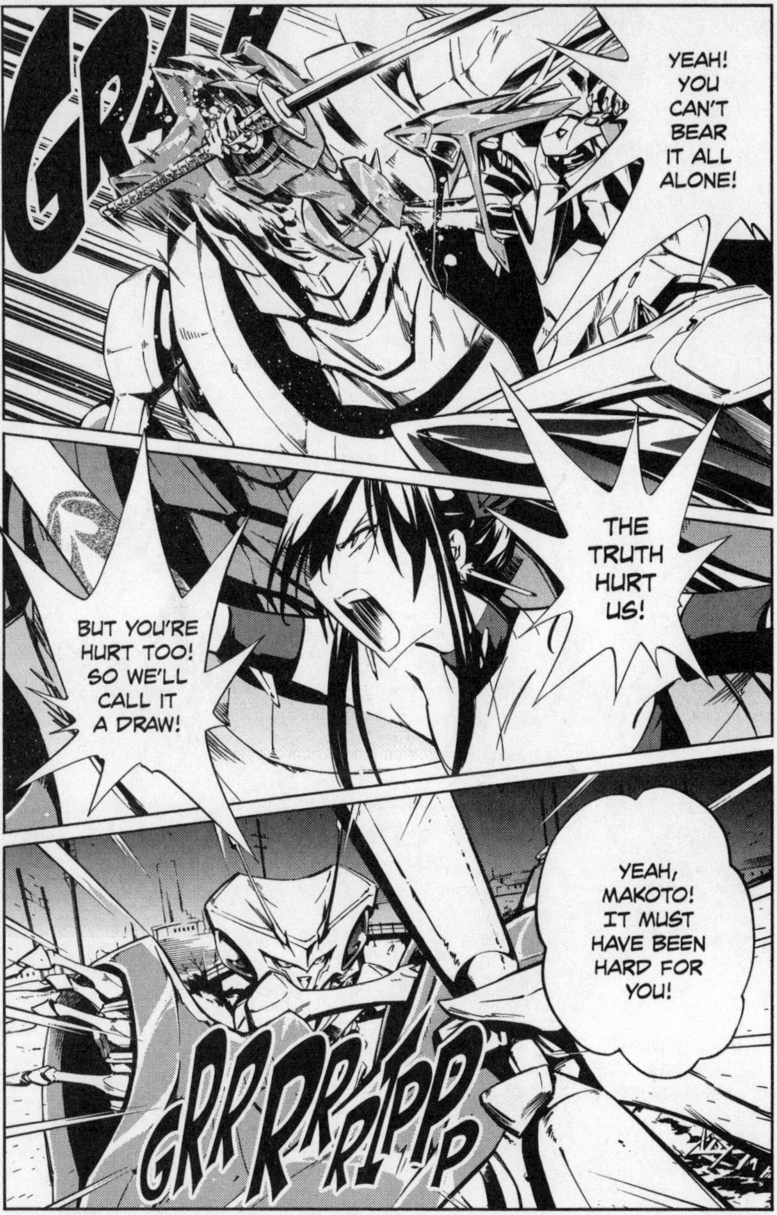
YEAH! YOU CAN'T BEAR IT ALL ALONE!
THE TRUTH HURT US!
BUT YOU'RE HURT TOO! SO WE'LL CALL IT A DRAW!
YEAH, MAKOTO! IT MUST HAVE BEEN HARD FOR YOU!

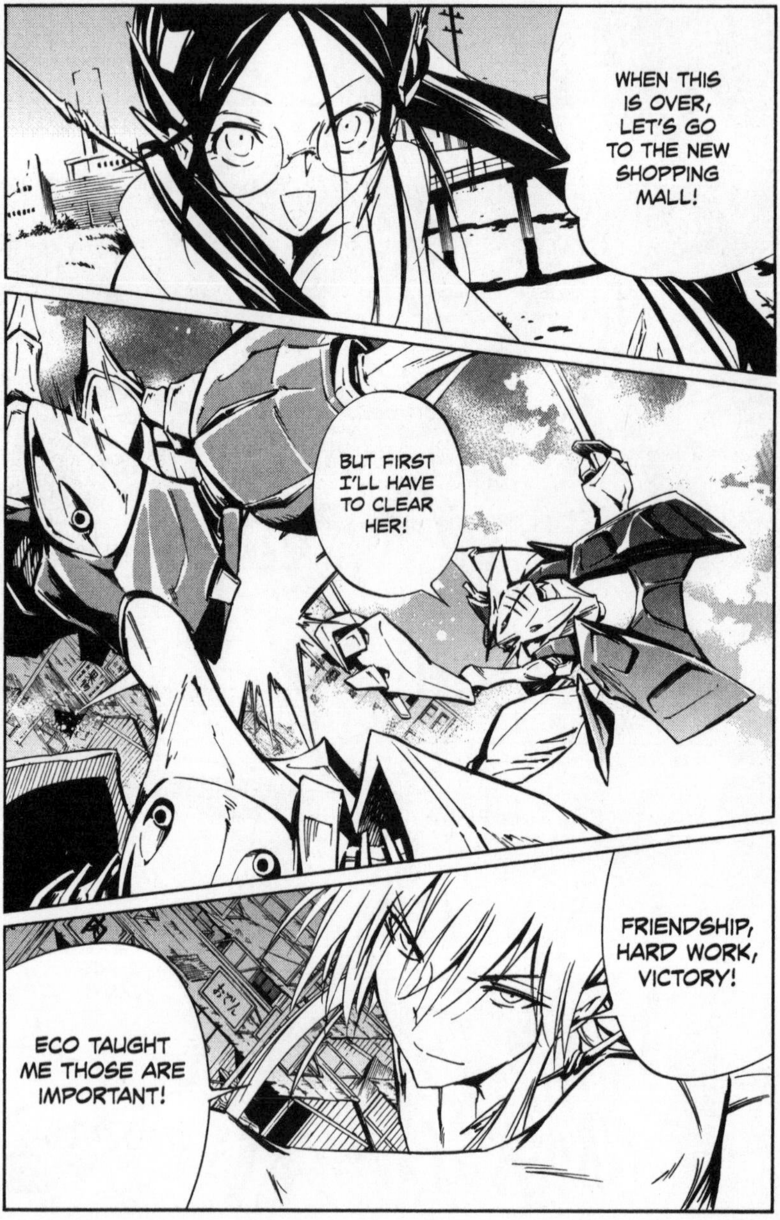
WHEN THIS IS OVER, LET'S GO TO THE NEW SHOPPING MALL!
BUT FIRST I'LL HAVE TO CLEAR HER!
FRIENDSHIP, HARD WORK, VICTORY!
ECO TAUGHT ME THOSE ARE IMPORTANT!

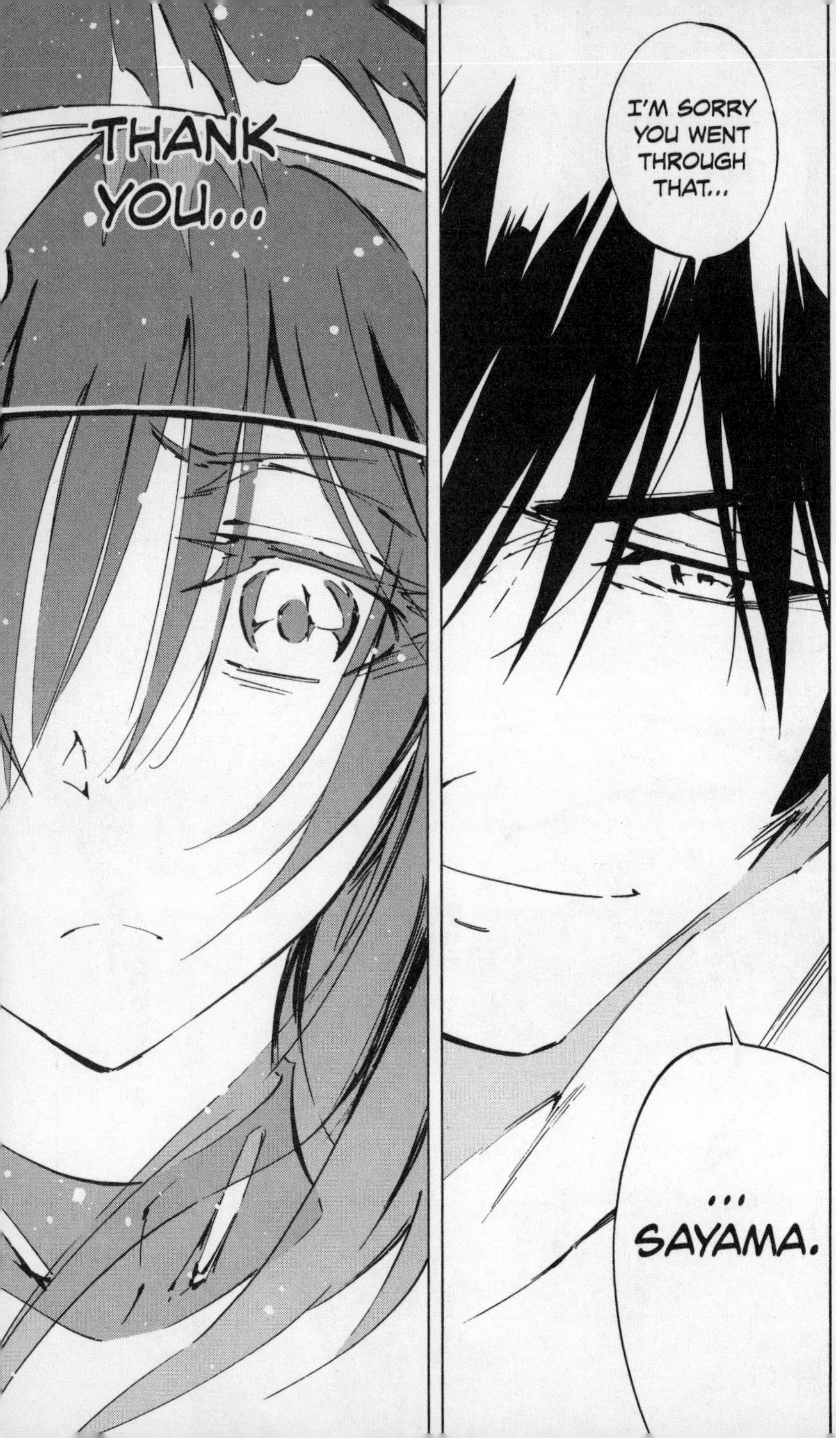
I'M SORRY YOU WENT THROUGH THAT...
...SAYAMA.
THANK YOU...

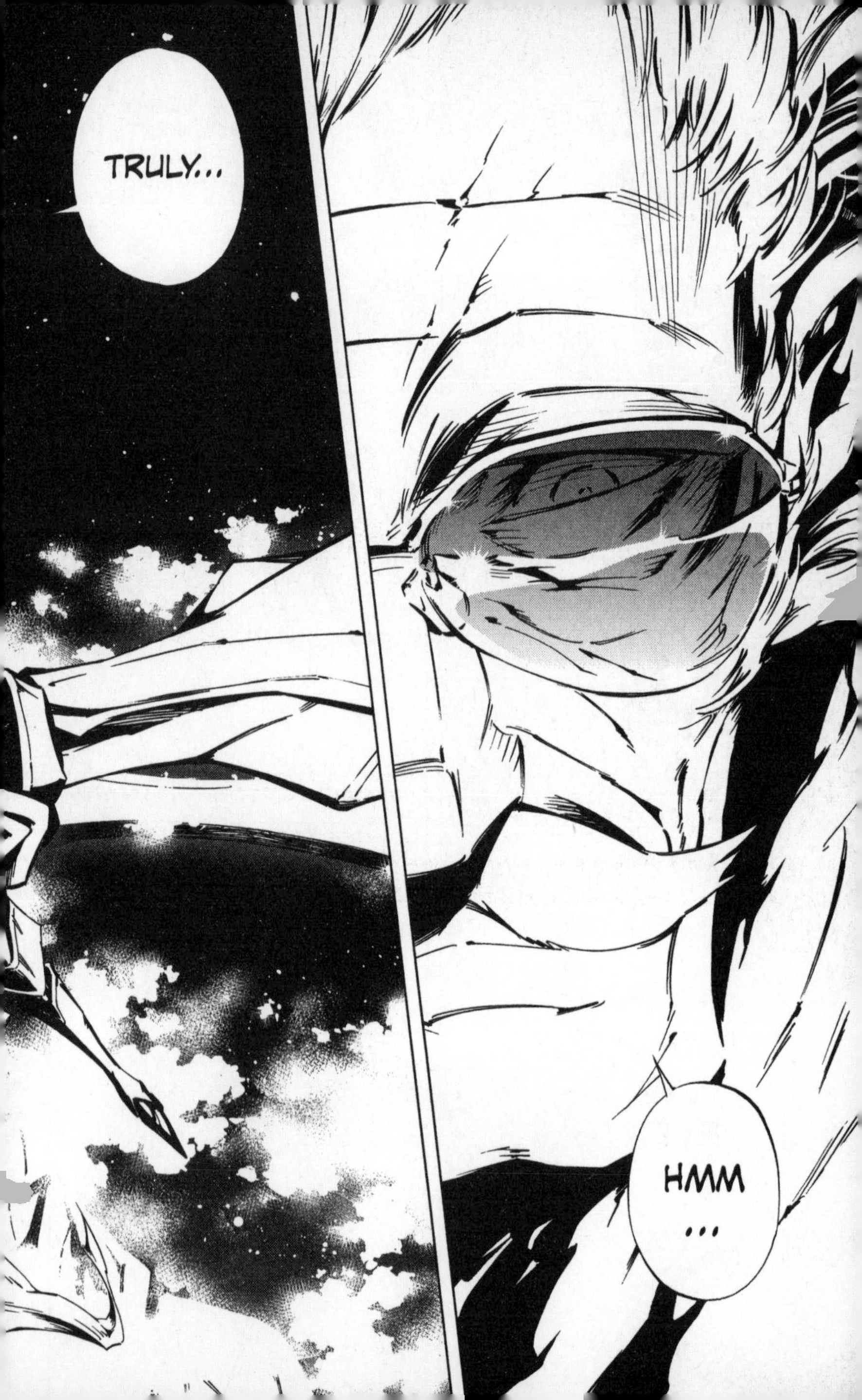
HMM
...
TRULY...

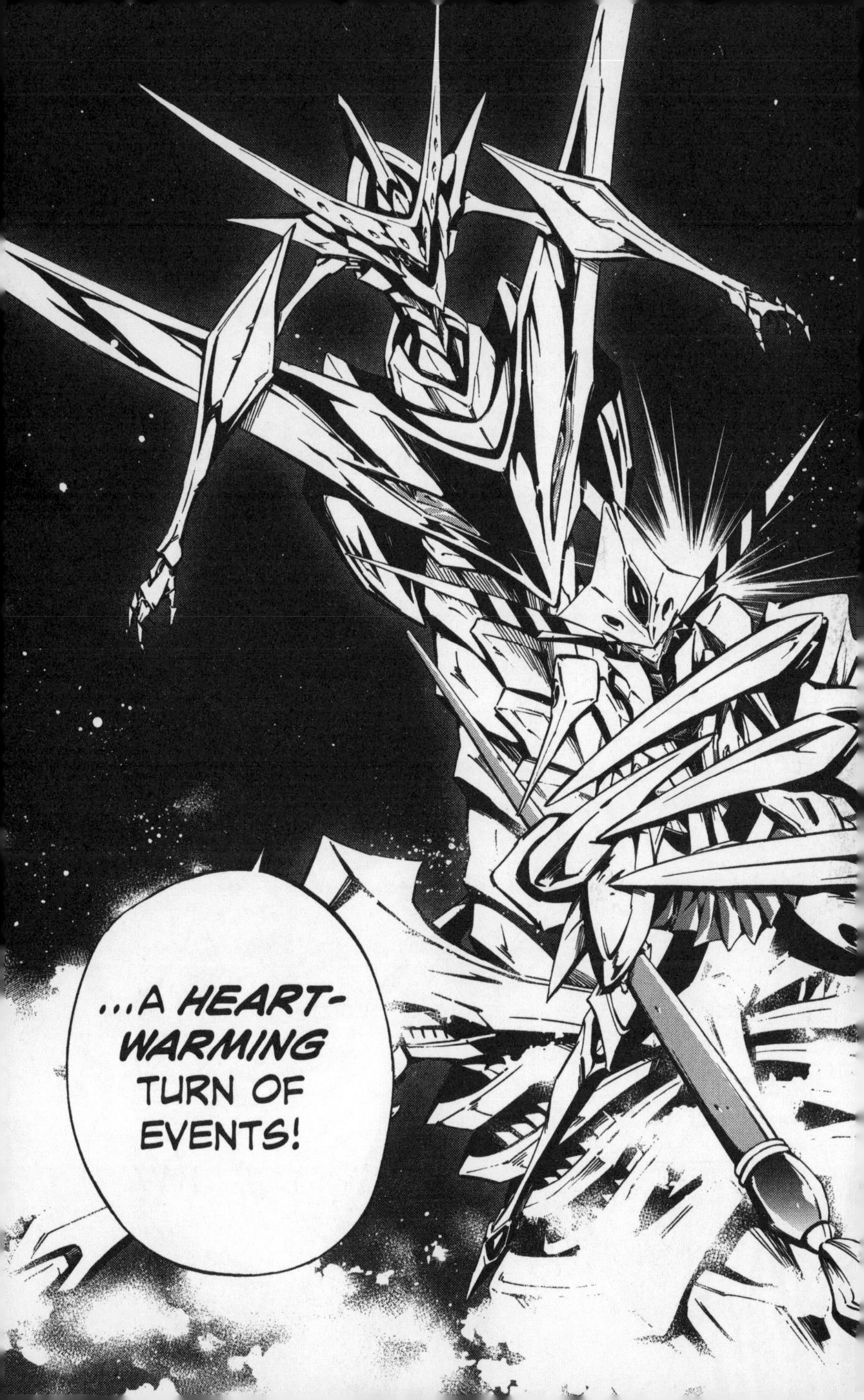
...A HEART-WARMING TURN OF EVENTS!

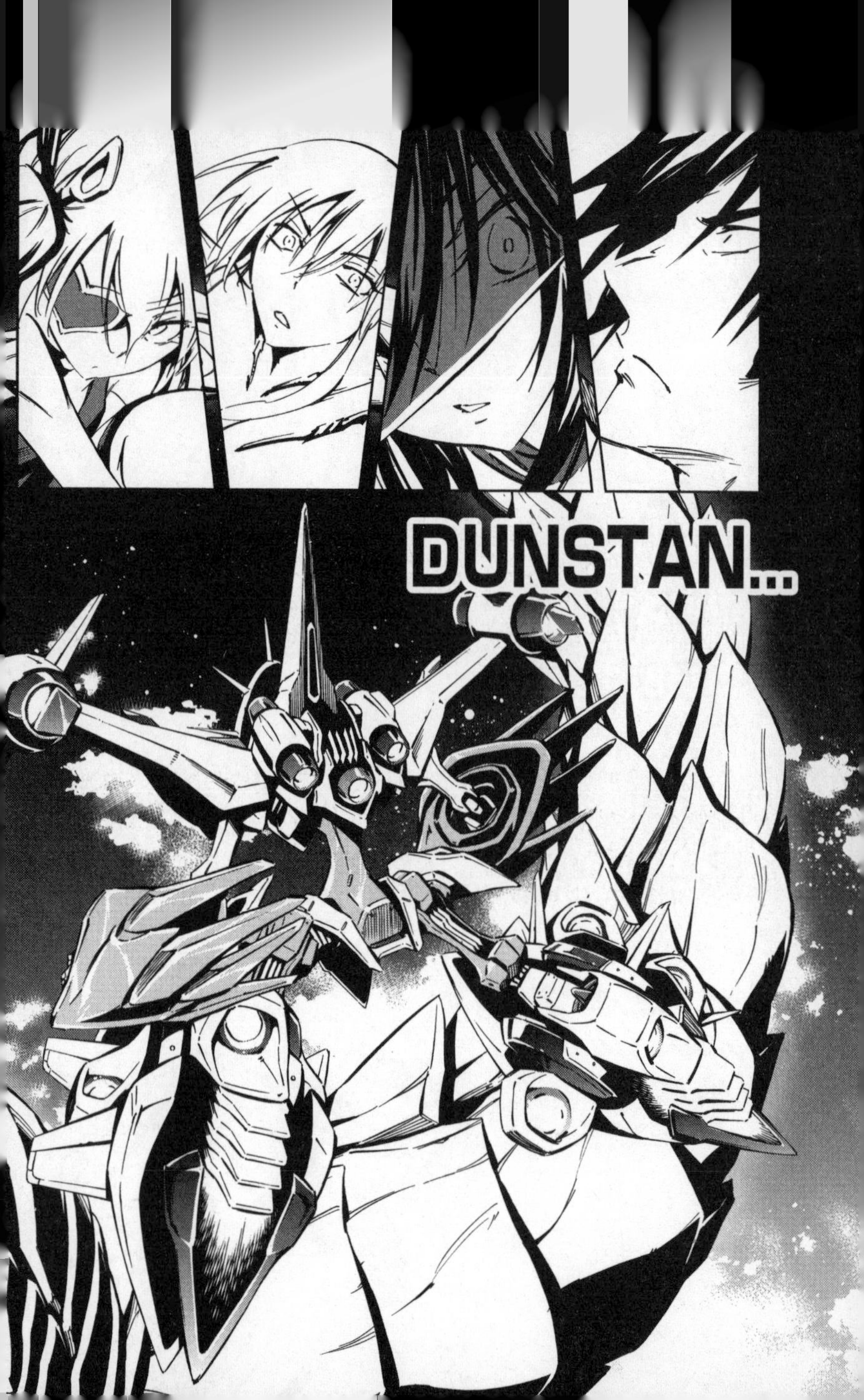
DUNSTAN...

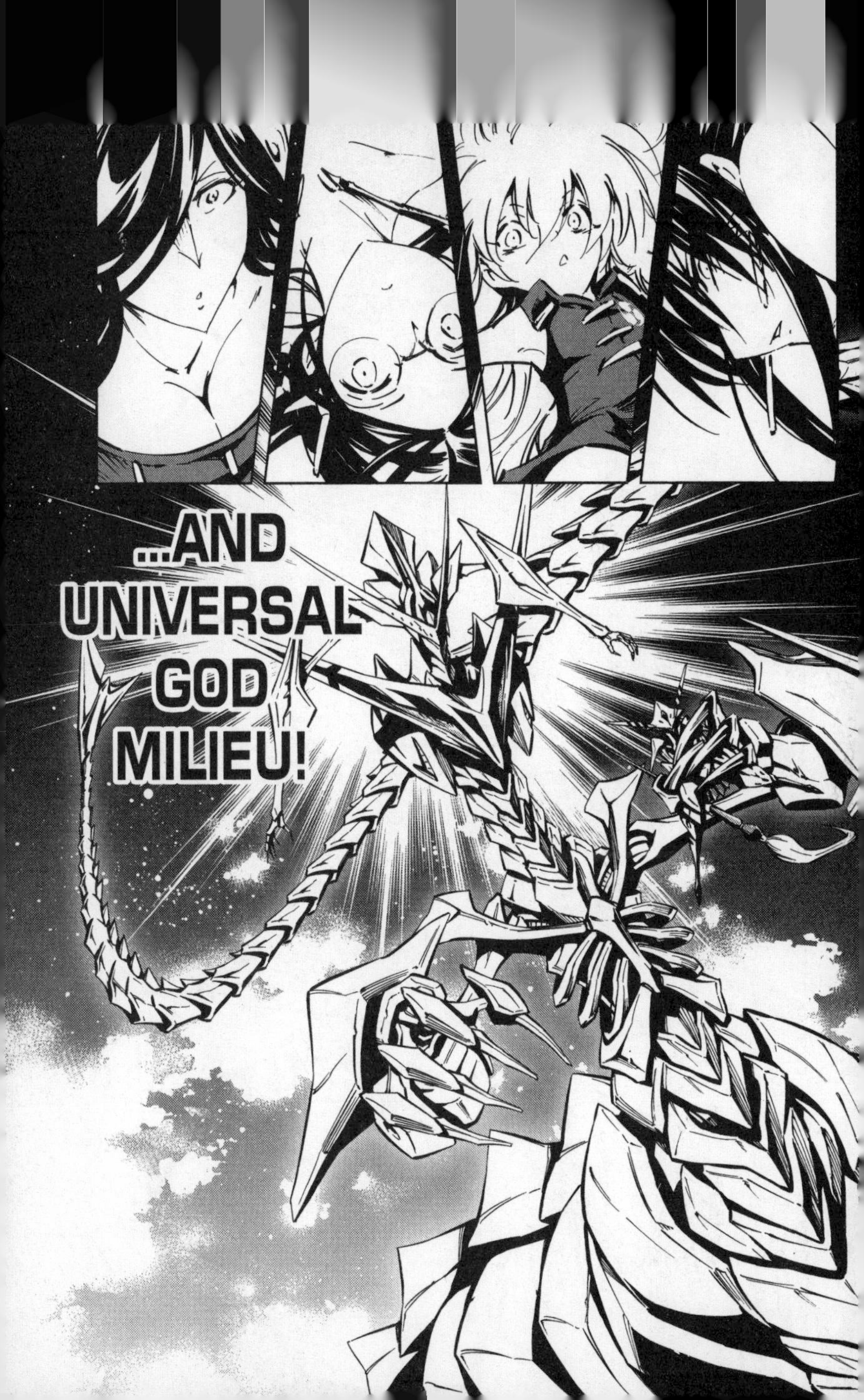
...AND UNIVERSAL GOD MILIEU!

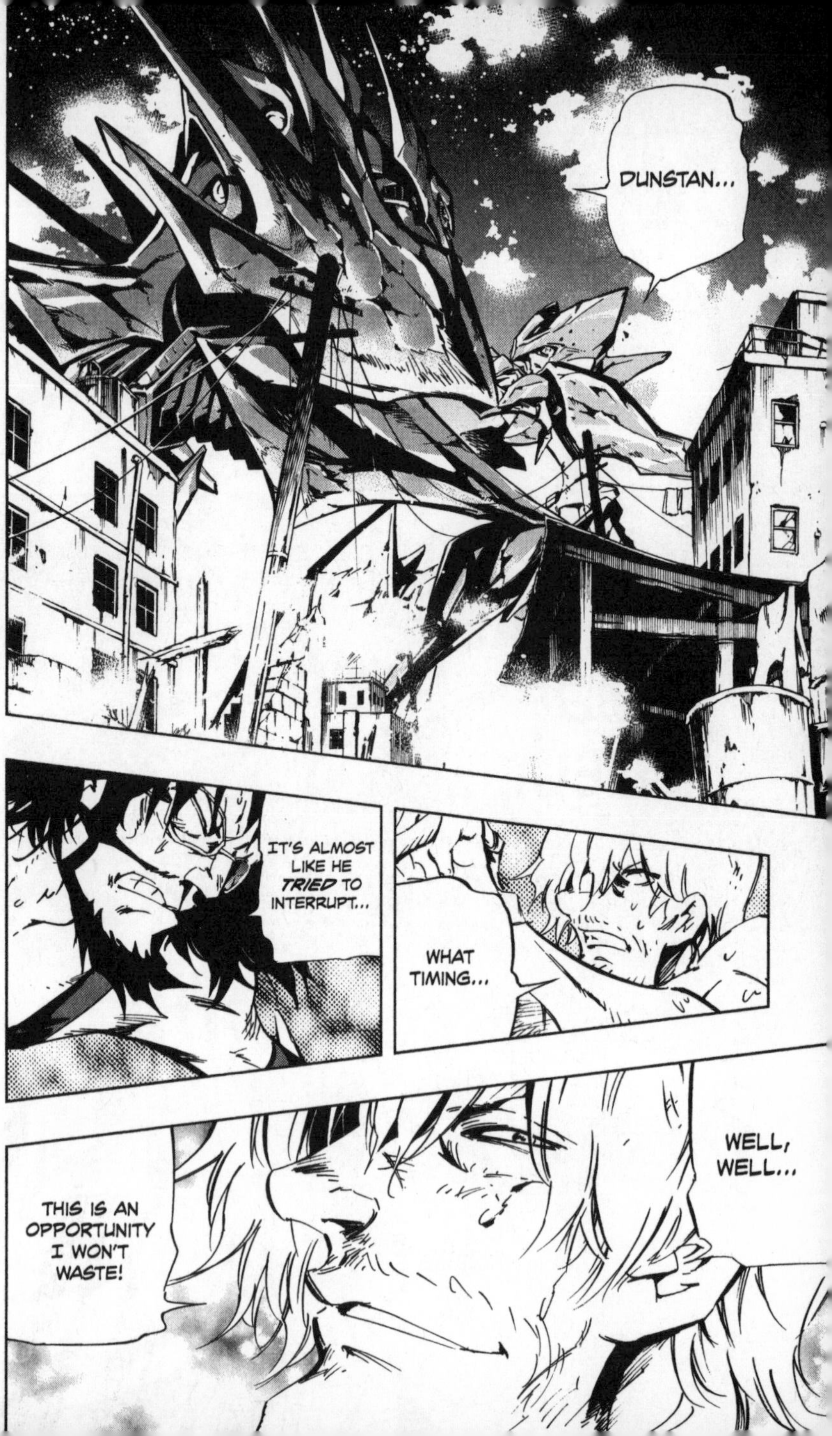
DUNSTAN...
WHAT TIMING...
IT'S ALMOST LIKE HE *TRIED* TO INTERRUPT...
WELL, WELL...
THIS IS AN OPPORTUNITY I WON'T WASTE!

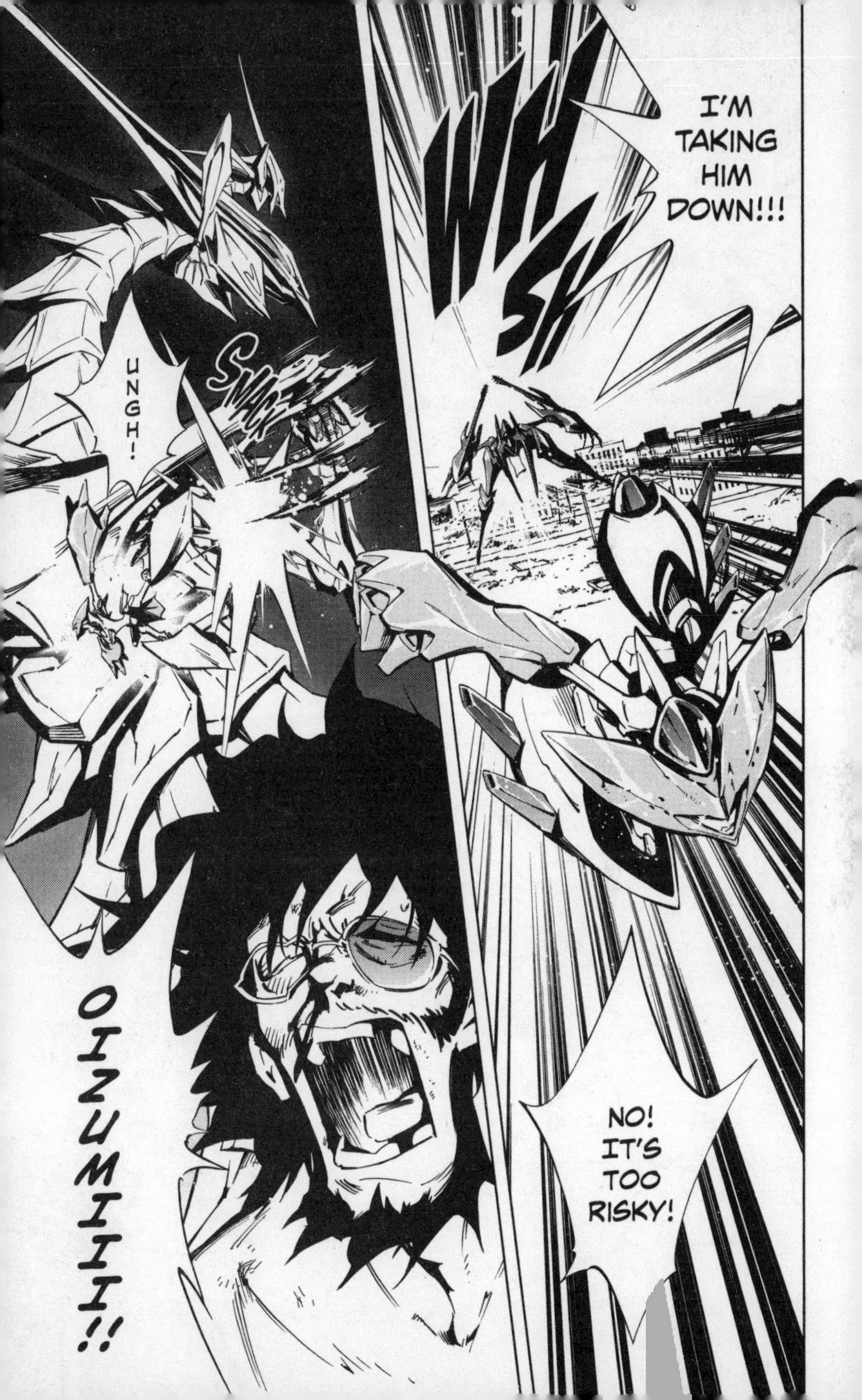
I'M TAKING HIM DOWN!!!
NO! IT'S TOO RISKY!
SMACK
UNGH!
OIZUMIII!!

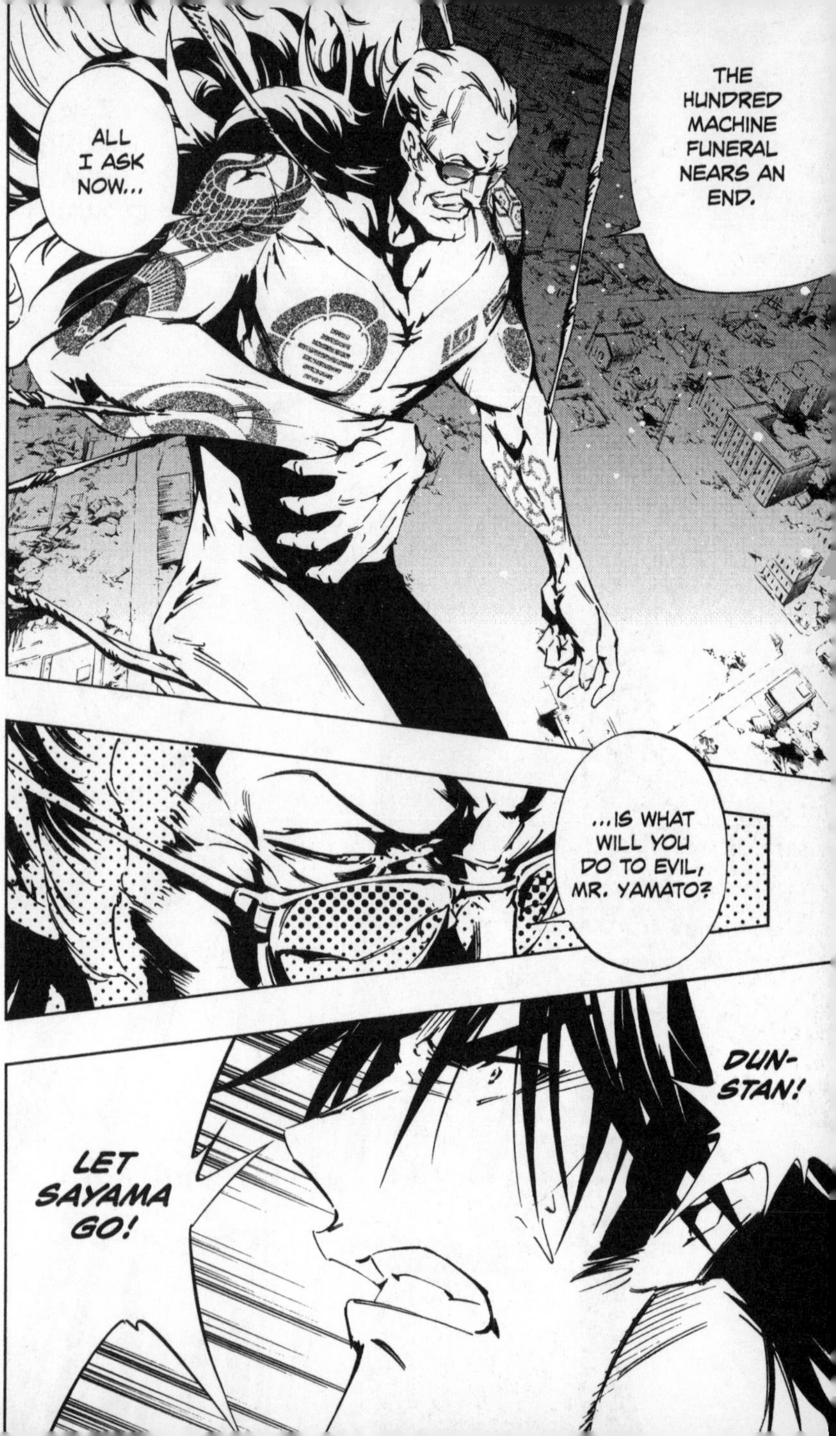
THE HUNDRED MACHINE FUNERAL NEARS AN END.
ALL I ASK NOW...
...IS WHAT WILL YOU DO TO EVIL, MR. YAMATO?
DUN-STAN!
LET SAYAMA GO!

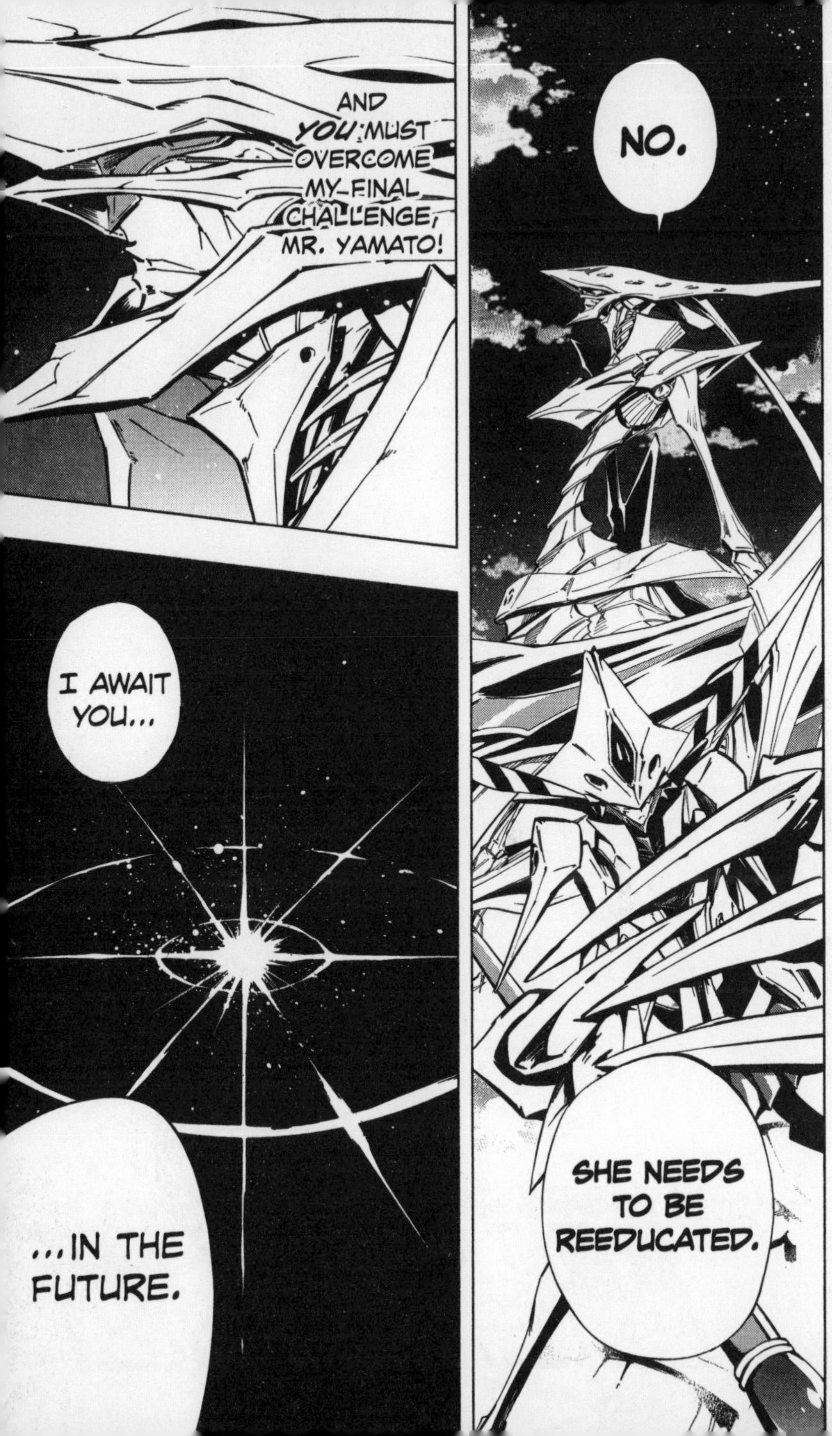
NO.
SHE NEEDS TO BE REEDUCATED.
AND YOU MUST OVERCOME MY FINAL CHALLENGE, MR. YAMATO!
I AWAIT YOU...
...IN THE FUTURE.

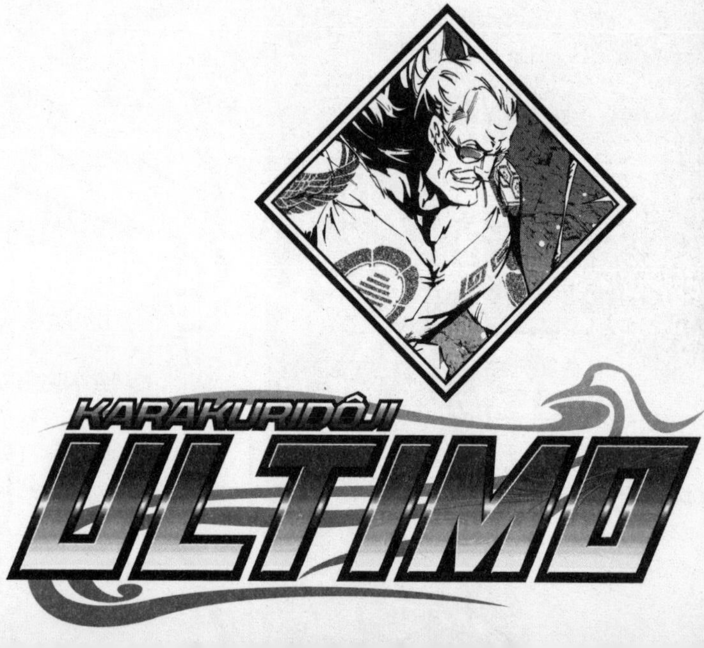

KARAKURIDÔJI
ULTIMO

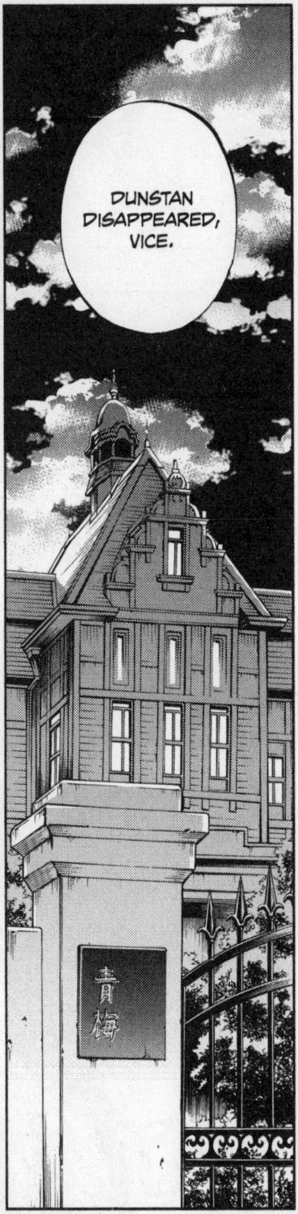
DUNSTAN DISAPPEARED, VICE.

ACT 50
ONE REALIZATION

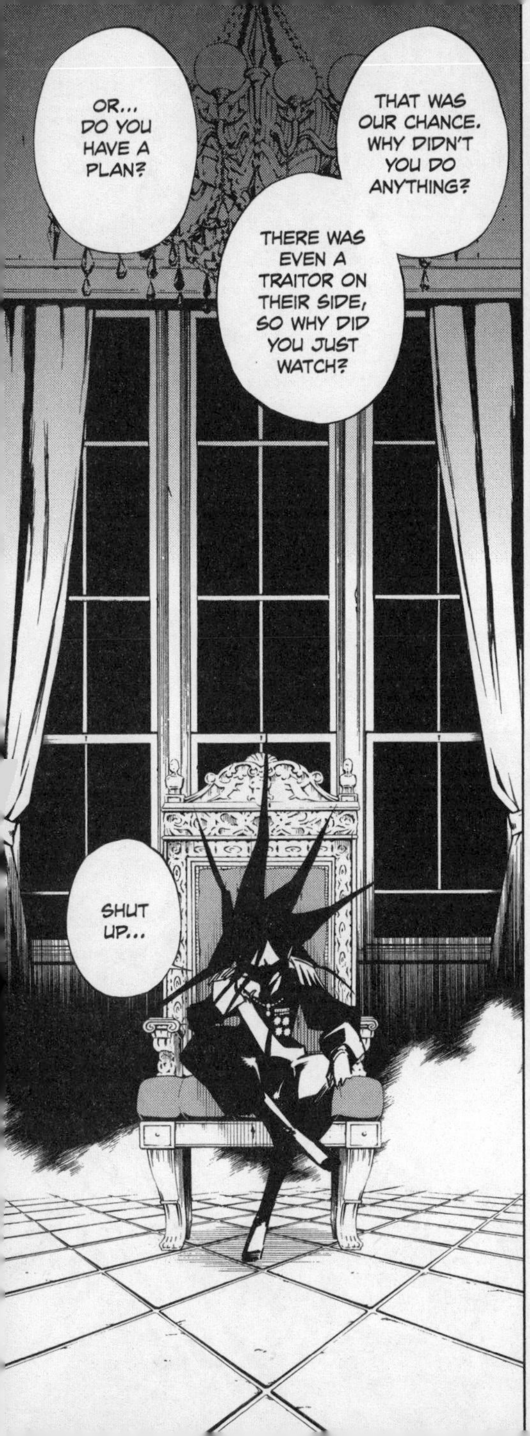
THAT WAS OUR CHANCE. WHY DIDN'T YOU DO ANYTHING?
OR... DO YOU HAVE A PLAN?
THERE WAS EVEN A TRAITOR ON THEIR SIDE, SO WHY DID YOU JUST WATCH?
SHUT UP...

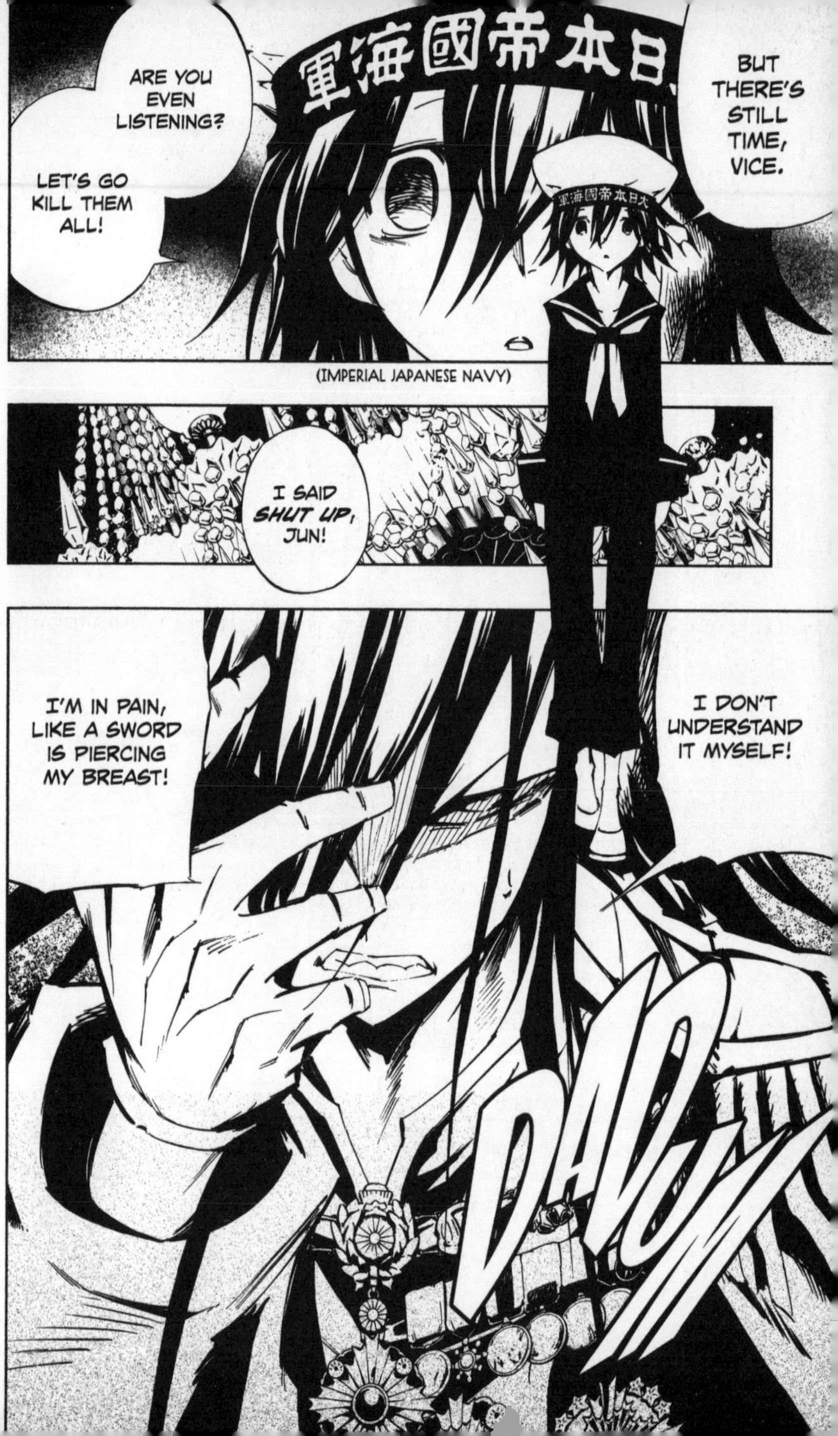
BUT THERE'S STILL TIME, VICE.
日本帝國海軍
大日本帝國海軍
ARE YOU EVEN LISTENING?
LET'S GO KILL THEM ALL!
(IMPERIAL JAPANESE NAVY)
I SAID *SHUT UP*, JUN!
I DON'T UNDERSTAND IT MYSELF!
I'M IN PAIN, LIKE A SWORD IS PIERCING MY BREAST!
DAN

ONE REALIZATION

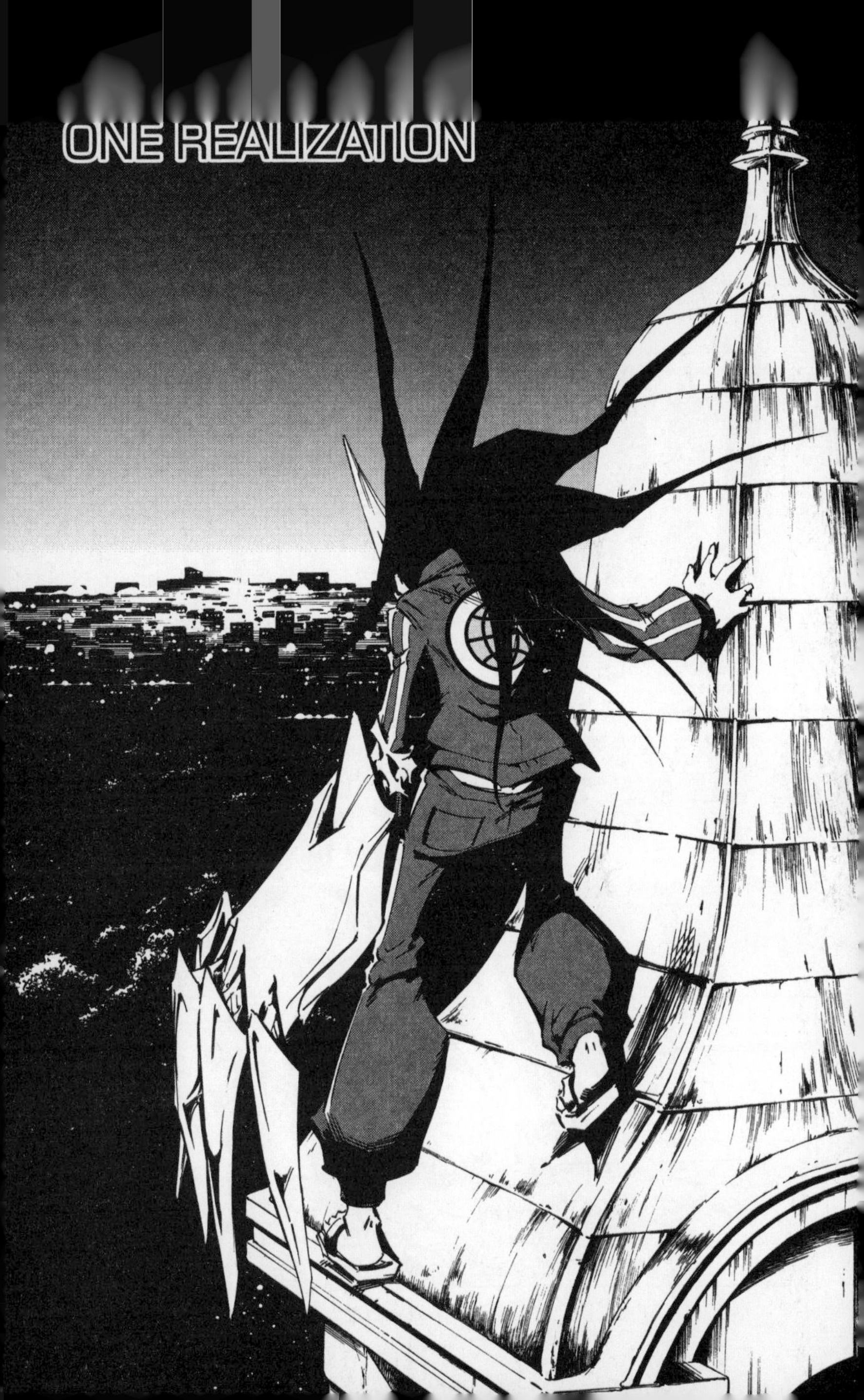

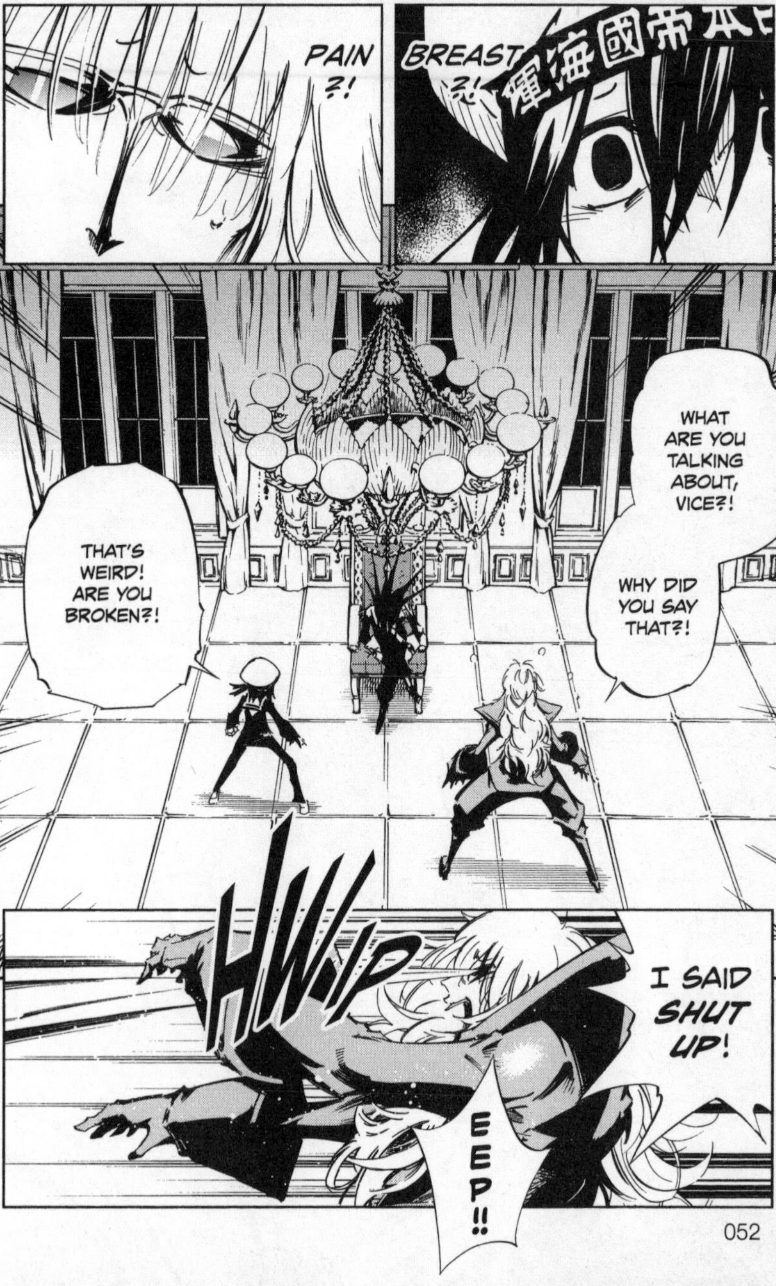
BREAST ?!
PAIN ?!
WHAT ARE YOU TALKING ABOUT, VICE?!
WHY DID YOU SAY THAT?!
THAT'S WEIRD! ARE YOU BROKEN?!
I SAID SHUT UP!
HWIP
EEP!!

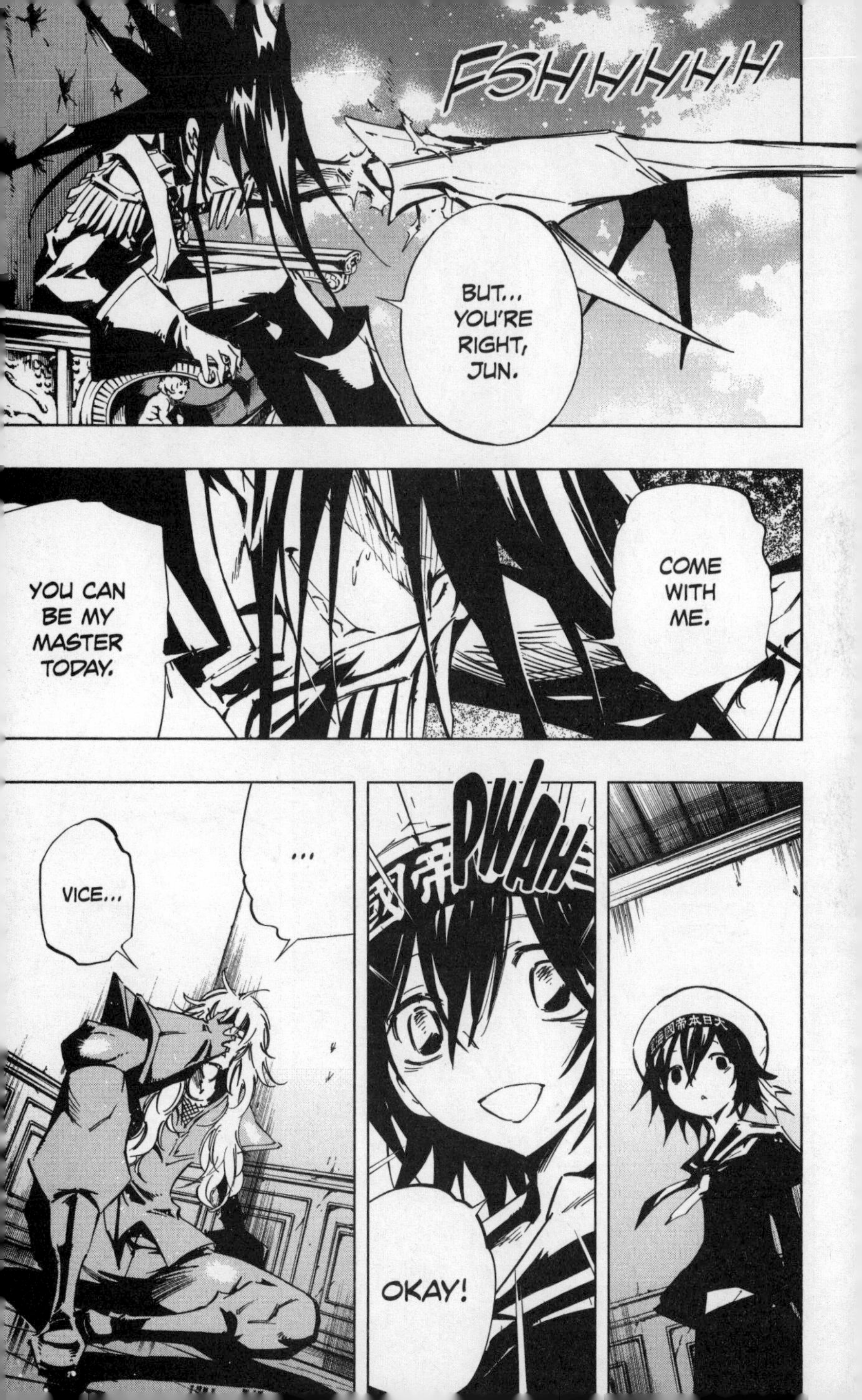
FSHHHHH
BUT... YOU'RE RIGHT, JUN.
COME WITH ME.
YOU CAN BE MY MASTER TODAY.
PWAH
OKAY!
...
VICE...

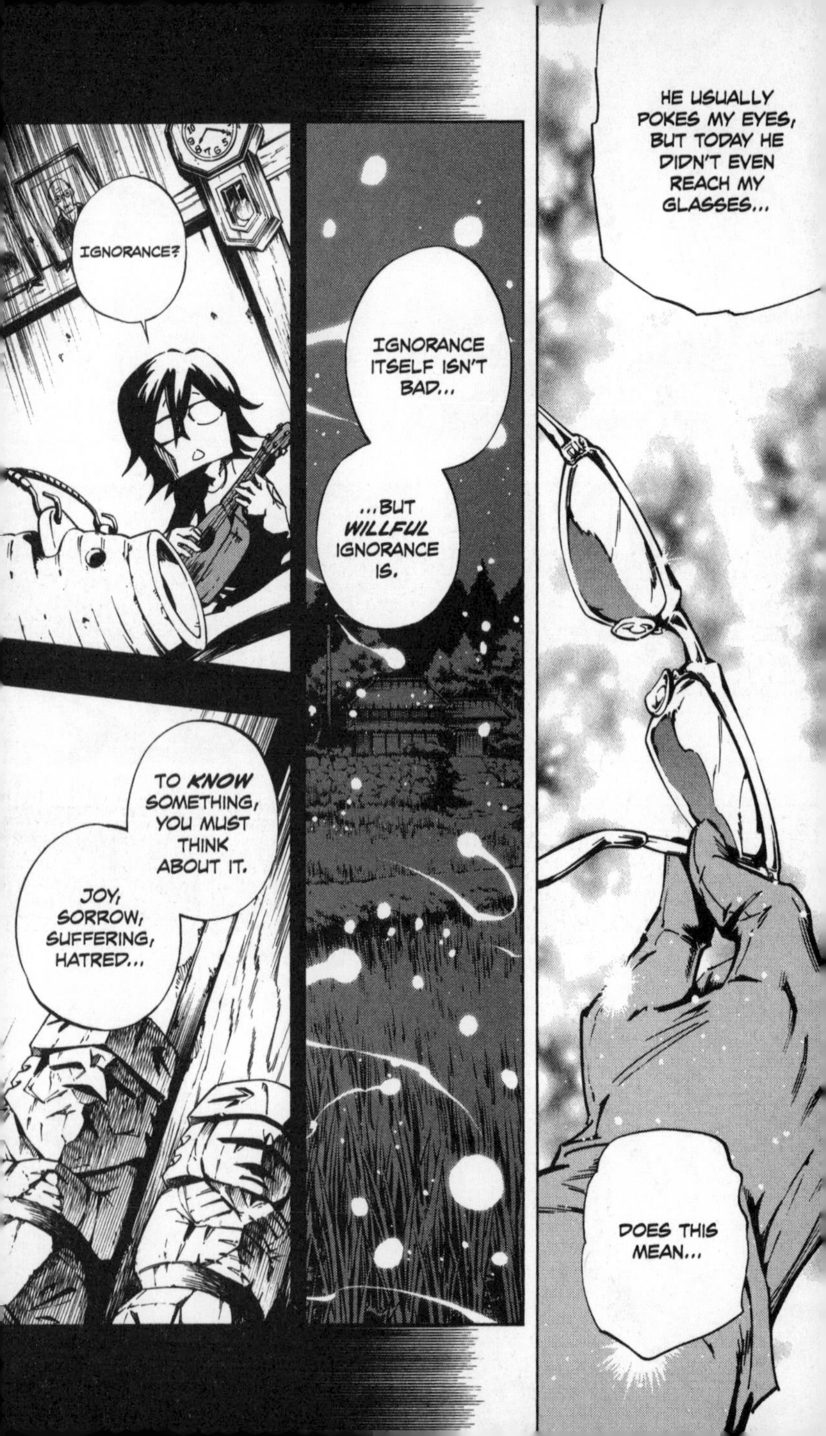
HE USUALLY POKES MY EYES, BUT TODAY HE DIDN'T EVEN REACH MY GLASSES...
DOES THIS MEAN...
IGNORANCE ITSELF ISN'T BAD...
...BUT *WILLFUL* IGNORANCE IS.
IGNORANCE?
TO *KNOW* SOMETHING, YOU MUST THINK ABOUT IT.
JOY, SORROW, SUFFERING, HATRED...

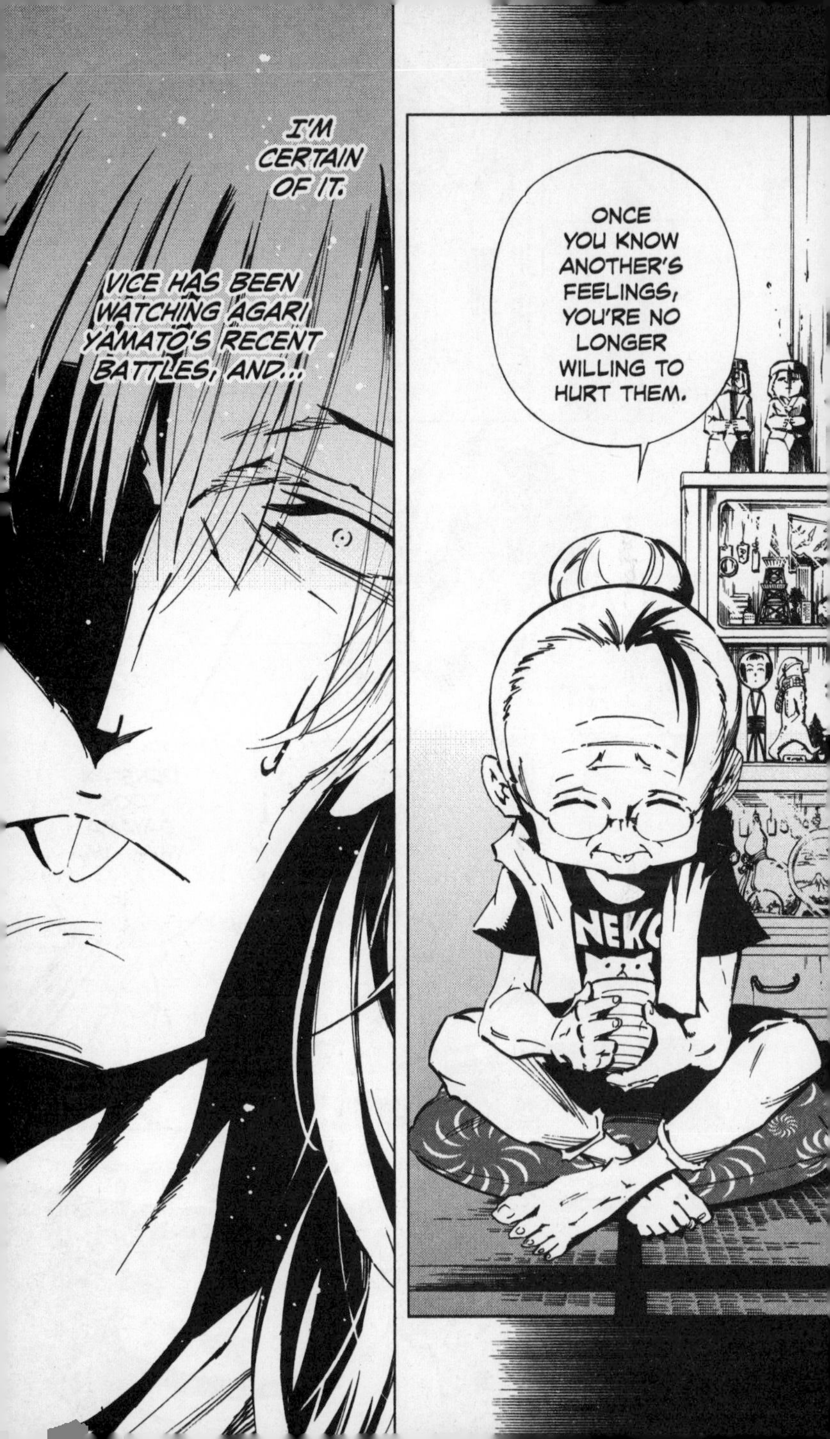
ONCE YOU KNOW ANOTHER'S FEELINGS, YOU'RE NO LONGER WILLING TO HURT THEM.
I'M CERTAIN OF IT.
VICE HAS BEEN WATCHING AGARI YAMATO'S RECENT BATTLES, AND...

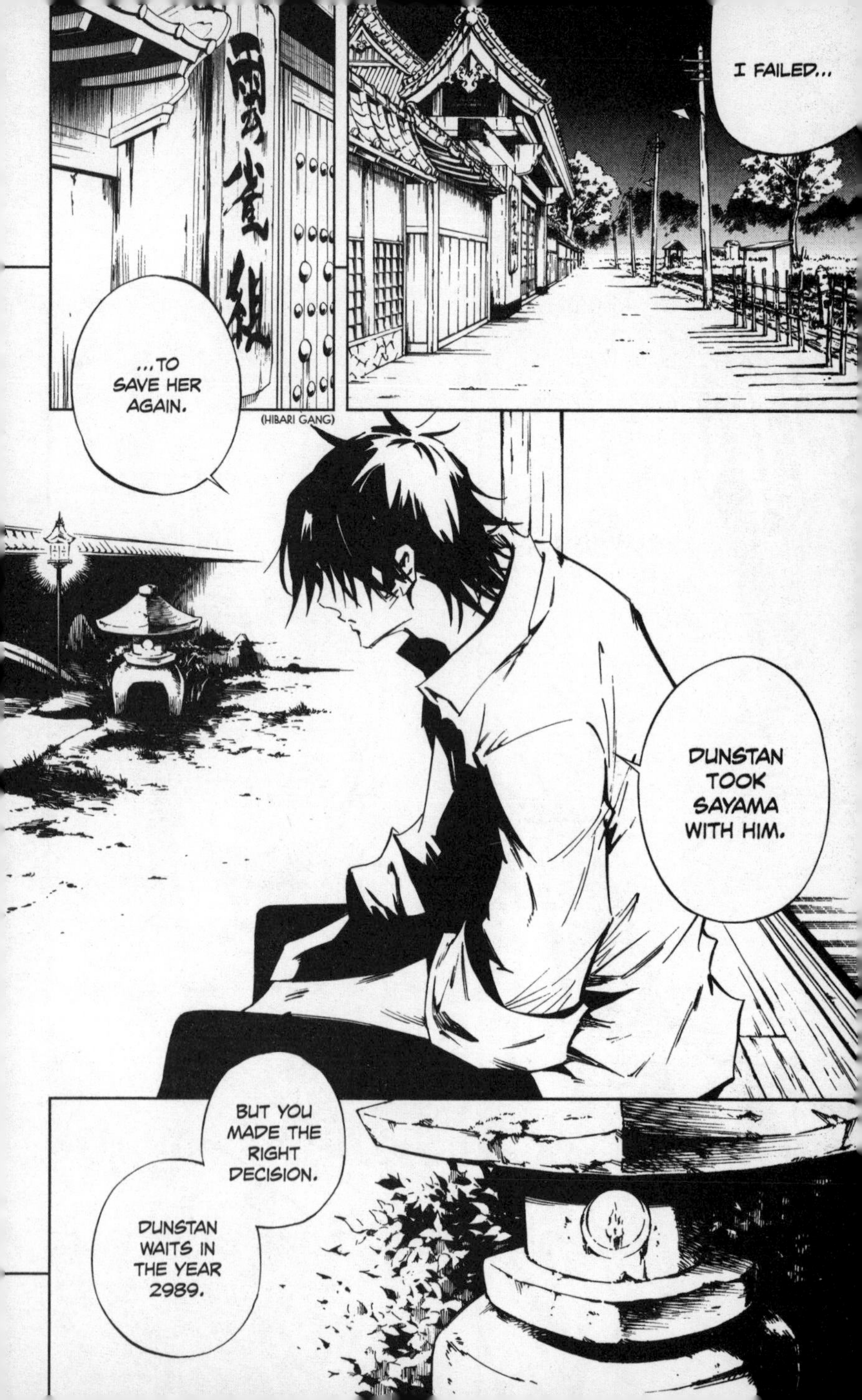
I FAILED...
...TO SAVE HER AGAIN.
(HIBARI GANG)
DUNSTAN TOOK SAYAMA WITH HIM.
BUT YOU MADE THE RIGHT DECISION.
DUNSTAN WAITS IN THE YEAR 2989.

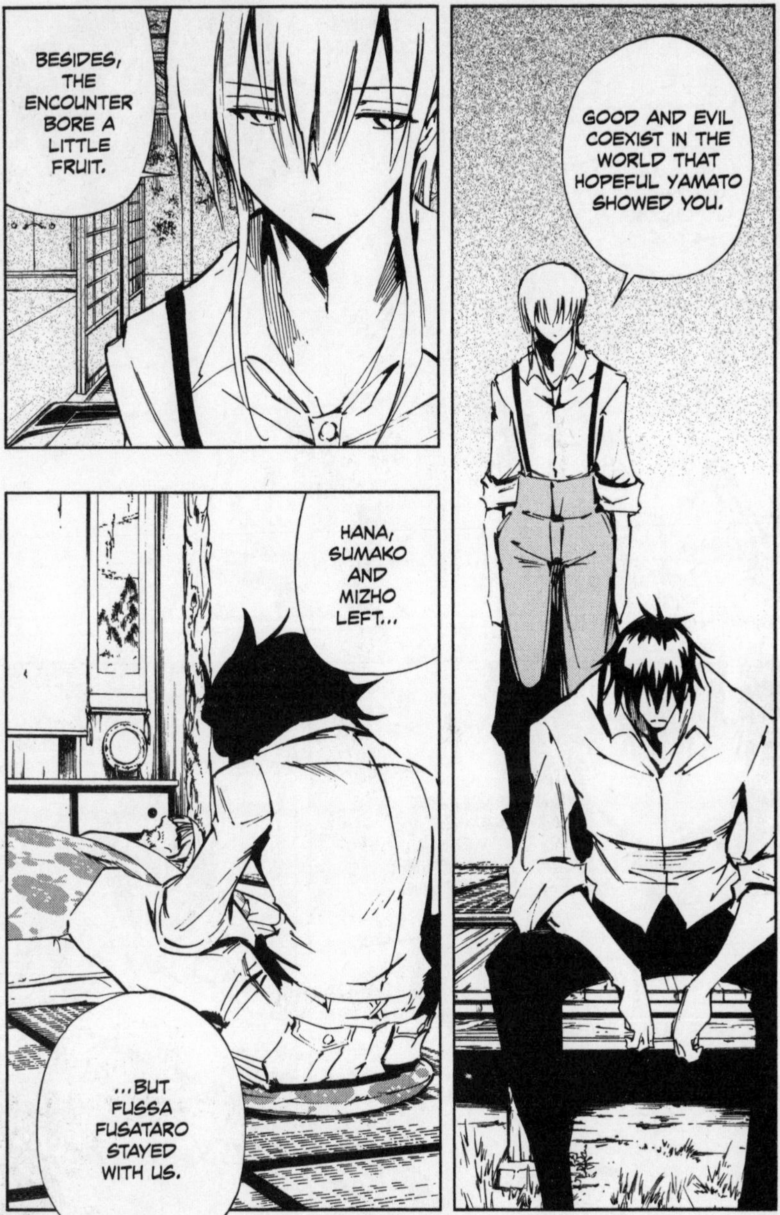
GOOD AND EVIL COEXIST IN THE WORLD THAT HOPEFUL YAMATO SHOWED YOU.
BESIDES, THE ENCOUNTER BORE A LITTLE FRUIT.
HANA, SUMAKO AND MIZHO LEFT...
...BUT FUSSA FUSATARO STAYED WITH US.

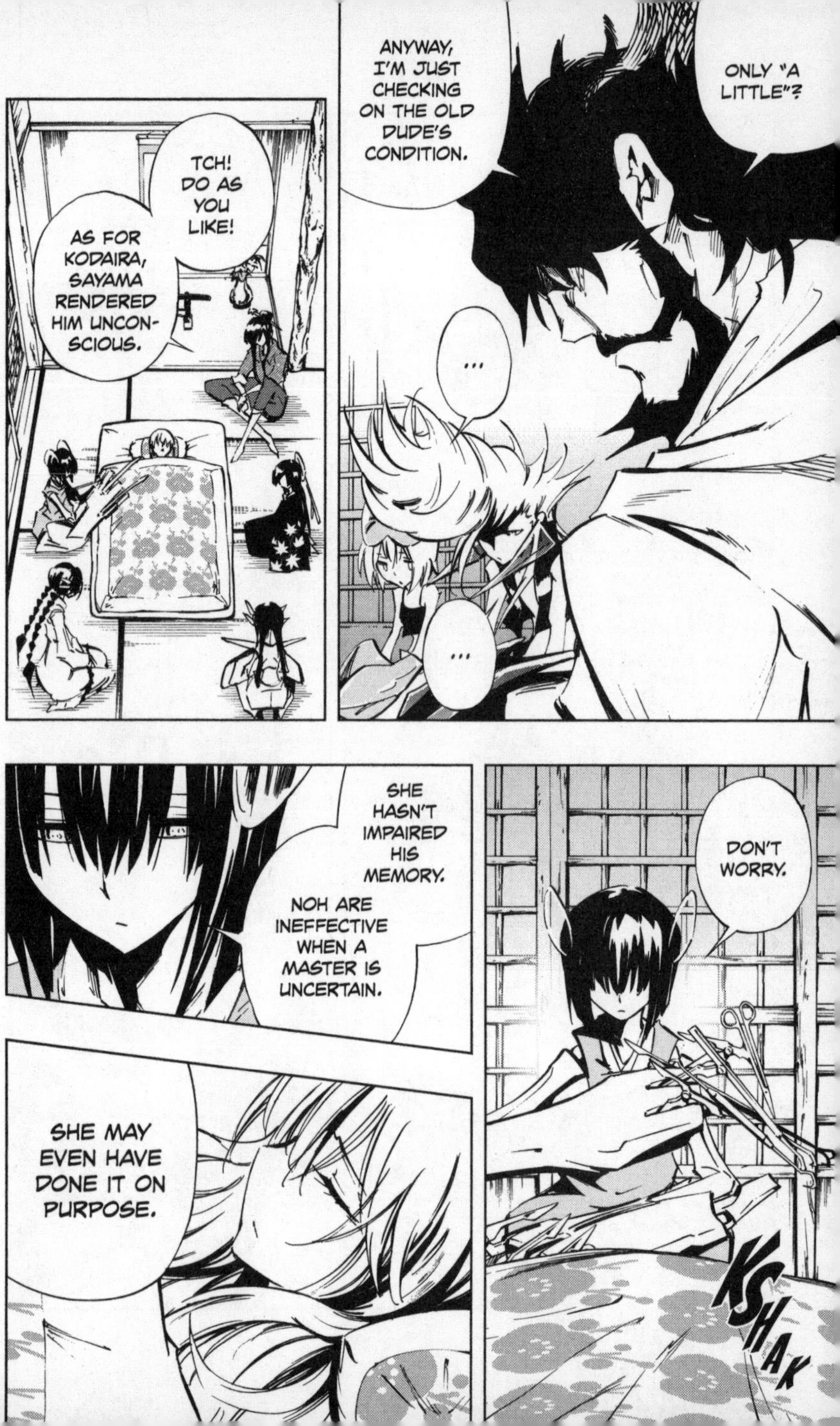
ONLY "A LITTLE"?
ANYWAY, I'M JUST CHECKING ON THE OLD DUDE'S CONDITION.
...
...
TCH! DO AS YOU LIKE!
AS FOR KODAIRA, SAYAMA RENDERED HIM UNCONSCIOUS.
DON'T WORRY.
KSHAK
SHE HASN'T IMPAIRED HIS MEMORY.
NOH ARE INEFFECTIVE WHEN A MASTER IS UNCERTAIN.
SHE MAY EVEN HAVE DONE IT ON PURPOSE.

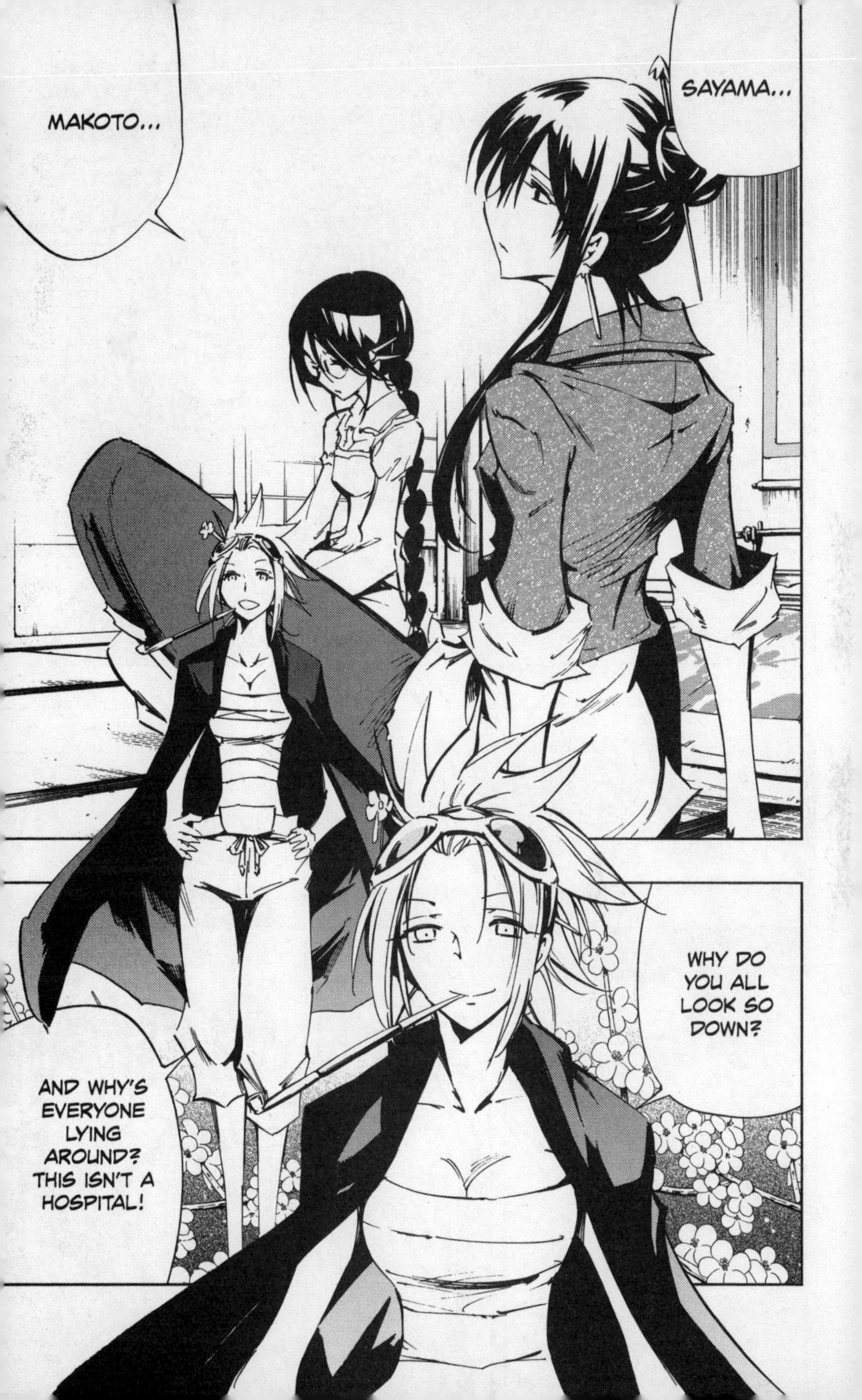
SAYAMA...
MAKOTO...
WHY DO YOU ALL LOOK SO DOWN?
AND WHY'S EVERYONE LYING AROUND? THIS ISN'T A HOSPITAL!

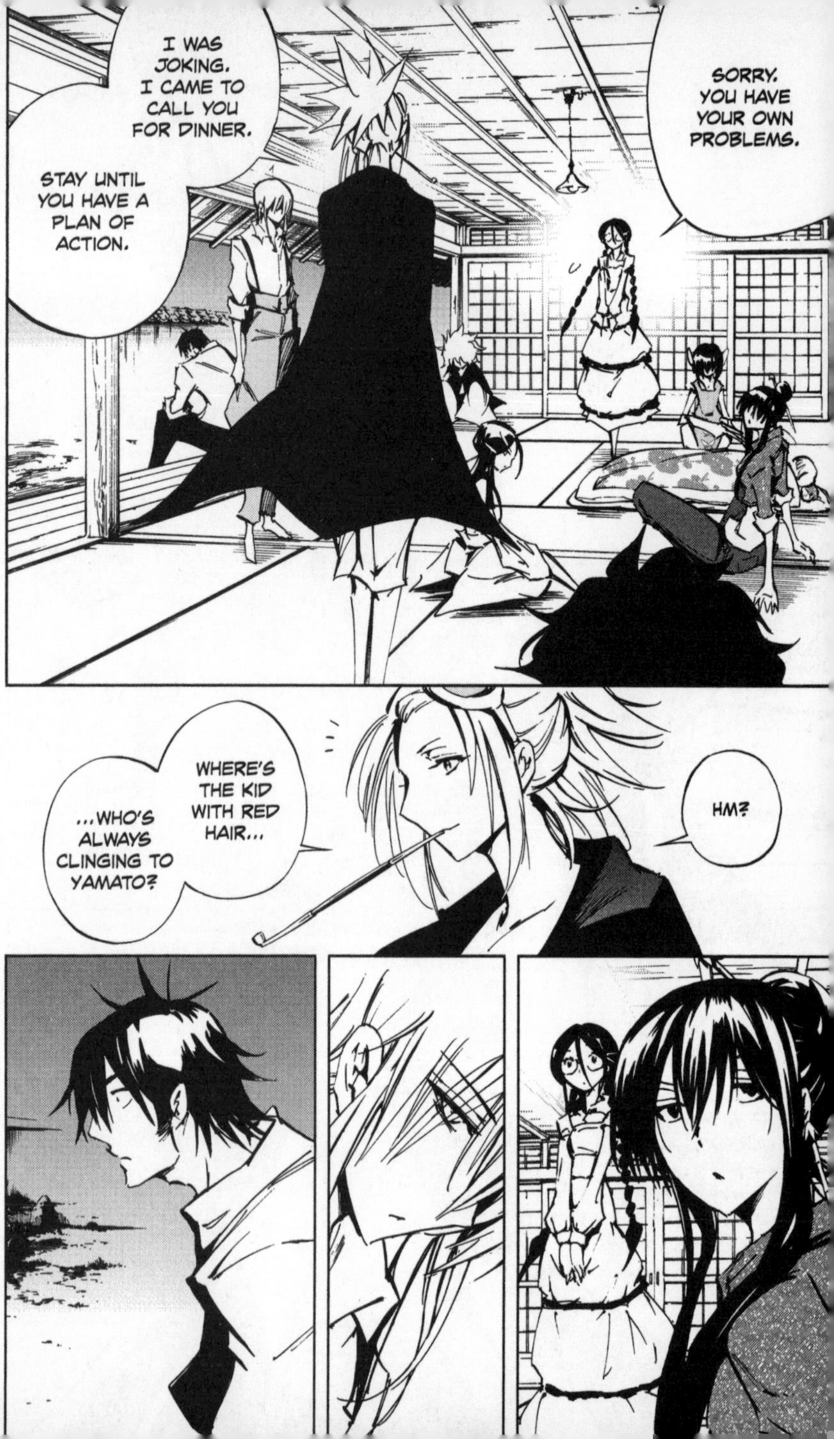
SORRY. YOU HAVE YOUR OWN PROBLEMS.
I WAS JOKING. I CAME TO CALL YOU FOR DINNER.
STAY UNTIL YOU HAVE A PLAN OF ACTION.
HM?
WHERE'S THE KID WITH RED HAIR...
...WHO'S ALWAYS CLINGING TO YAMATO?

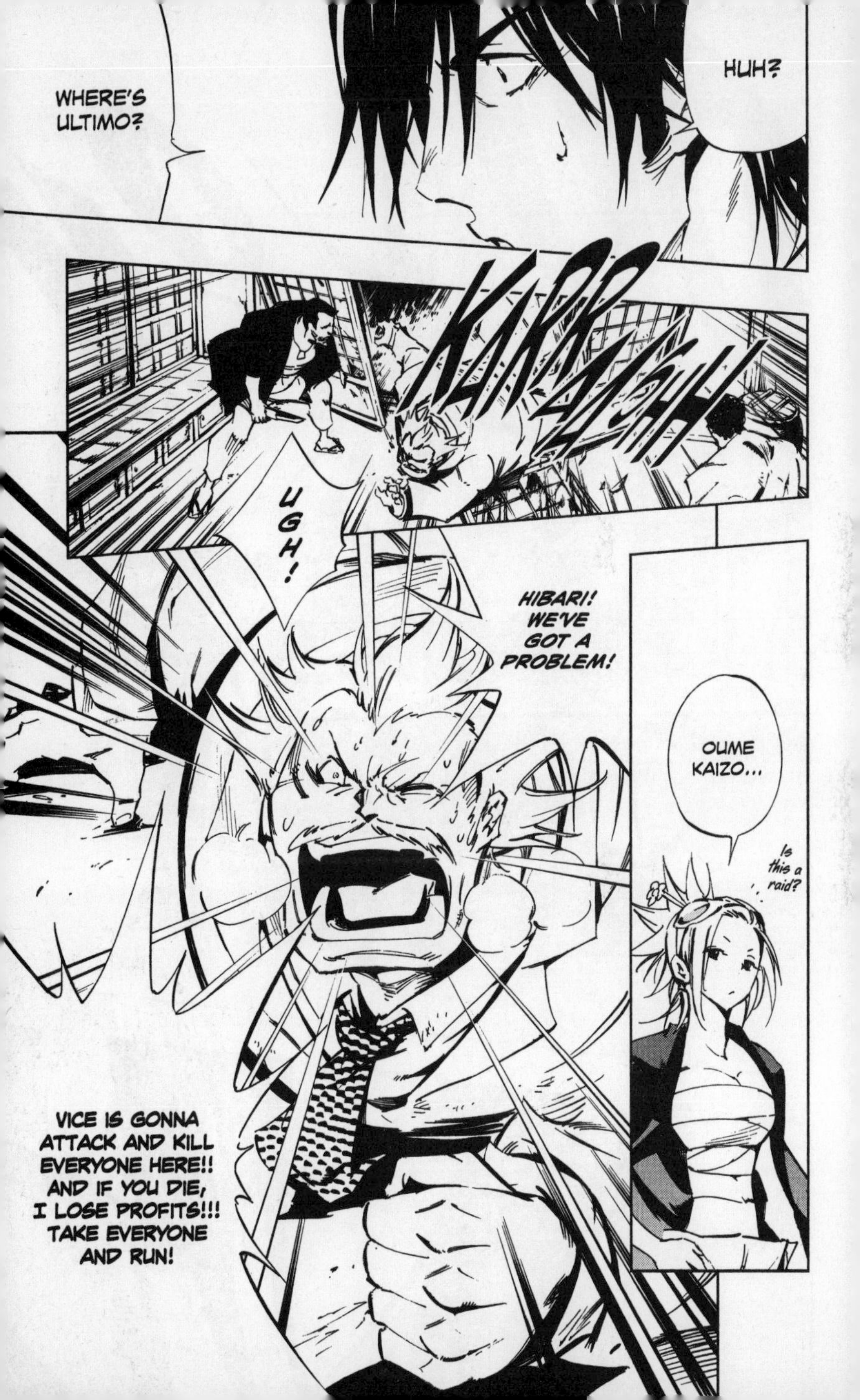
HUH?
WHERE'S ULTIMO?
UGH!
OUME KAIZO...
Is this a raid?
HIBARI! WE'VE GOT A PROBLEM!
VICE IS GONNA ATTACK AND KILL EVERYONE HERE!! AND IF YOU DIE, I LOSE PROFITS!!! TAKE EVERYONE AND RUN!

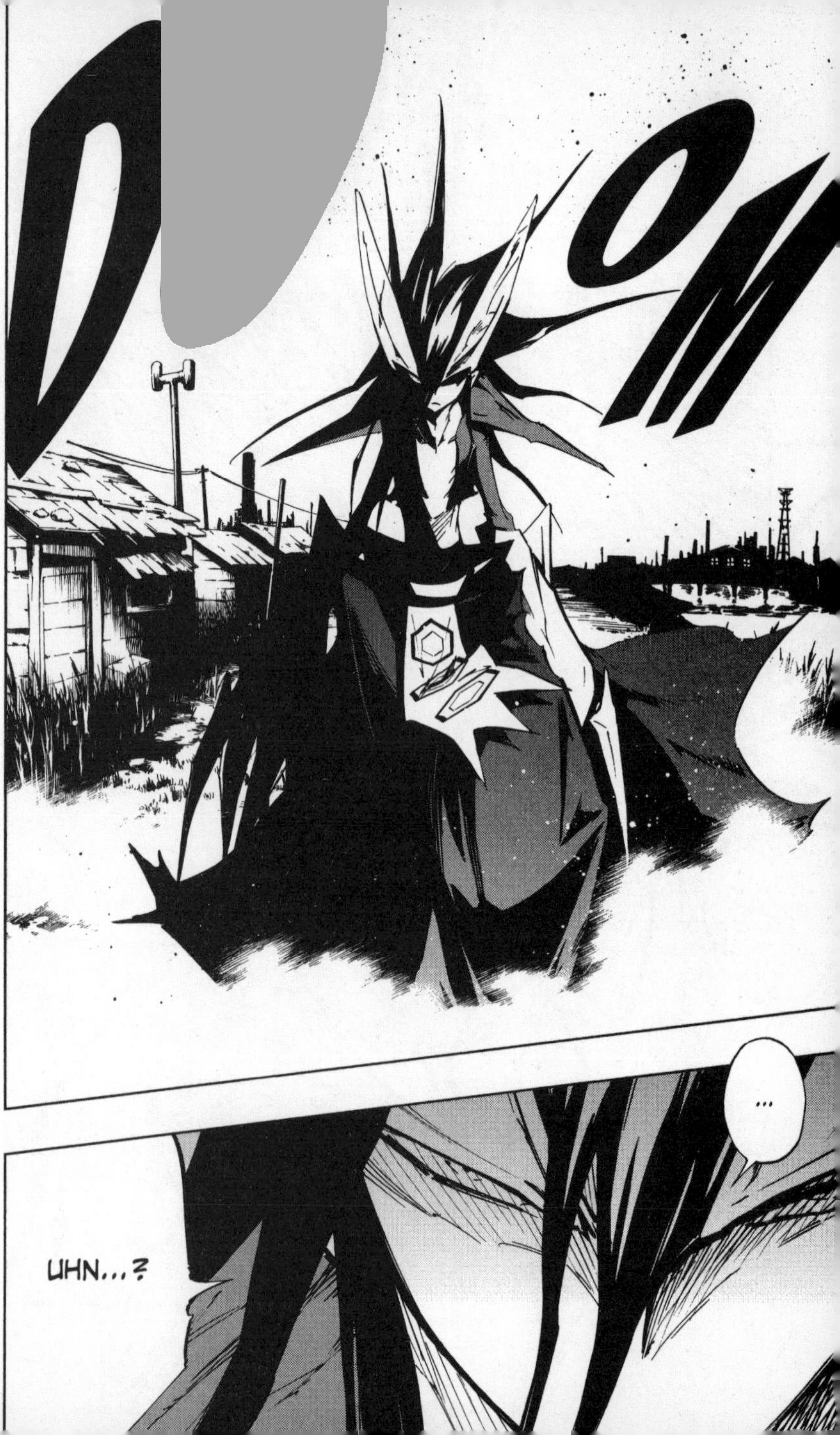
DOM
...
UHN...?

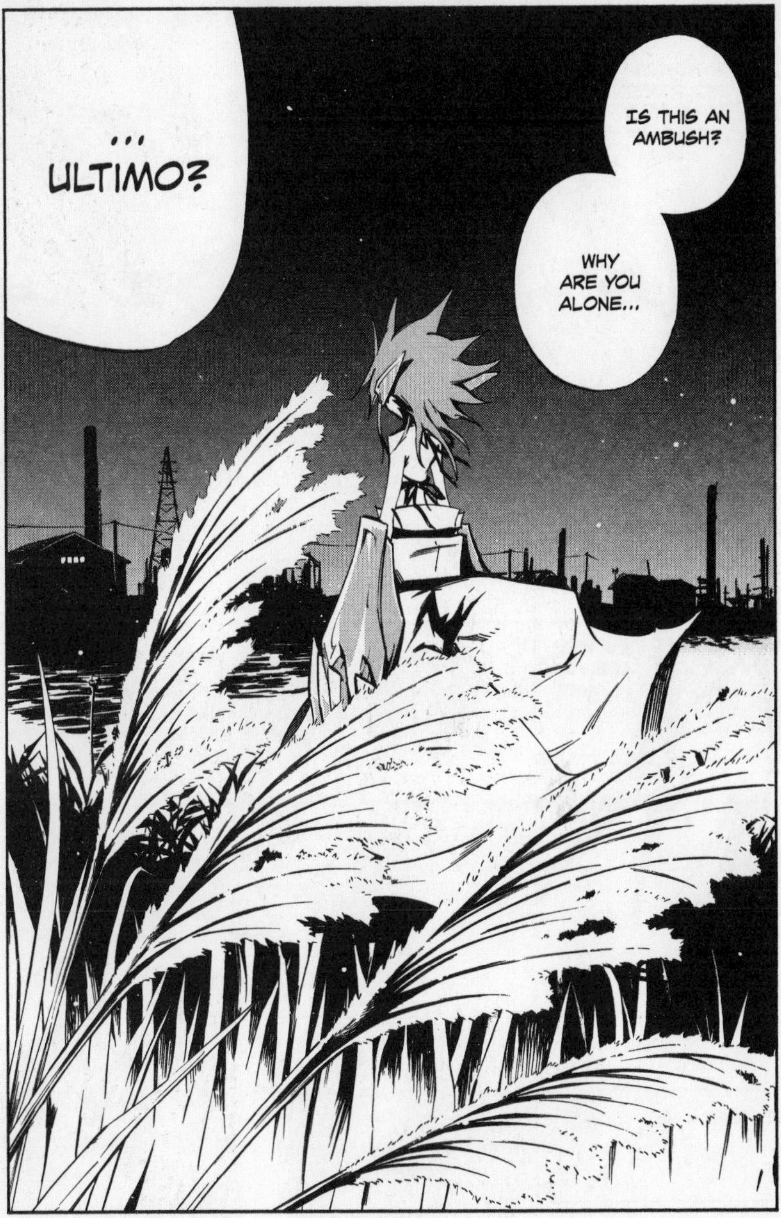
IS THIS AN AMBUSH?
WHY ARE YOU ALONE...
...ULTIMO?

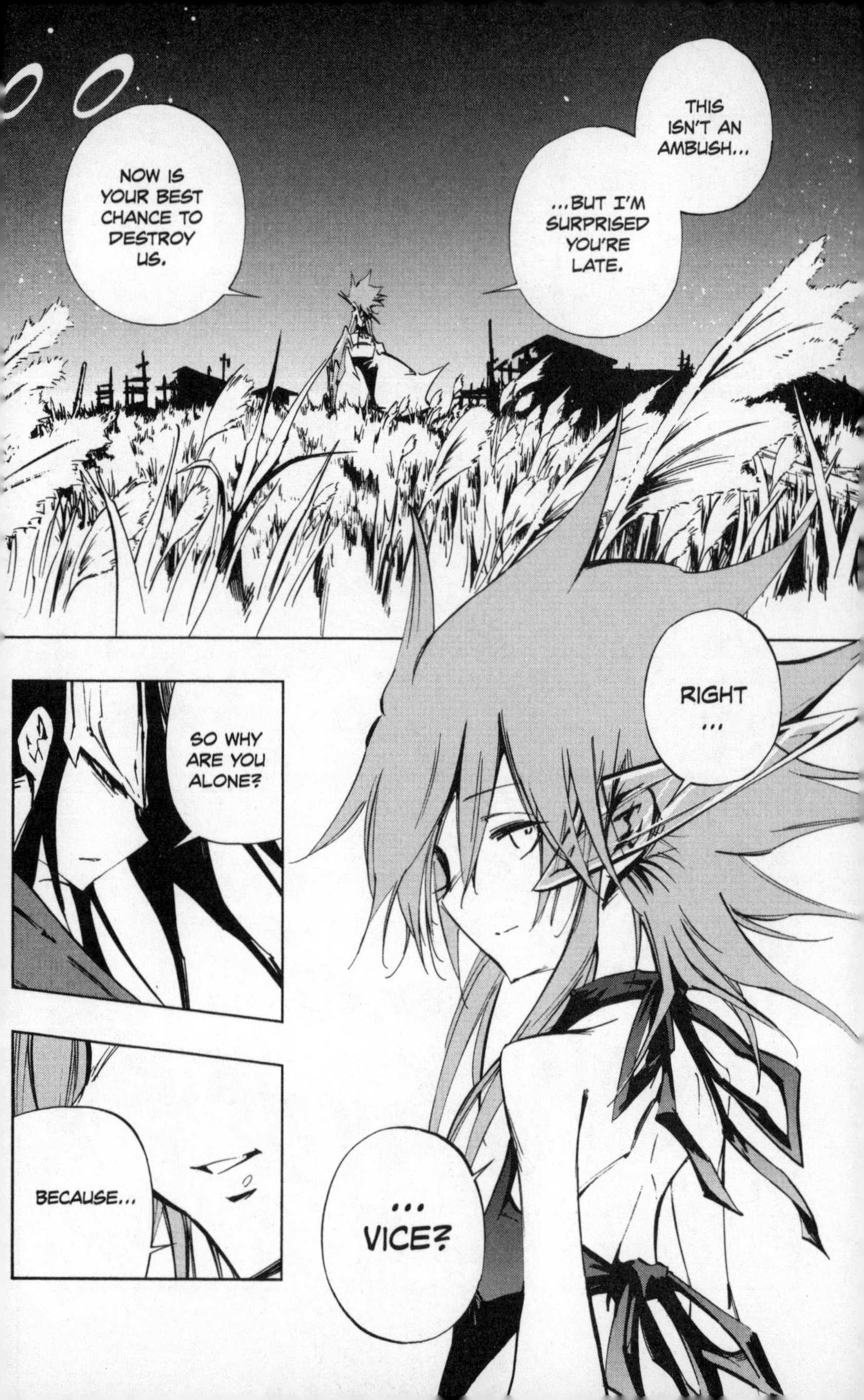
THIS ISN'T AN AMBUSH...
...BUT I'M SURPRISED YOU'RE LATE.
NOW IS YOUR BEST CHANCE TO DESTROY US.
RIGHT...
...VICE?
SO WHY ARE YOU ALONE?
BECAUSE...

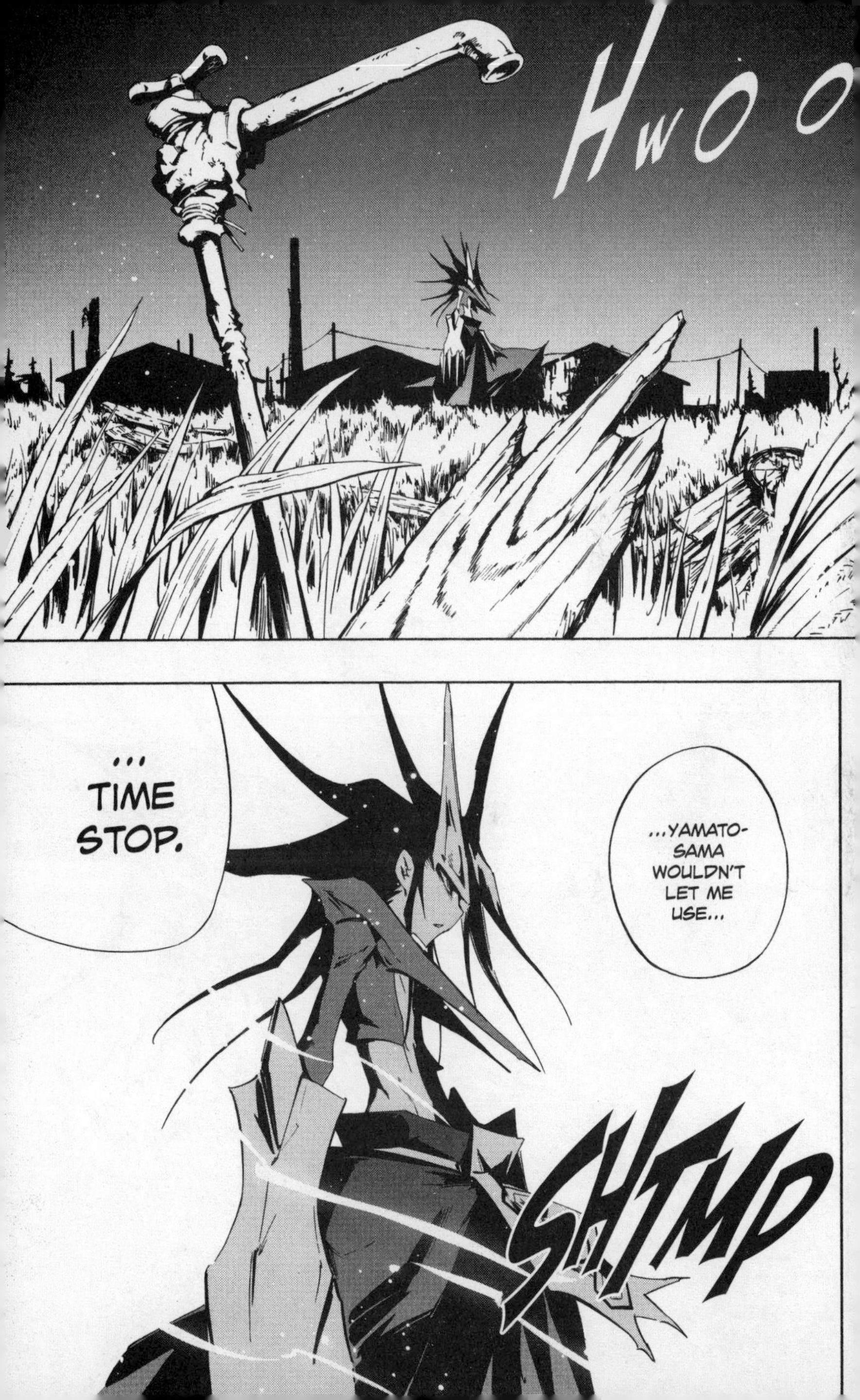
HWOO
...YAMATO-SAMA WOULDN'T LET ME USE...
... TIME STOP.
SHTMP

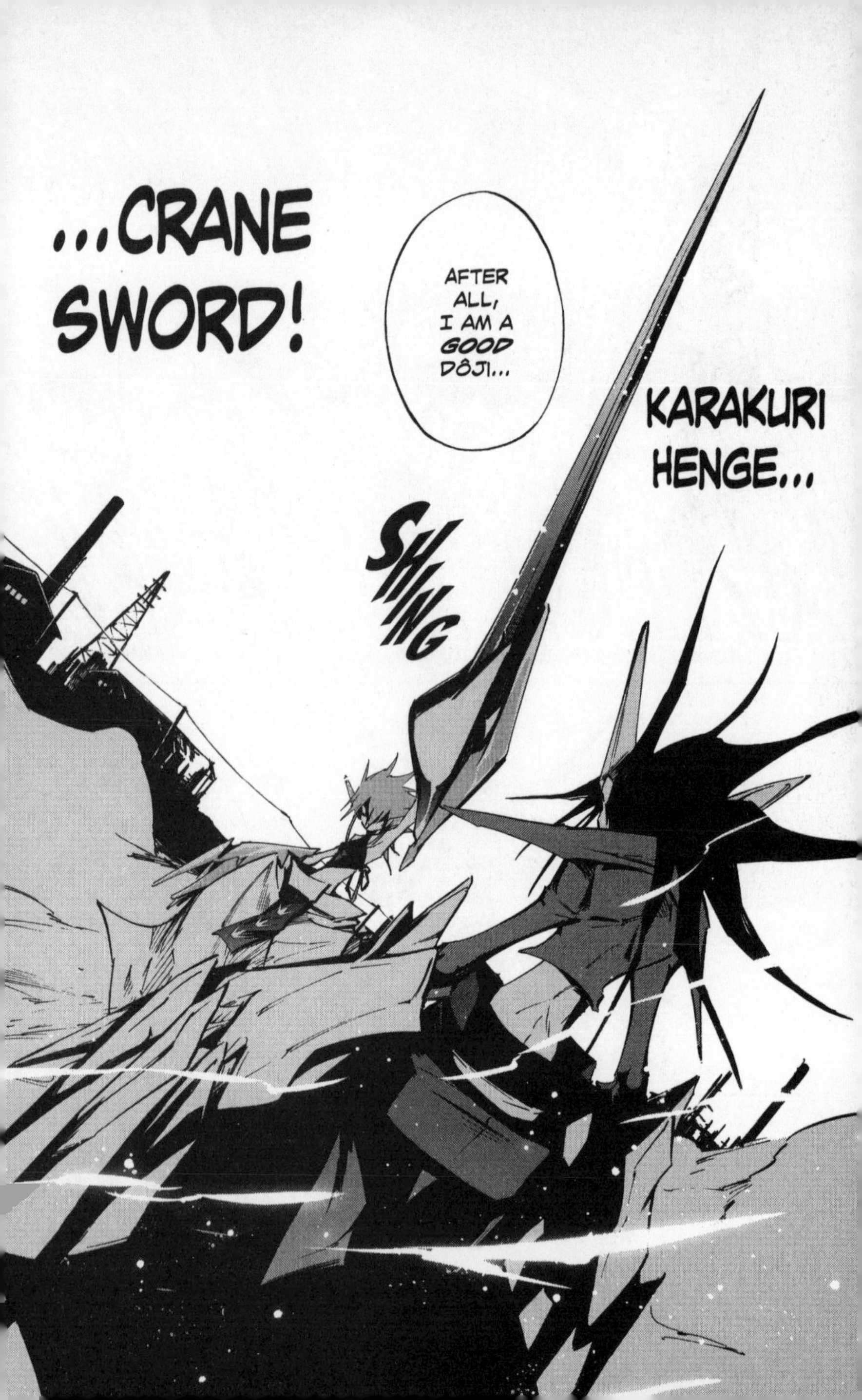
AFTER ALL, I AM A *GOOD* DÔJI...
KARAKURI HENGE...
...CRANE SWORD!
SHING

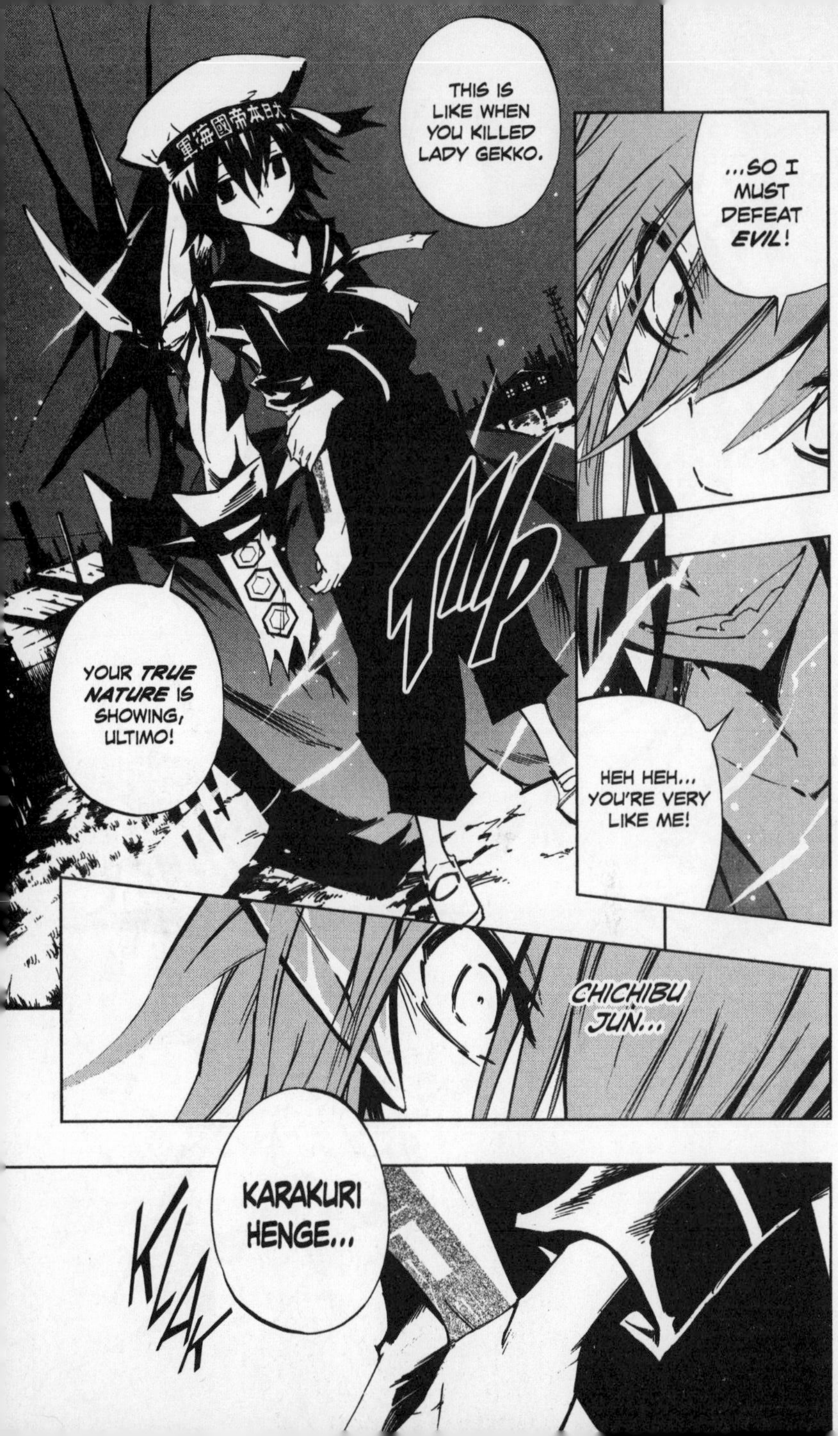
...SO I MUST DEFEAT *EVIL*!
HEH HEH... YOU'RE VERY LIKE ME!
THIS IS LIKE WHEN YOU KILLED LADY GEKKO.
大日本帝國海軍
JUMP
YOUR *TRUE NATURE* IS SHOWING, ULTIMO!
CHICHIBU JUN...
KARAKURI HENGE...
KLAK

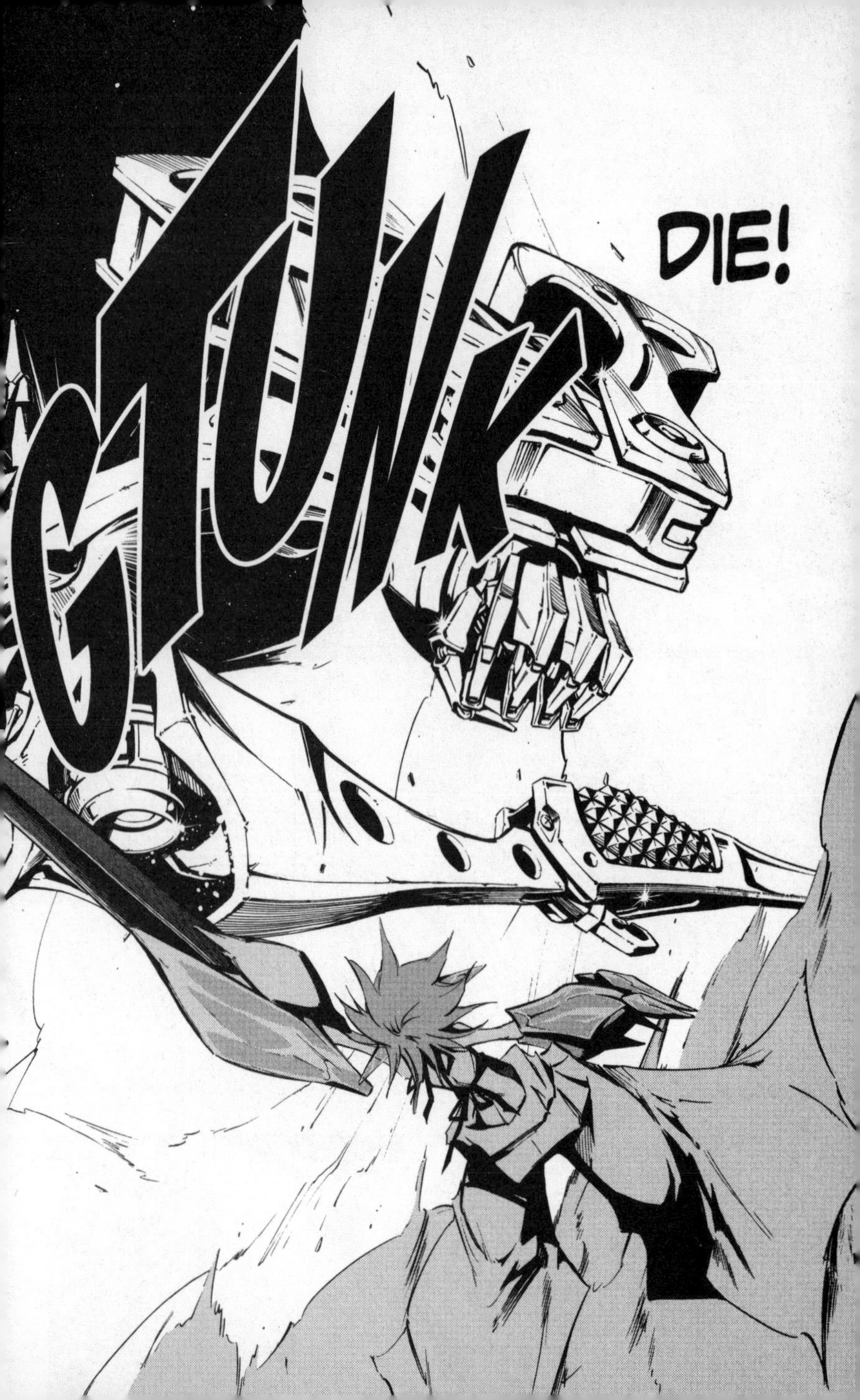
DIE!
GTUNK

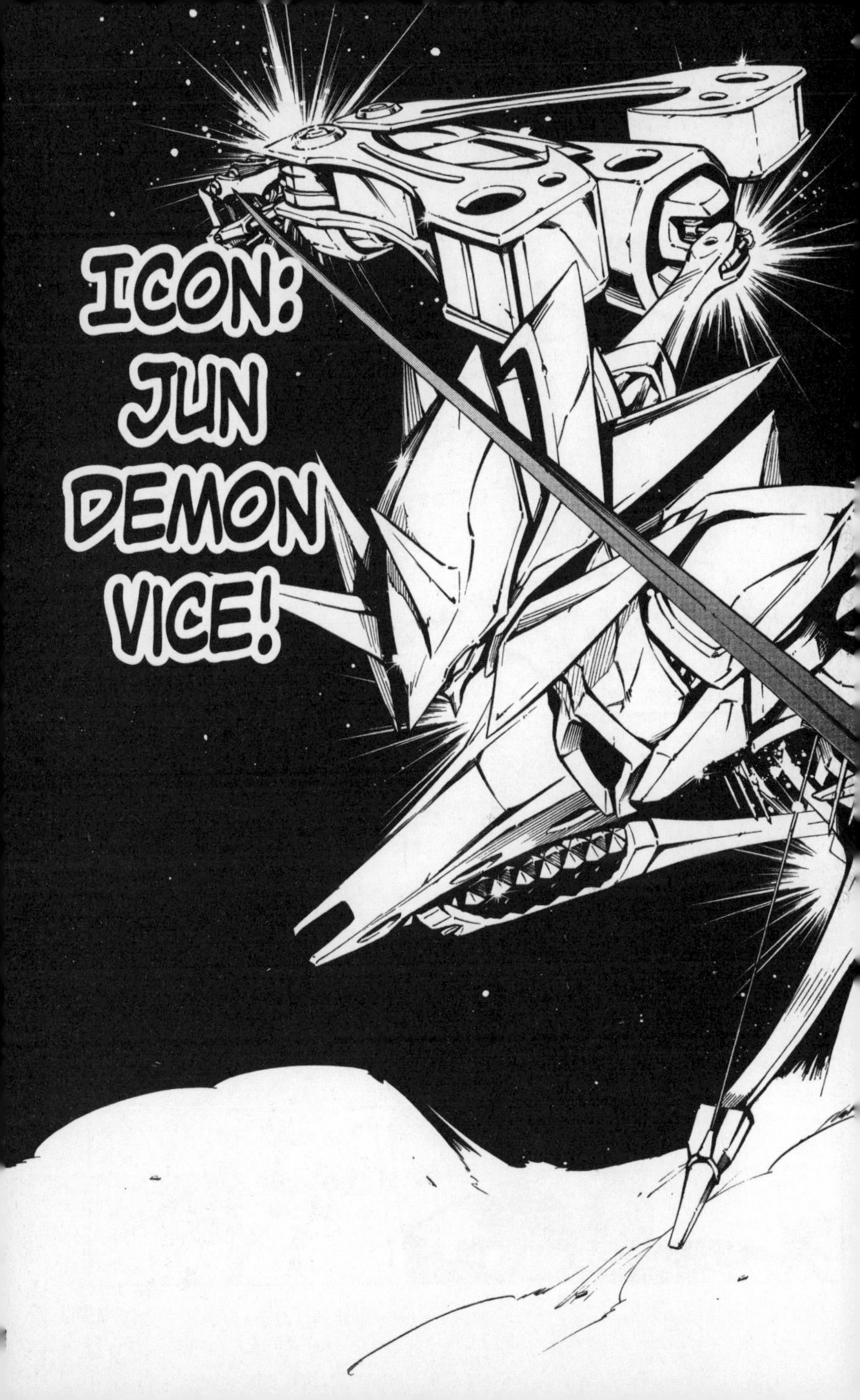
ICON: JUN DEMON VICE!

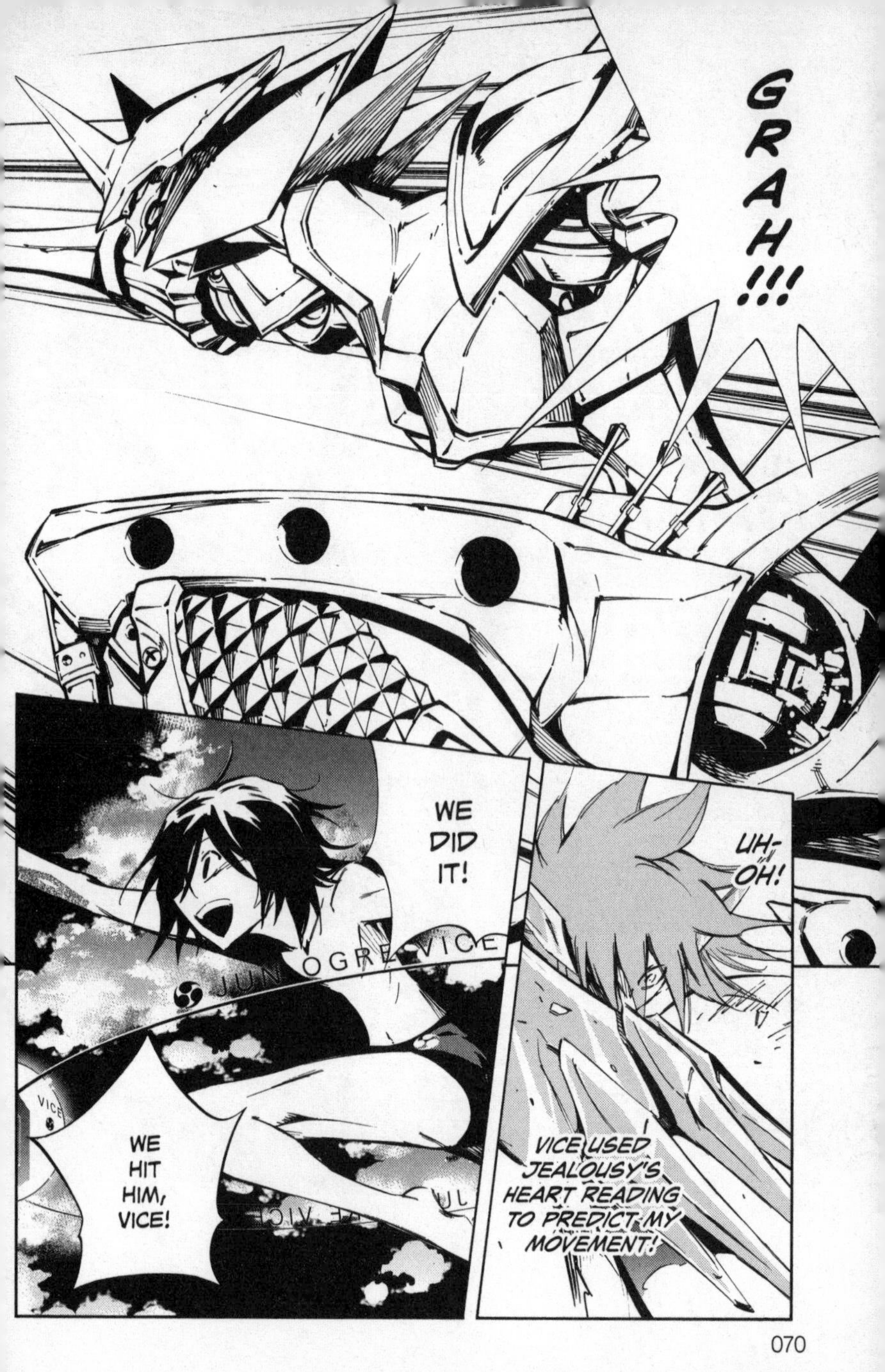
GRAH!!!
UH-OH!
VICE USED JEALOUSY'S HEART READING TO PREDICT MY MOVEMENT!
WE DID IT!
JUN OGRE VICE
WE HIT HIM, VICE!

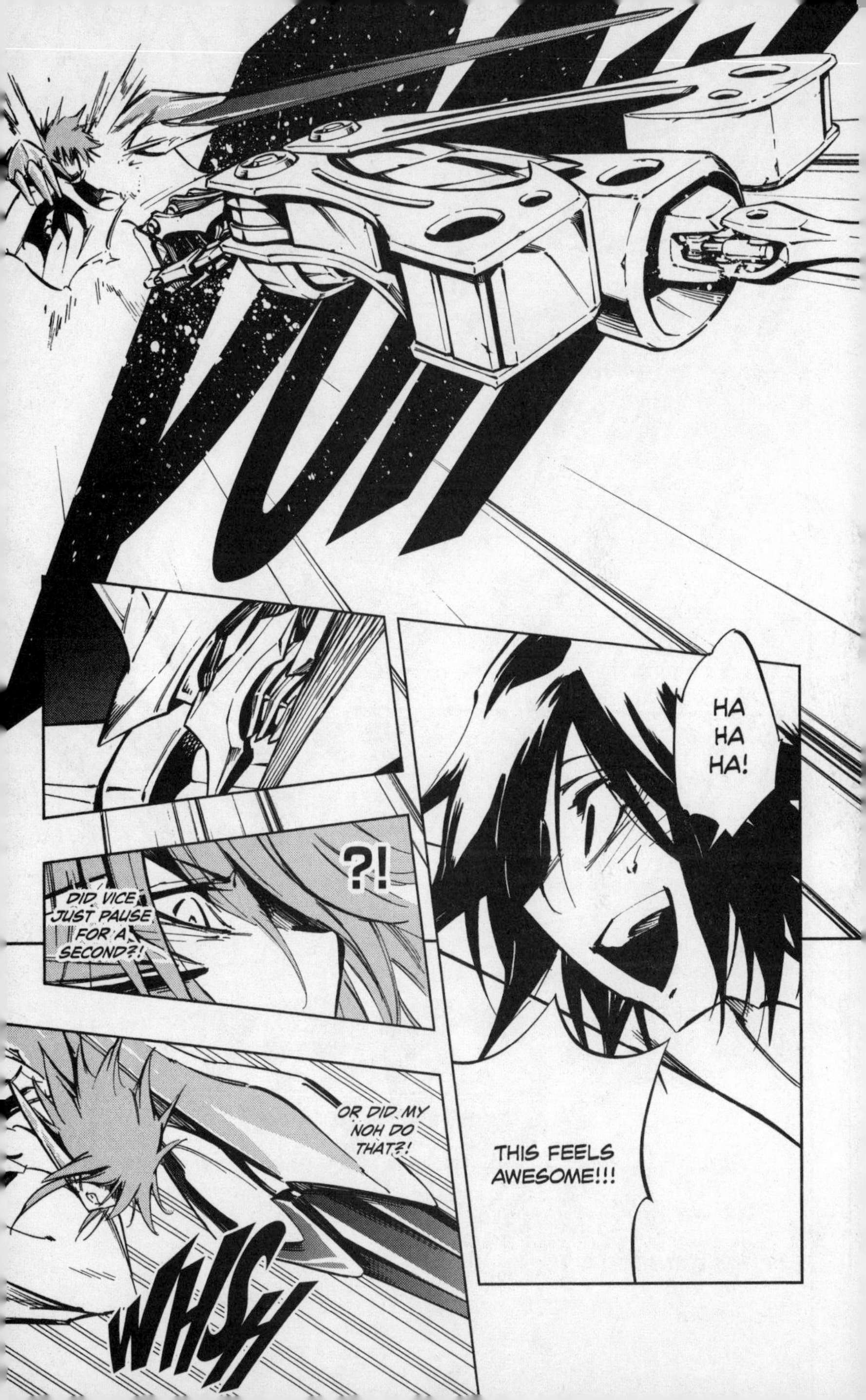
HA HA HA!
THIS FEELS AWESOME!!!
?!
DID VICE JUST PAUSE FOR A SECOND?!
OR DID MY NOH DO THAT?!
WHSH

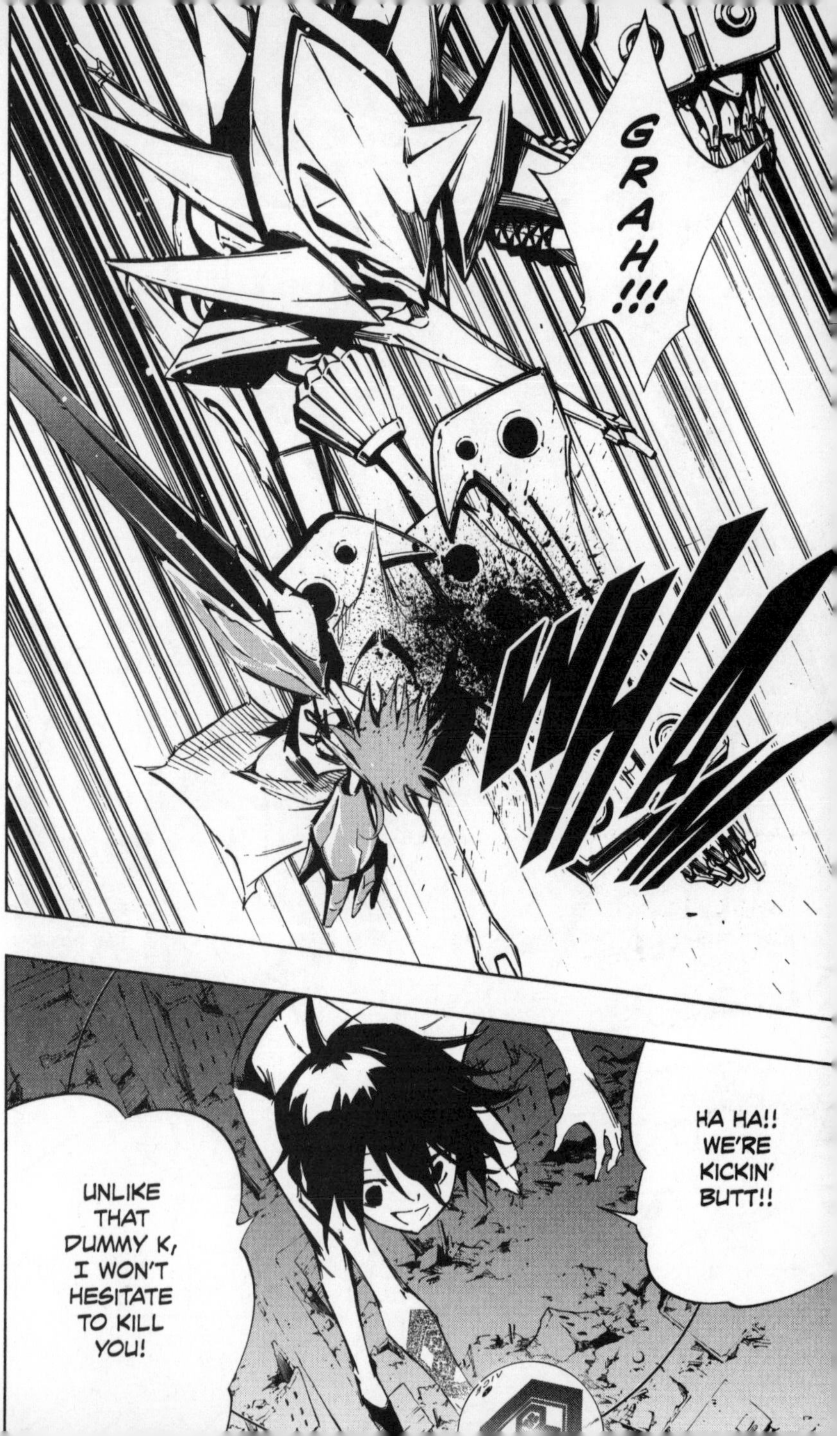
GRAH!!!
WHAM
HA HA!! WE'RE KICKIN' BUTT!!
UNLIKE THAT DUMMY K, I WON'T HESITATE TO KILL YOU!

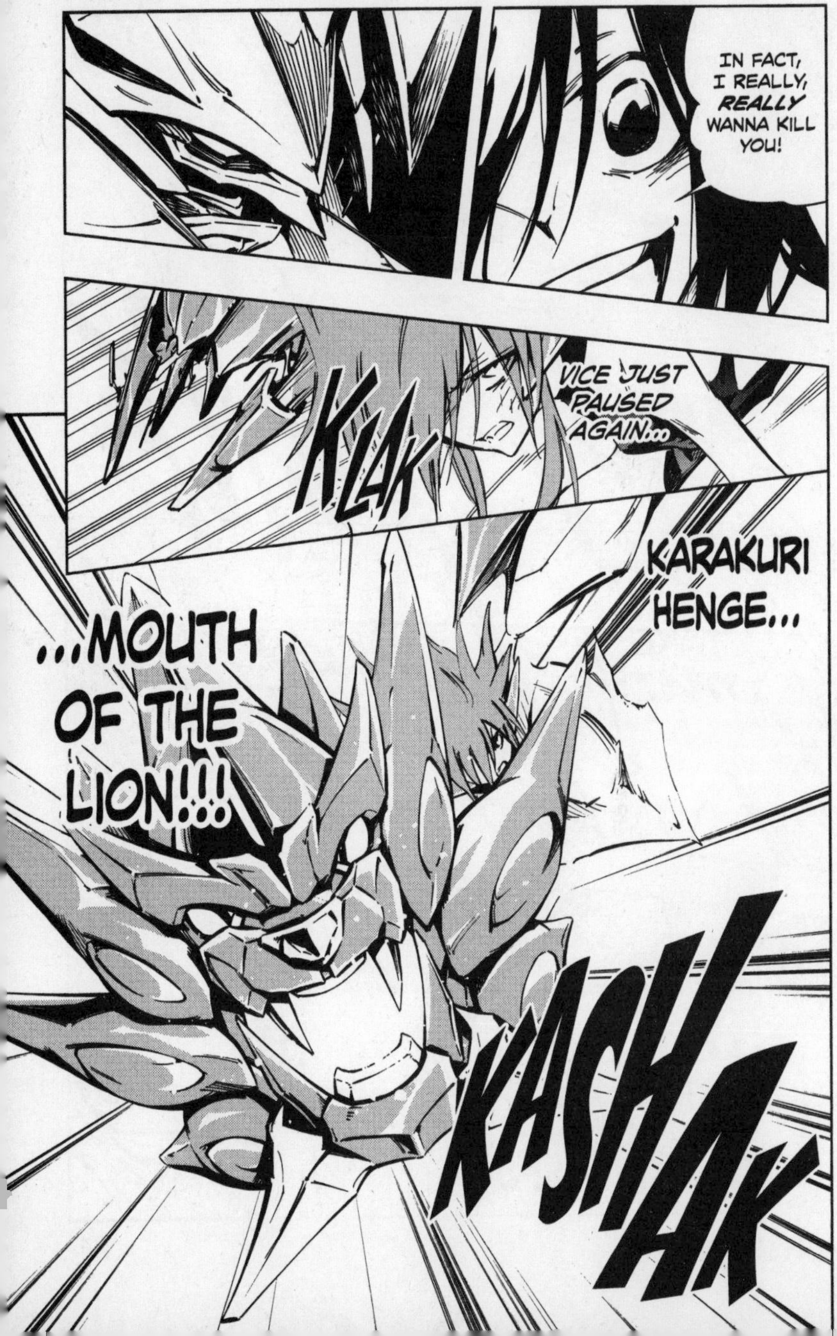
IN FACT, I REALLY, REALLY WANNA KILL YOU!
VICE JUST PAUSED AGAIN...
KLAK
KARAKURI HENGE...
...MOUTH OF THE LION!!!
KASHAK

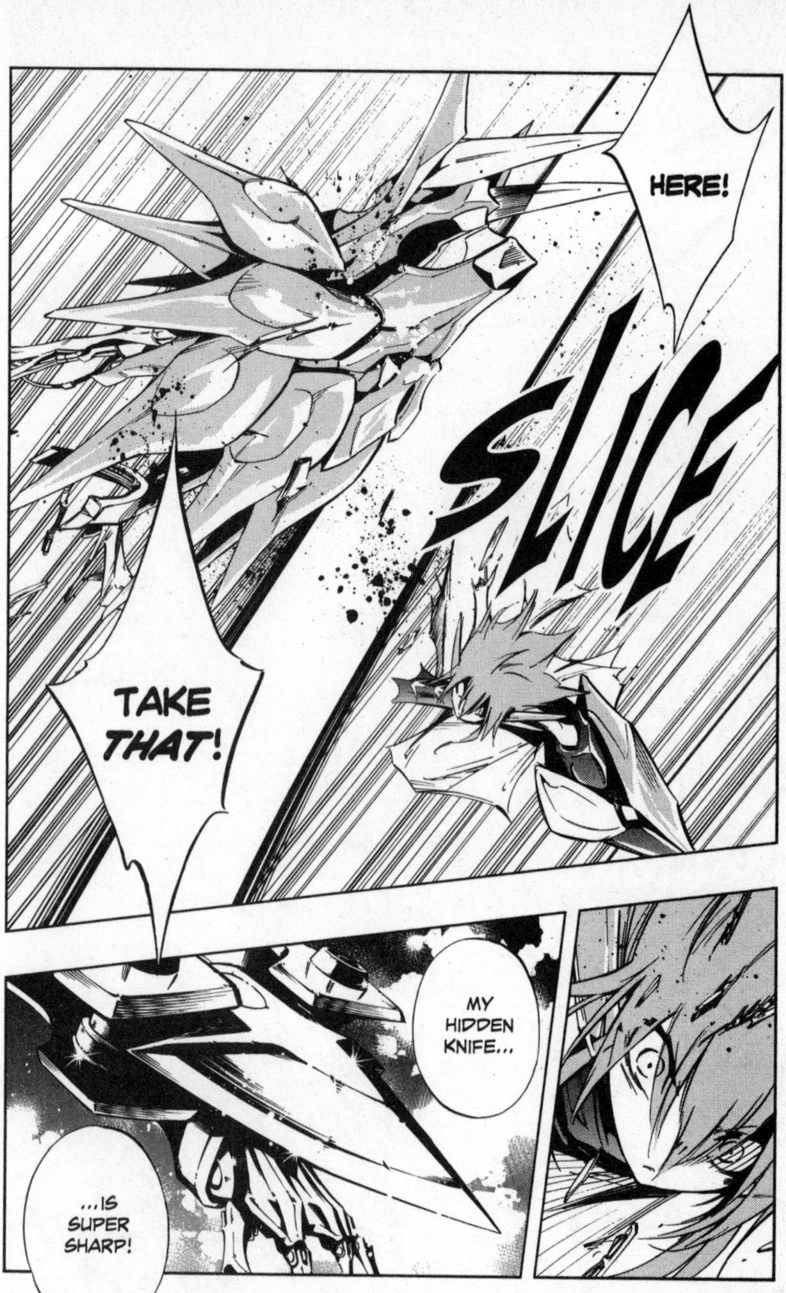
HERE!
SLICE
TAKE *THAT*!
MY HIDDEN KNIFE...
...IS SUPER SHARP!

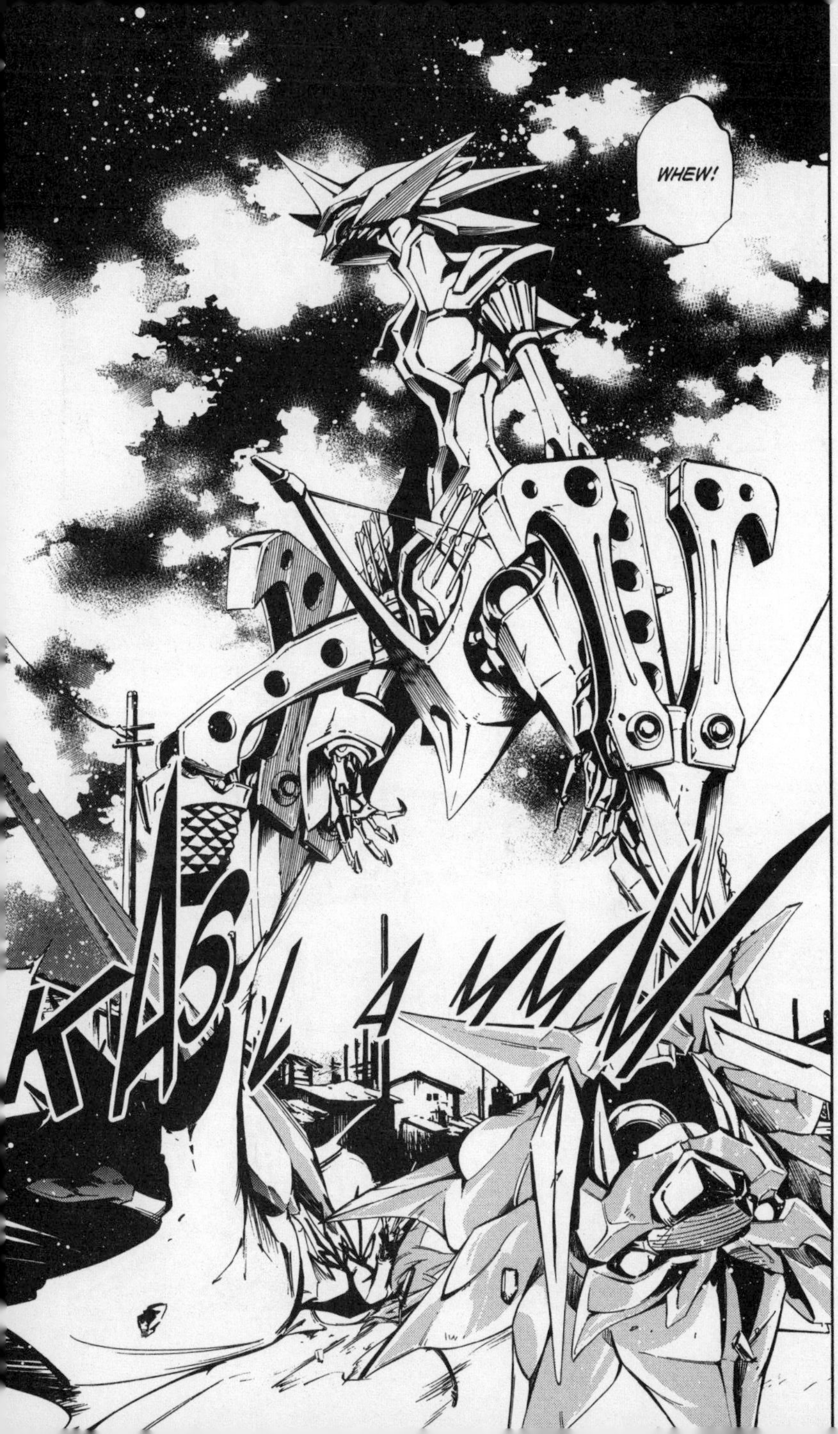
WHEW!
KASHUNN

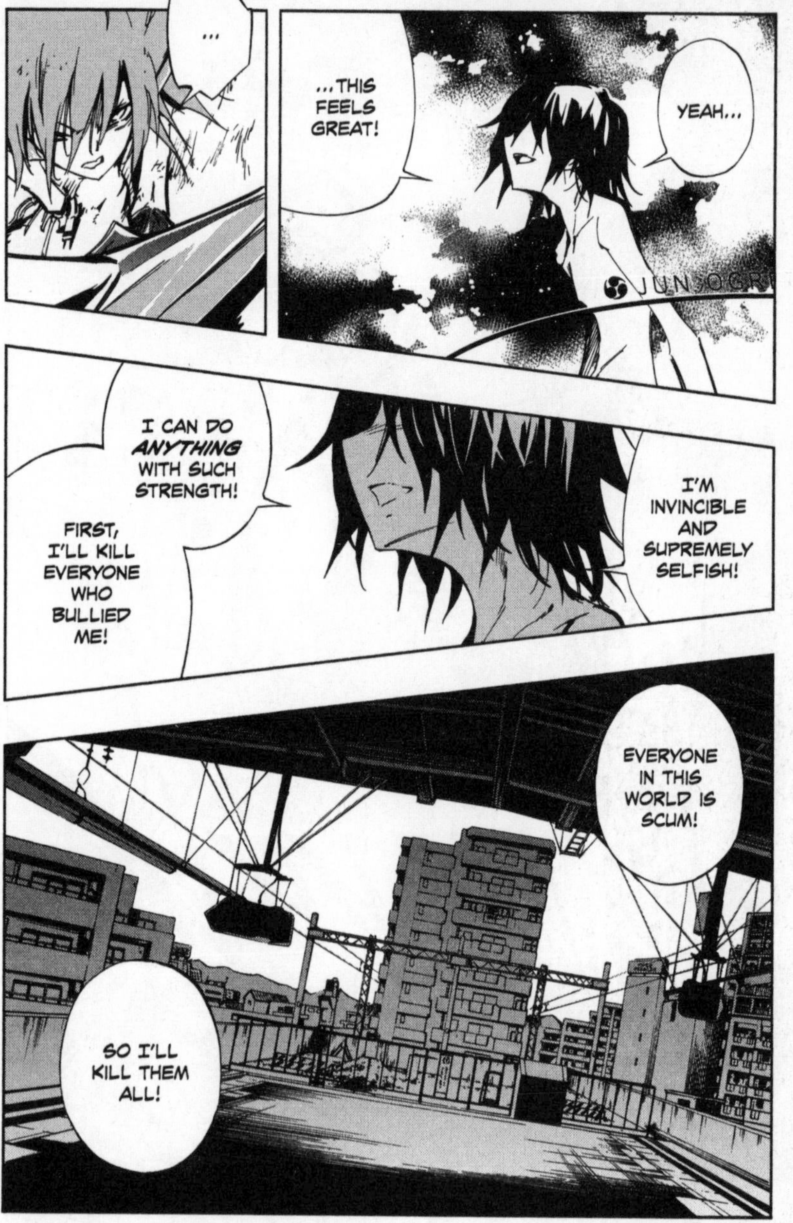
YEAH...
...THIS FEELS GREAT!
...
I'M INVINCIBLE AND SUPREMELY SELFISH!
I CAN DO *ANYTHING* WITH SUCH STRENGTH!
FIRST, I'LL KILL EVERYONE WHO BULLIED ME!
EVERYONE IN THIS WORLD IS SCUM!
SO I'LL KILL THEM ALL!

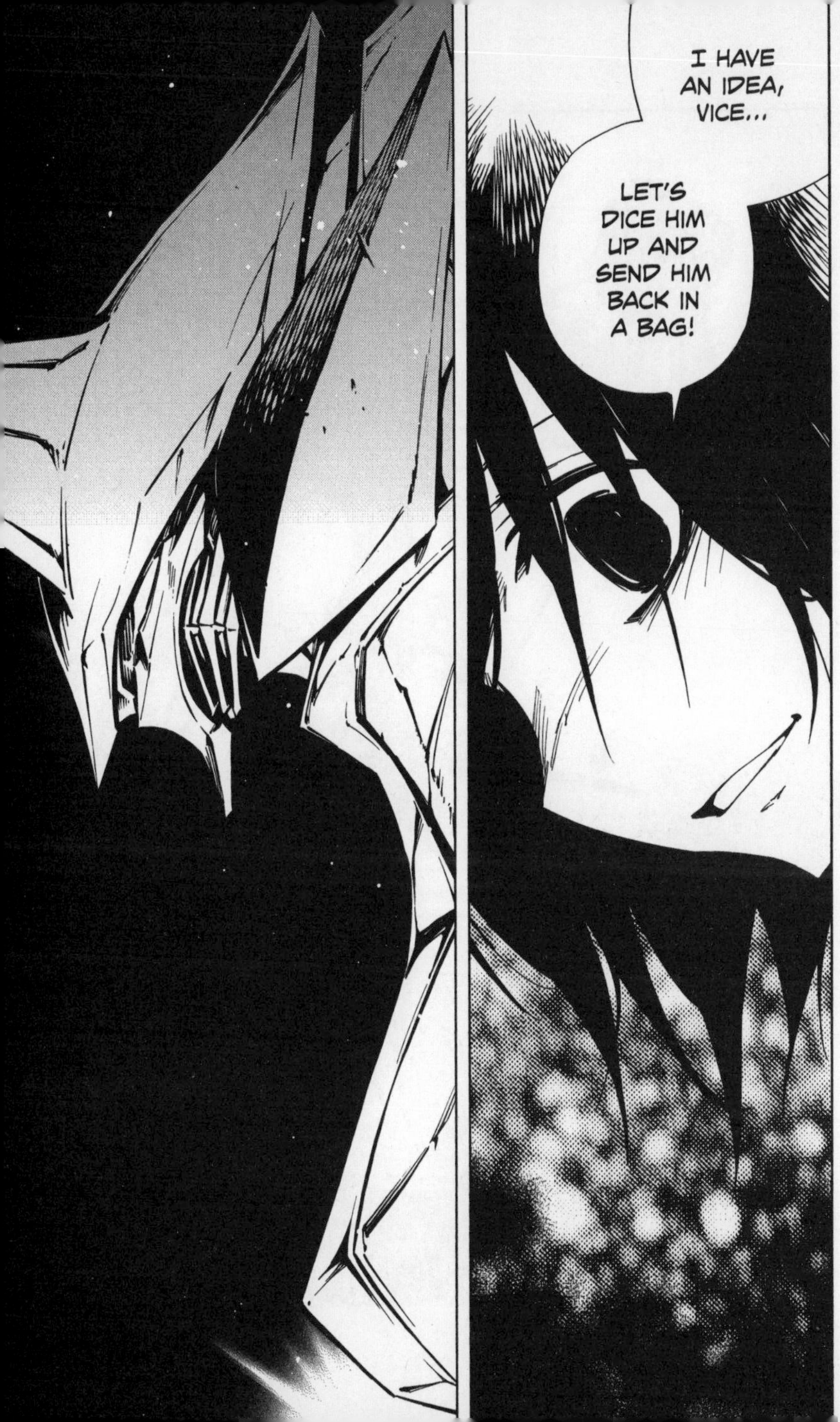
I HAVE AN IDEA, VICE...
LET'S DICE HIM UP AND SEND HIM BACK IN A BAG!

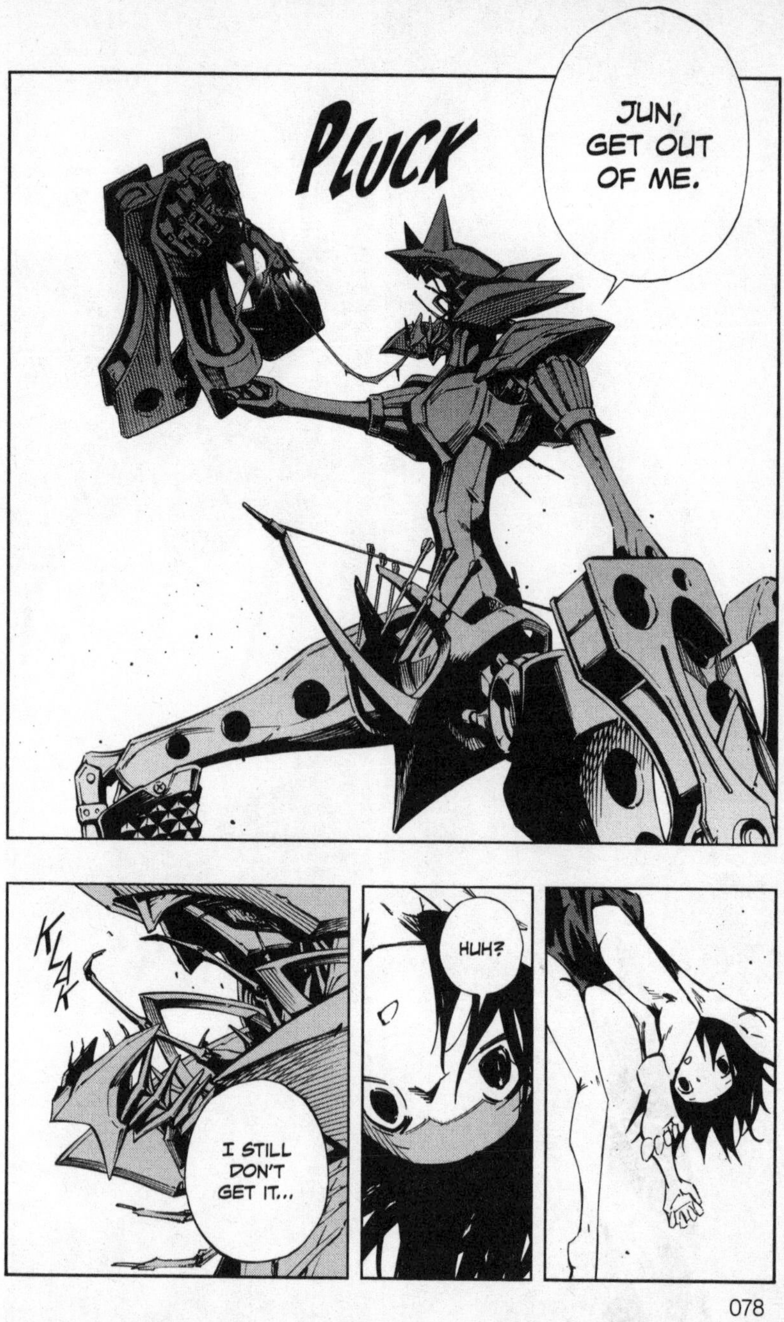
PLUCK
JUN, GET OUT OF ME.
HUH?
KLAK
I STILL DON'T GET IT...

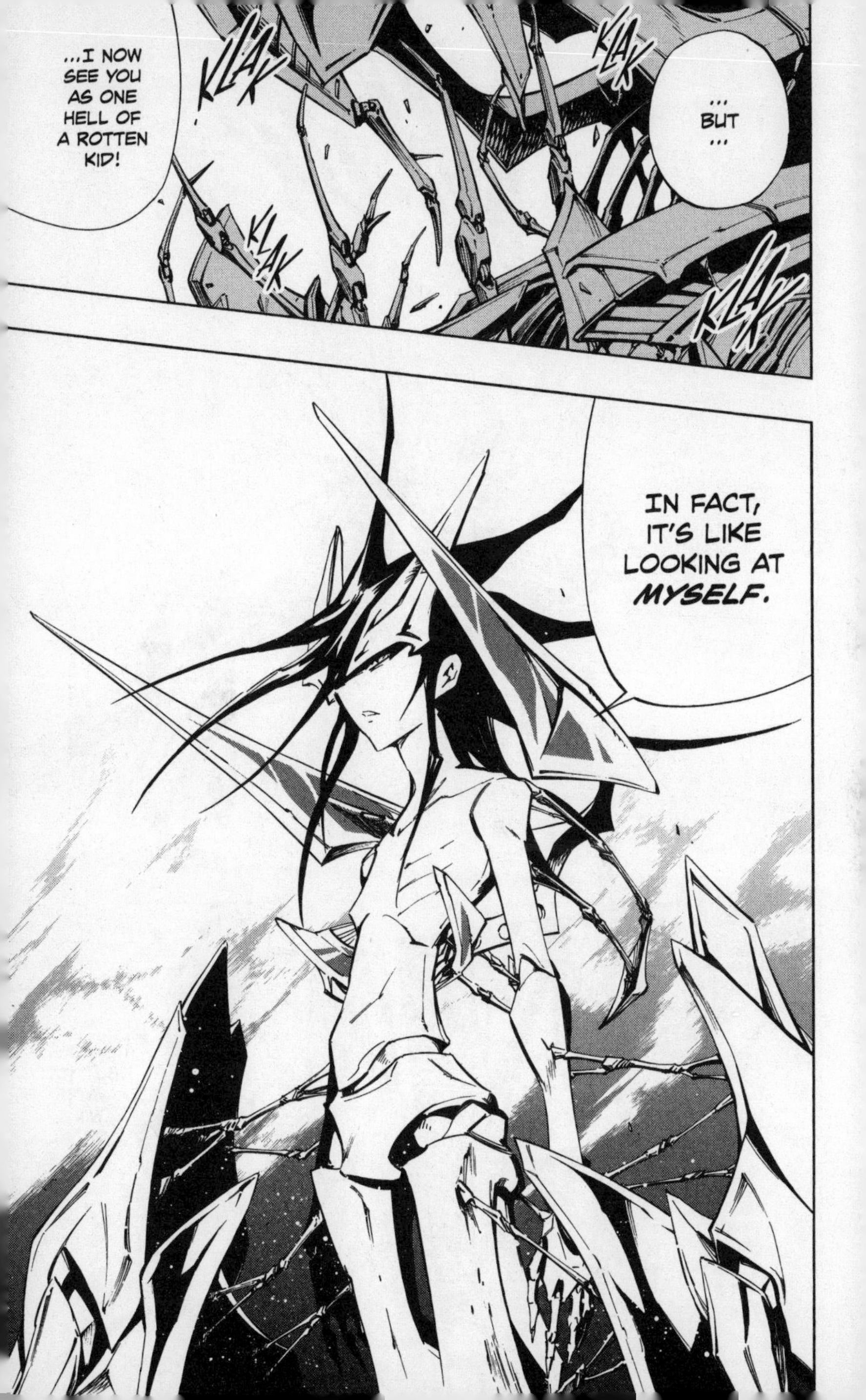
KLAK
... BUT ...
KLAK
...I NOW SEE YOU AS ONE HELL OF A ROTTEN KID!
KLAK
KLAK
IN FACT, IT'S LIKE LOOKING AT *MYSELF*.

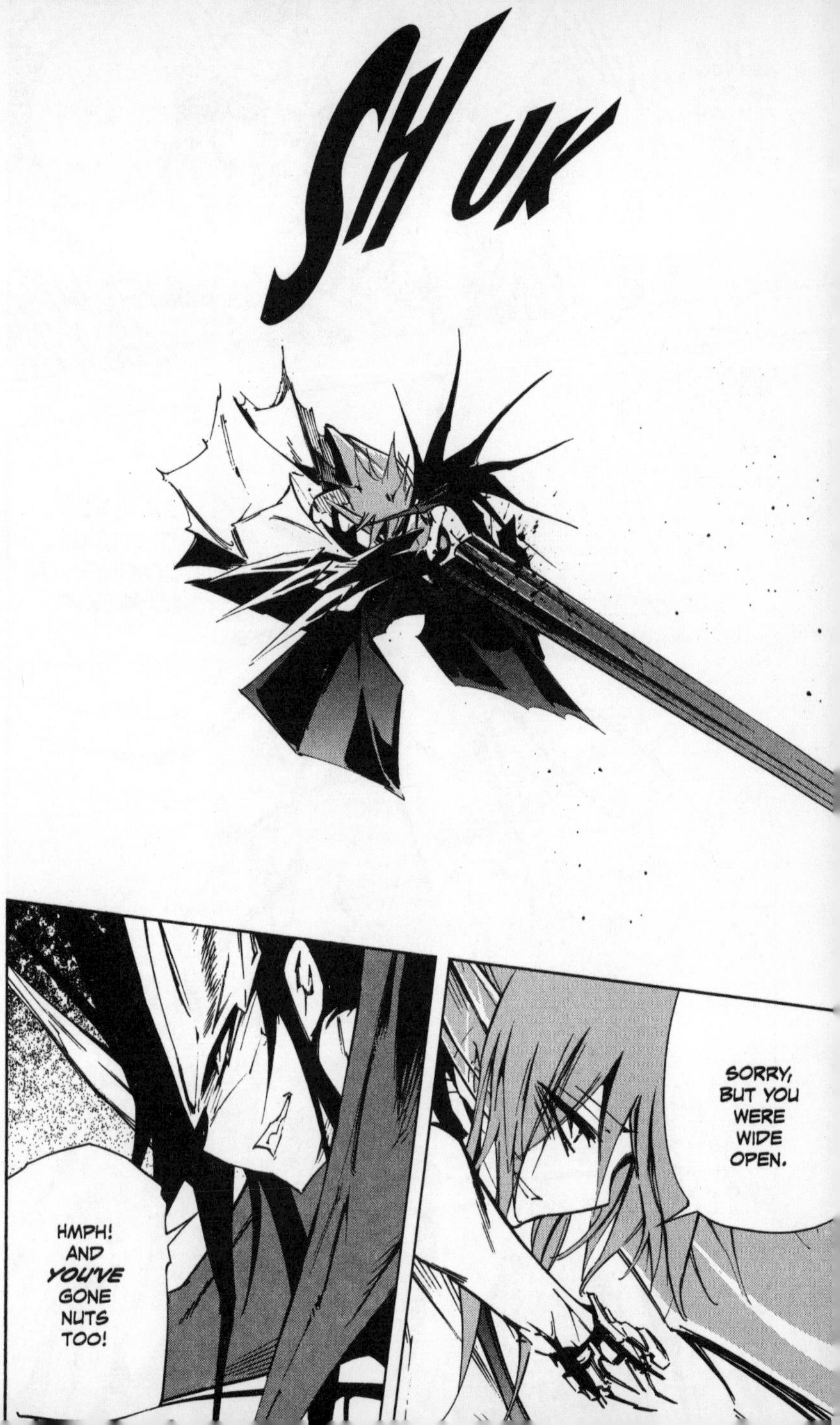
SHUK
SORRY, BUT YOU WERE WIDE OPEN.
HMPH! AND *YOU'VE* GONE NUTS TOO!

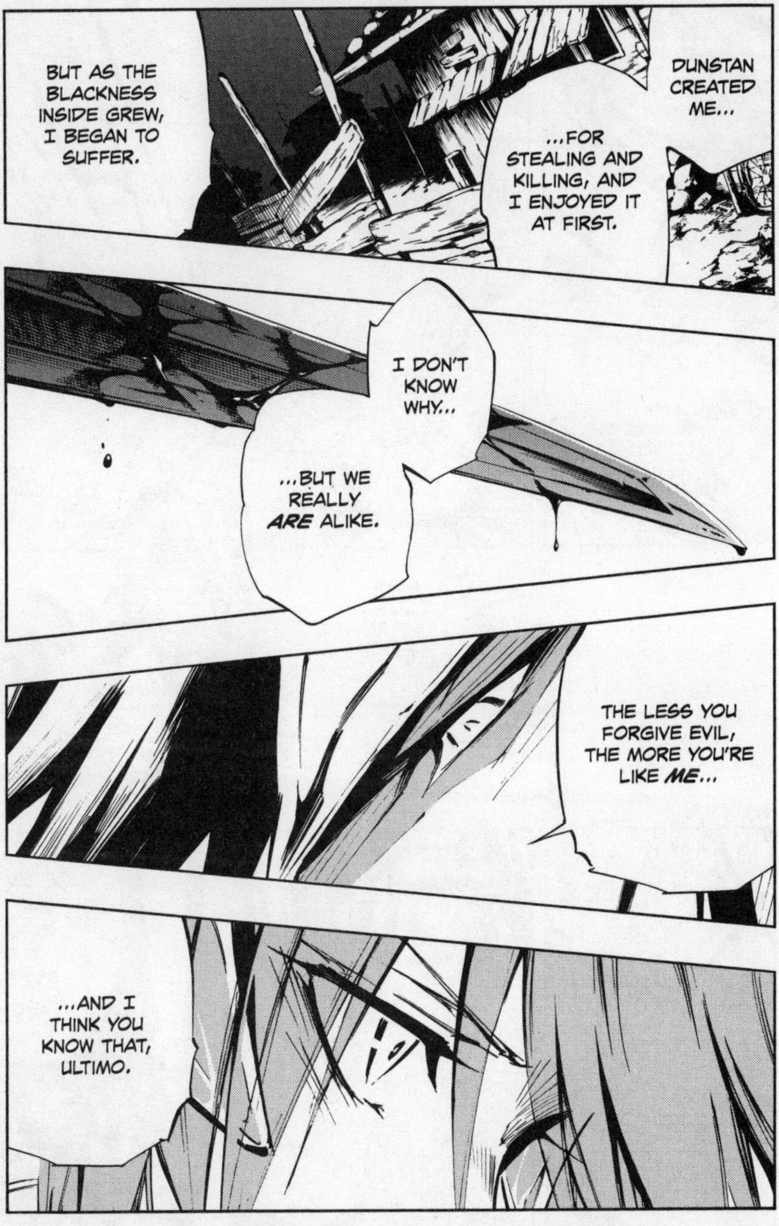
DUNSTAN CREATED ME...
...FOR STEALING AND KILLING, AND I ENJOYED IT AT FIRST.
BUT AS THE BLACKNESS INSIDE GREW, I BEGAN TO SUFFER.
I DON'T KNOW WHY...
...BUT WE REALLY *ARE* ALIKE.
THE LESS YOU FORGIVE EVIL, THE MORE YOU'RE LIKE *ME*...
...AND I THINK YOU KNOW THAT, ULTIMO.

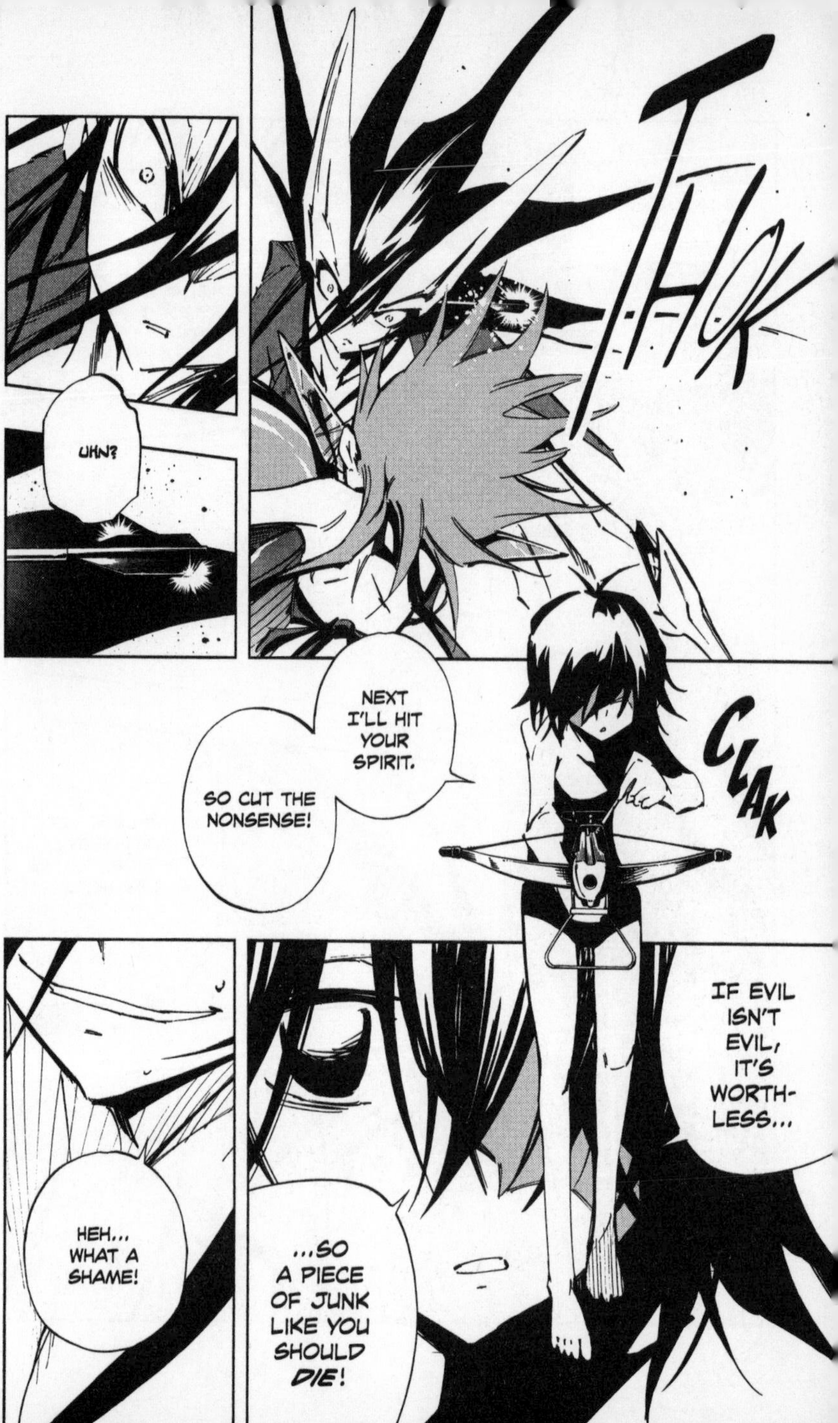
THOK
UHN?
CLAK
NEXT I'LL HIT YOUR SPIRIT.
SO CUT THE NONSENSE!
IF EVIL ISN'T EVIL, IT'S WORTH-LESS...
...SO A PIECE OF JUNK LIKE YOU SHOULD *DIE*!
HEH... WHAT A SHAME!

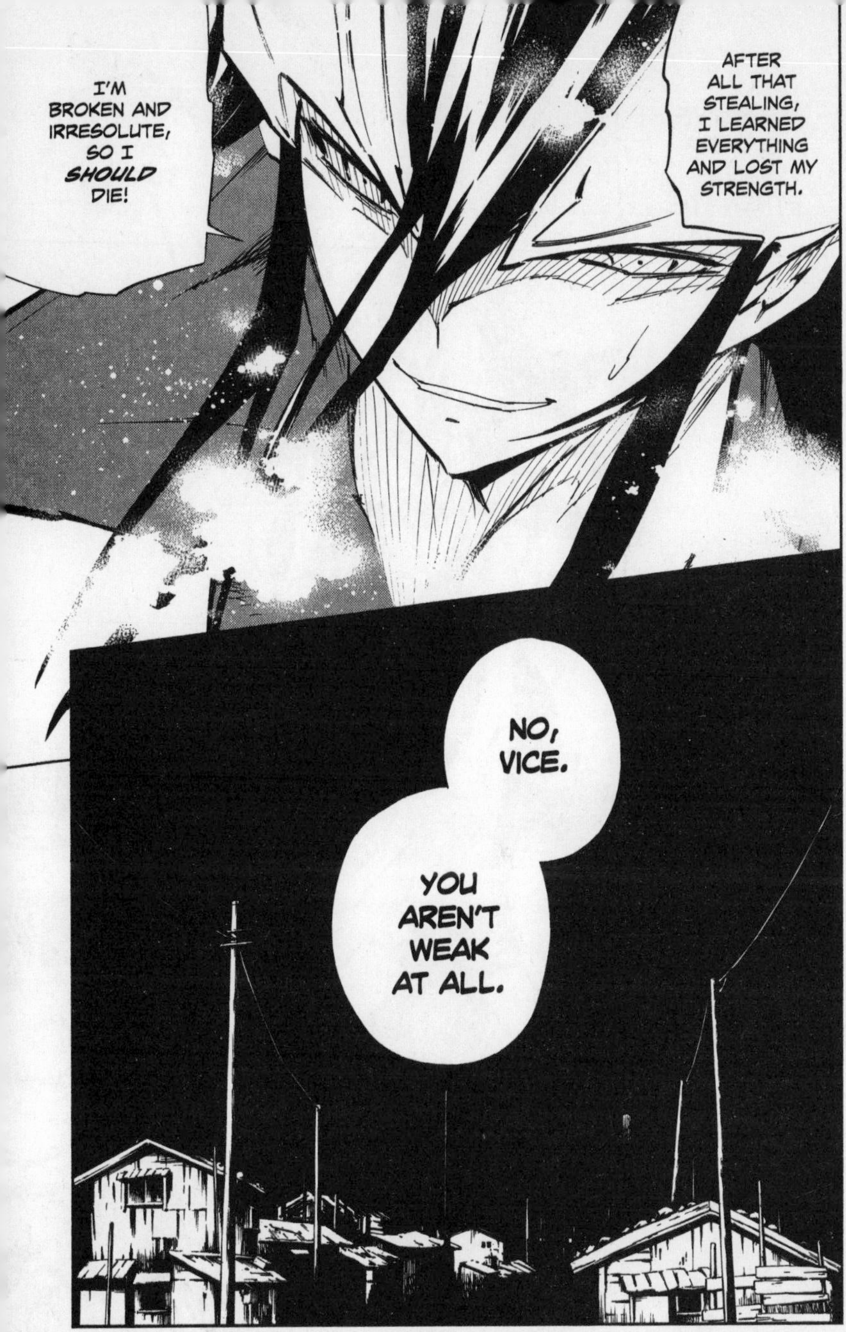
AFTER ALL THAT STEALING, I LEARNED EVERYTHING AND LOST MY STRENGTH.
I'M BROKEN AND IRRESOLUTE, SO I SHOULD DIE!
NO, VICE.
YOU AREN'T WEAK AT ALL.

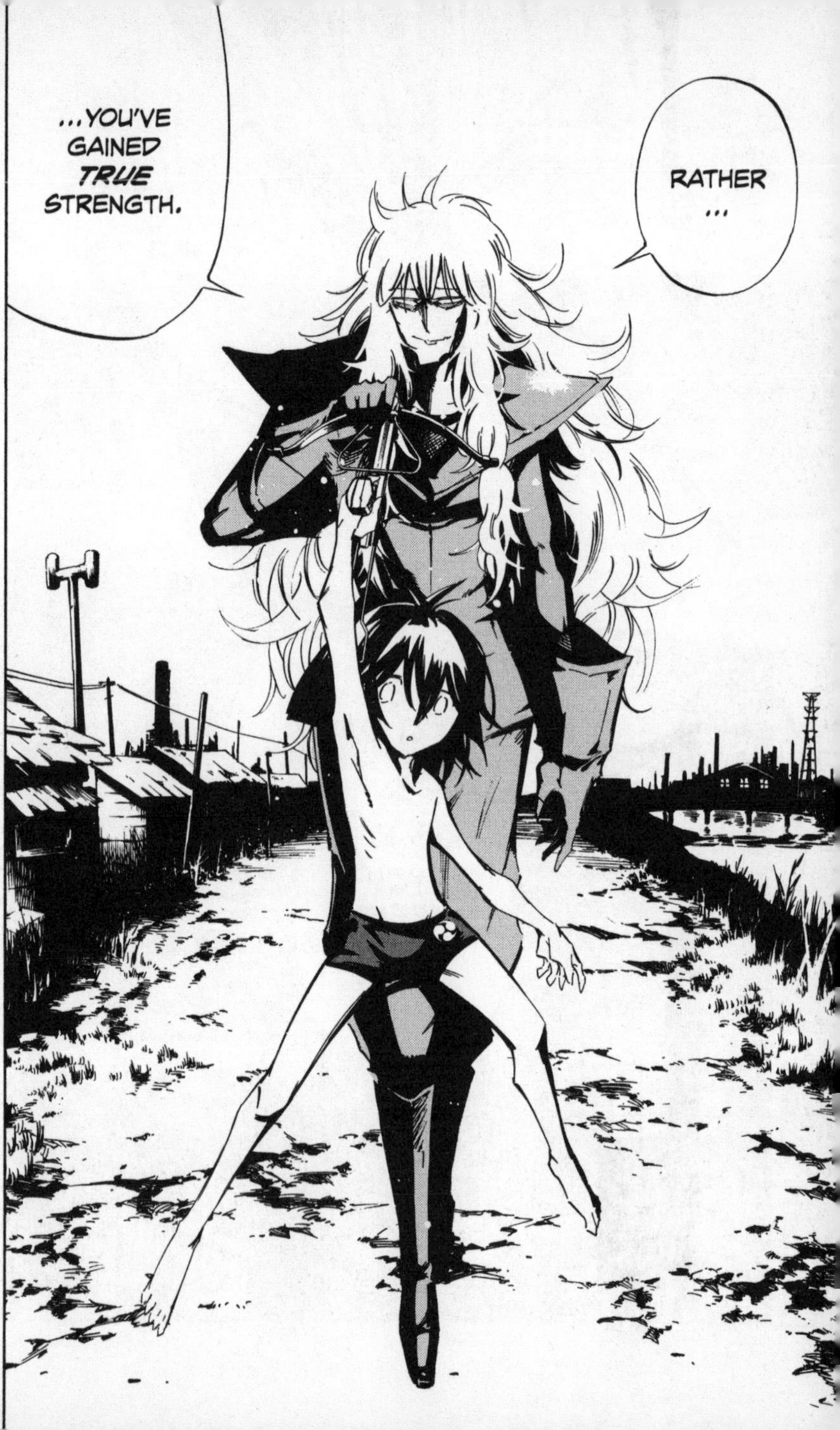
RATHER ...
...YOU'VE GAINED *TRUE* STRENGTH.

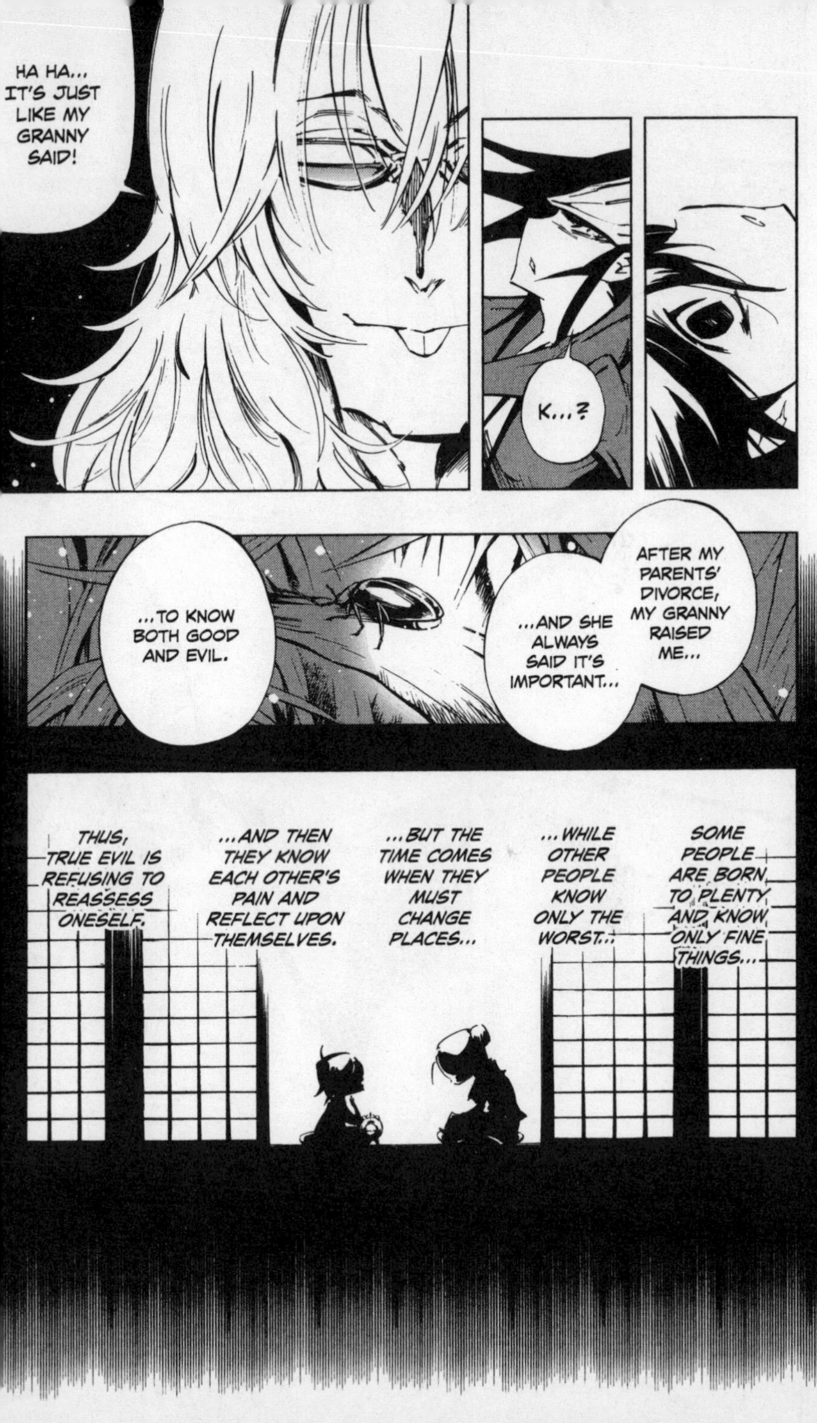
K...?
HA HA... IT'S JUST LIKE MY GRANNY SAID!
AFTER MY PARENTS' DIVORCE, MY GRANNY RAISED ME...
...AND SHE ALWAYS SAID IT'S IMPORTANT...
...TO KNOW BOTH GOOD AND EVIL.
SOME PEOPLE ARE BORN TO PLENTY AND KNOW ONLY FINE THINGS...
...WHILE OTHER PEOPLE KNOW ONLY THE WORST...
...BUT THE TIME COMES WHEN THEY MUST CHANGE PLACES...
...AND THEN THEY KNOW EACH OTHER'S PAIN AND REFLECT UPON THEMSELVES.
THUS, TRUE EVIL IS REFUSING TO REASSESS ONESELF.

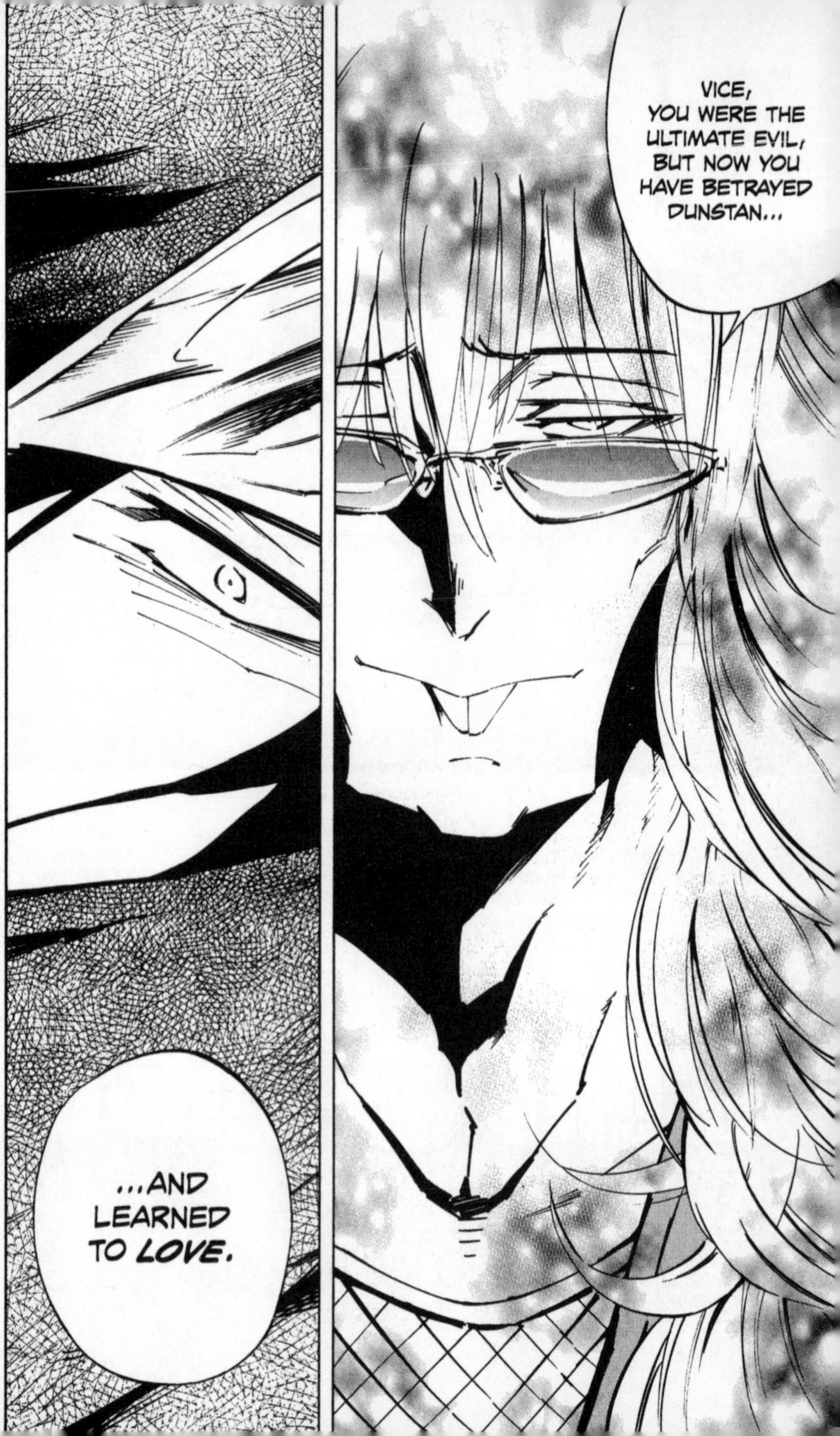
VICE, YOU WERE THE ULTIMATE EVIL, BUT NOW YOU HAVE BETRAYED DUNSTAN...
...AND LEARNED TO *LOVE*.

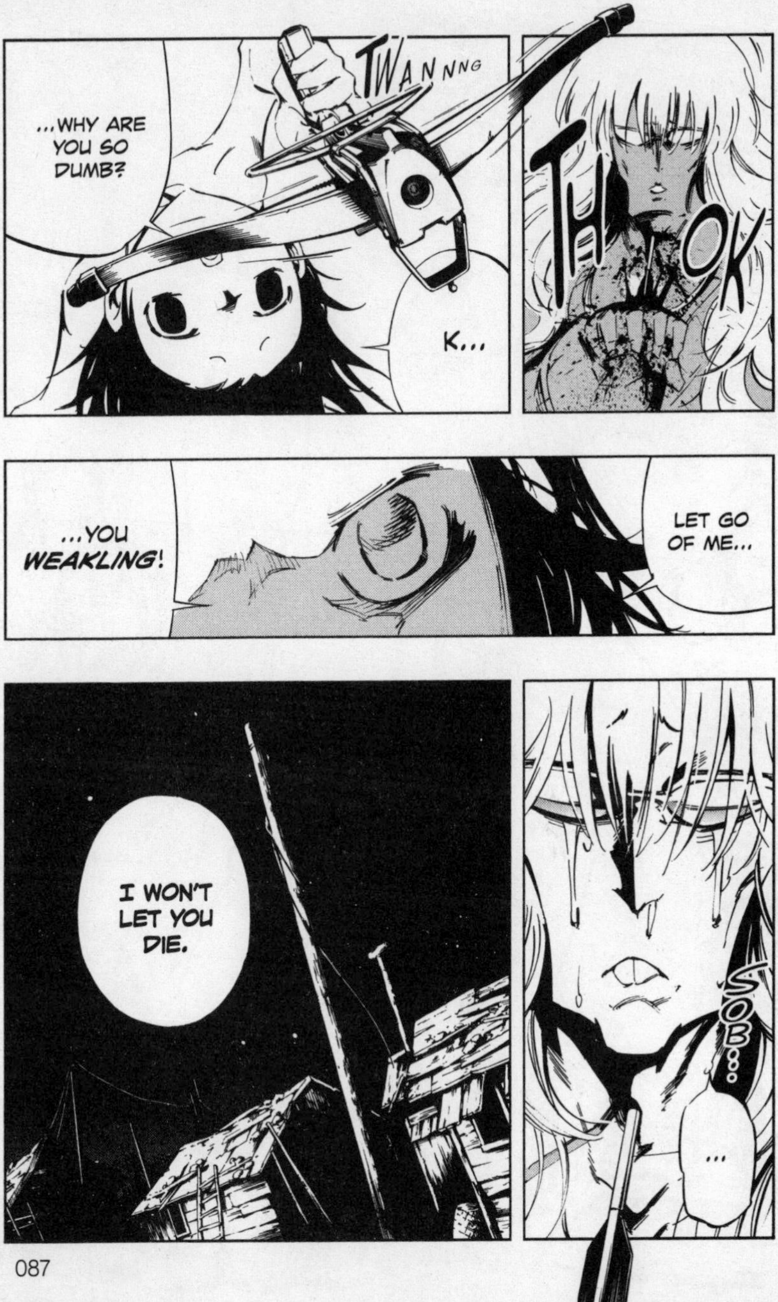
THOK
...WHY ARE YOU SO DUMB?
TWANNNG
K...
LET GO OF ME...
...YOU WEAKLING!
SOB...
...
I WON'T LET YOU DIE.

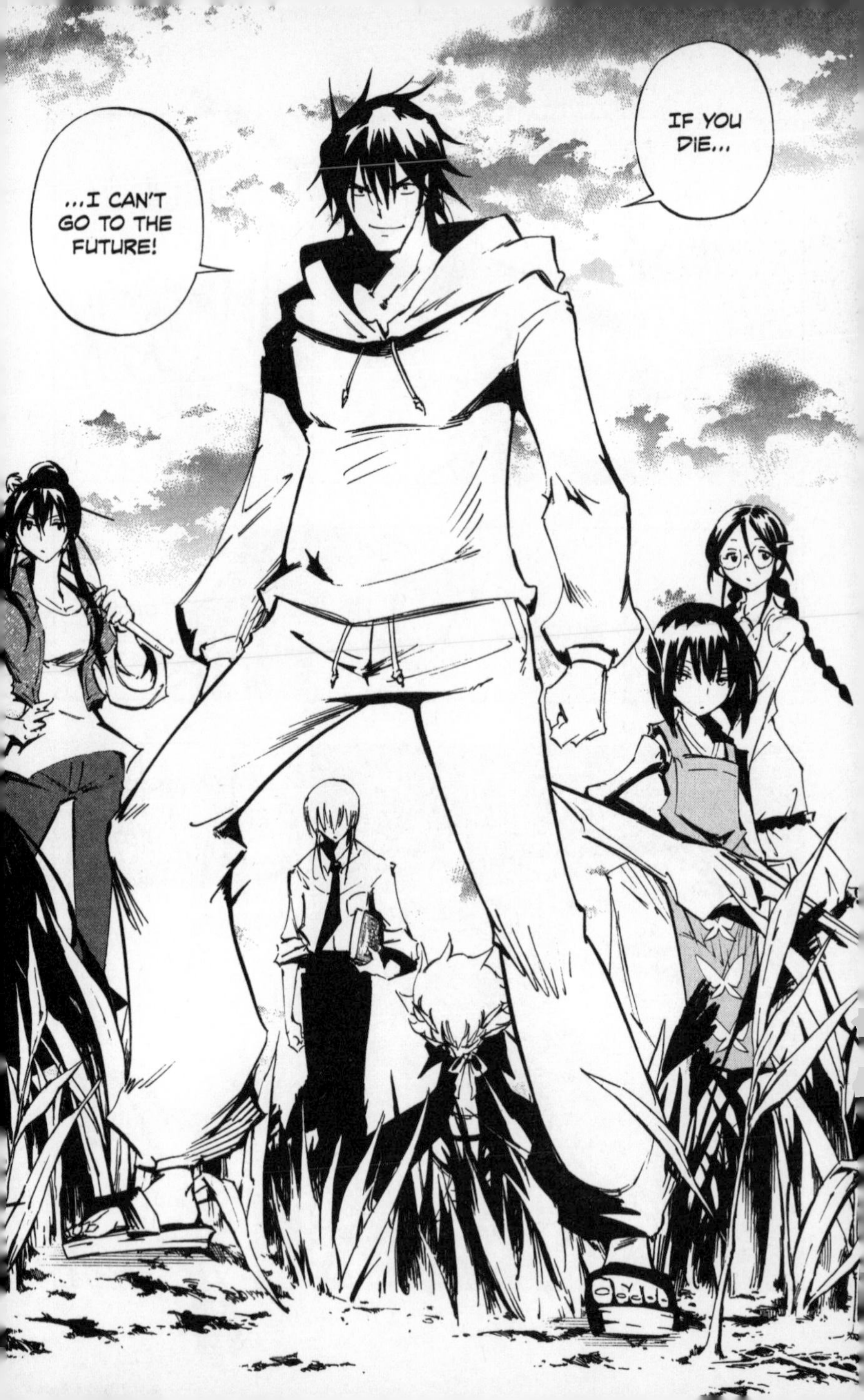
IF YOU DIE...
...I CAN'T GO TO THE FUTURE!

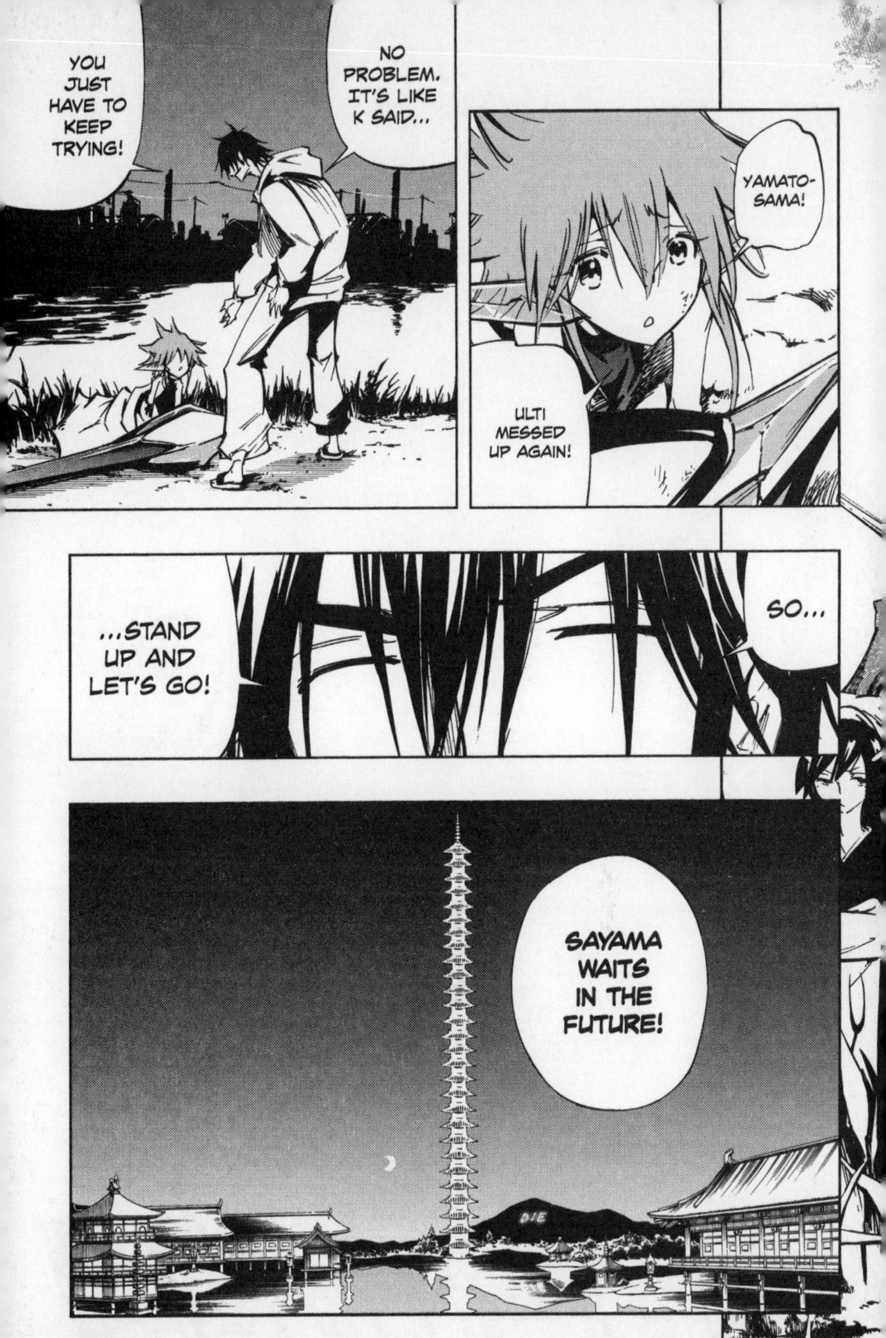
YAMATO-SAMA!
ULTI MESSED UP AGAIN!
NO PROBLEM. IT'S LIKE K SAID...
YOU JUST HAVE TO KEEP TRYING!
SO...
...STAND UP AND LET'S GO!
SAYAMA WAITS IN THE FUTURE!

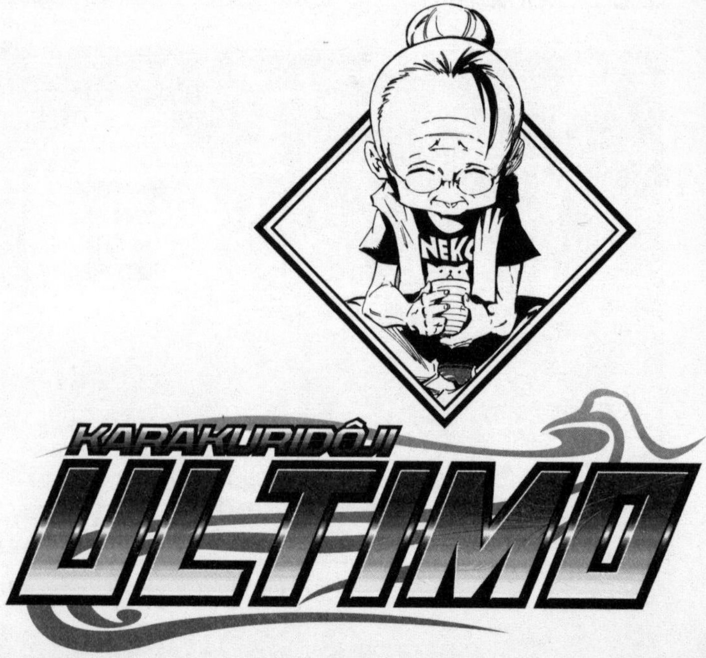

KARAKURIDÔJI
ULTIMO

FINAL ACT
BEYOND EXTREMES,
GOOD AND EVIL CONNECT

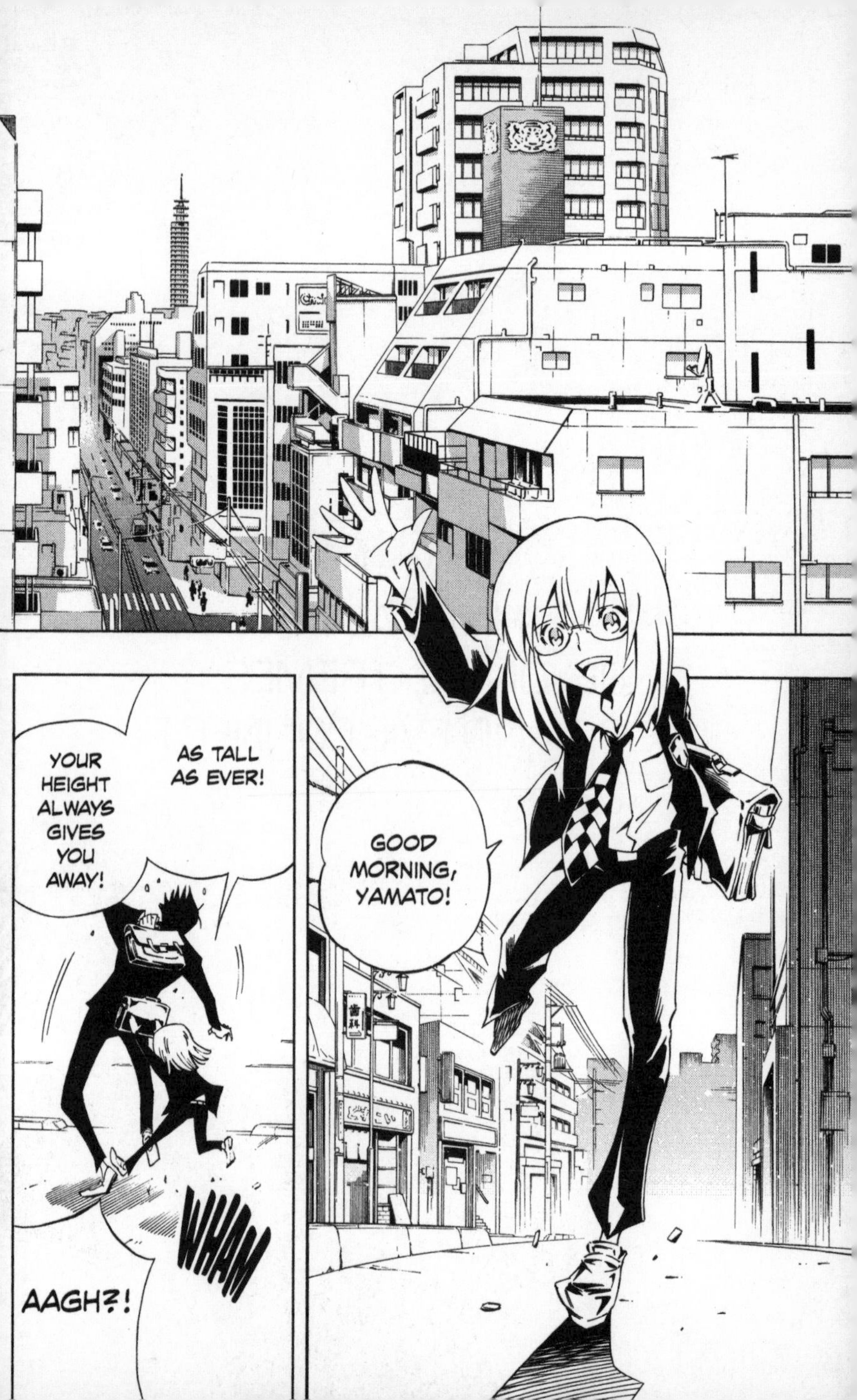
GOOD MORNING, YAMATO!
AS TALL AS EVER!
YOUR HEIGHT ALWAYS GIVES YOU AWAY!
WHAM
AAGH?!

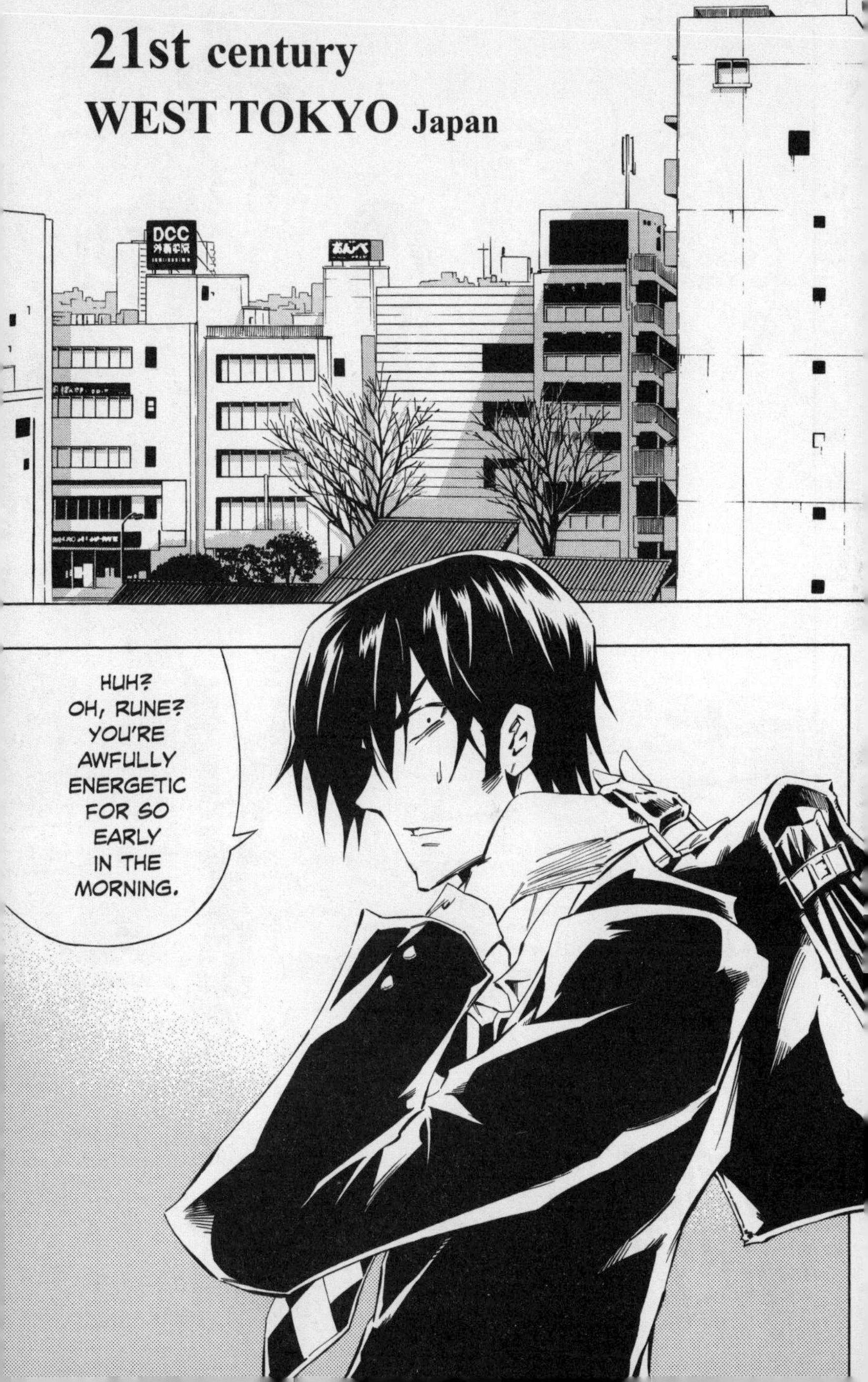
21st century
WEST TOKYO Japan
DCC
HUH? OH, RUNE? YOU'RE AWFULLY ENERGETIC FOR SO EARLY IN THE MORNING.

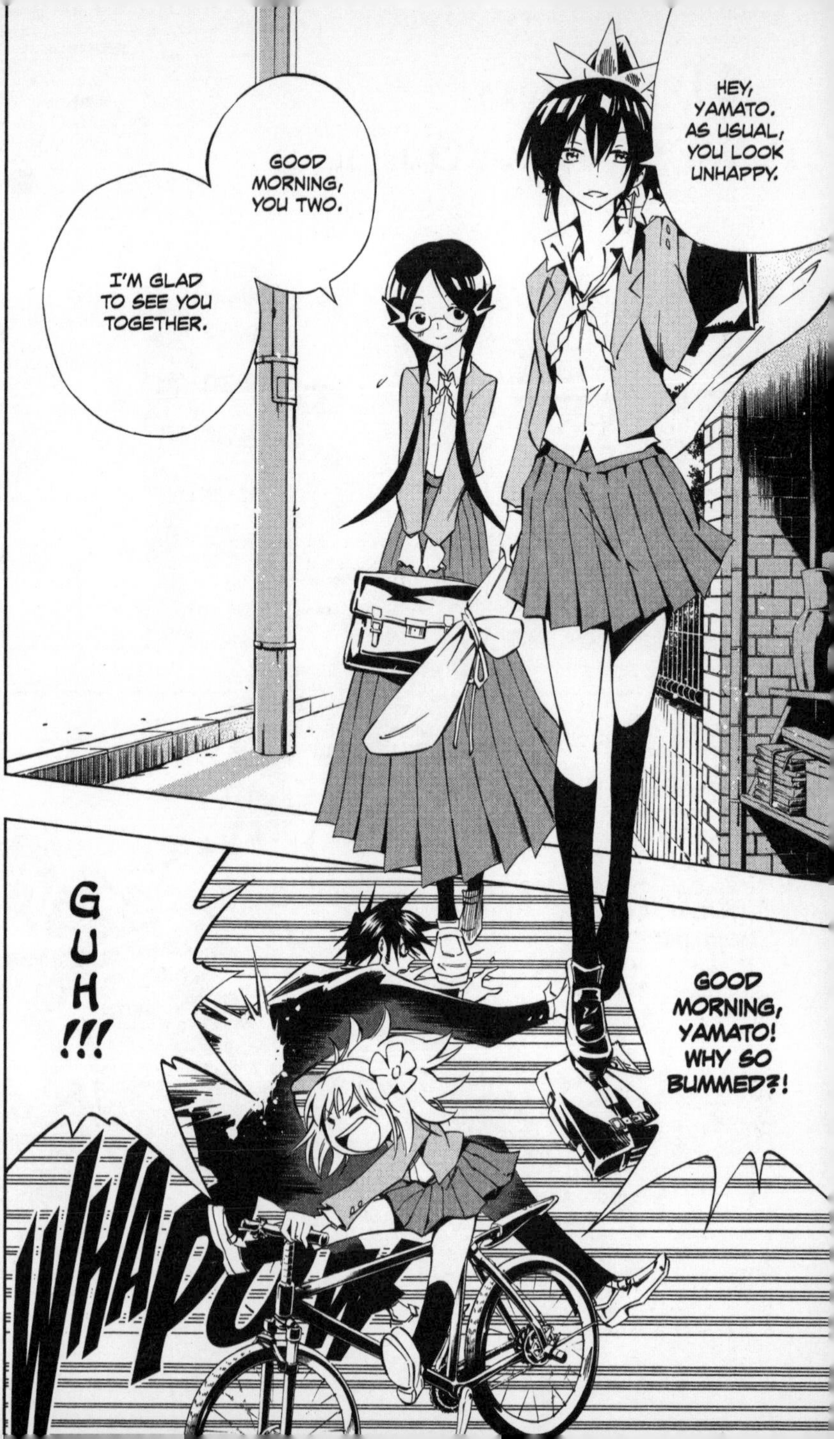
HEY, YAMATO. AS USUAL, YOU LOOK UNHAPPY.
GOOD MORNING, YOU TWO.
I'M GLAD TO SEE YOU TOGETHER.
GOOD MORNING, YAMATO! WHY SO BUMMED?!
GUH!!!

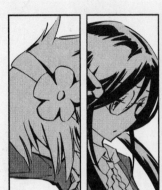

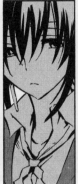

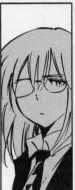

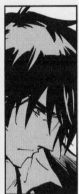

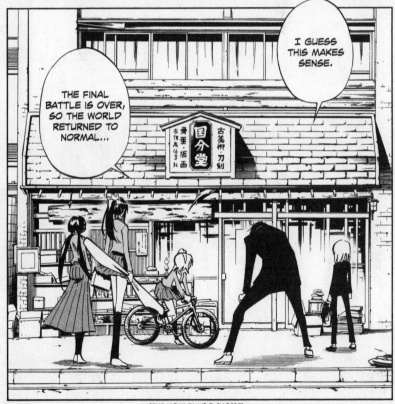

I GUESS THIS MAKES SENSE.
THE FINAL BATTLE IS OVER, SO THE WORLD RETURNED TO NORMAL...
国分堂
古美術・刀剣
骨董・版画
(THE KOKUBUNDO SHOPPE)

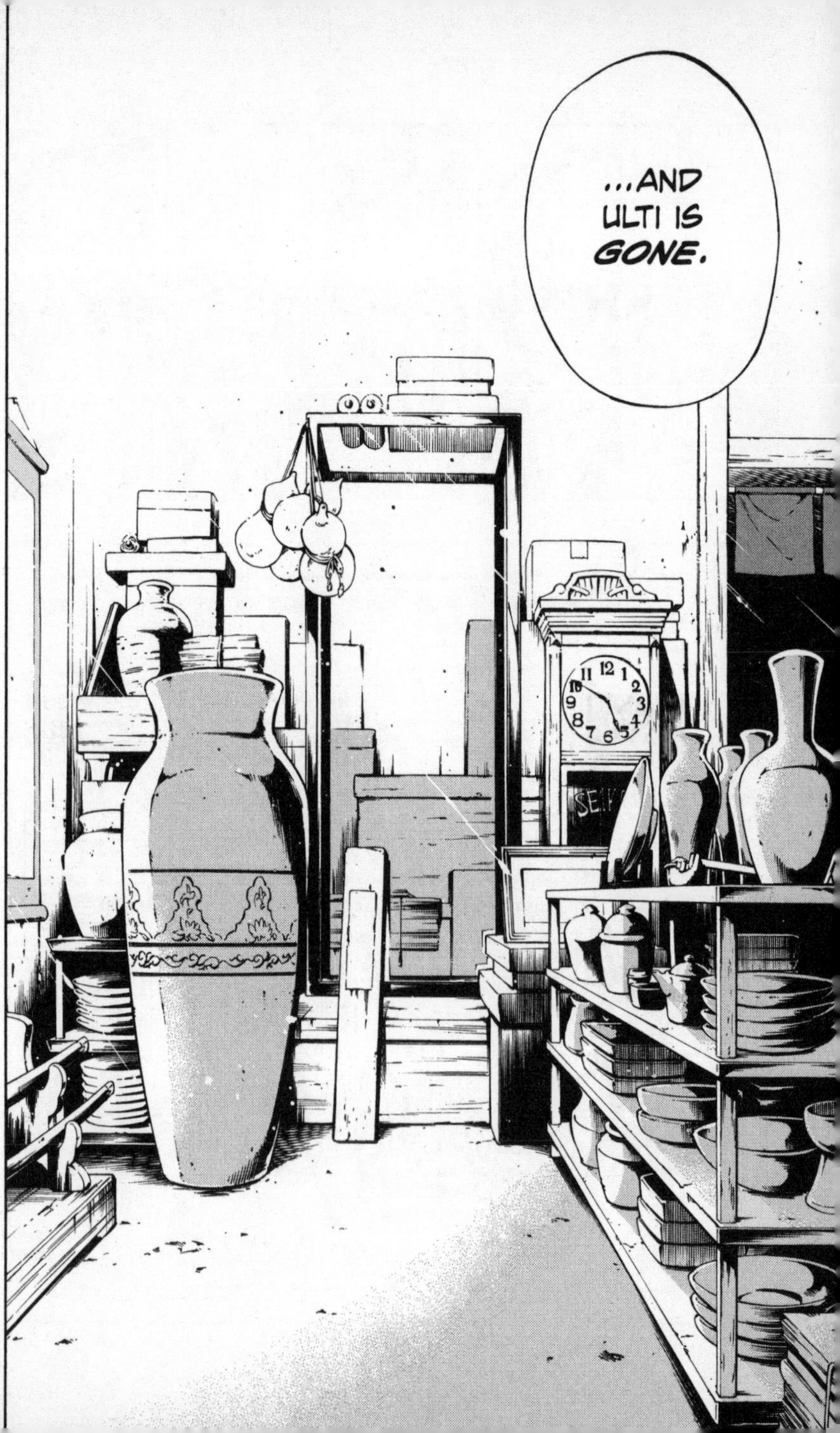
...AND ULTI IS GONE.
SEIK

20th century
SHINBASHI Japan

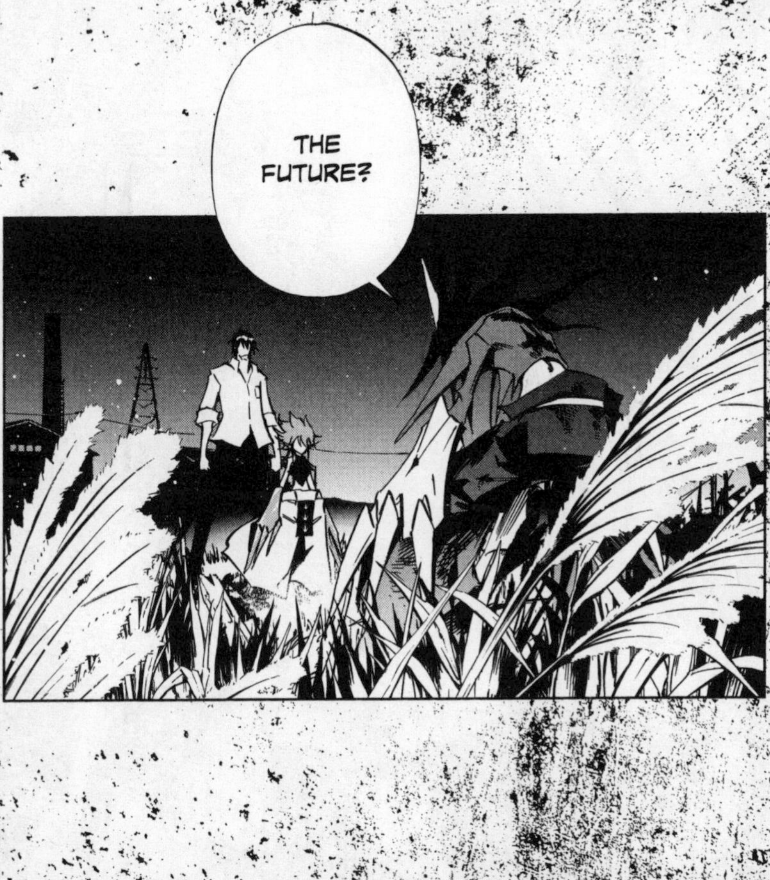
THE FUTURE?

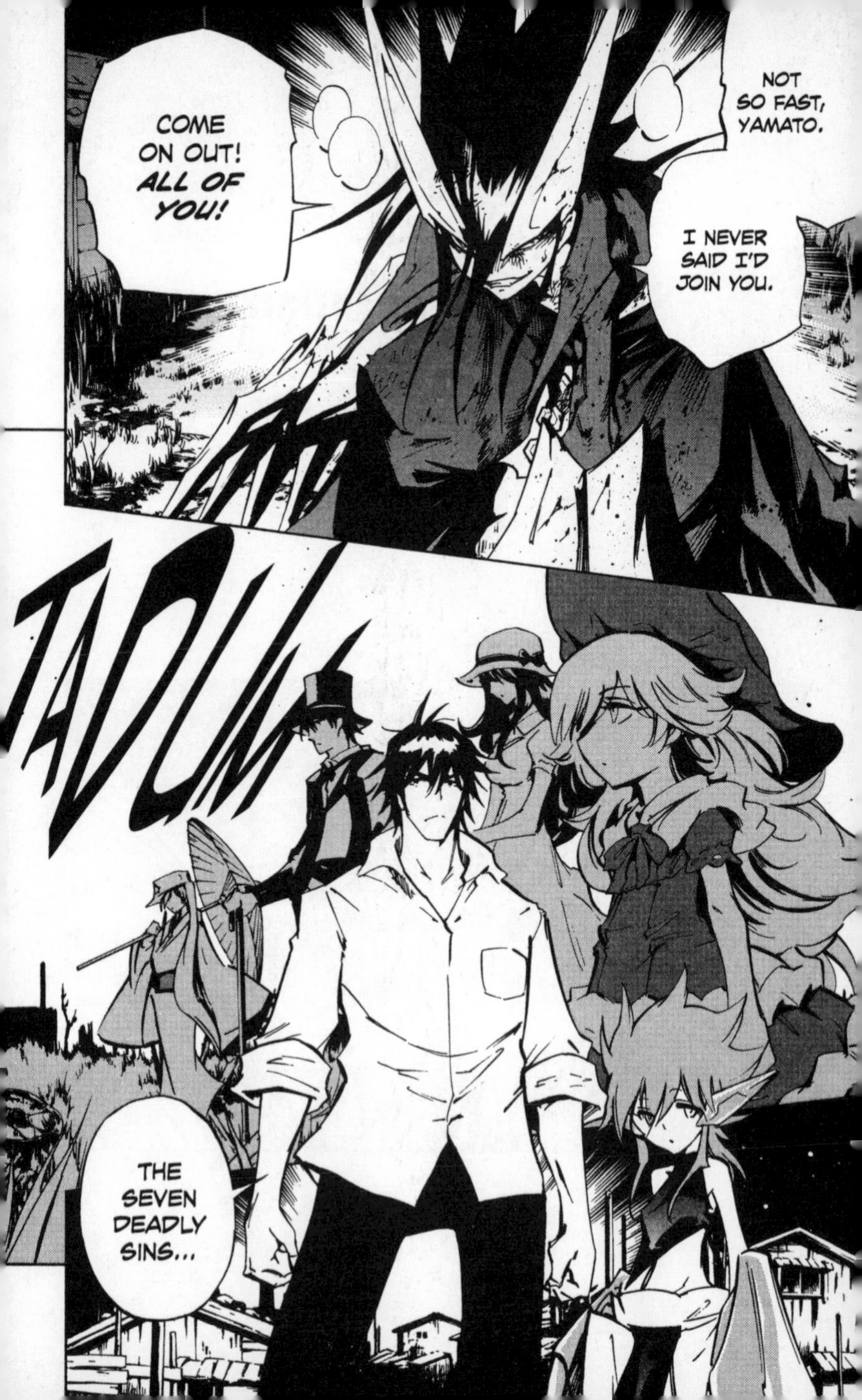
NOT SO FAST, YAMATO.
I NEVER SAID I'D JOIN YOU.
COME ON OUT! ALL OF YOU!
TADUM
THE SEVEN DEADLY SINS...

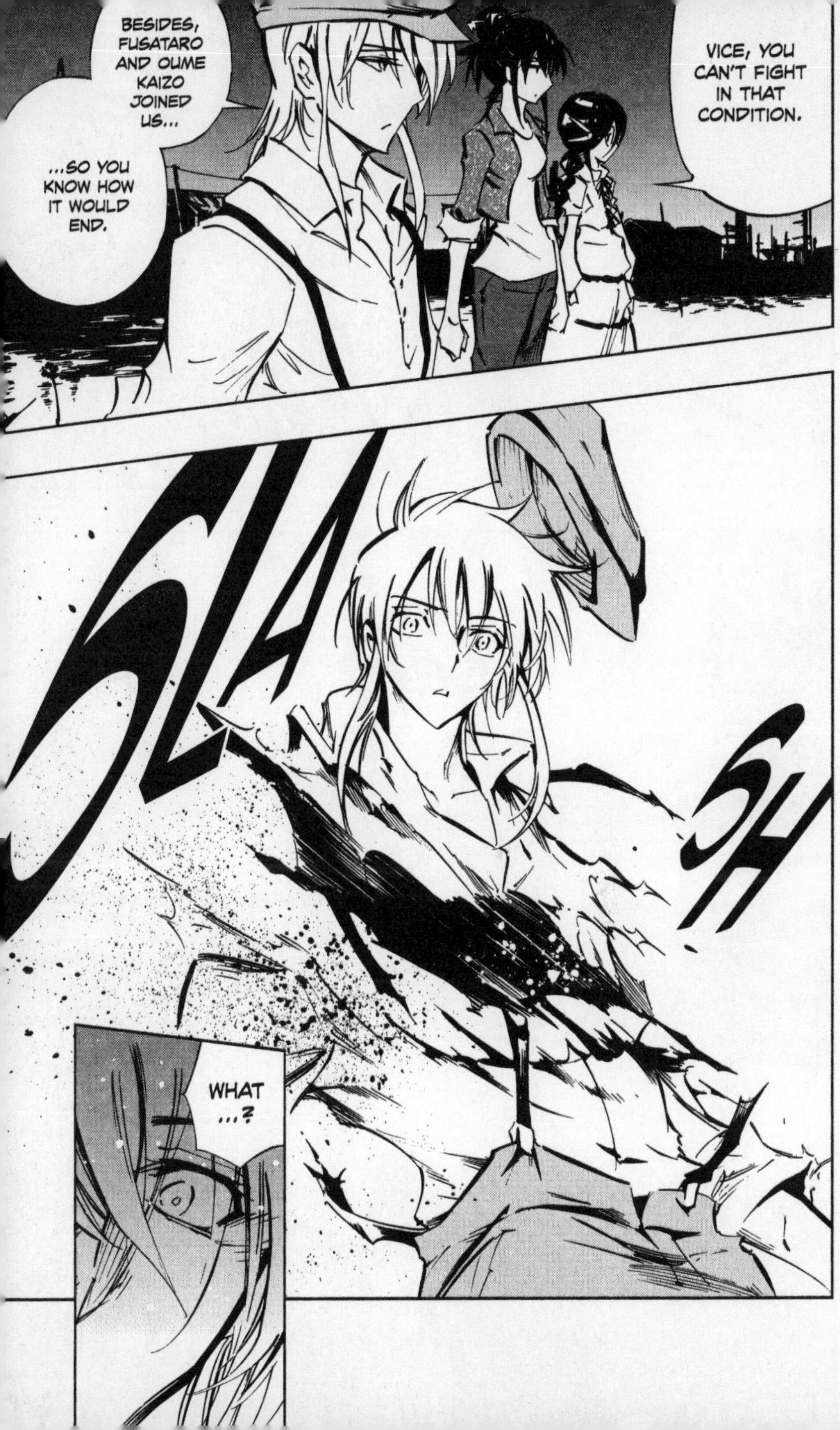
VICE, YOU CAN'T FIGHT IN THAT CONDITION.
BESIDES, FUSATARO AND OUME KAIZO JOINED US...
...SO YOU KNOW HOW IT WOULD END.
SLA
SH
WHAT ...?

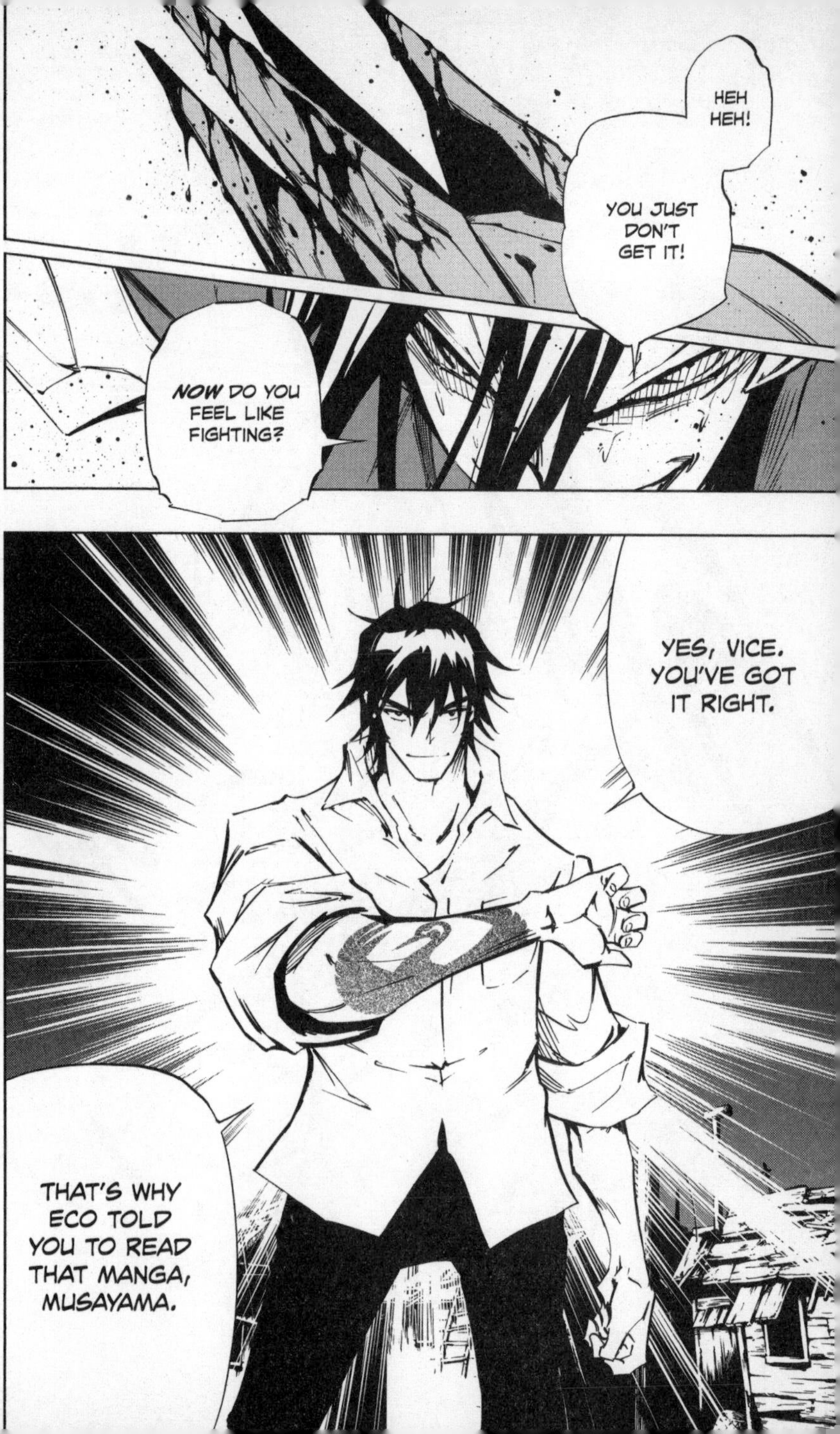
HEH HEH!
YOU JUST DON'T GET IT!
NOW DO YOU FEEL LIKE FIGHTING?
YES, VICE. YOU'VE GOT IT RIGHT.
THAT'S WHY ECO TOLD YOU TO READ THAT MANGA, MUSAYAMA.

30th century
NORTH ISLAND

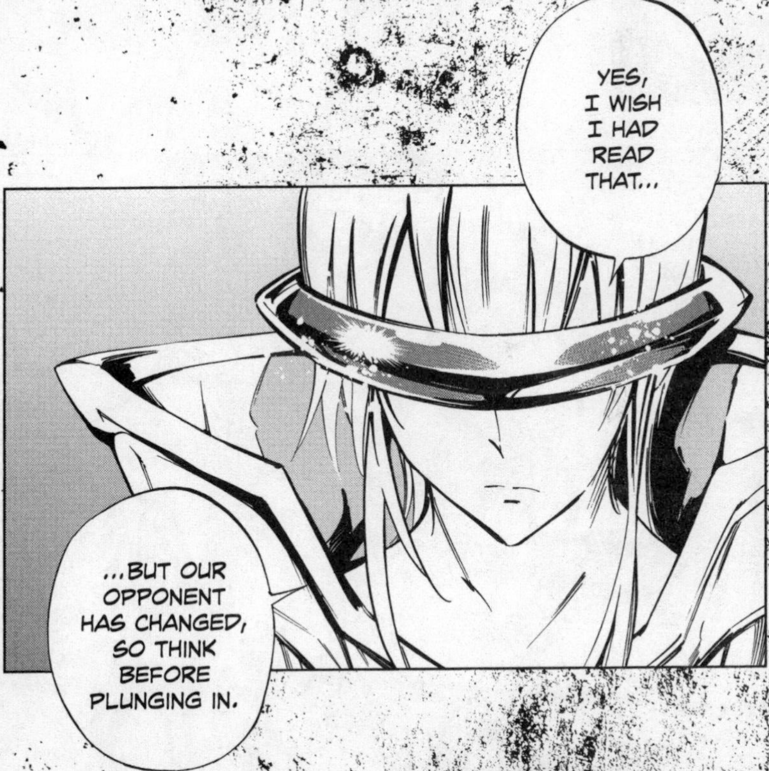
YES, I WISH I HAD READ THAT...
...BUT OUR OPPONENT HAS CHANGED, SO THINK BEFORE PLUNGING IN.

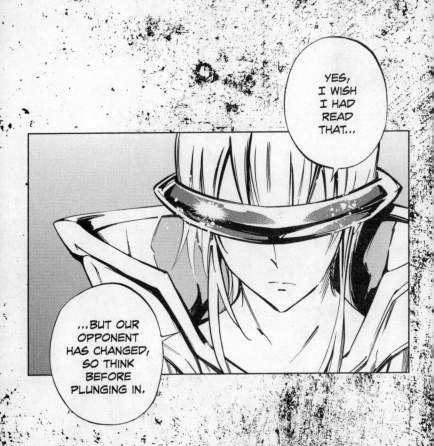

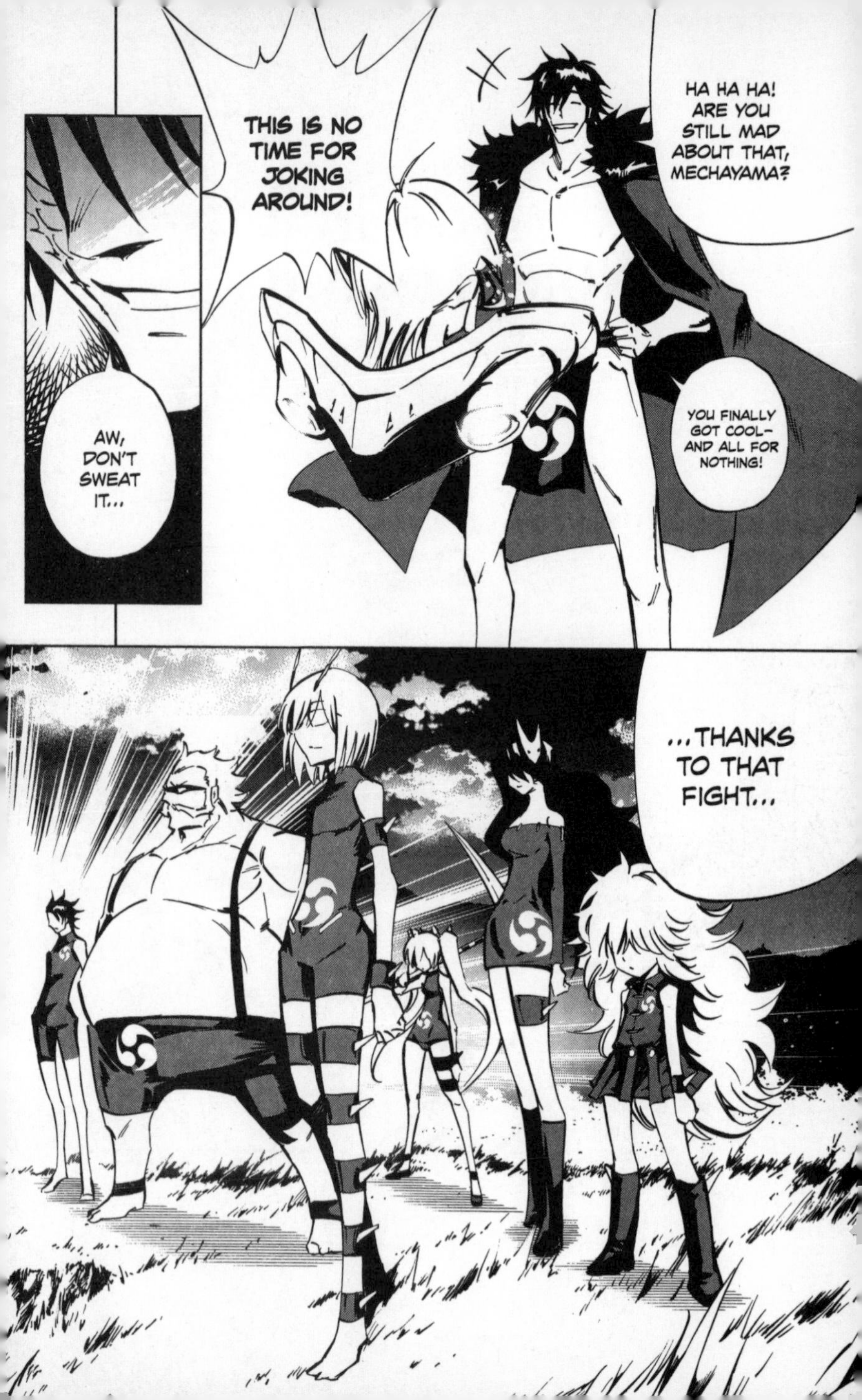
HA HA HA! ARE YOU STILL MAD ABOUT THAT, MECHAYAMA?
THIS IS NO TIME FOR JOKING AROUND!
YOU FINALLY GOT COOL—AND ALL FOR NOTHING!
AW, DON'T SWEAT IT...
...THANKS TO THAT FIGHT...

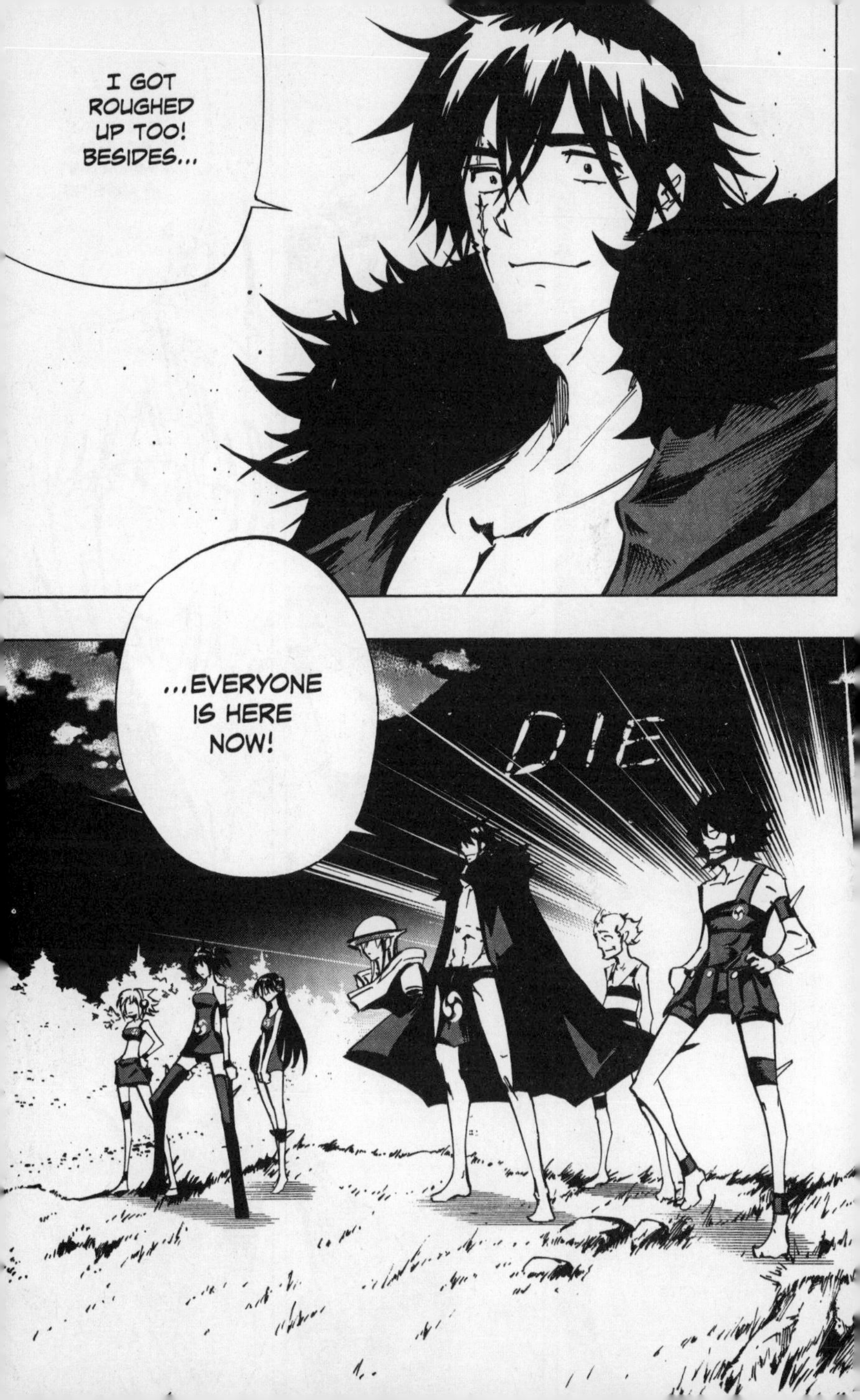
I GOT ROUGHED UP TOO! BESIDES...
...EVERYONE IS HERE NOW!
DIE

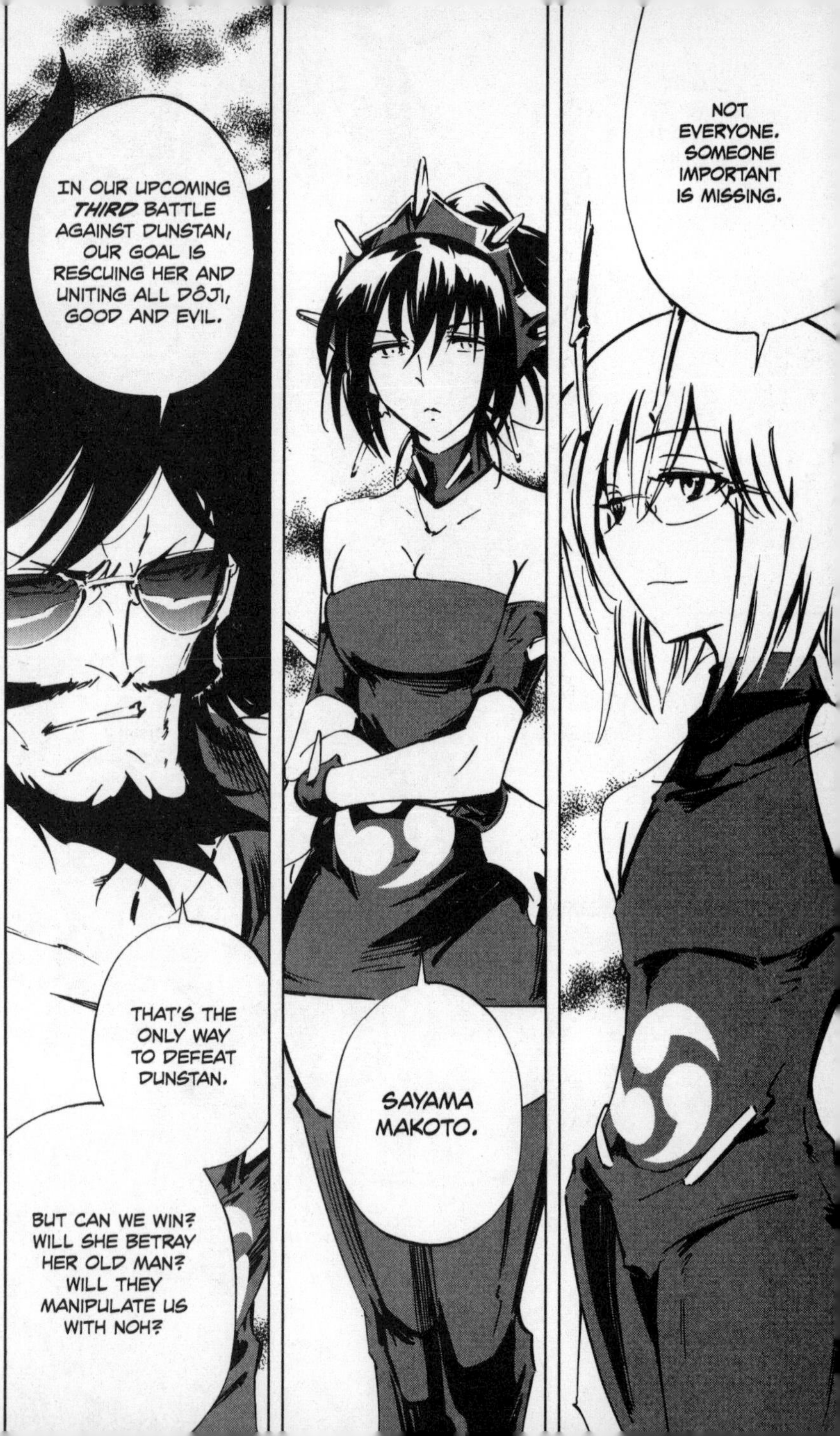
NOT EVERYONE. SOMEONE IMPORTANT IS MISSING.
SAYAMA MAKOTO.
IN OUR UPCOMING *THIRD* BATTLE AGAINST DUNSTAN, OUR GOAL IS RESCUING HER AND UNITING ALL DÔJI, GOOD AND EVIL.
THAT'S THE ONLY WAY TO DEFEAT DUNSTAN.
BUT CAN WE WIN? WILL SHE BETRAY HER OLD MAN? WILL THEY MANIPULATE US WITH NOH?

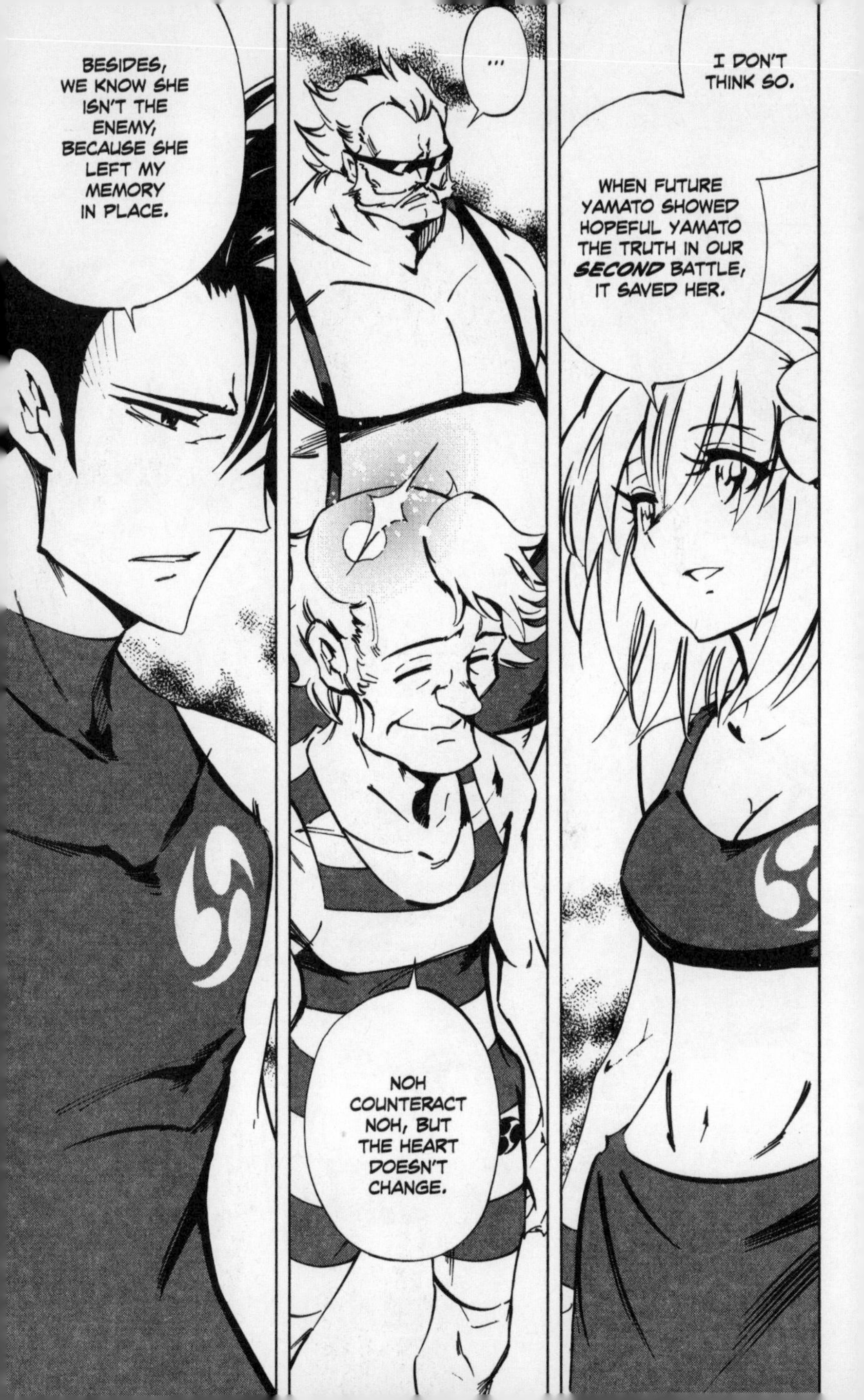
I DON'T THINK SO.
WHEN FUTURE YAMATO SHOWED HOPEFUL YAMATO THE TRUTH IN OUR *SECOND* BATTLE, IT SAVED HER.
...
NOH COUNTERACT NOH, BUT THE HEART DOESN'T CHANGE.
BESIDES, WE KNOW SHE ISN'T THE ENEMY, BECAUSE SHE LEFT MY MEMORY IN PLACE.

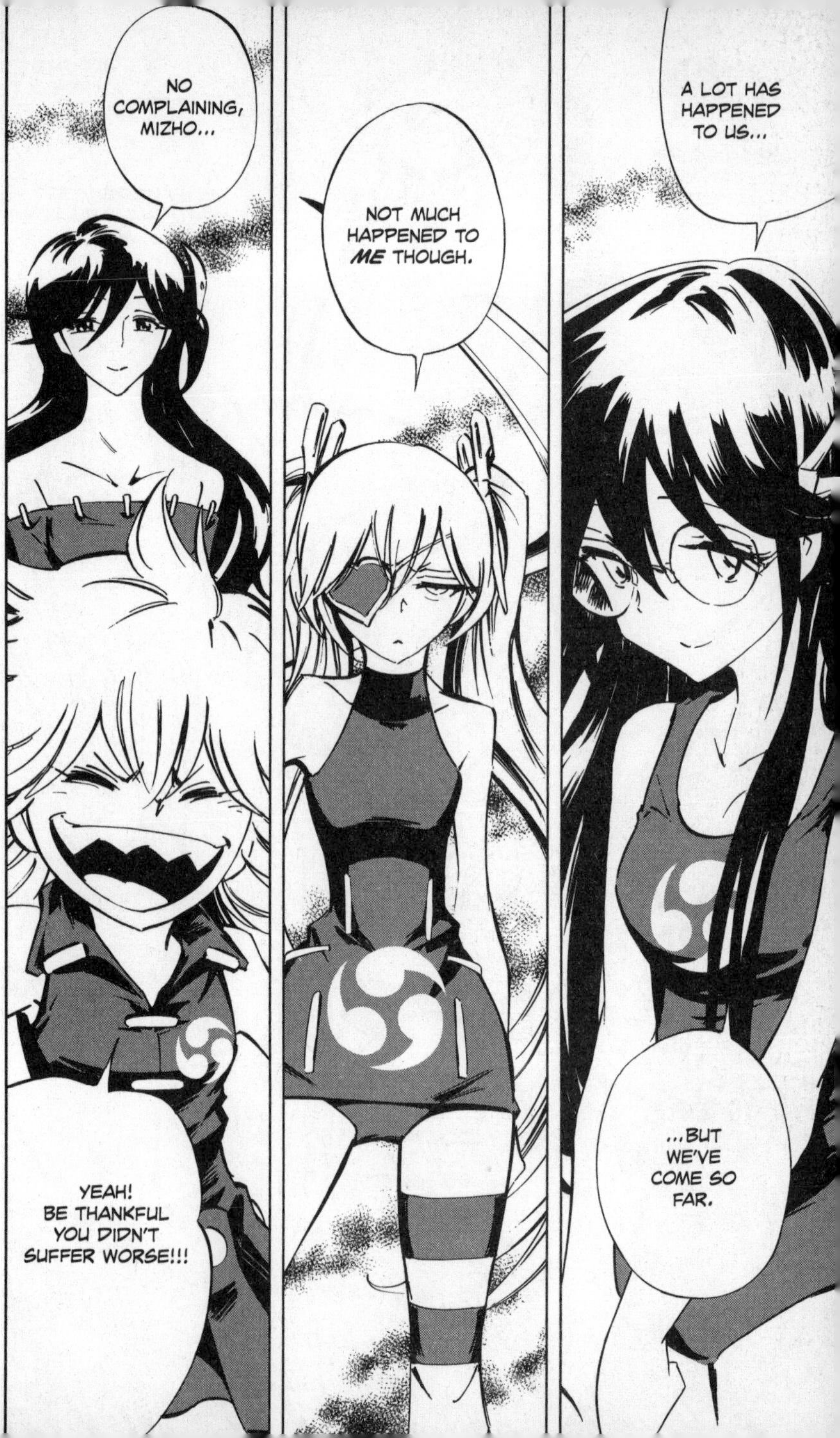
A LOT HAS HAPPENED TO US...
...BUT WE'VE COME SO FAR.
NOT MUCH HAPPENED TO *ME* THOUGH.
NO COMPLAINING, MIZHO...
YEAH! BE THANKFUL YOU DIDN'T SUFFER WORSE!!!

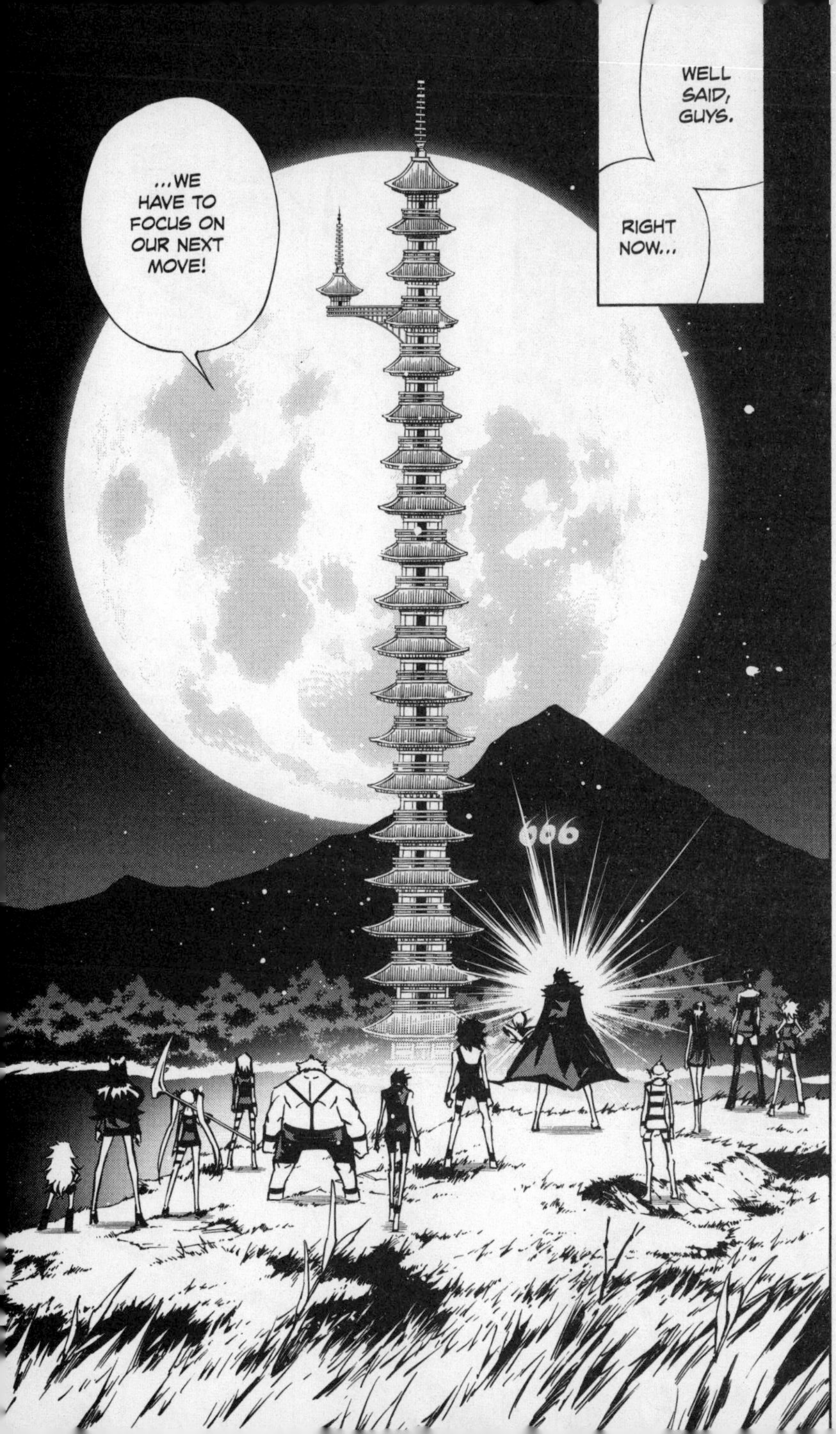
WELL SAID, GUYS.
RIGHT NOW...
...WE HAVE TO FOCUS ON OUR NEXT MOVE!

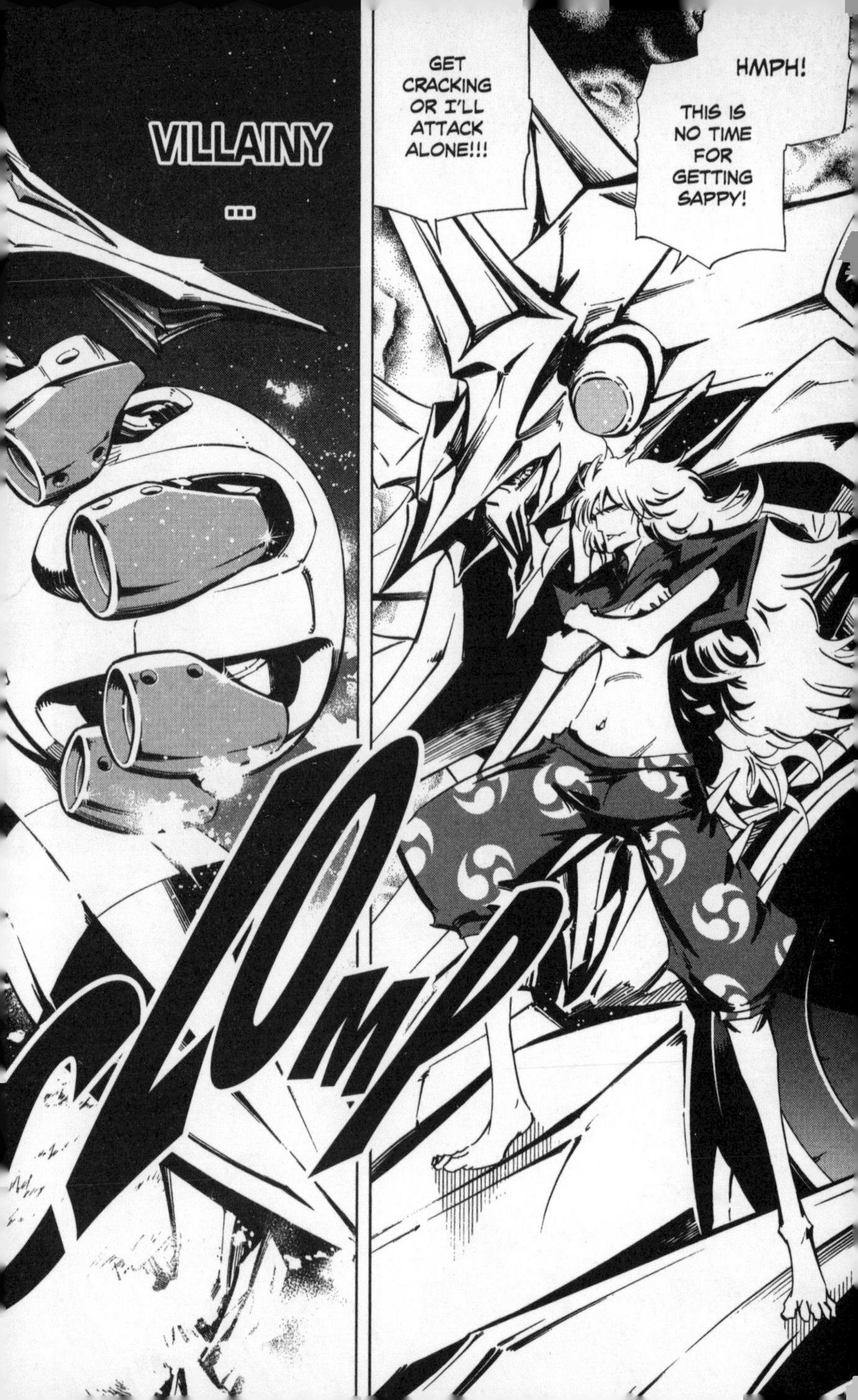
HMPH!
THIS IS NO TIME FOR GETTING SAPPY!
GET CRACKING OR I'LL ATTACK ALONE!!!
VILLAINY
...

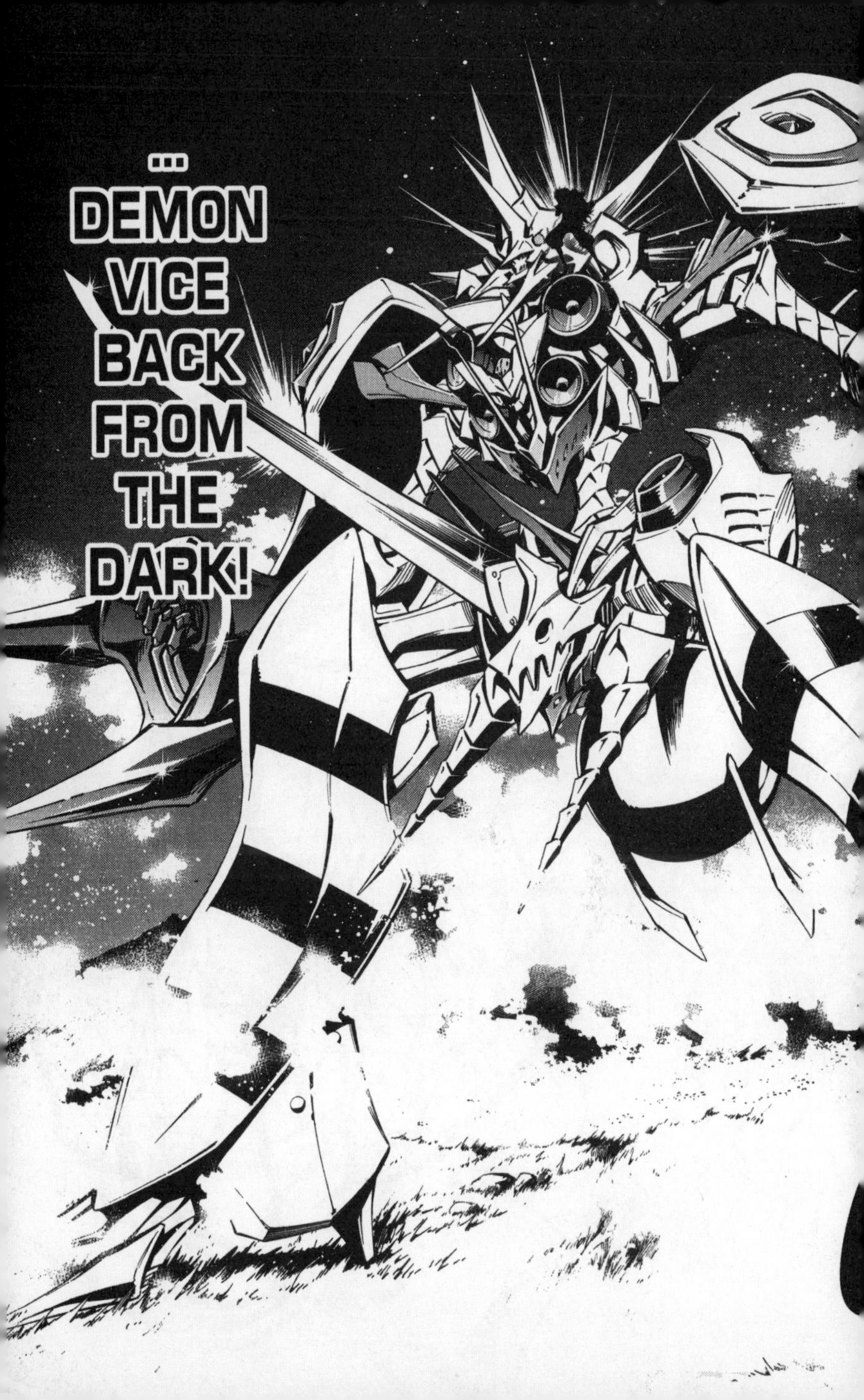
...DEMON VICE BACK FROM THE DARK!

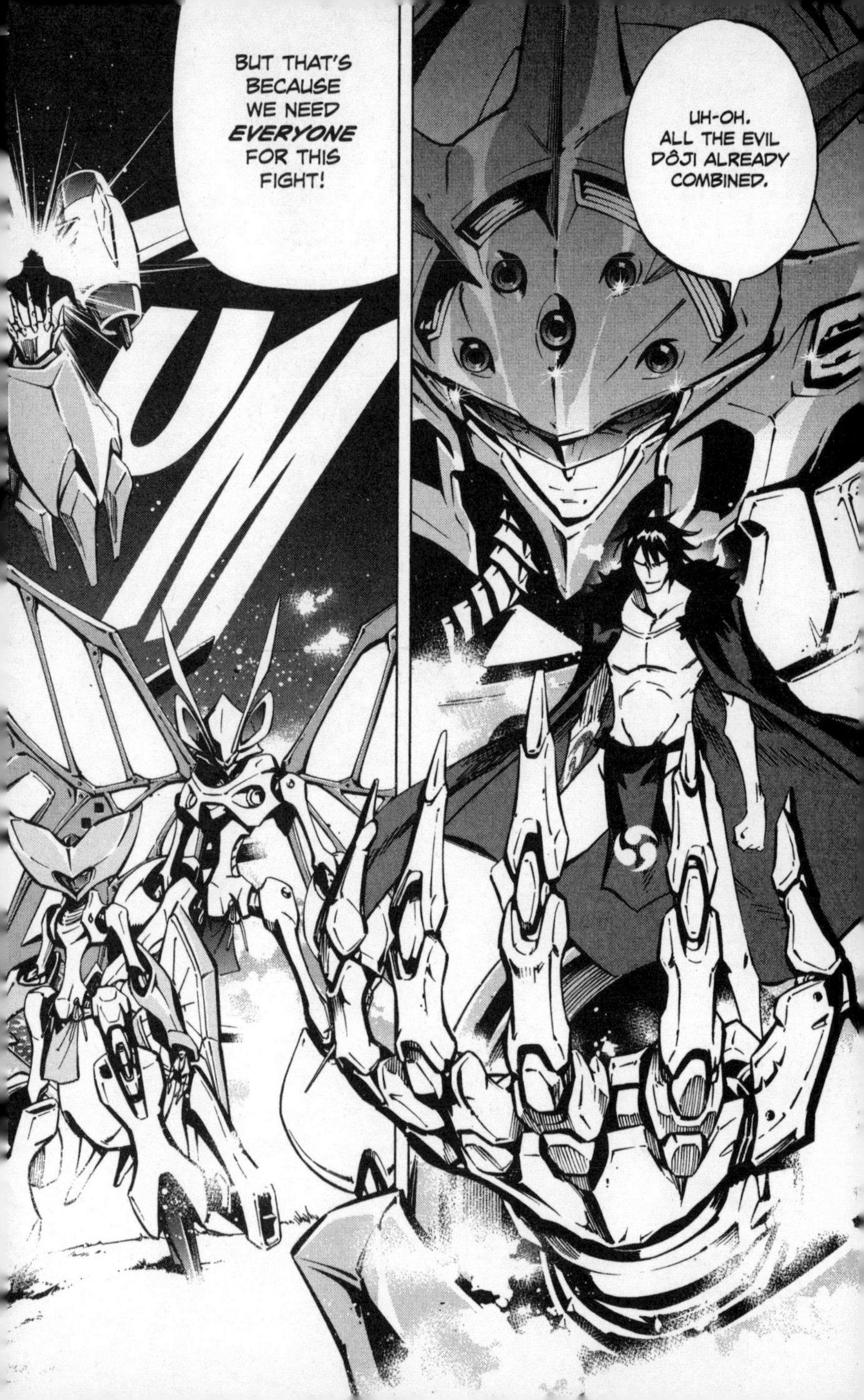
UH-OH. ALL THE EVIL DÔJI ALREADY COMBINED.
BUT THAT'S BECAUSE WE NEED *EVERYONE* FOR THIS FIGHT!

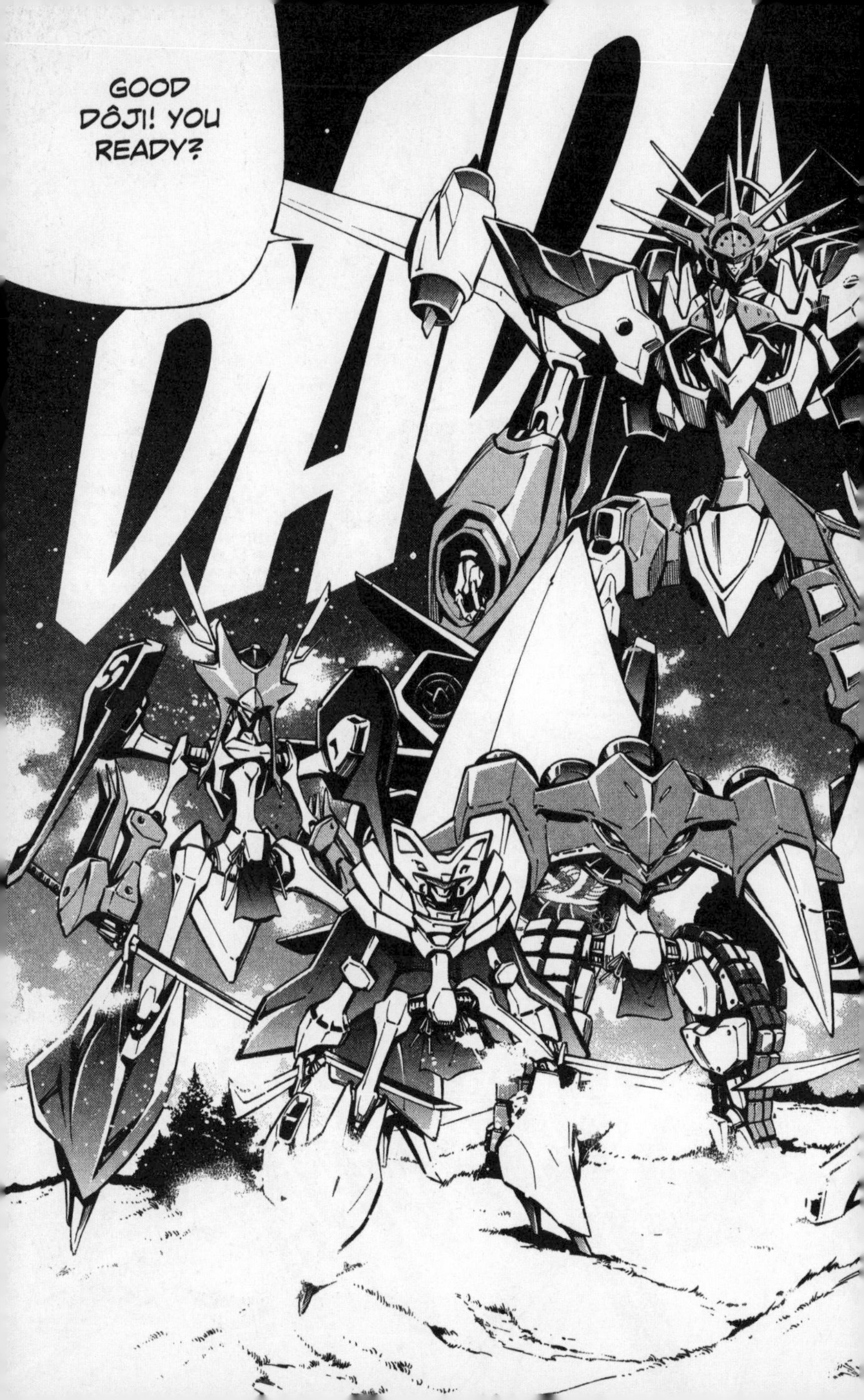
GOOD DÔJI! YOU READY?

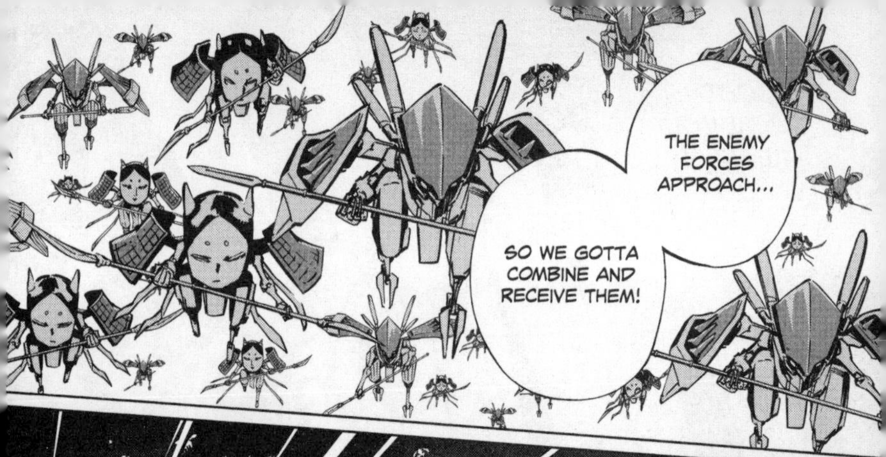
THE ENEMY FORCES APPROACH...
SO WE GOTTA COMBINE AND RECEIVE THEM!

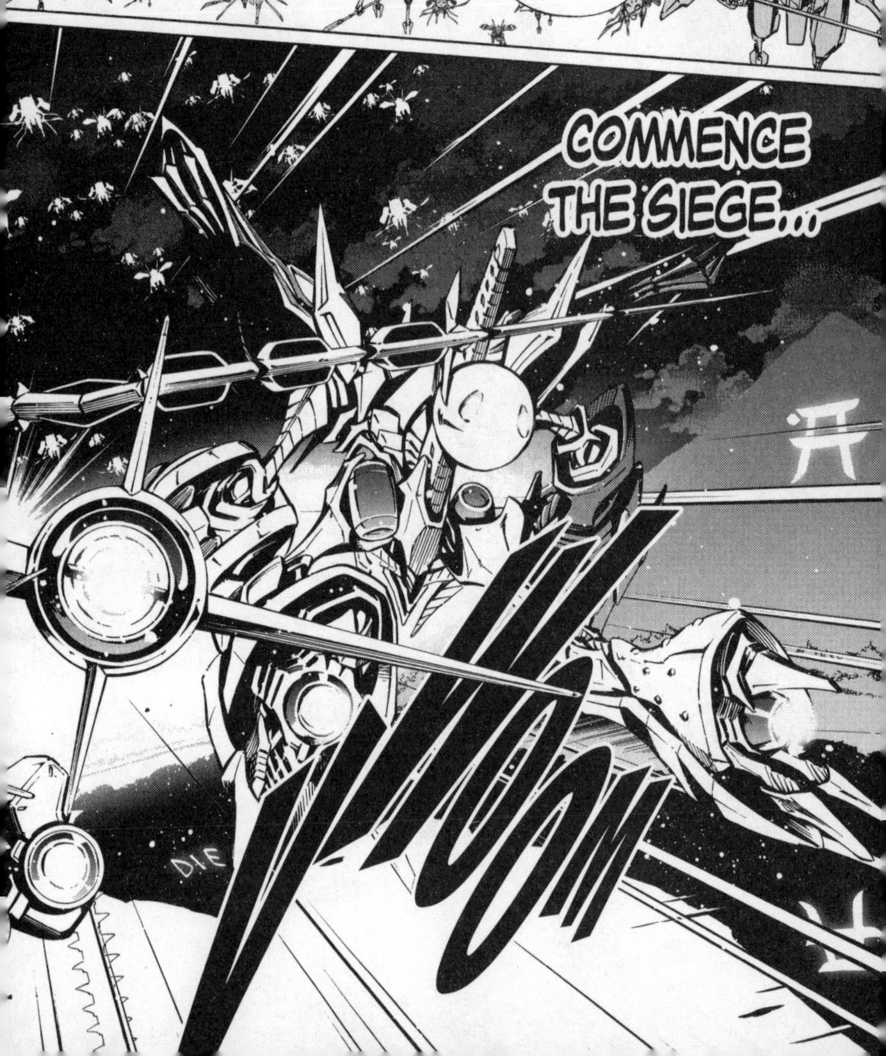
COMMENCE THE SIEGE...
DIE

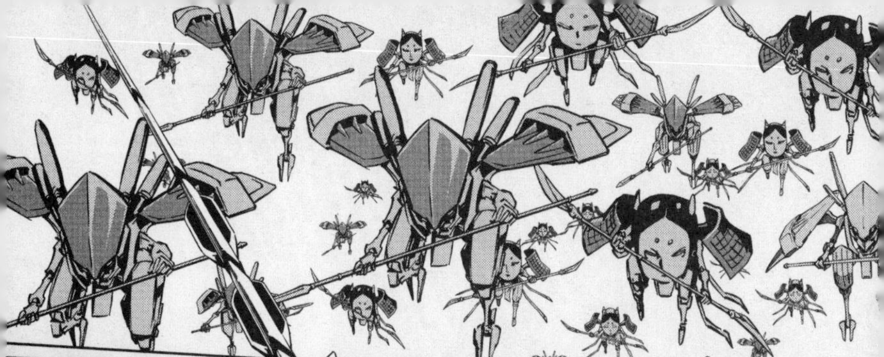
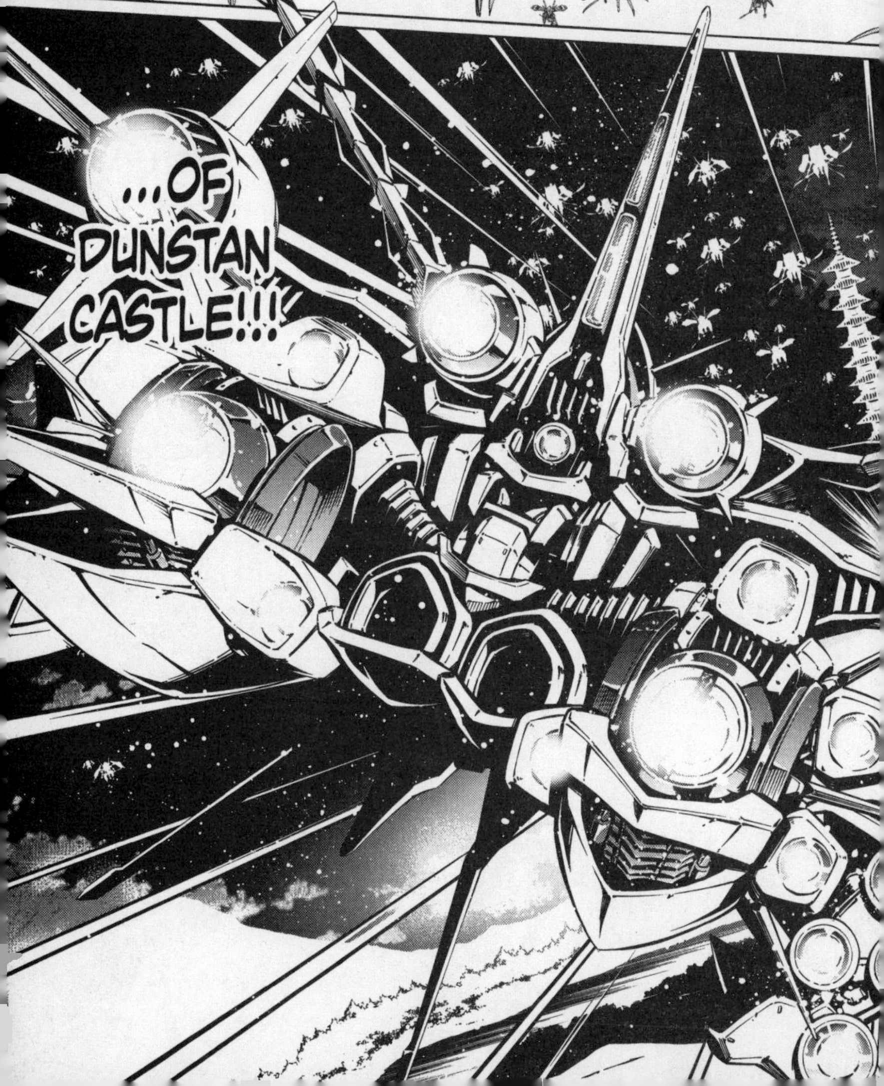
...OF DUNSTAN CASTLE!!!

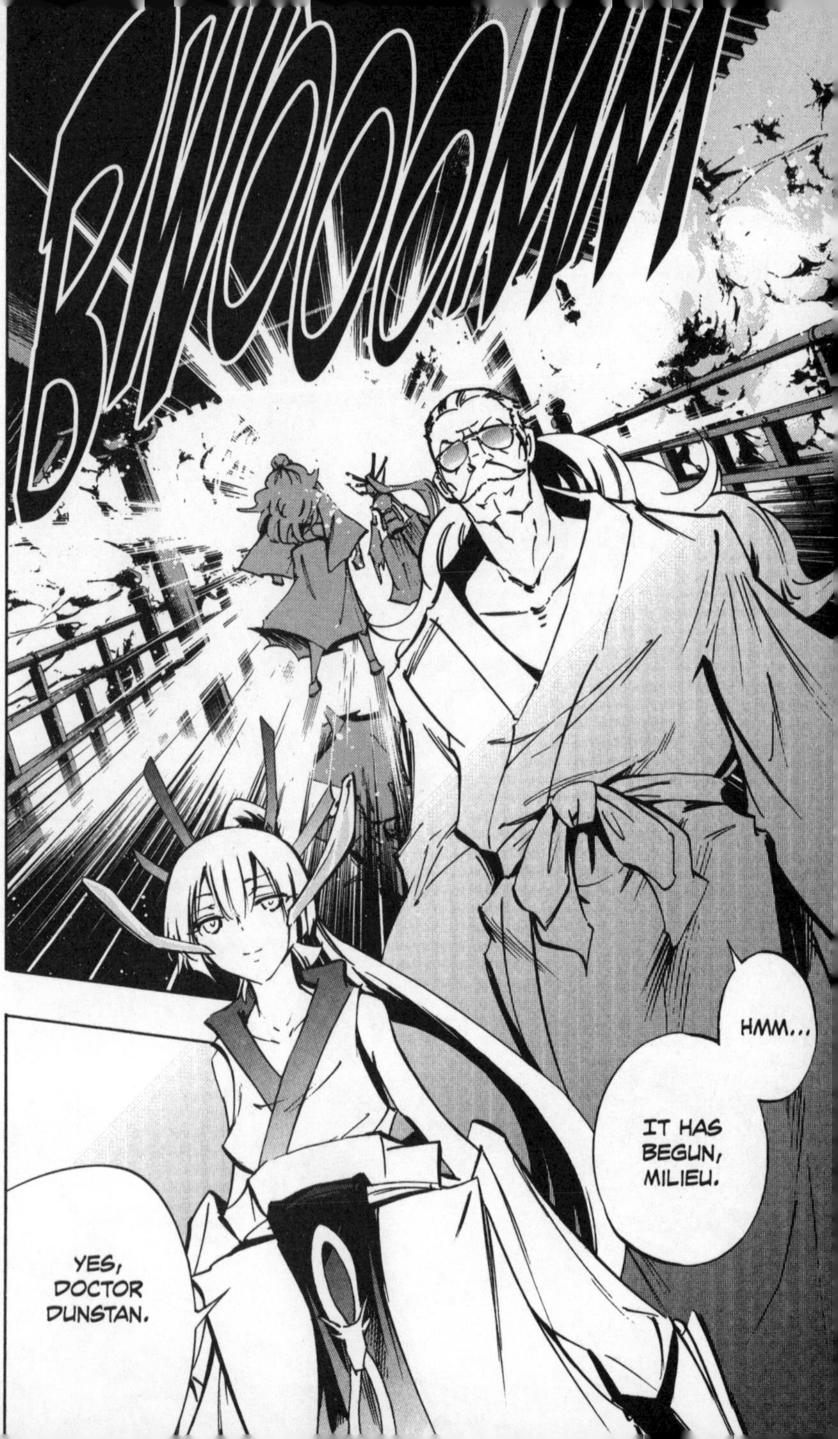
BWOOOOMM
HMM...
IT HAS BEGUN, MILIEU.
YES, DOCTOR DUNSTAN.

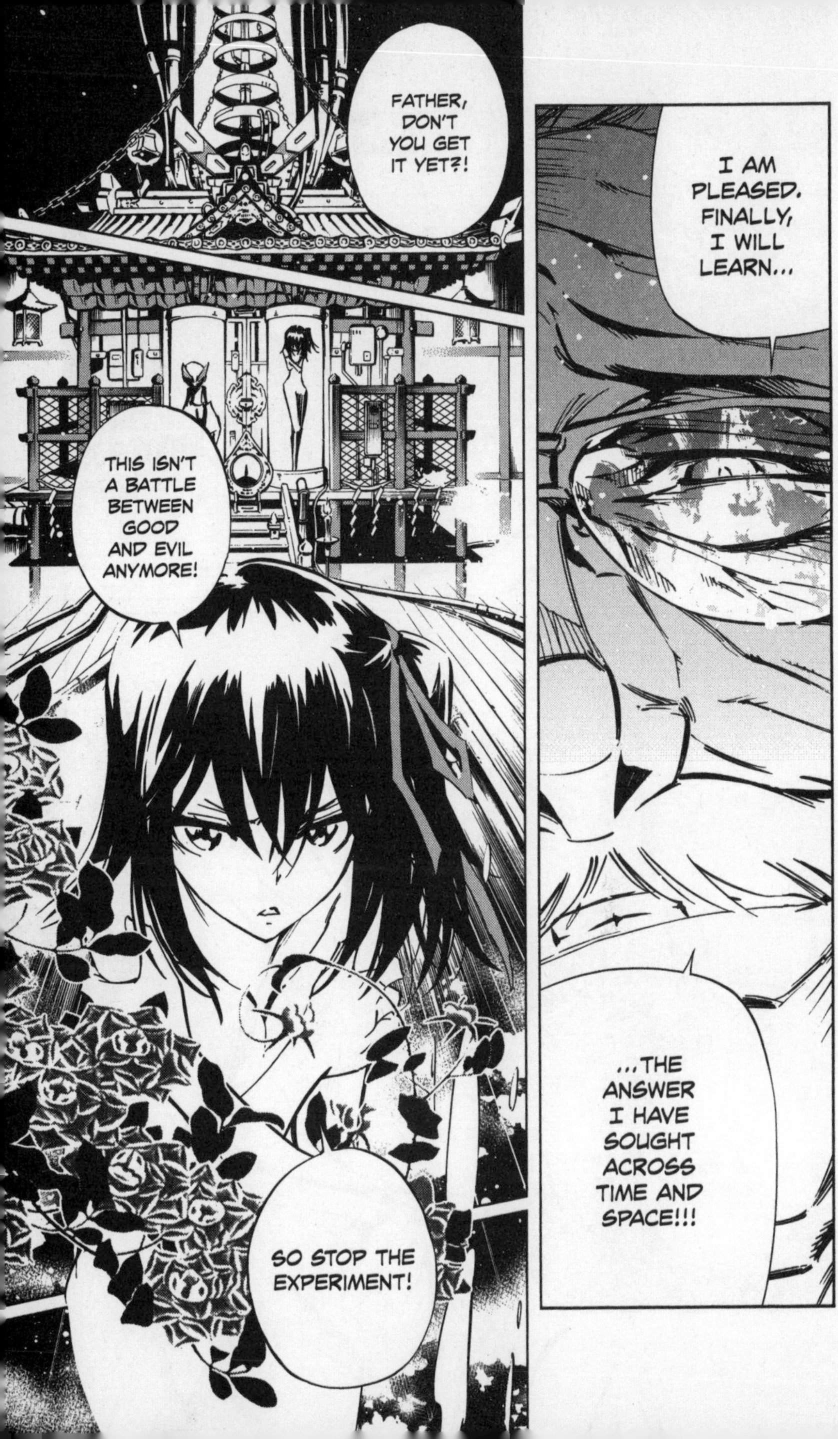
I AM PLEASED. FINALLY, I WILL LEARN...
...THE ANSWER I HAVE SOUGHT ACROSS TIME AND SPACE!!!
FATHER, DON'T YOU GET IT YET?!
THIS ISN'T A BATTLE BETWEEN GOOD AND EVIL ANYMORE!
SO STOP THE EXPERIMENT!

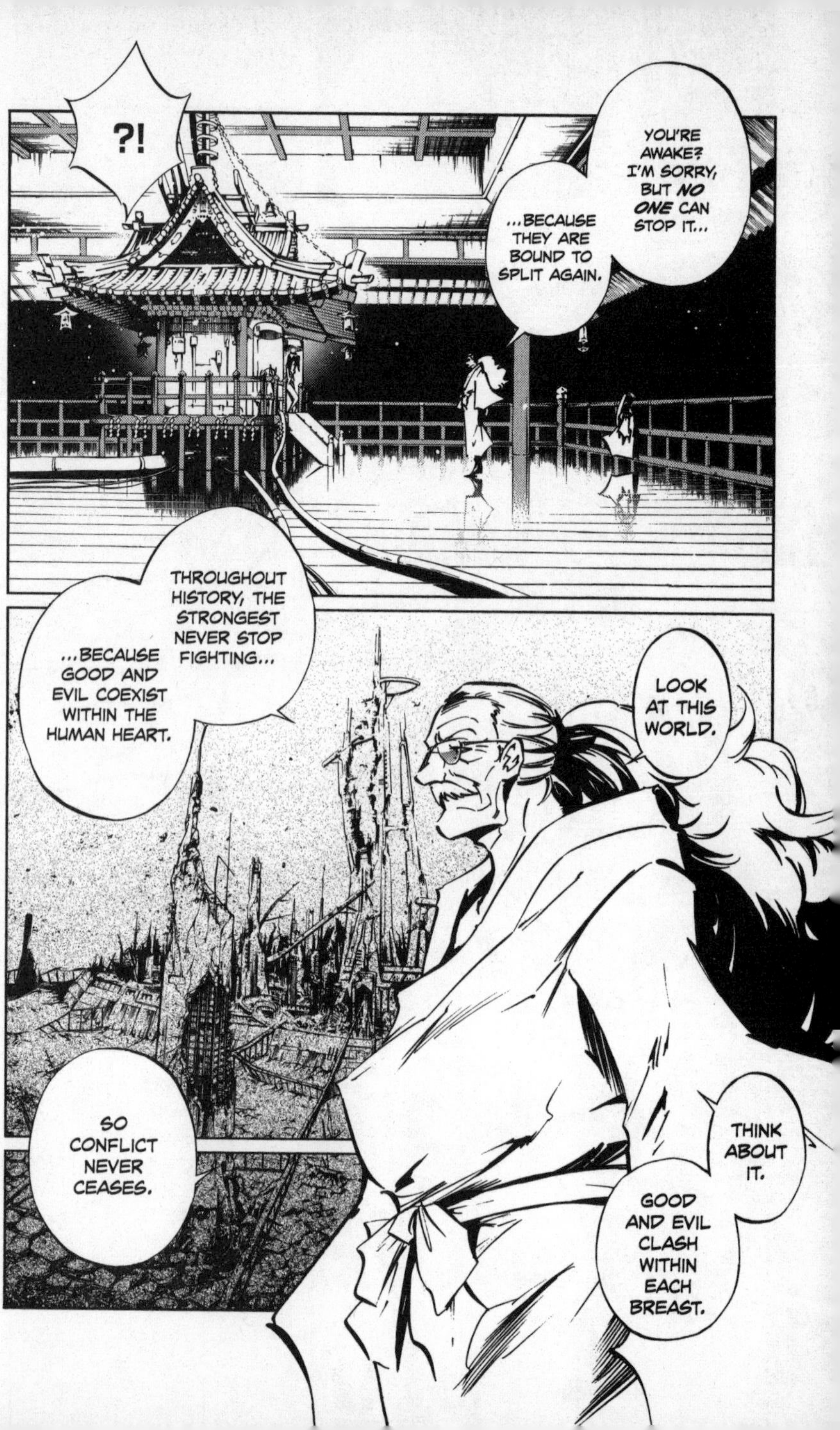
?!
YOU'RE AWAKE? I'M SORRY, BUT *NO ONE* CAN STOP IT...
...BECAUSE THEY ARE BOUND TO SPLIT AGAIN.
LOOK AT THIS WORLD.
THROUGHOUT HISTORY, THE STRONGEST NEVER STOP FIGHTING...
...BECAUSE GOOD AND EVIL COEXIST WITHIN THE HUMAN HEART.
THINK ABOUT IT.
GOOD AND EVIL CLASH WITHIN EACH BREAST.
SO CONFLICT NEVER CEASES.

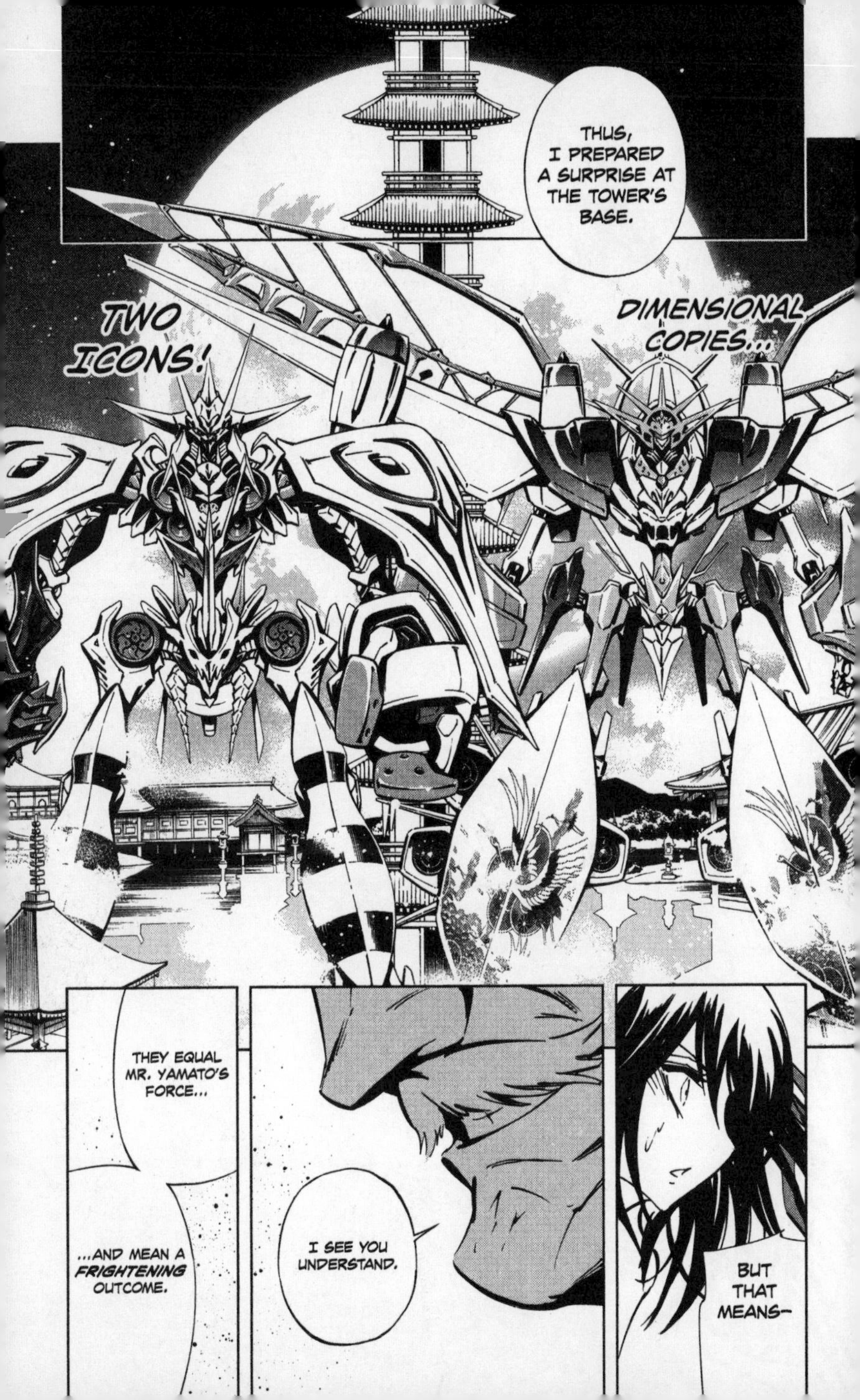
THUS, I PREPARED A SURPRISE AT THE TOWER'S BASE.
DIMENSIONAL COPIES...
TWO ICONS!
BUT THAT MEANS—
I SEE YOU UNDERSTAND.
THEY EQUAL MR. YAMATO'S FORCE...
...AND MEAN A FRIGHTENING OUTCOME.

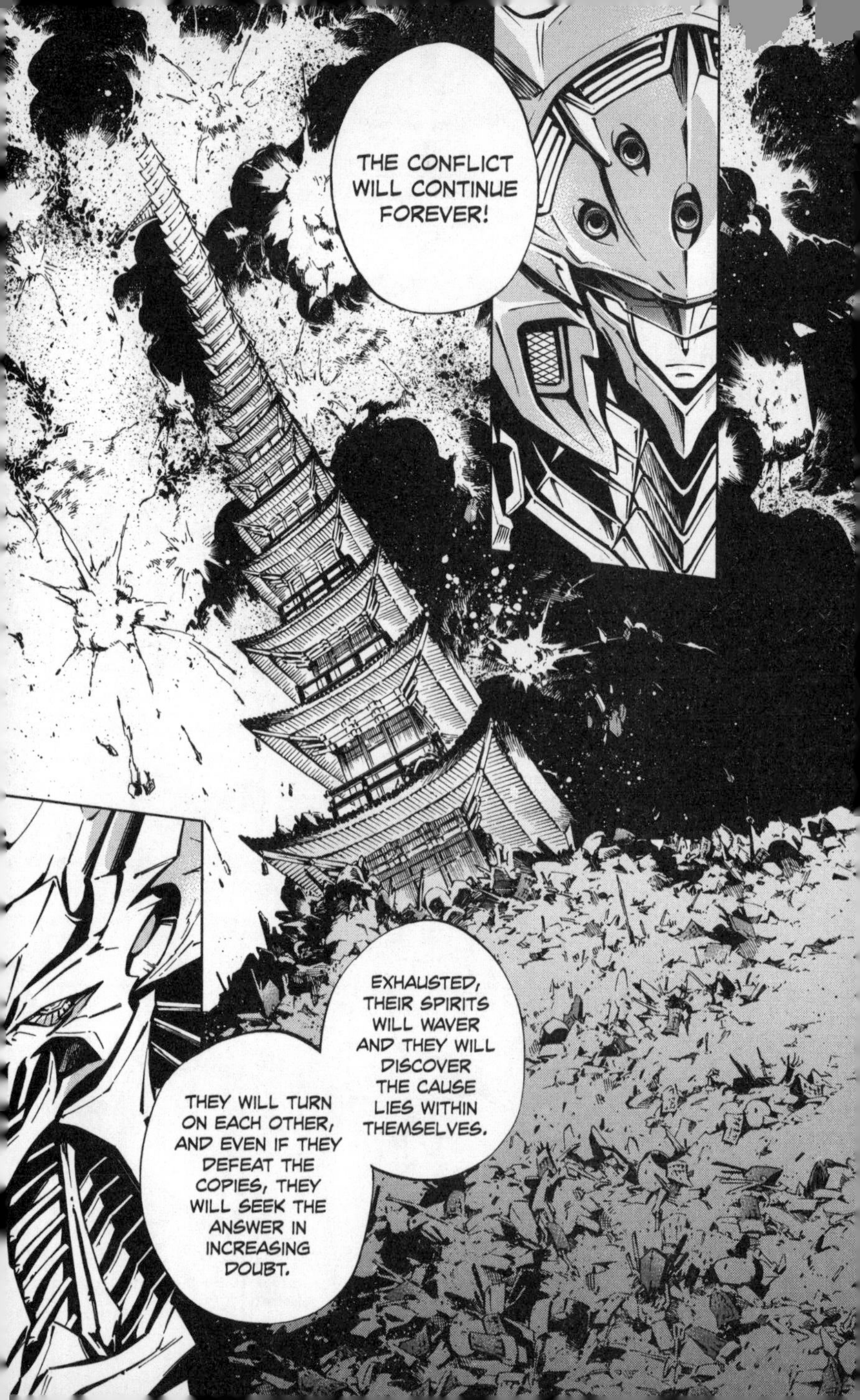
THE CONFLICT WILL CONTINUE FOREVER!
EXHAUSTED, THEIR SPIRITS WILL WAVER AND THEY WILL DISCOVER THE CAUSE LIES WITHIN THEMSELVES.
THEY WILL TURN ON EACH OTHER, AND EVEN IF THEY DEFEAT THE COPIES, THEY WILL SEEK THE ANSWER IN INCREASING DOUBT.

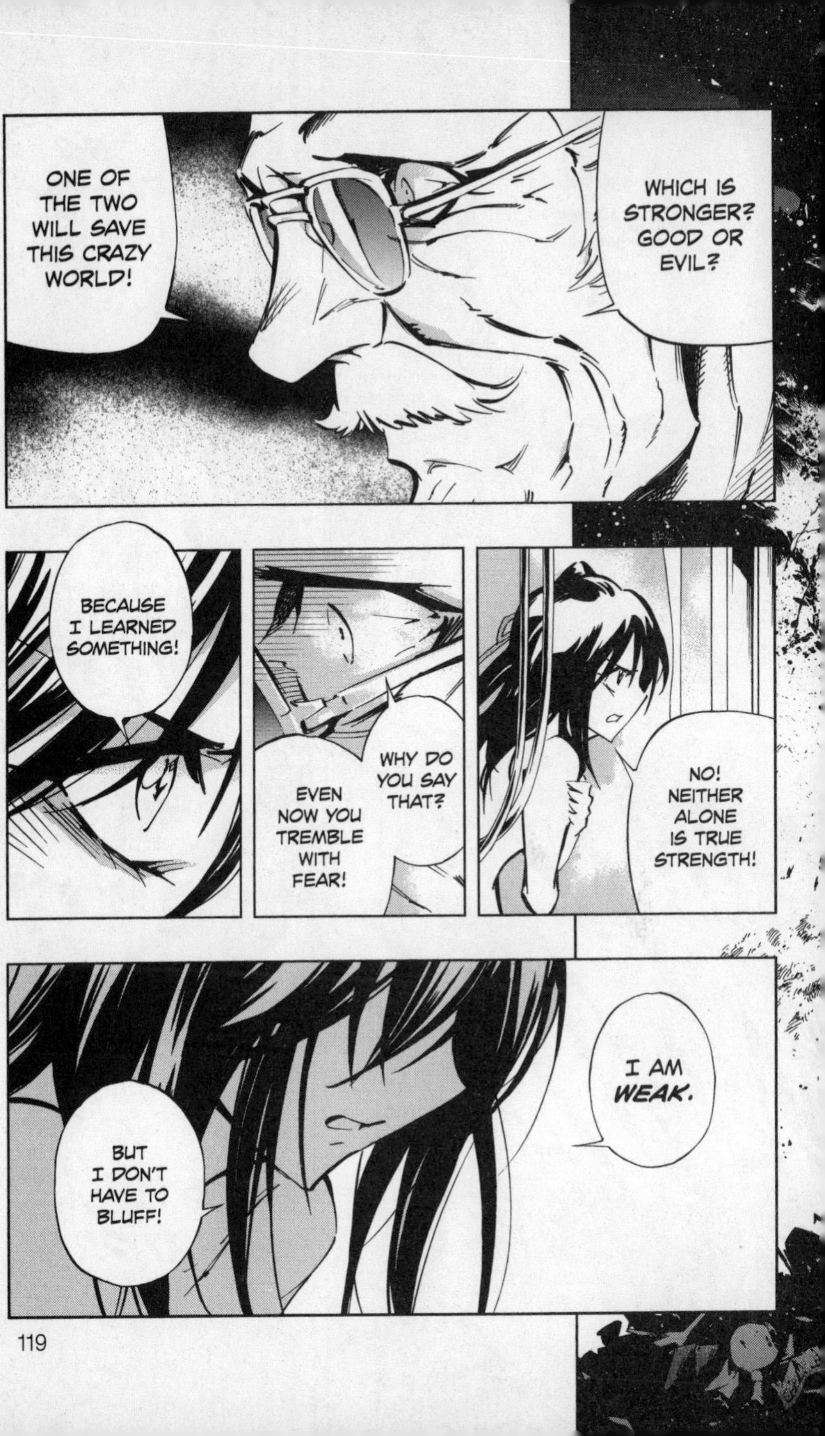
WHICH IS STRONGER? GOOD OR EVIL?
ONE OF THE TWO WILL SAVE THIS CRAZY WORLD!
NO! NEITHER ALONE IS TRUE STRENGTH!
WHY DO YOU SAY THAT?
EVEN NOW YOU TREMBLE WITH FEAR!
BECAUSE I LEARNED SOMETHING!
I AM *WEAK.*
BUT I DON'T HAVE TO BLUFF!

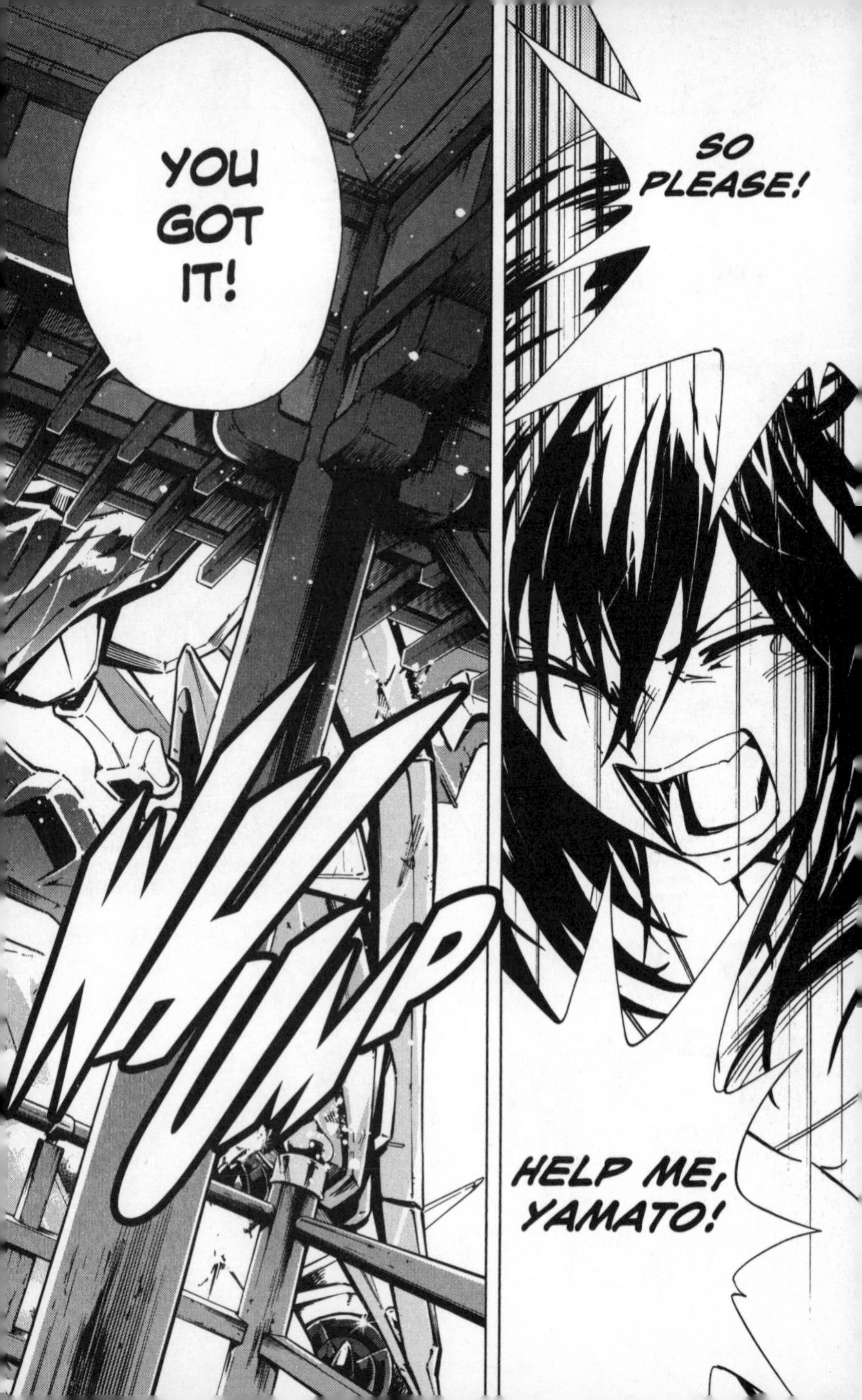
SO PLEASE!
HELP ME, YAMATO!
YOU GOT IT!
WHUMP

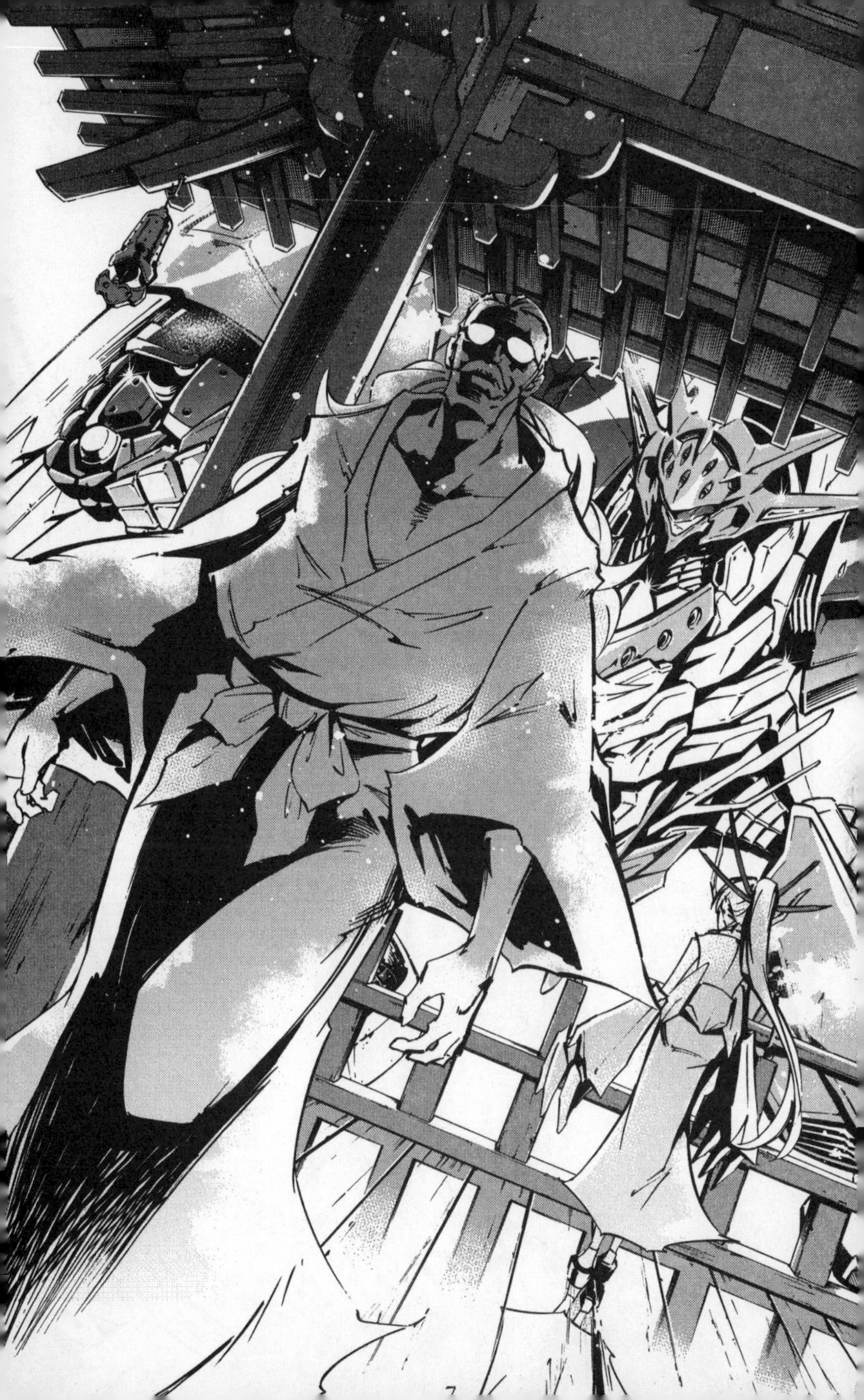

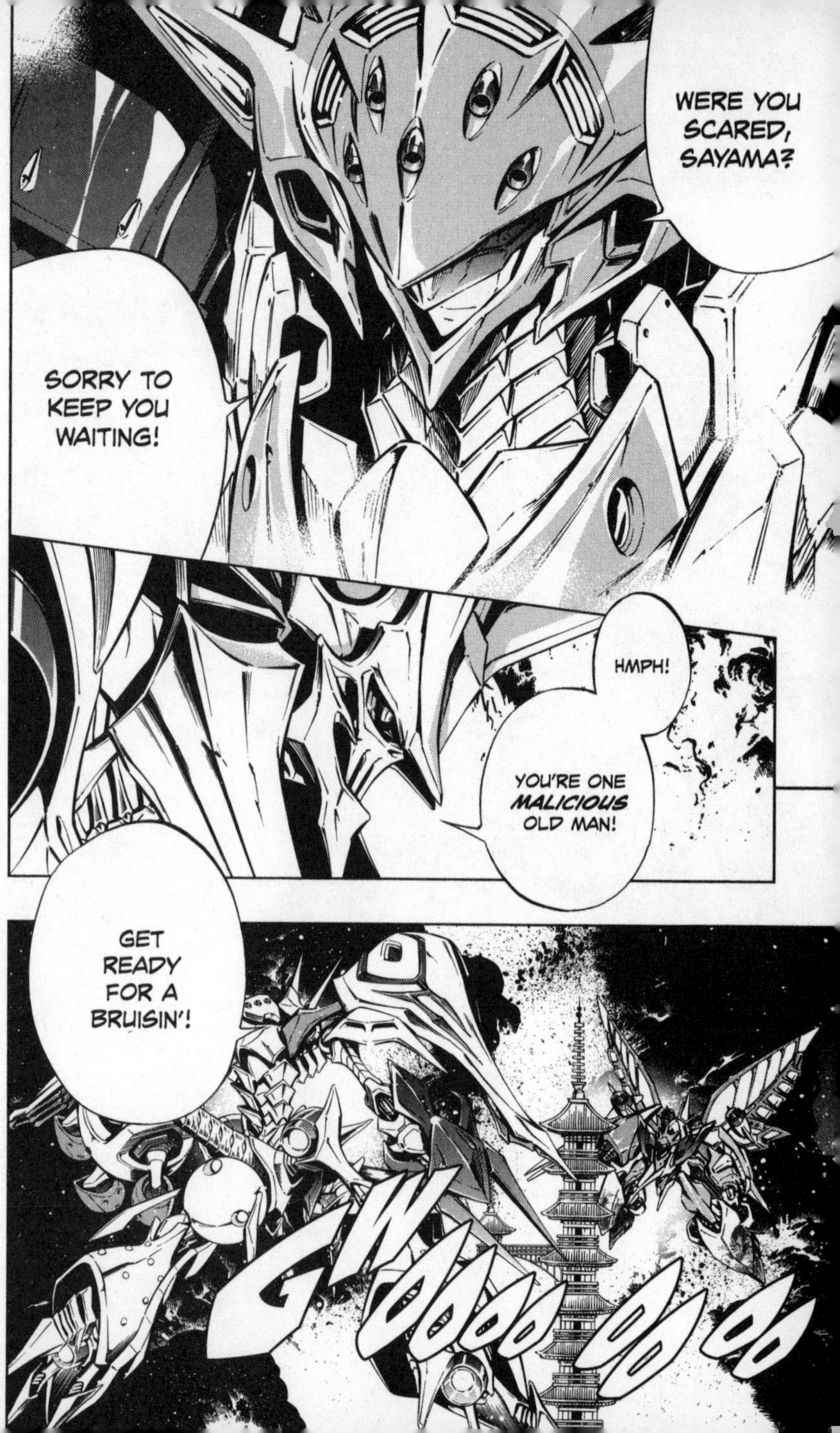
WERE YOU SCARED, SAYAMA?
SORRY TO KEEP YOU WAITING!
HMPH!
YOU'RE ONE *MALICIOUS* OLD MAN!
GET READY FOR A BRUISIN'!

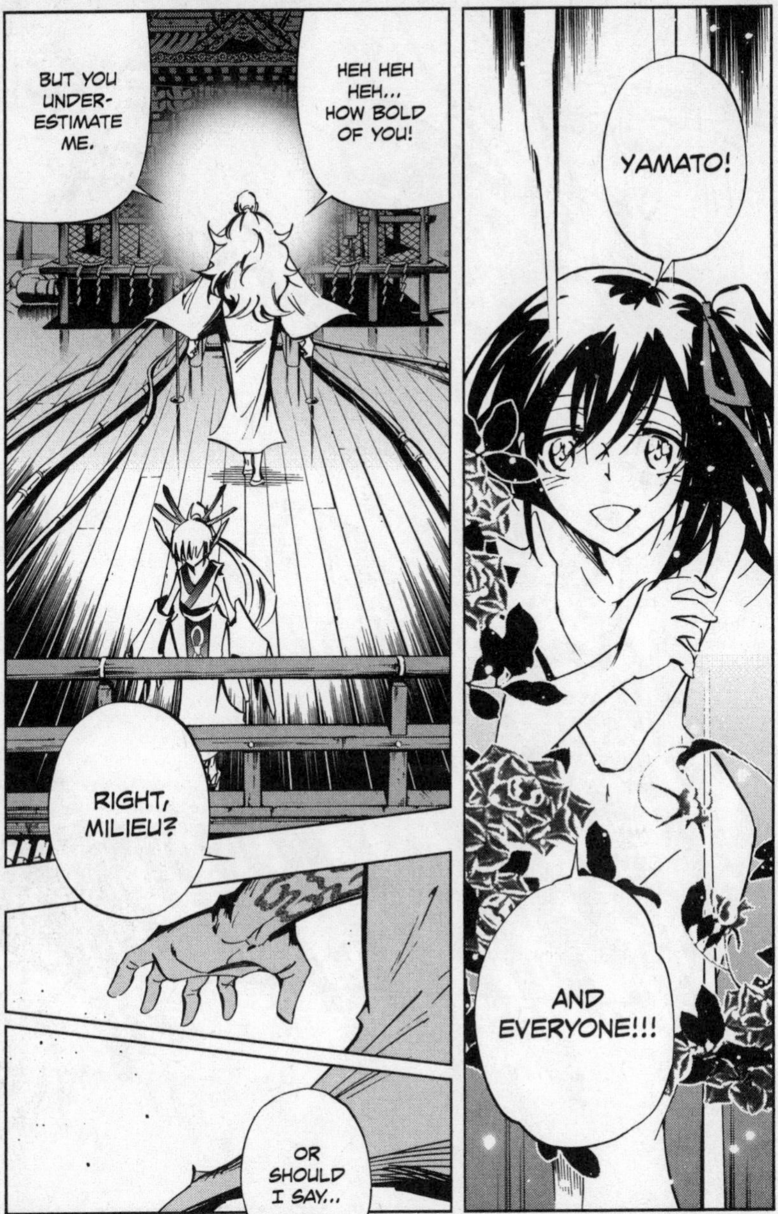
HEH HEH HEH... HOW BOLD OF YOU!
BUT YOU UNDER-ESTIMATE ME.
RIGHT, MILIEU?
OR SHOULD I SAY...
YAMATO!
AND EVERYONE!!!

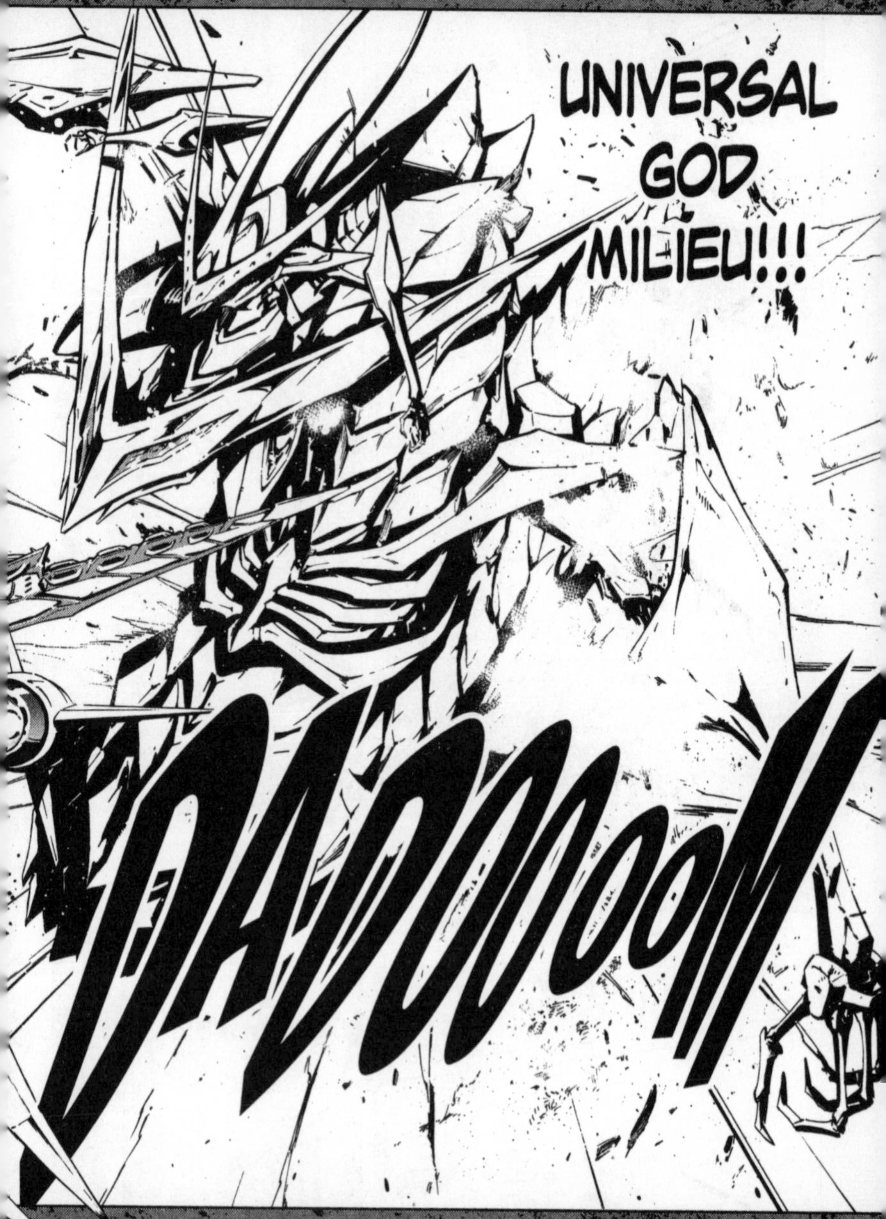
UNIVERSAL GOD MILIEU!!!
DHOOOOM

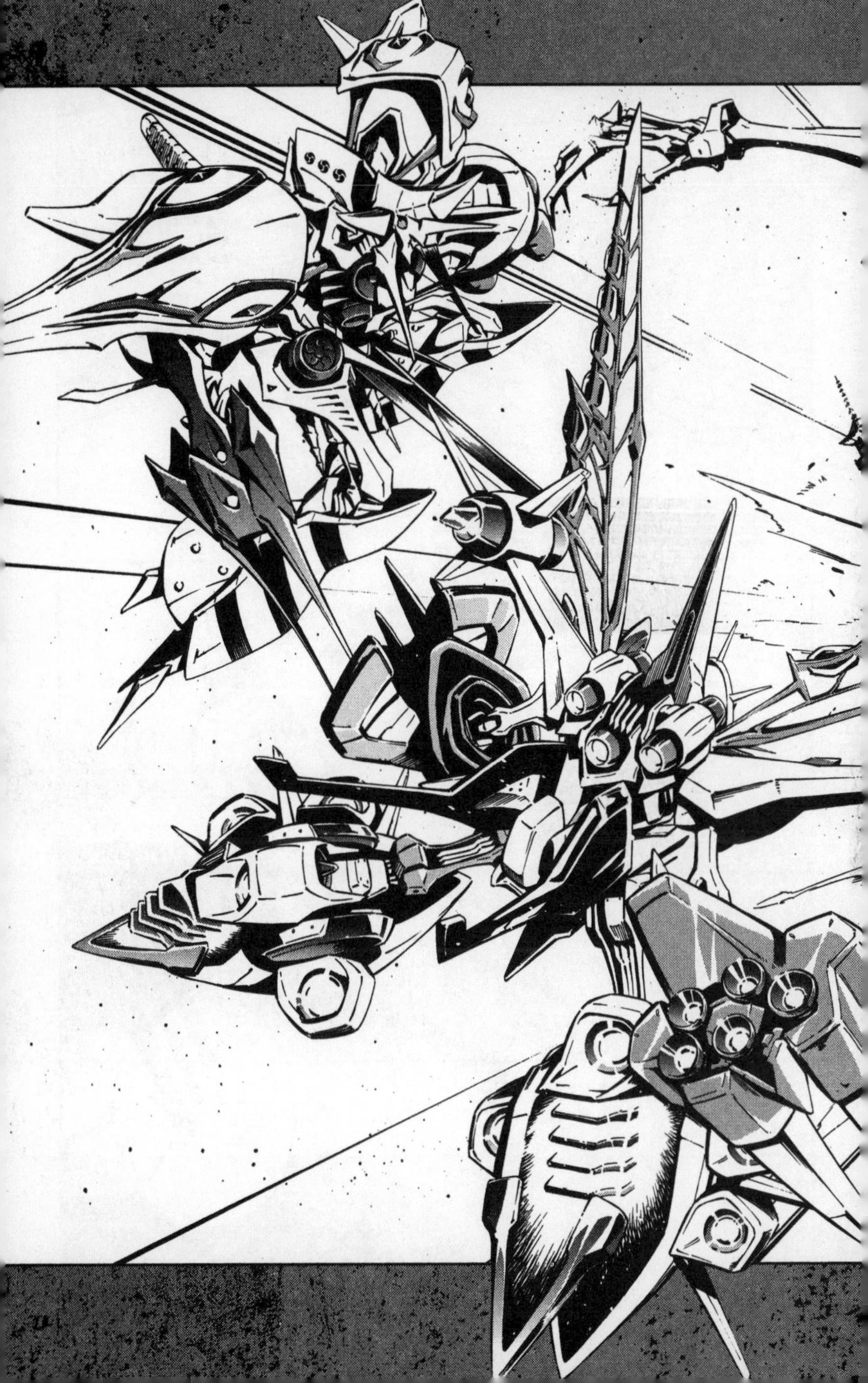

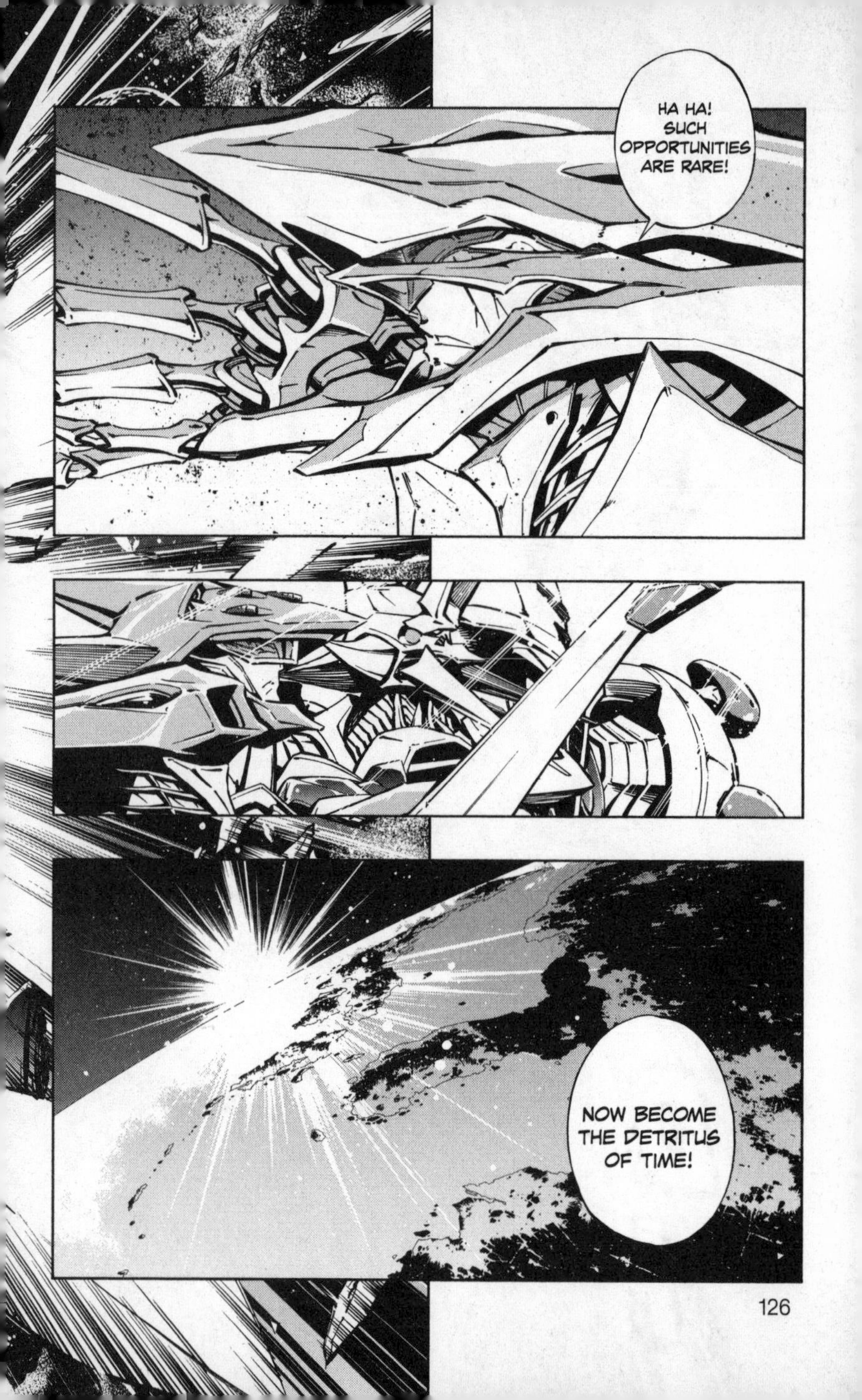
HA HA! SUCH OPPORTUNITIES ARE RARE!
NOW BECOME THE DETRITUS OF TIME!

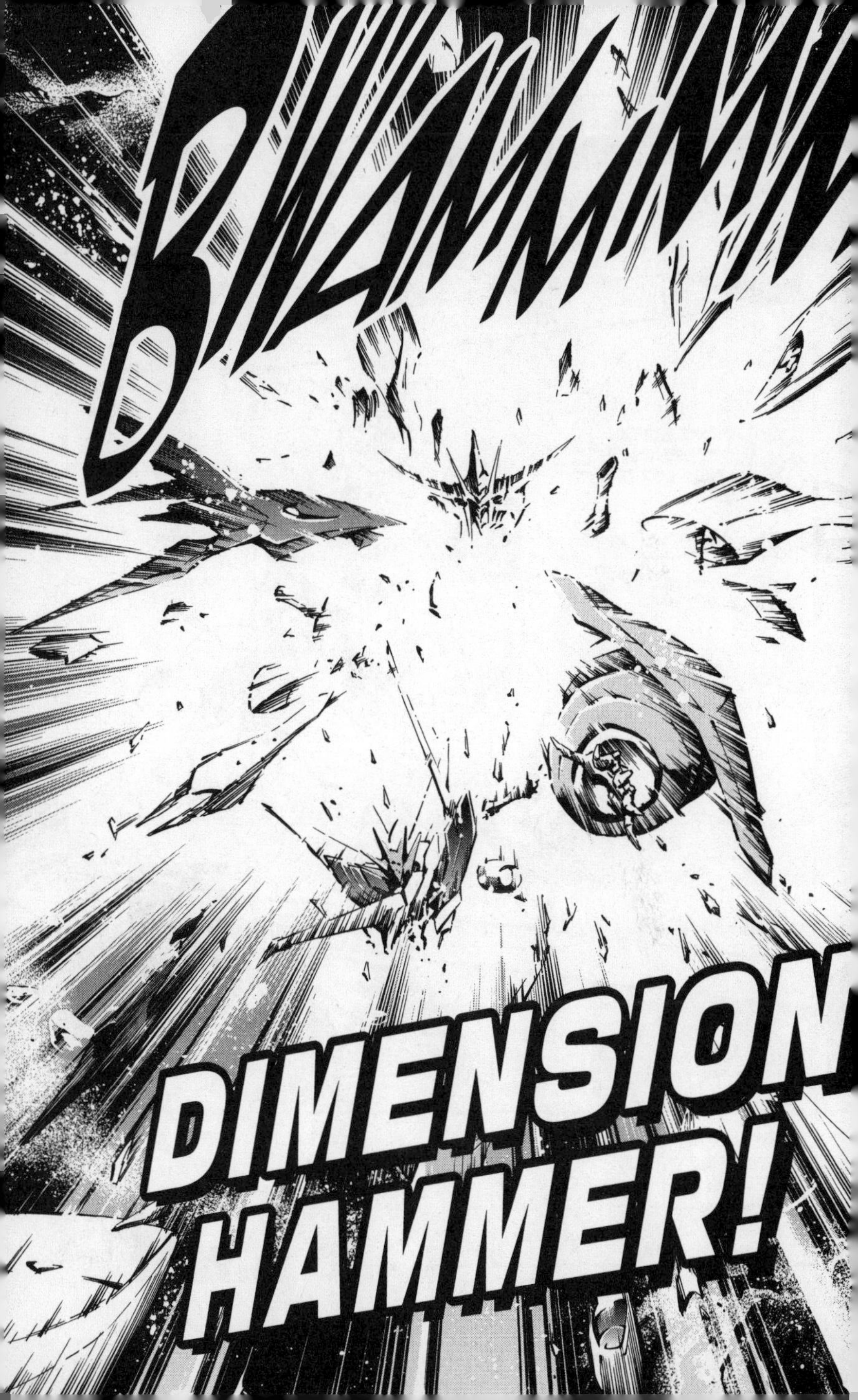
BAMMMM
DIMENSION HAMMER!

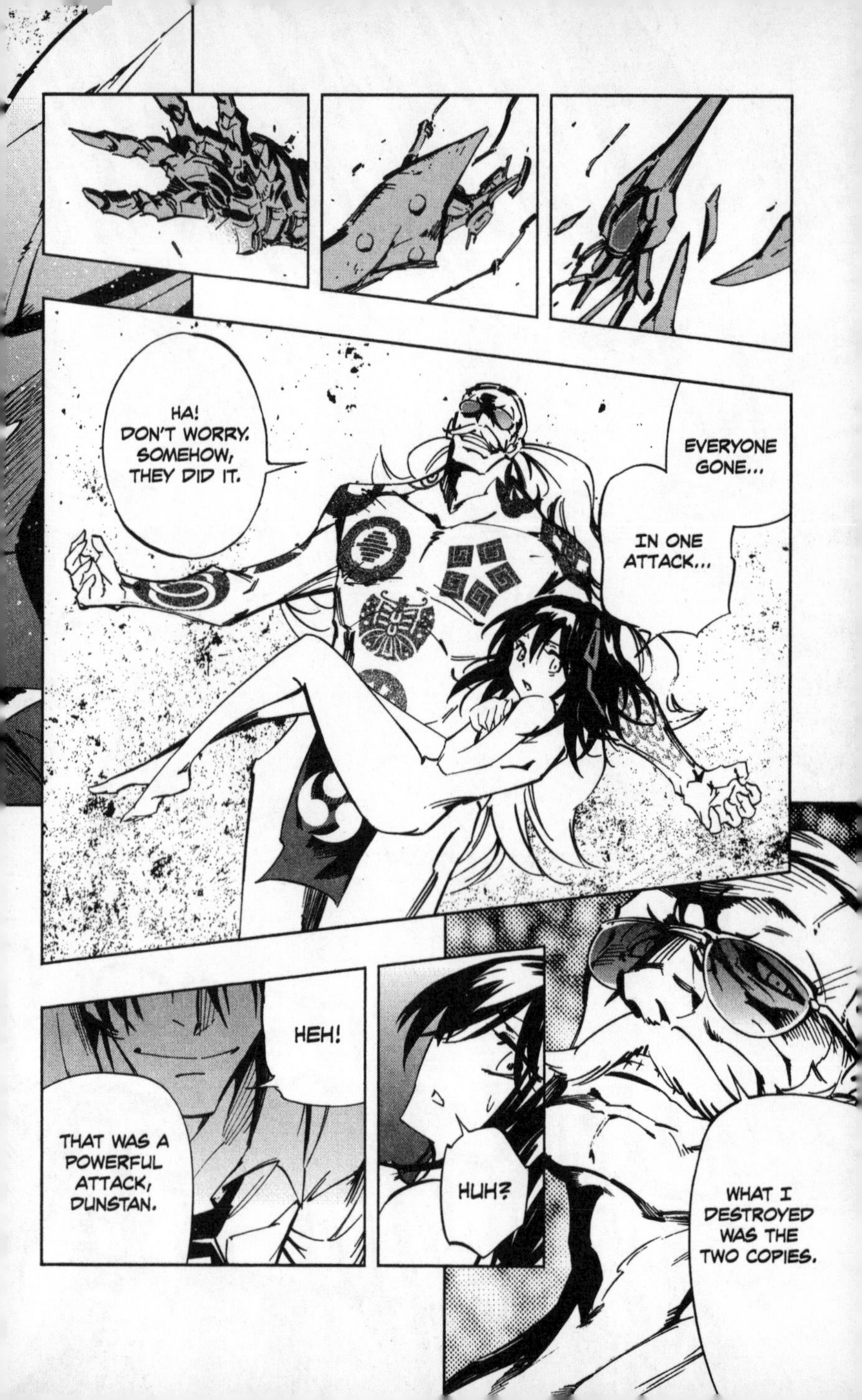
EVERYONE GONE...
IN ONE ATTACK...
HA! DON'T WORRY. SOMEHOW, THEY DID IT.
WHAT I DESTROYED WAS THE TWO COPIES.
HUH?
HEH!
THAT WAS A POWERFUL ATTACK, DUNSTAN.

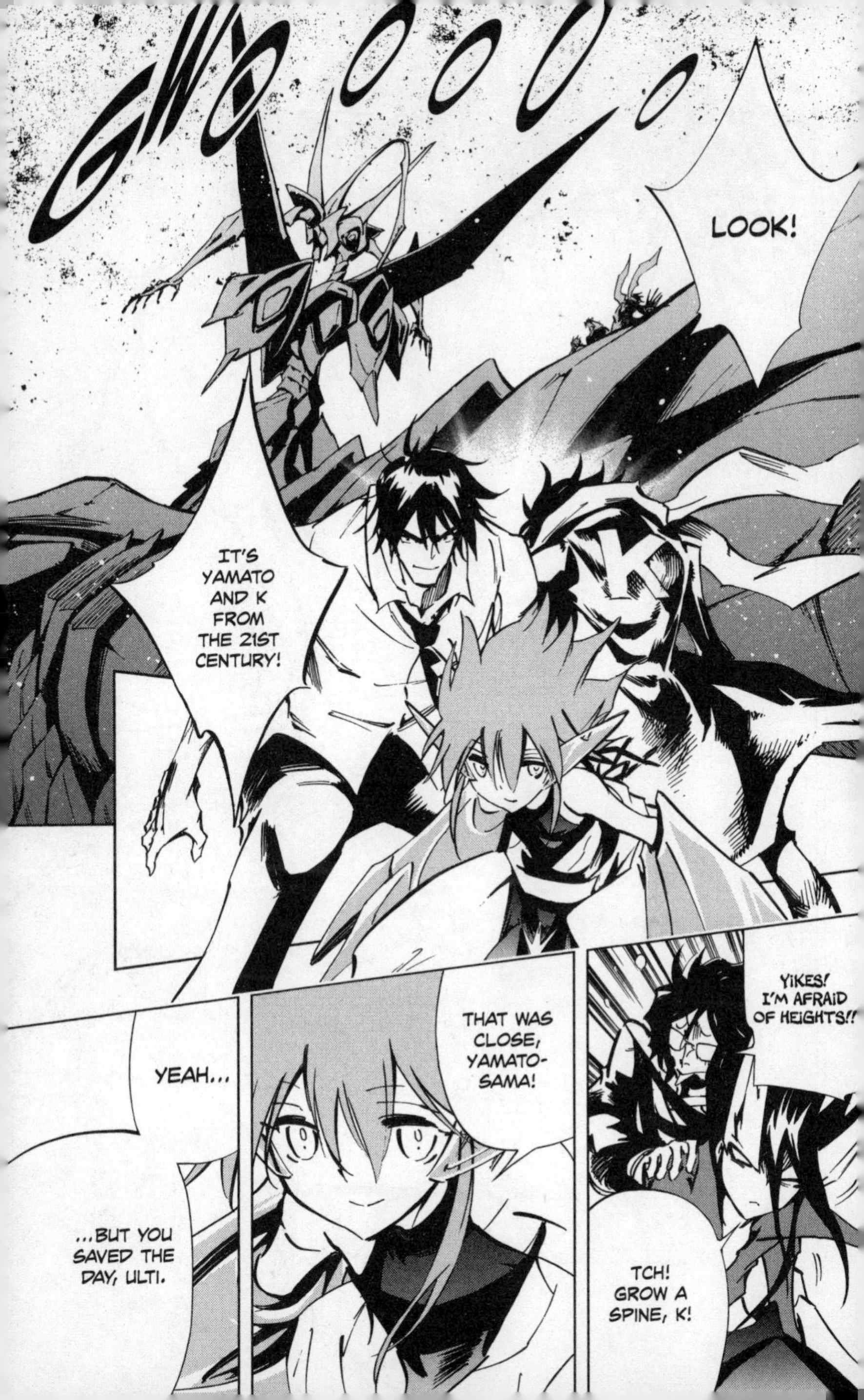
GWOOOOO
LOOK!
IT'S YAMATO AND K FROM THE 21ST CENTURY!
YIKES! I'M AFRAID OF HEIGHTS!!
TCH! GROW A SPINE, K!
THAT WAS CLOSE, YAMATO-SAMA!
YEAH...
...BUT YOU SAVED THE DAY, ULTI.

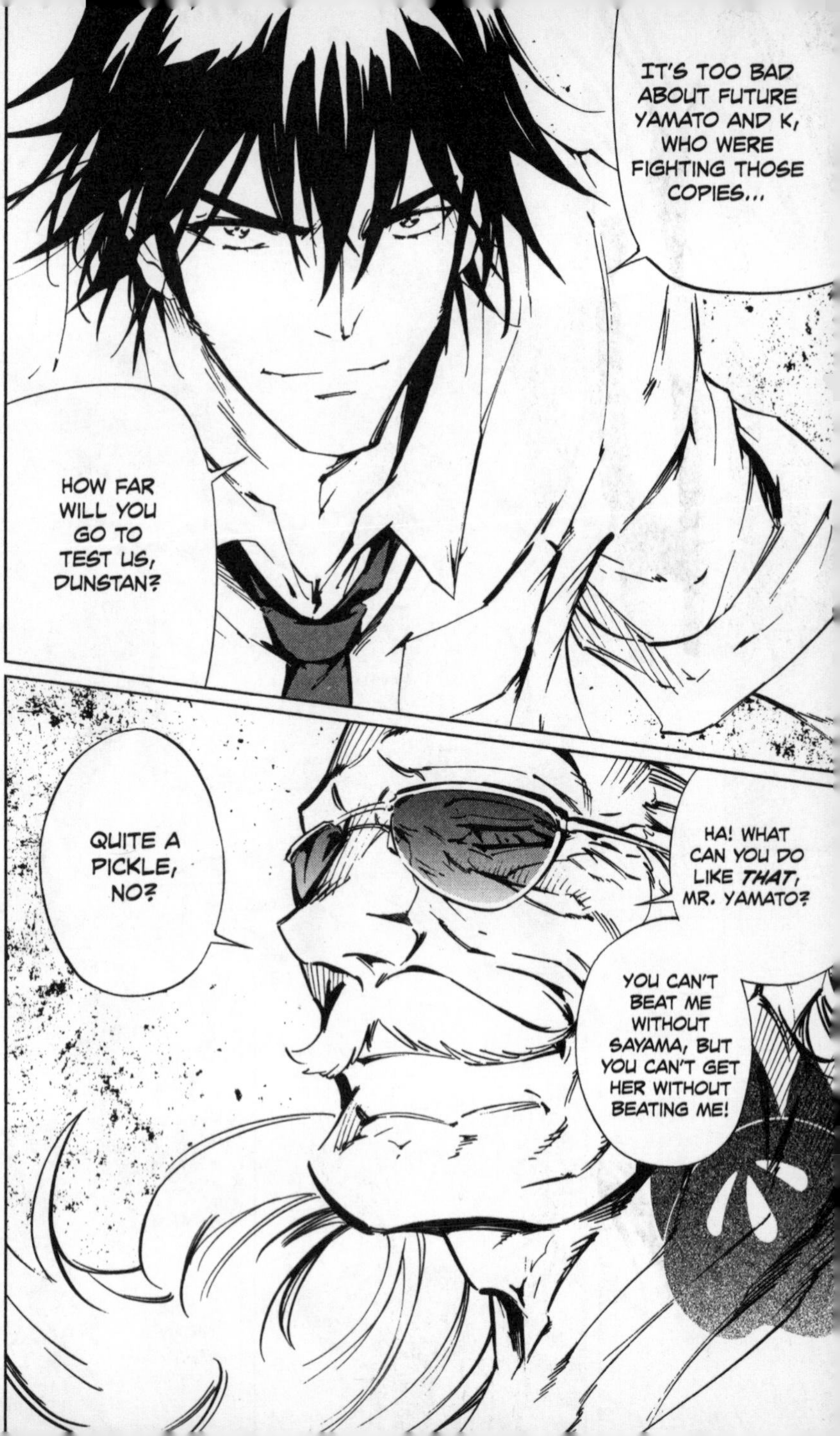
IT'S TOO BAD ABOUT FUTURE YAMATO AND K, WHO WERE FIGHTING THOSE COPIES...
HOW FAR WILL YOU GO TO TEST US, DUNSTAN?
HA! WHAT CAN YOU DO LIKE *THAT*, MR. YAMATO?
YOU CAN'T BEAT ME WITHOUT SAYAMA, BUT YOU CAN'T GET HER WITHOUT BEATING ME!
QUITE A PICKLE, NO?

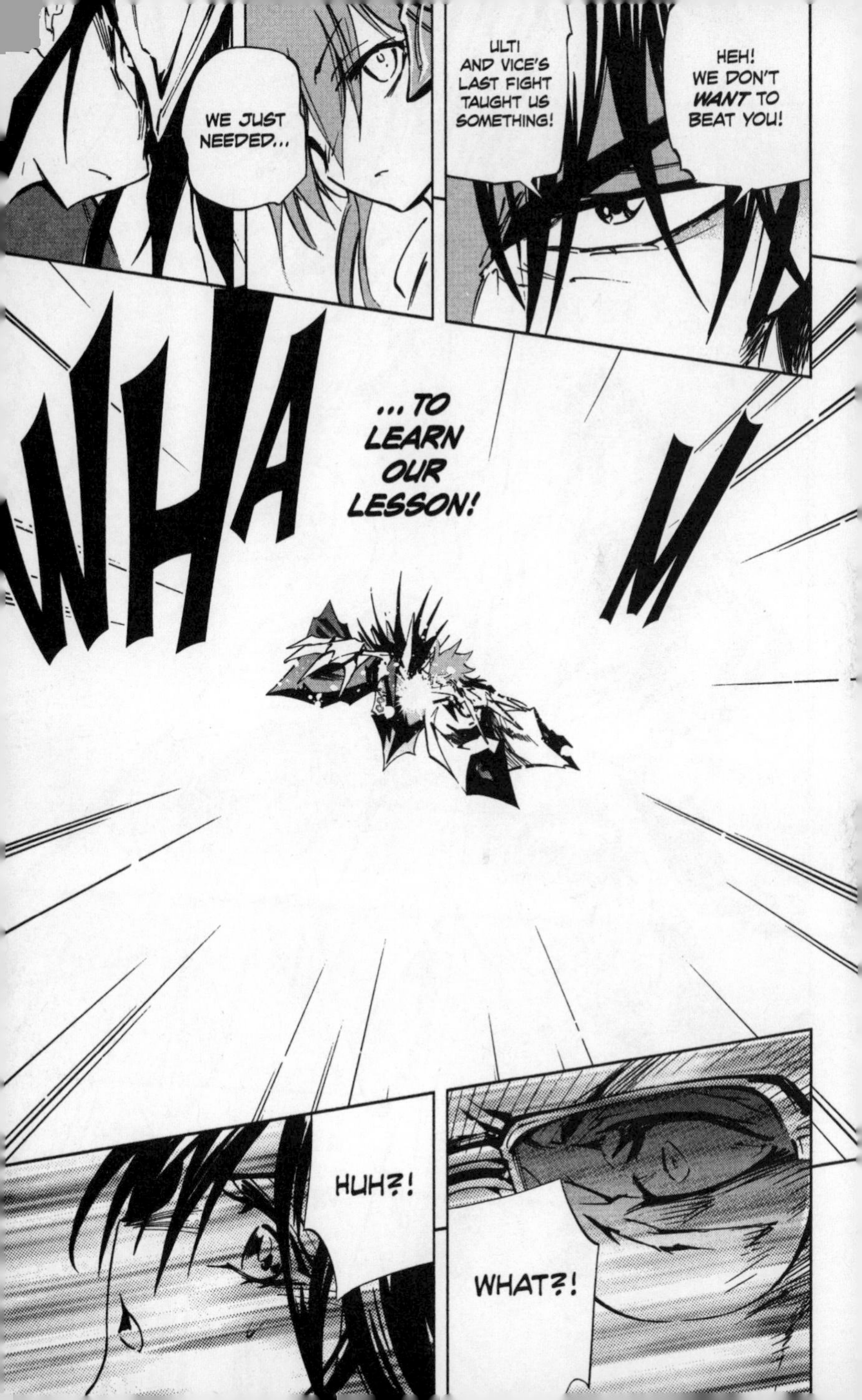
HEH! WE DON'T *WANT* TO BEAT YOU!
ULTI AND VICE'S LAST FIGHT TAUGHT US SOMETHING!
WE JUST NEEDED...
...TO LEARN OUR LESSON!
WHAM
WHAT?!
HUH?!

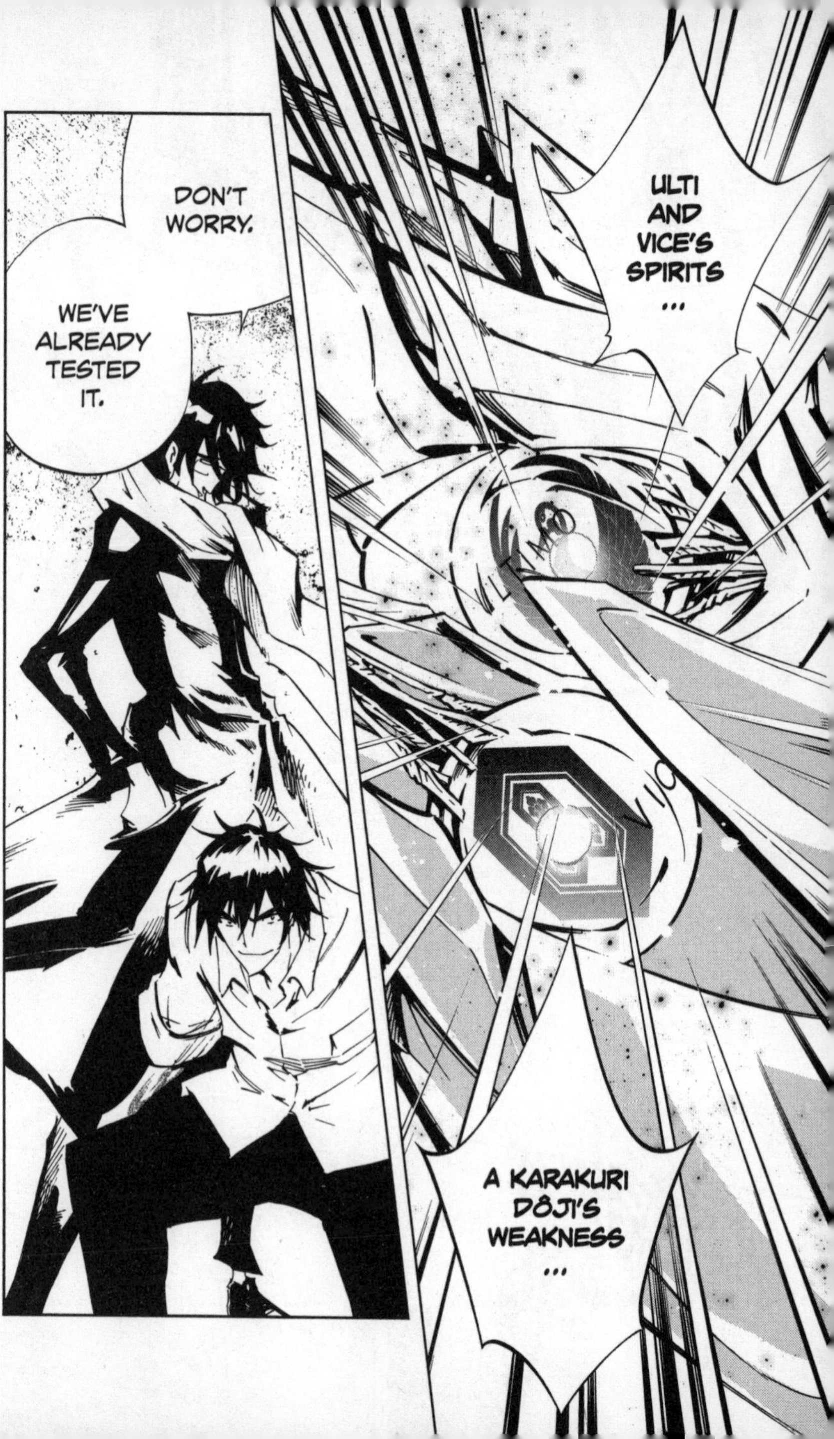
ULTI AND VICE'S SPIRITS ...
A KARAKURI DŌJI'S WEAKNESS ...
DON'T WORRY.
WE'VE ALREADY TESTED IT.

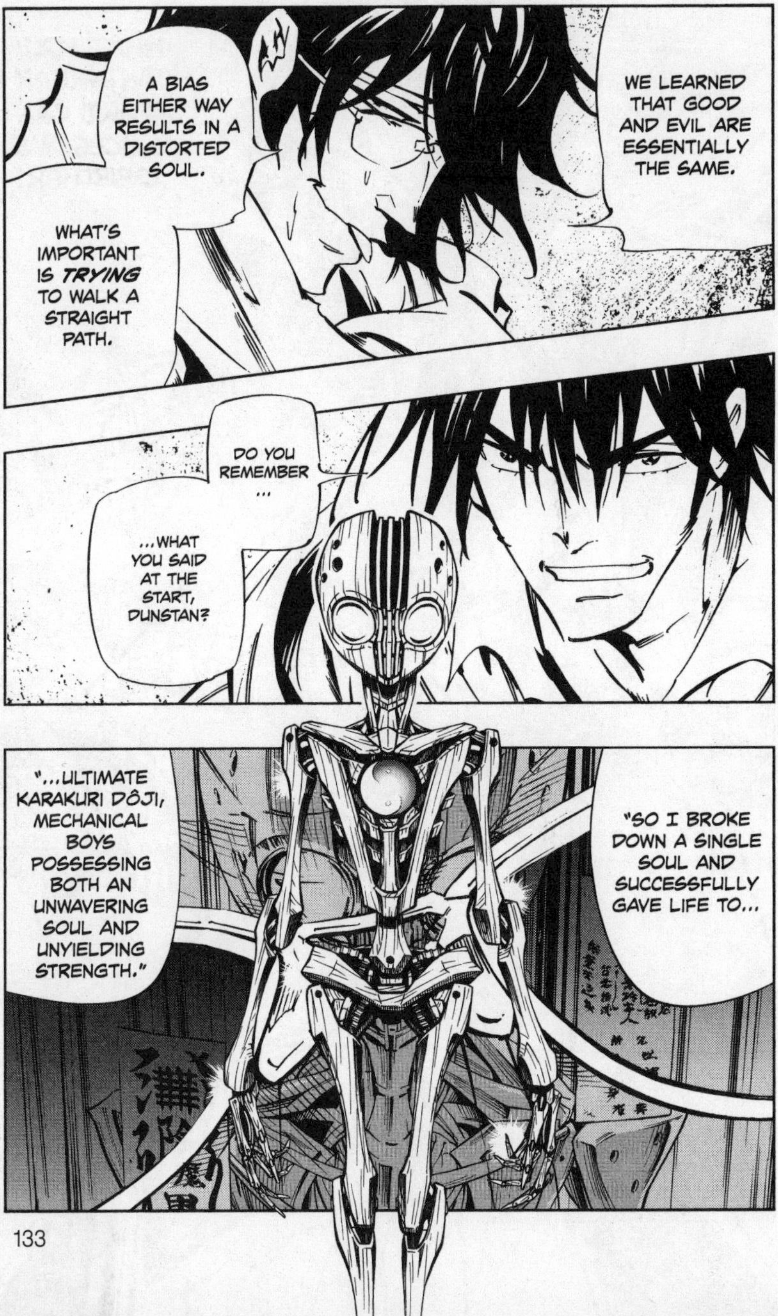
WE LEARNED THAT GOOD AND EVIL ARE ESSENTIALLY THE SAME.
A BIAS EITHER WAY RESULTS IN A DISTORTED SOUL.
WHAT'S IMPORTANT IS *TRYING* TO WALK A STRAIGHT PATH.
DO YOU REMEMBER ...
...WHAT YOU SAID AT THE START, DUNSTAN?
"SO I BROKE DOWN A SINGLE SOUL AND SUCCESSFULLY GAVE LIFE TO...
"...ULTIMATE KARAKURI DÔJI, MECHANICAL BOYS POSSESSING BOTH AN UNWAVERING SOUL AND UNYIELDING STRENGTH."

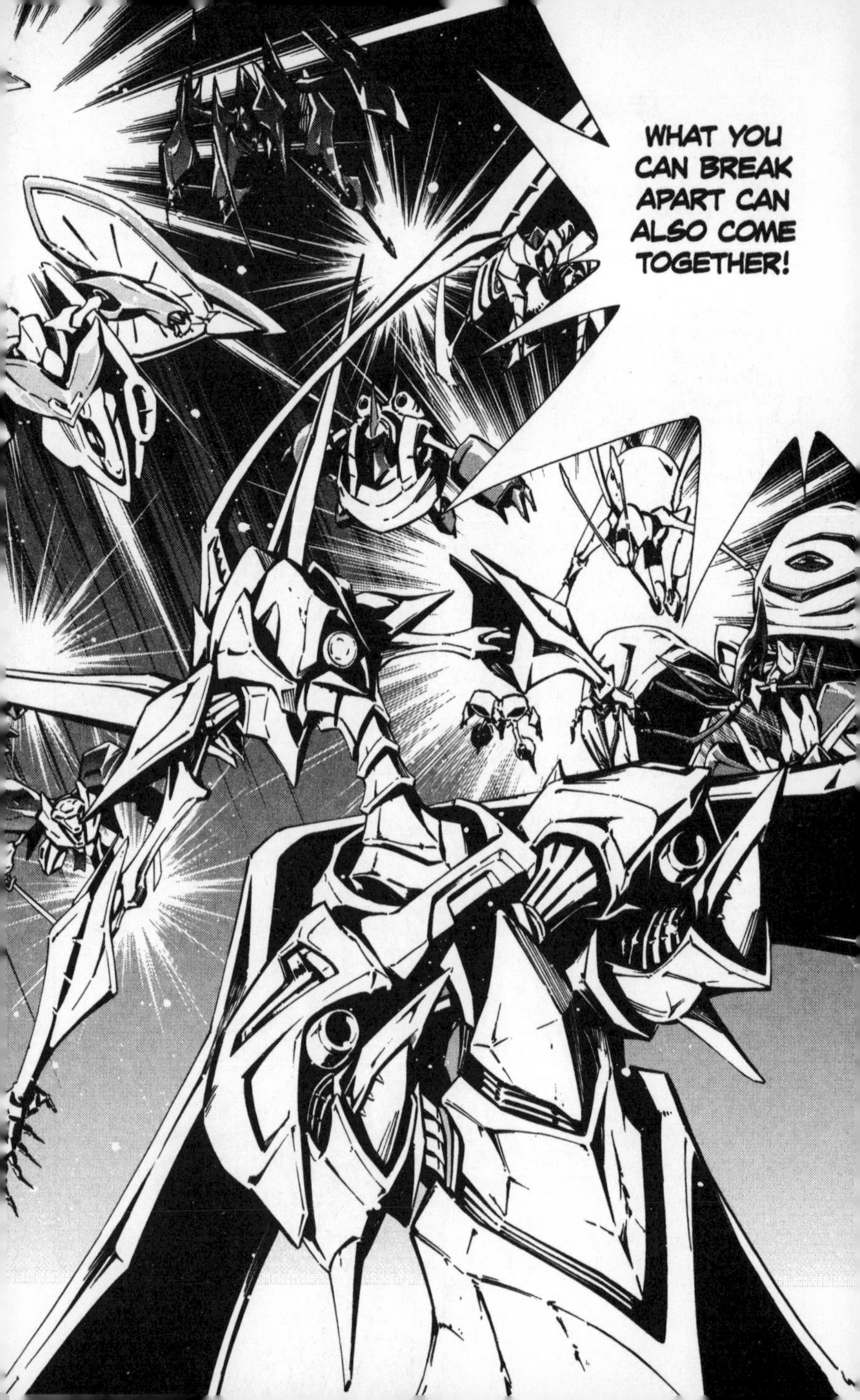
WHAT YOU CAN BREAK APART CAN ALSO COME TOGETHER!

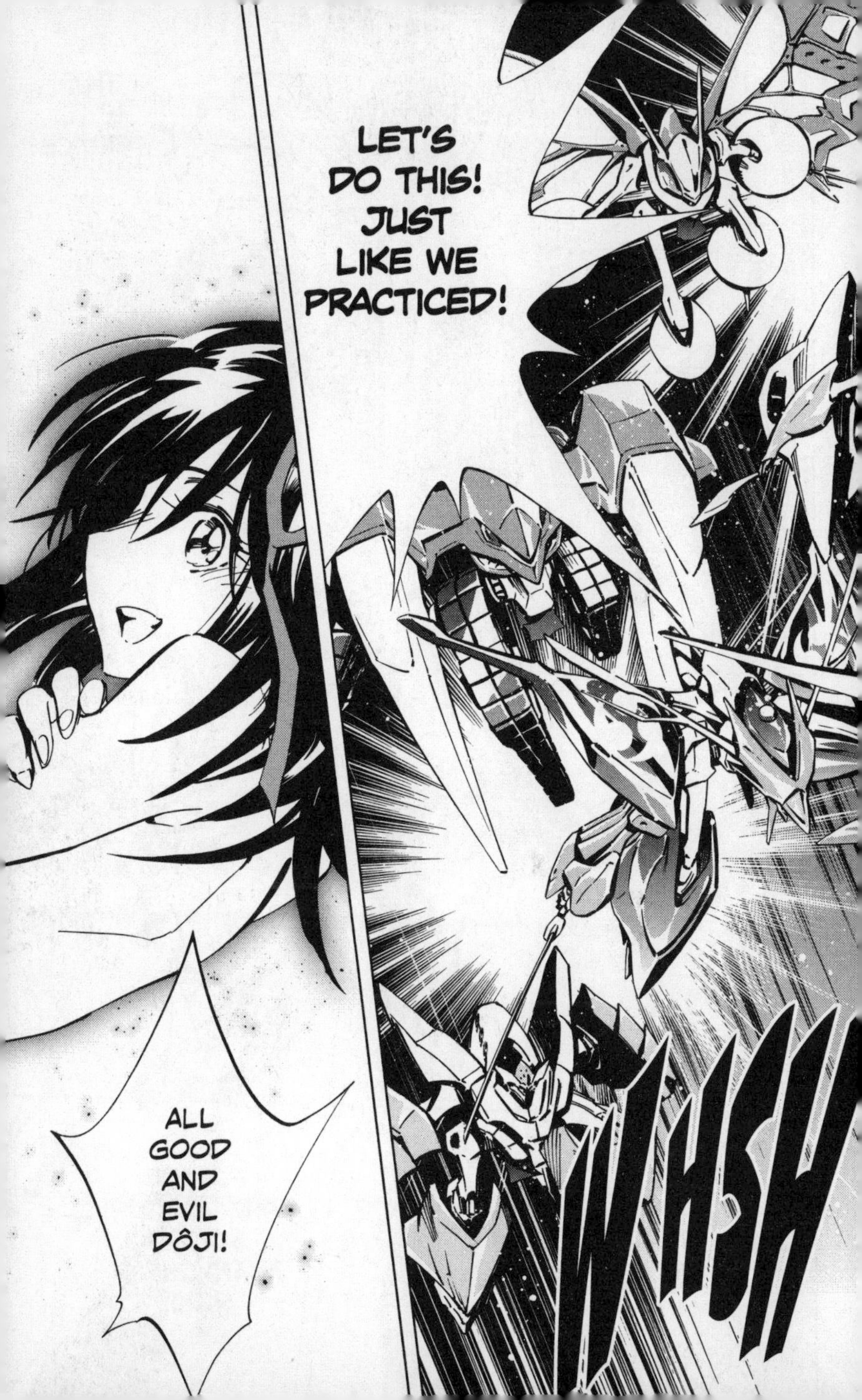
LET'S DO THIS! JUST LIKE WE PRACTICED!
WHSH
ALL GOOD AND EVIL DÔJI!

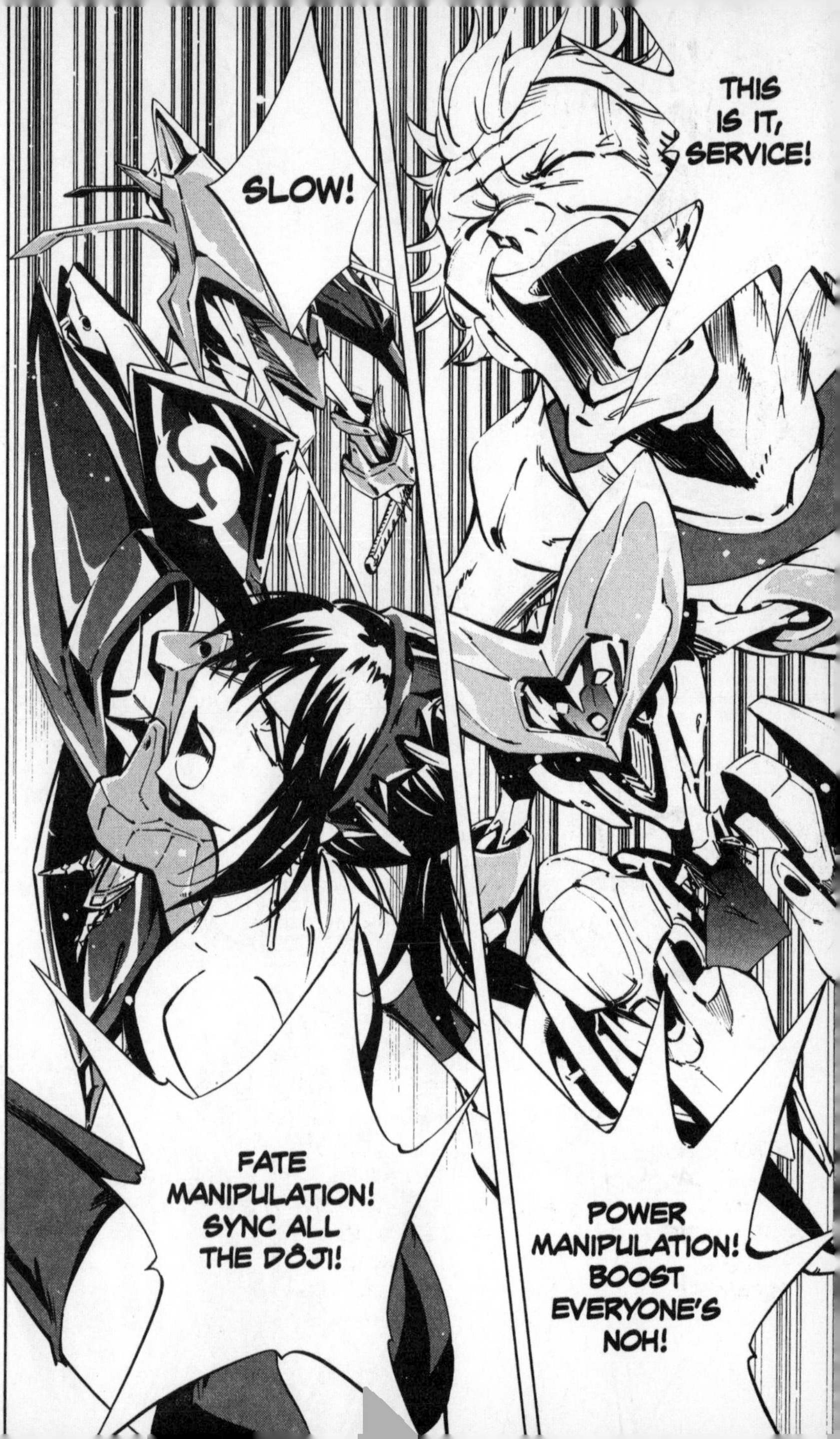
THIS IS IT, SERVICE!
SLOW!
POWER MANIPULATION! BOOST EVERYONE'S NOH!
FATE MANIPULATION! SYNC ALL THE DÔJI!

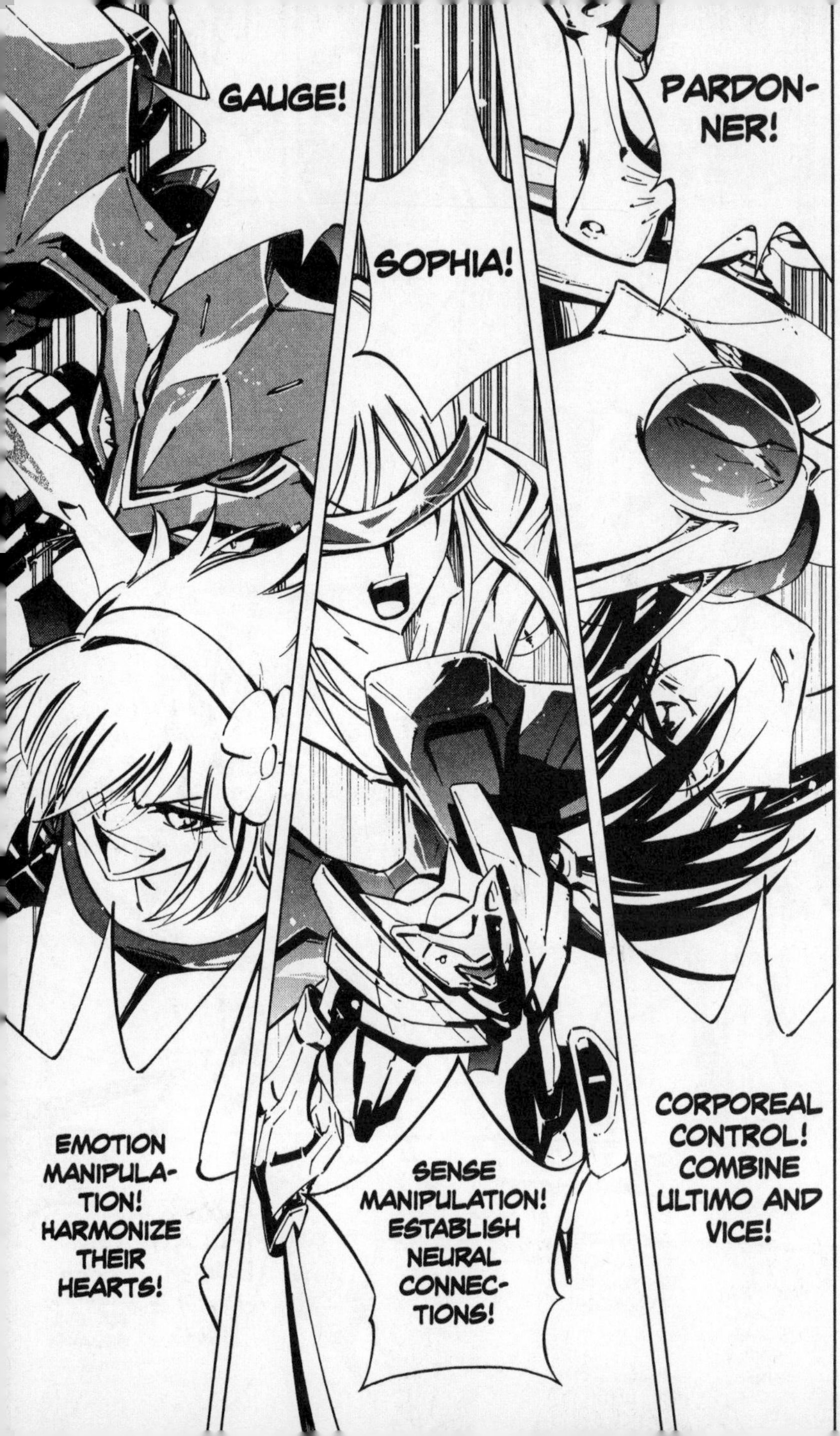
PARDON-
NER!
CORPOREAL CONTROL! COMBINE ULTIMO AND VICE!
SOPHIA!
SENSE MANIPULATION! ESTABLISH NEURAL CONNEC-TIONS!
GAUGE!
EMOTION MANIPULA-TION! HARMONIZE THEIR HEARTS!

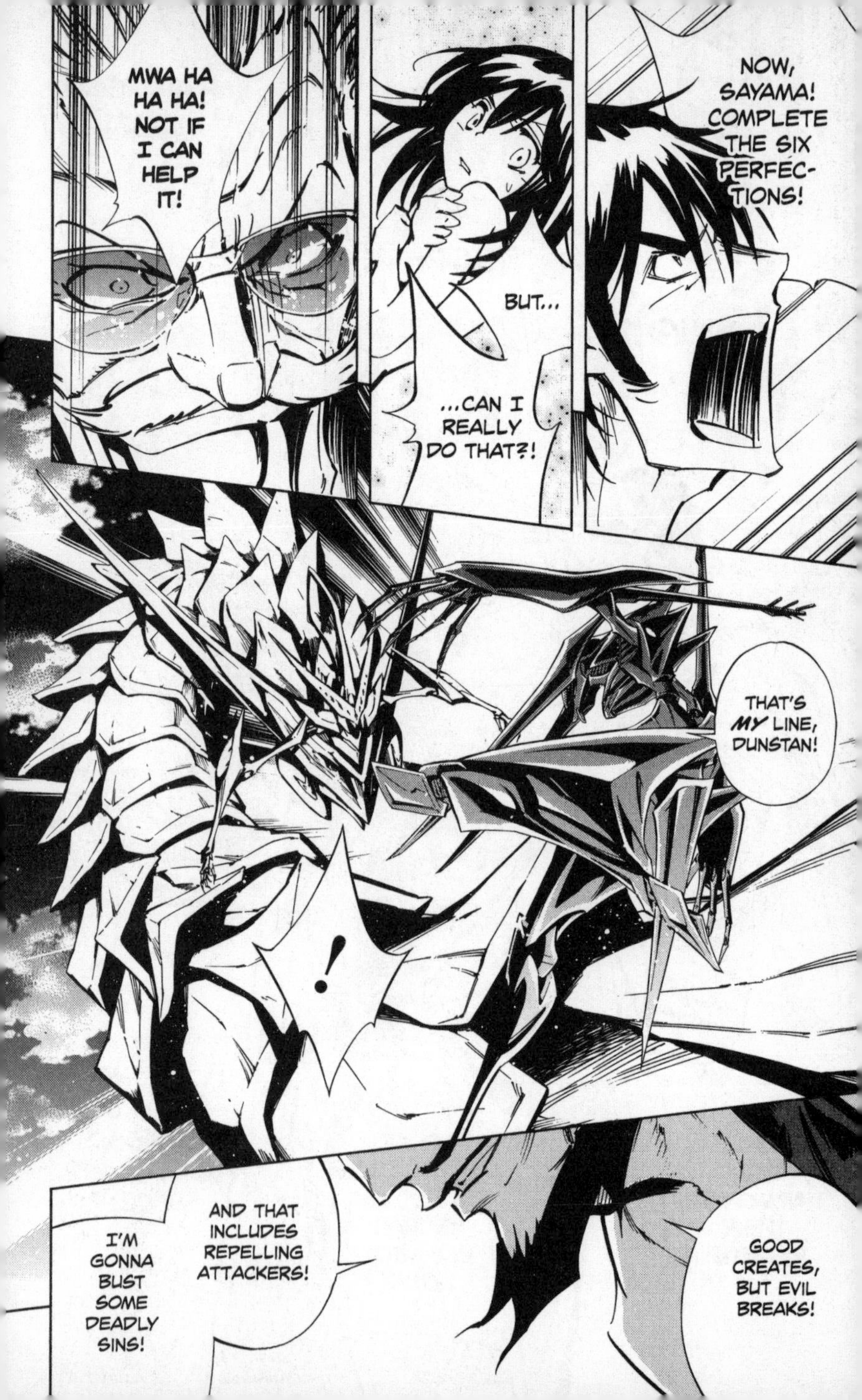
NOW, SAYAMA! COMPLETE THE SIX PERFEC-TIONS!
BUT...
...CAN I REALLY DO THAT?!
MWA HA HA HA! NOT IF I CAN HELP IT!
THAT'S MY LINE, DUNSTAN!
!
GOOD CREATES, BUT EVIL BREAKS!
AND THAT INCLUDES REPELLING ATTACKERS!
I'M GONNA BUST SOME DEADLY SINS!

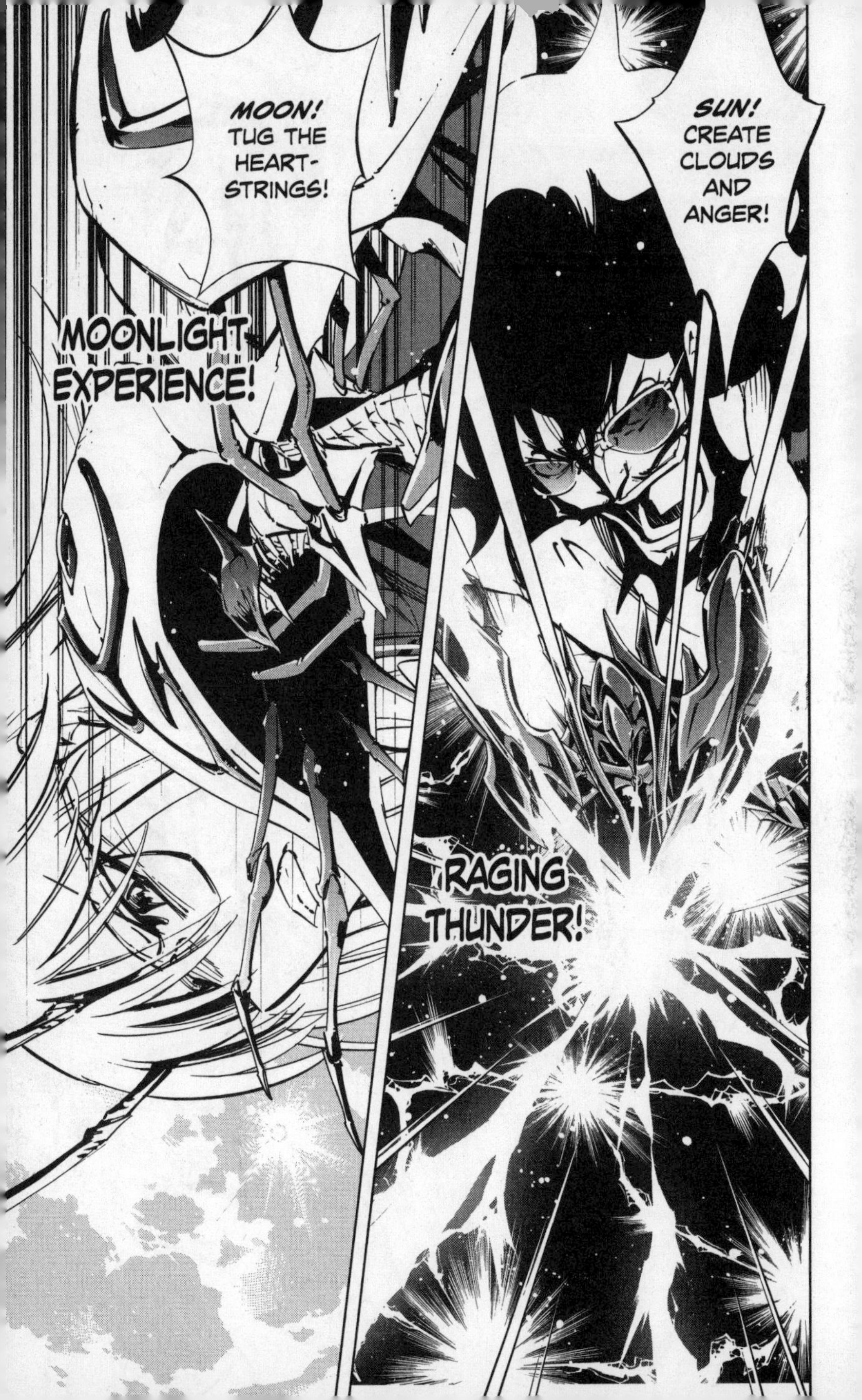
SUN! CREATE CLOUDS AND ANGER!
RAGING THUNDER!
MOON! TUG THE HEART-STRINGS!
MOONLIGHT EXPERIENCE!

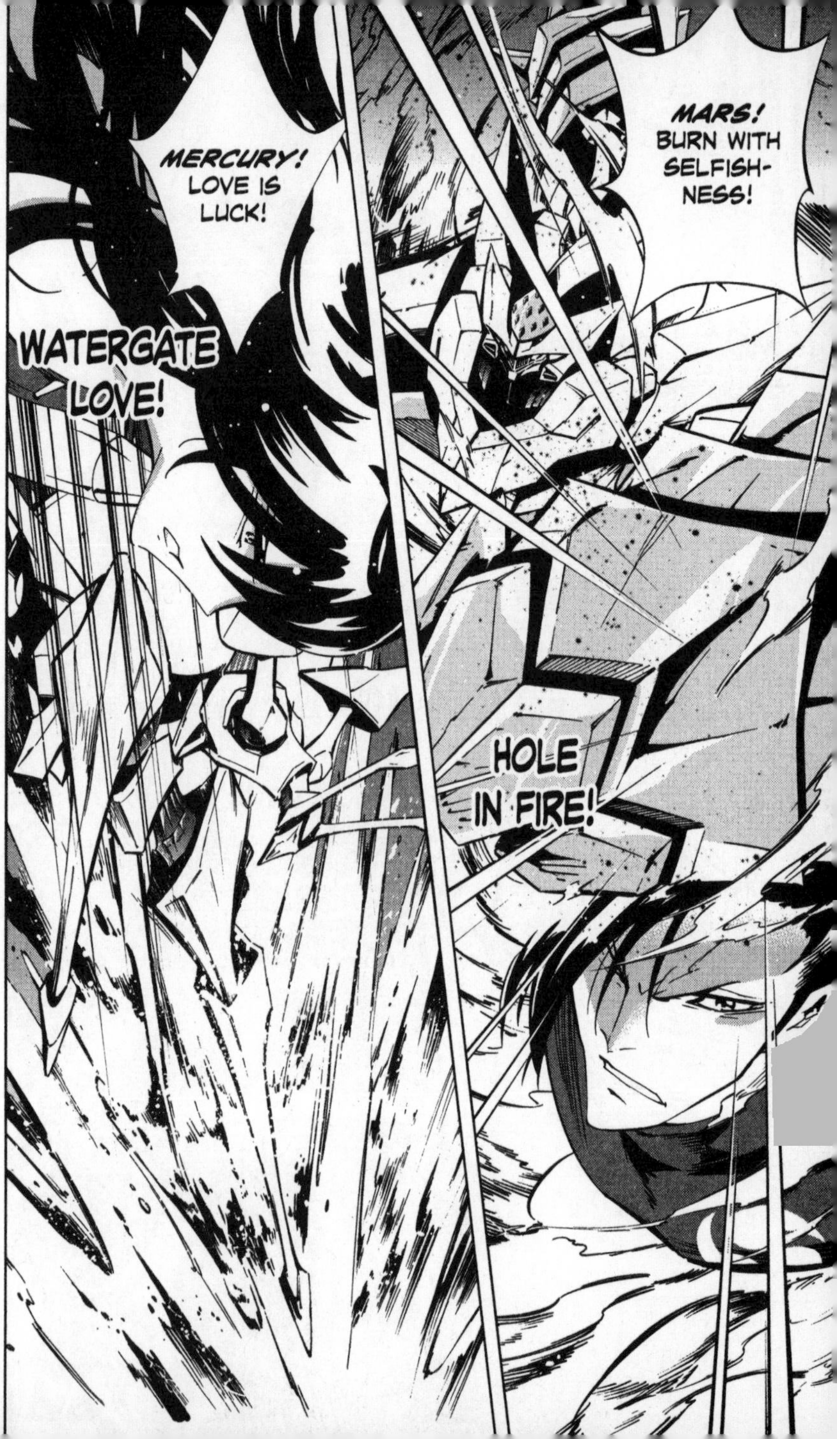
MARS! BURN WITH SELFISHNESS!
MERCURY! LOVE IS LUCK!
WATERGATE LOVE!
HOLE IN FIRE!

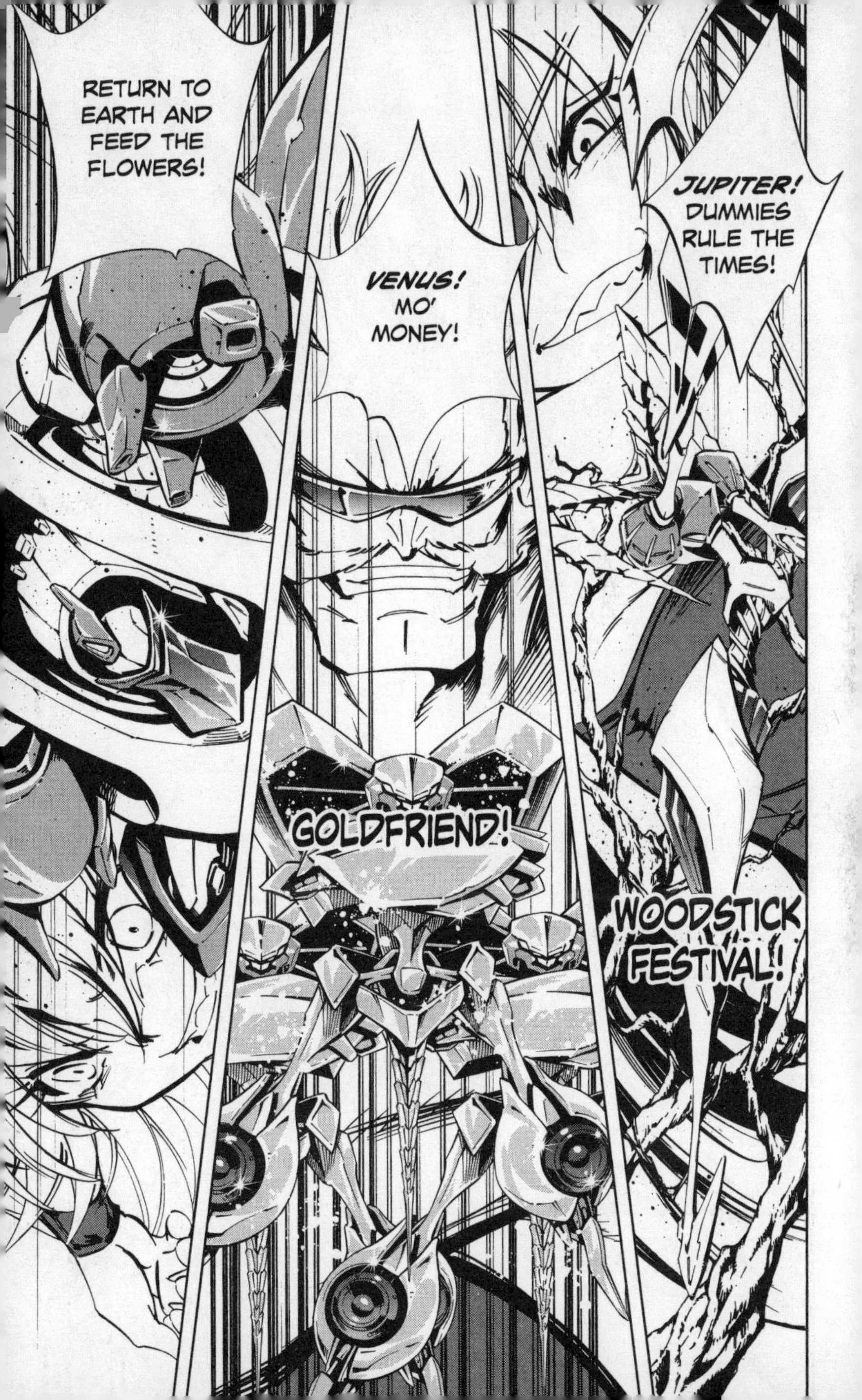
JUPITER! DUMMIES RULE THE TIMES!
WOODSTICK FESTIVAL!
VENUS! MO' MONEY!
GOLDFRIEND!
RETURN TO EARTH AND FEED THE FLOWERS!

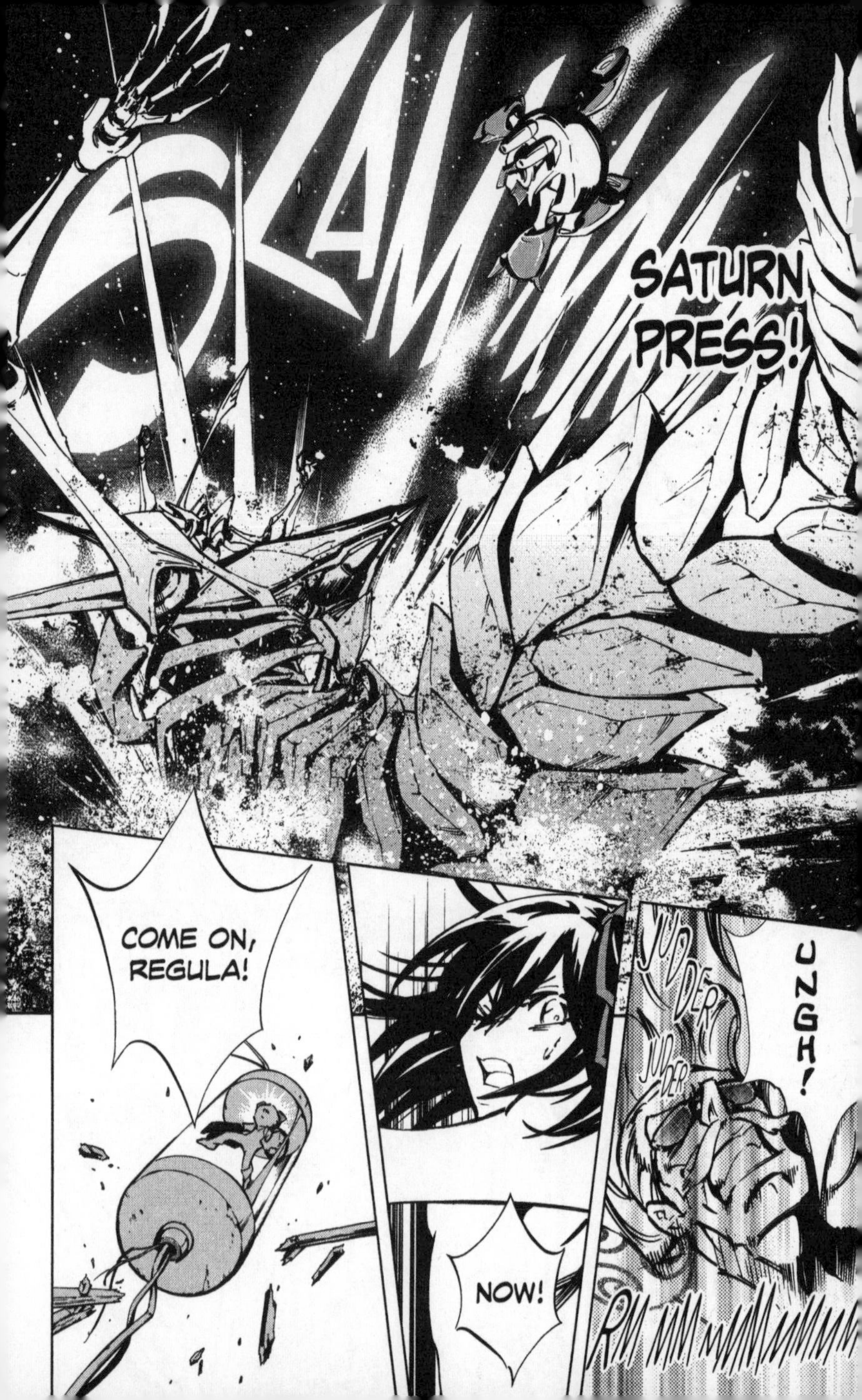
SATURN PRESS!
JUDDER
JUDDER
UNGH!
NOW!
COME ON, REGULA!

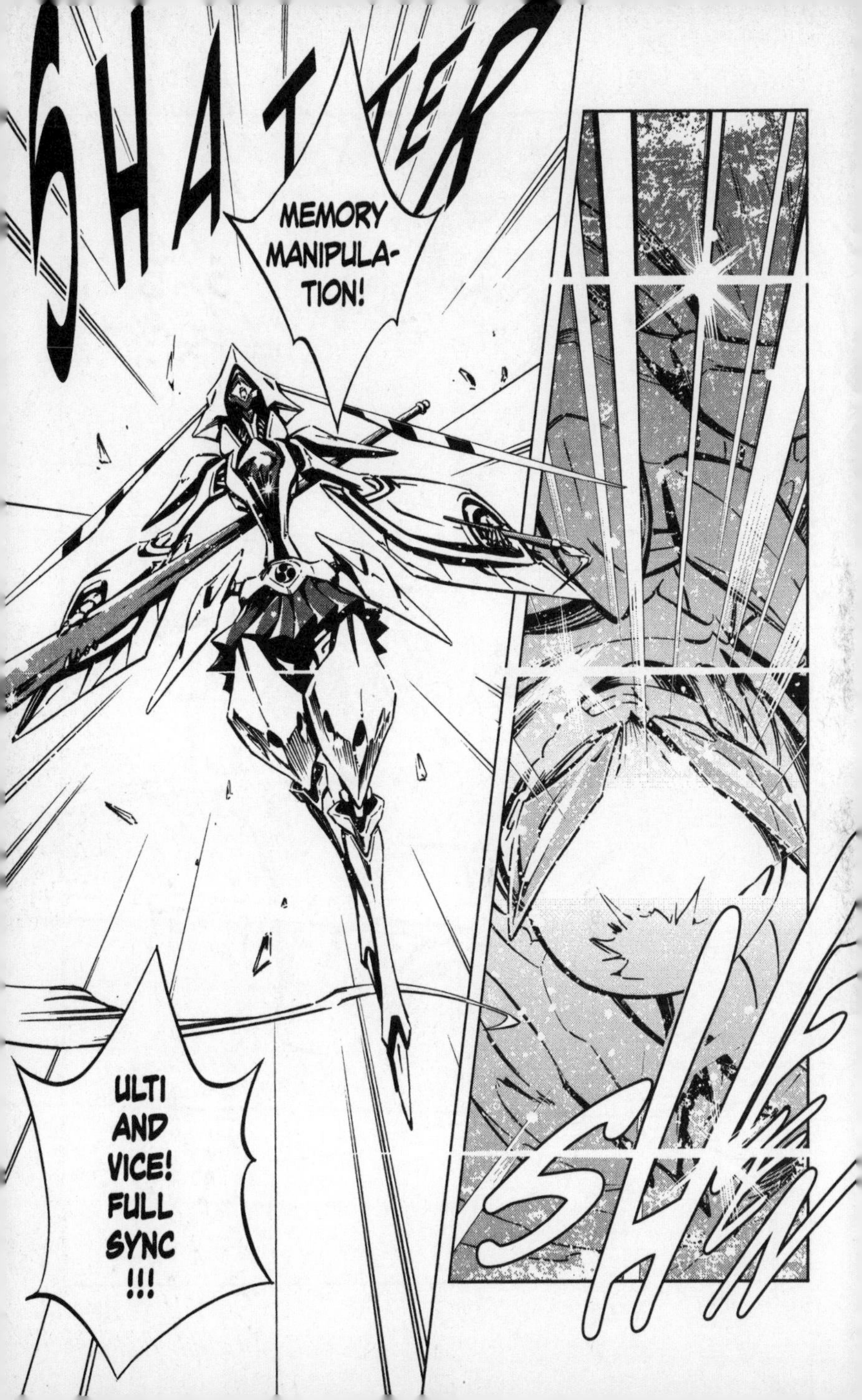
SHATTER
MEMORY MANIPULA-TION!
ULTI AND VICE! FULL SYNC!!!

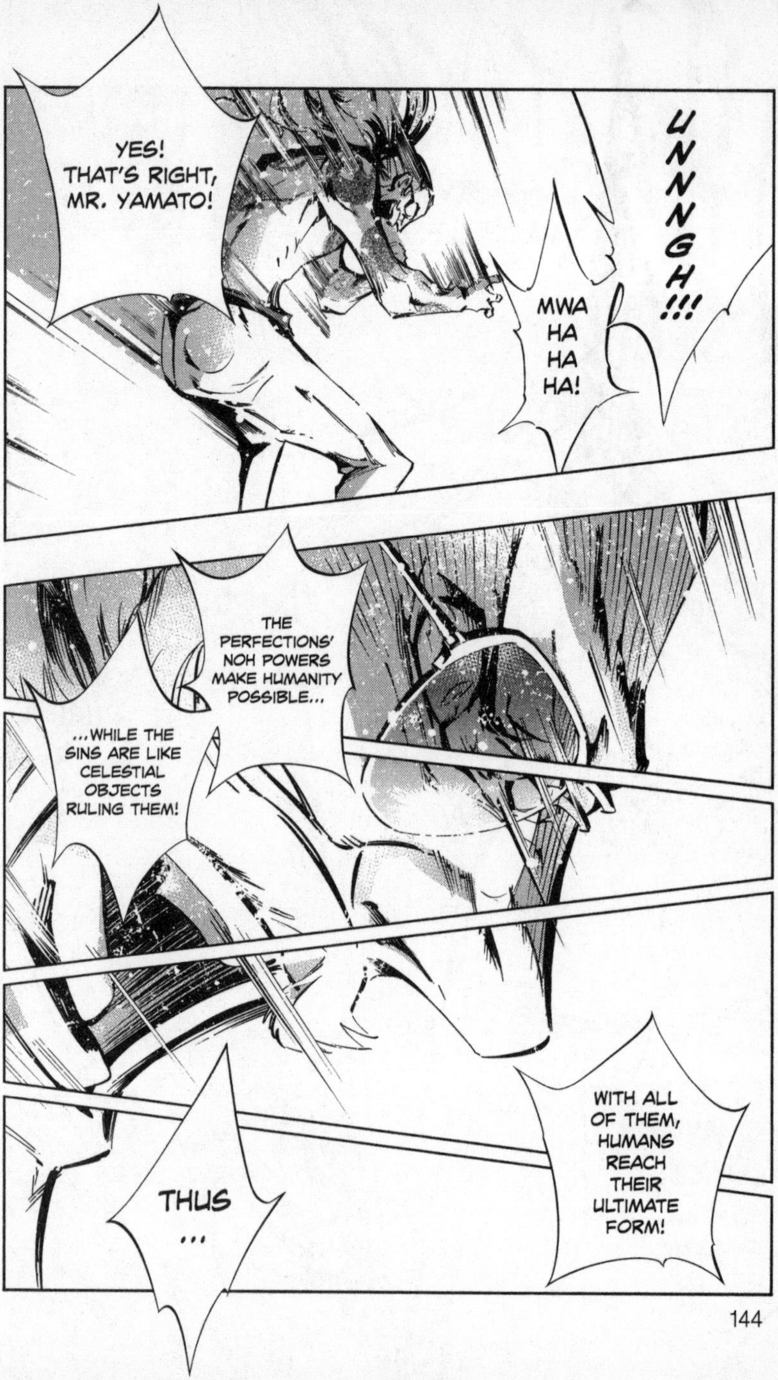
UNNNGH!!!
YES! THAT'S RIGHT, MR. YAMATO!
MWA HA HA HA!
THE PERFECTIONS' NOH POWERS MAKE HUMANITY POSSIBLE...
...WHILE THE SINS ARE LIKE CELESTIAL OBJECTS RULING THEM!
THUS...
WITH ALL OF THEM, HUMANS REACH THEIR ULTIMATE FORM!

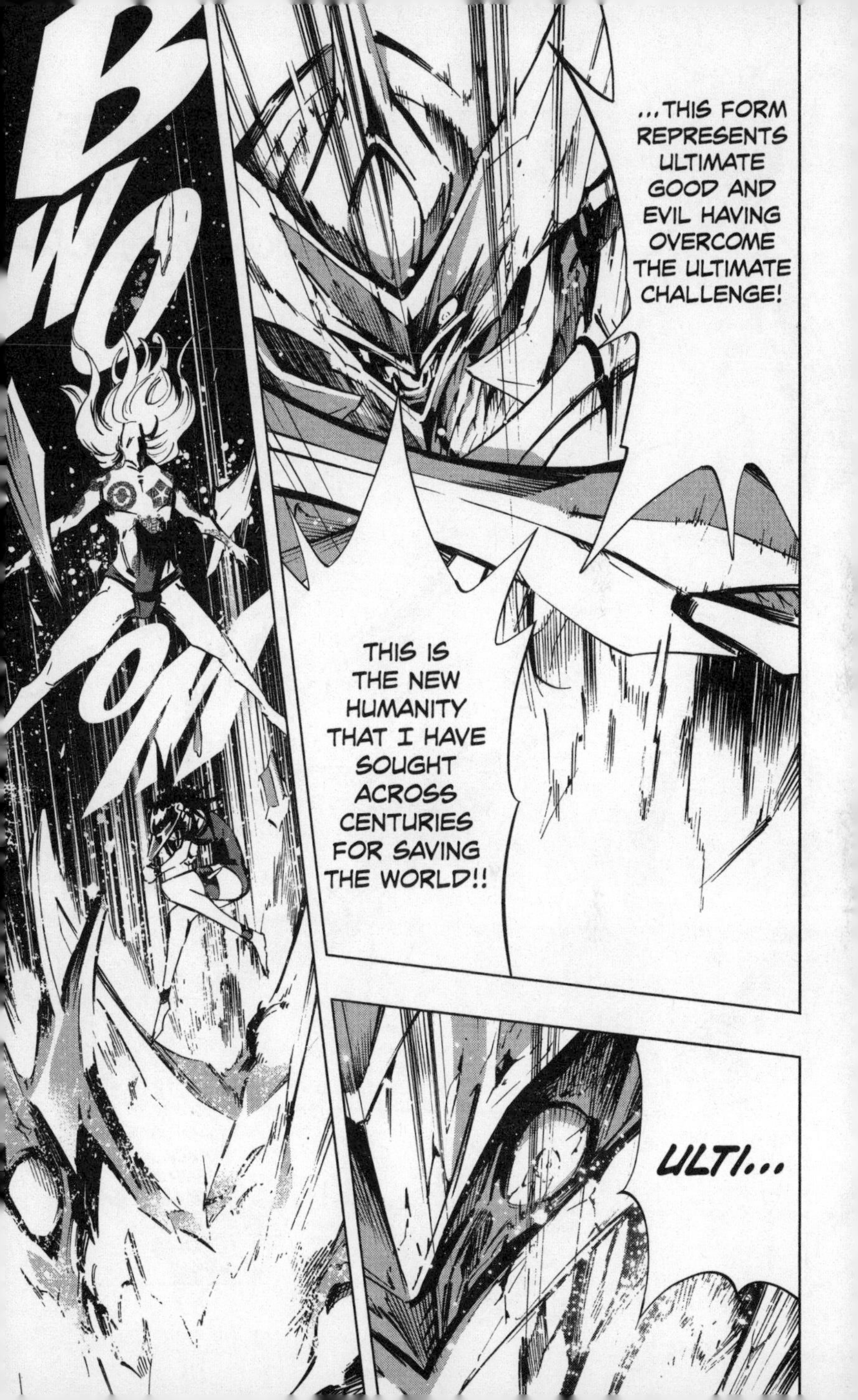
...THIS FORM REPRESENTS ULTIMATE GOOD AND EVIL HAVING OVERCOME THE ULTIMATE CHALLENGE!
THIS IS THE NEW HUMANITY THAT I HAVE SOUGHT ACROSS CENTURIES FOR SAVING THE WORLD!!
ULTI...

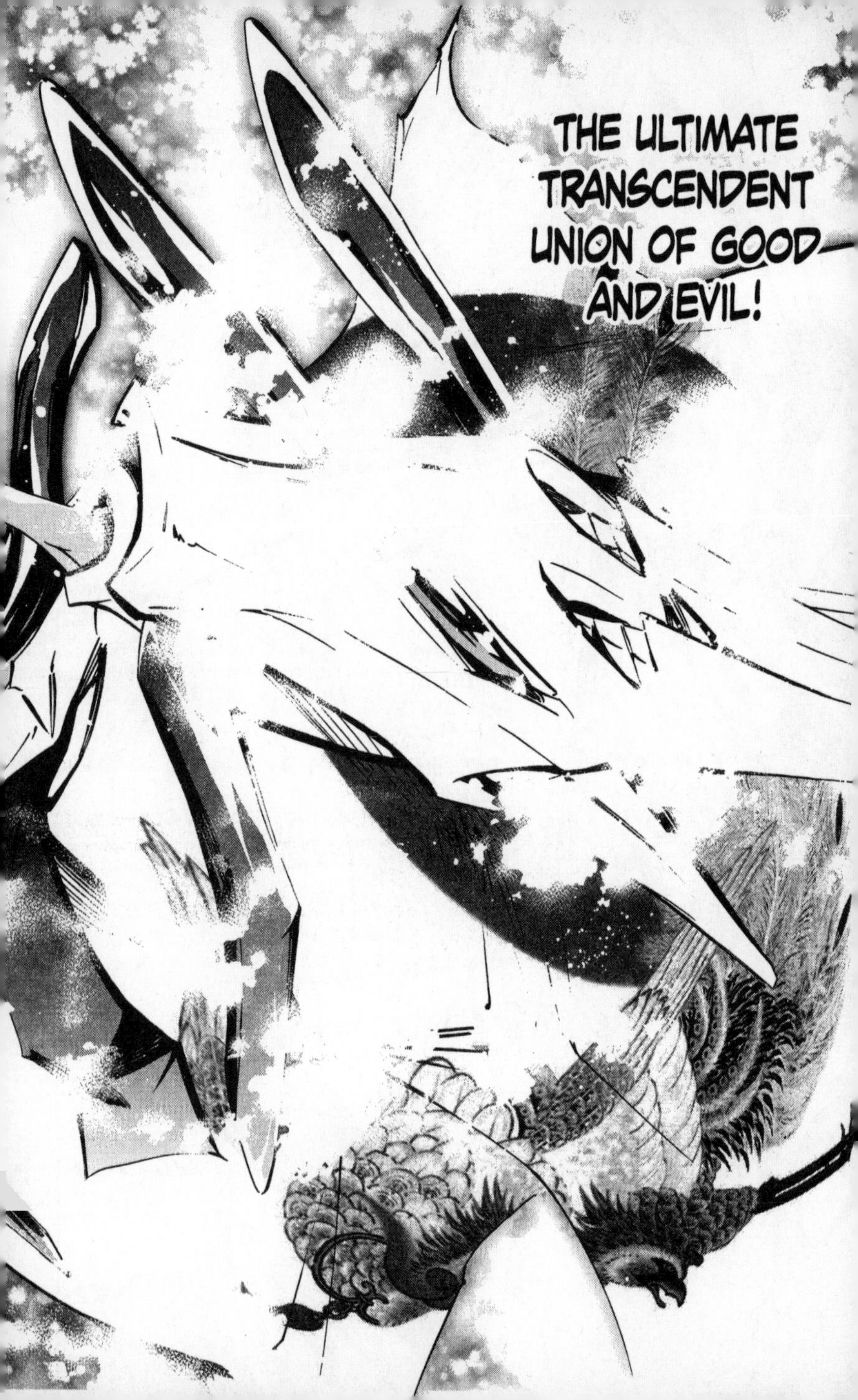
THE ULTIMATE TRANSCENDENT UNION OF GOOD AND EVIL!

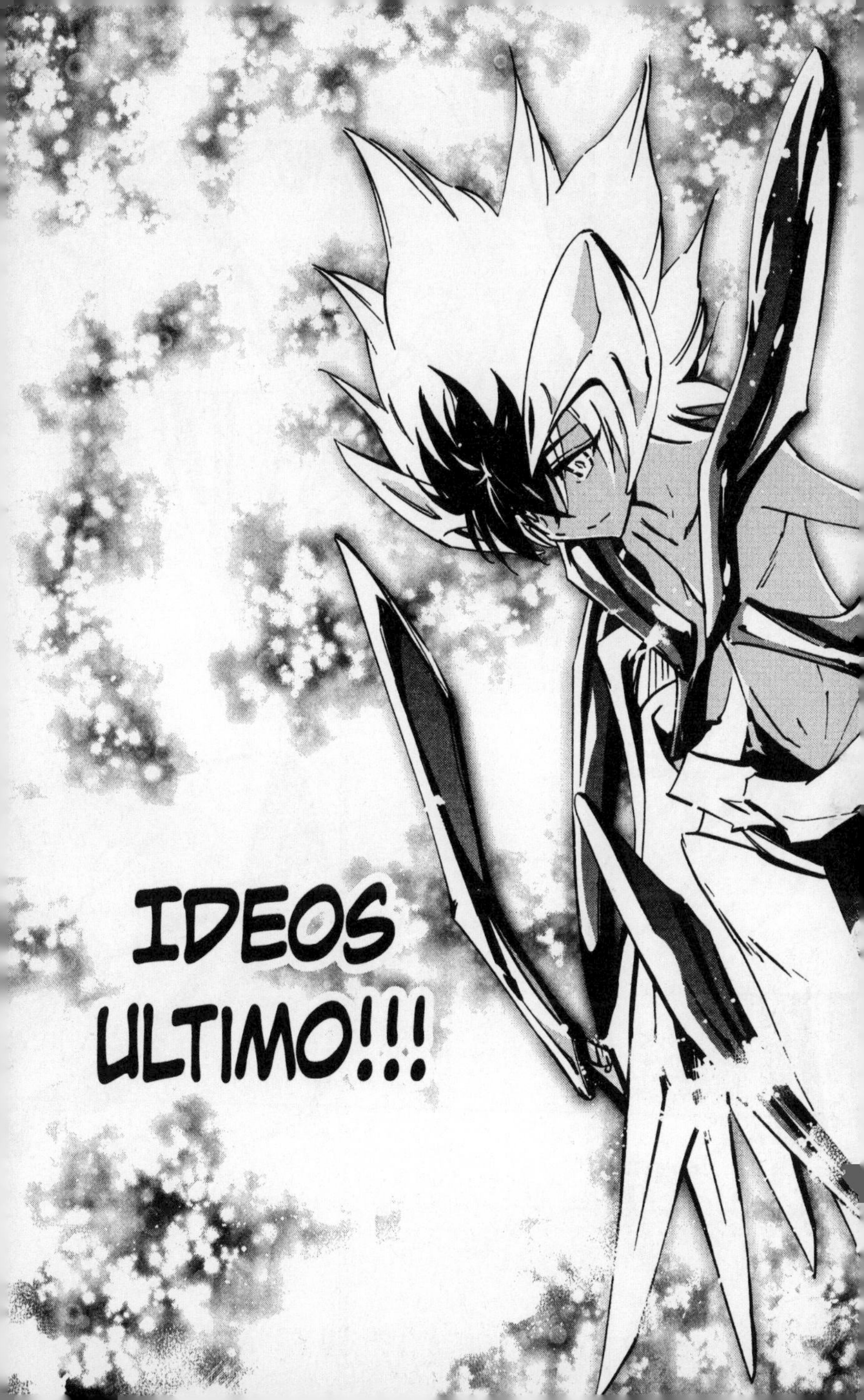
IDEOS ULTIMO!!!

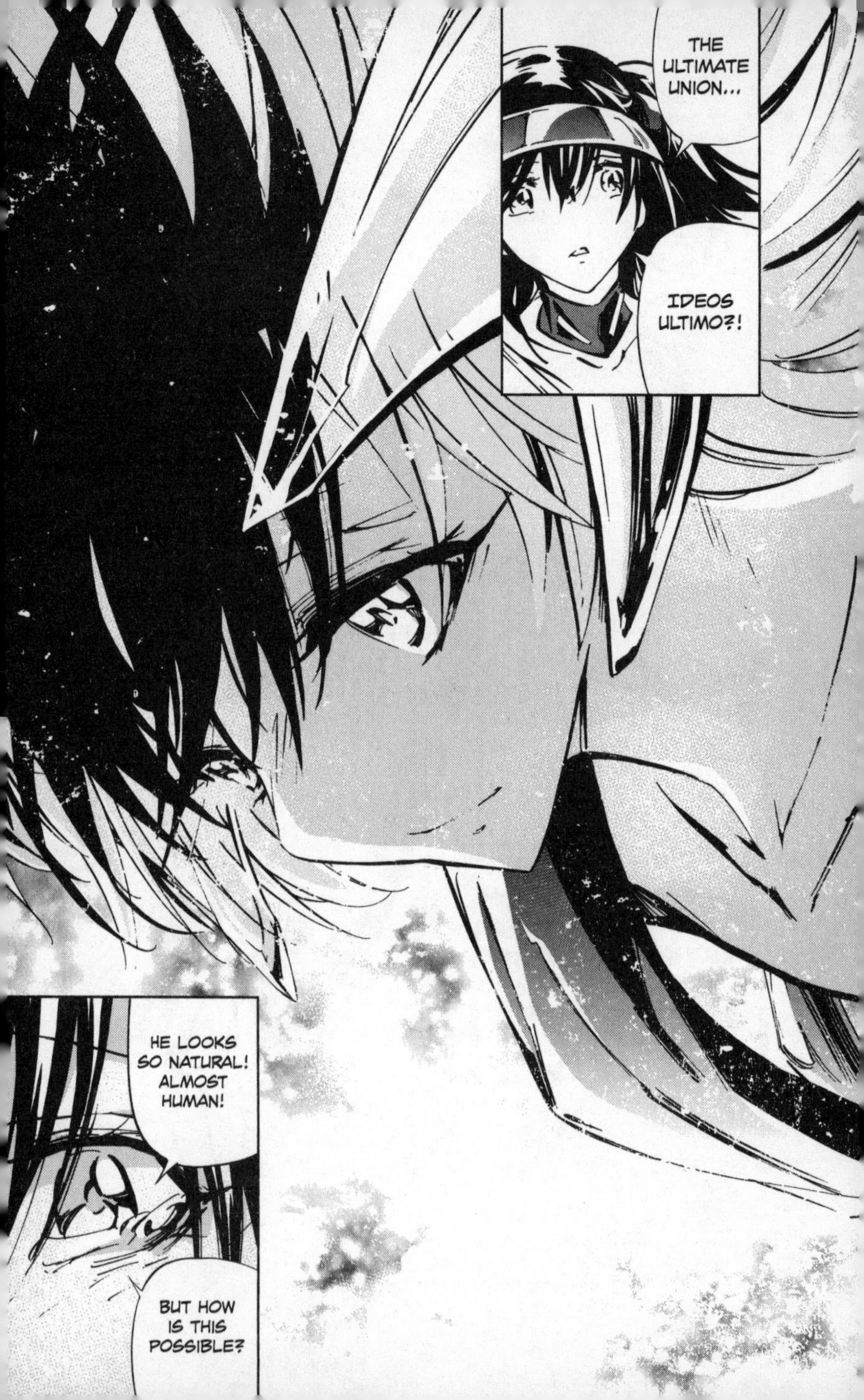
THE ULTIMATE UNION...
IDEOS ULTIMO?!
HE LOOKS SO NATURAL! ALMOST HUMAN!
BUT HOW IS THIS POSSIBLE?

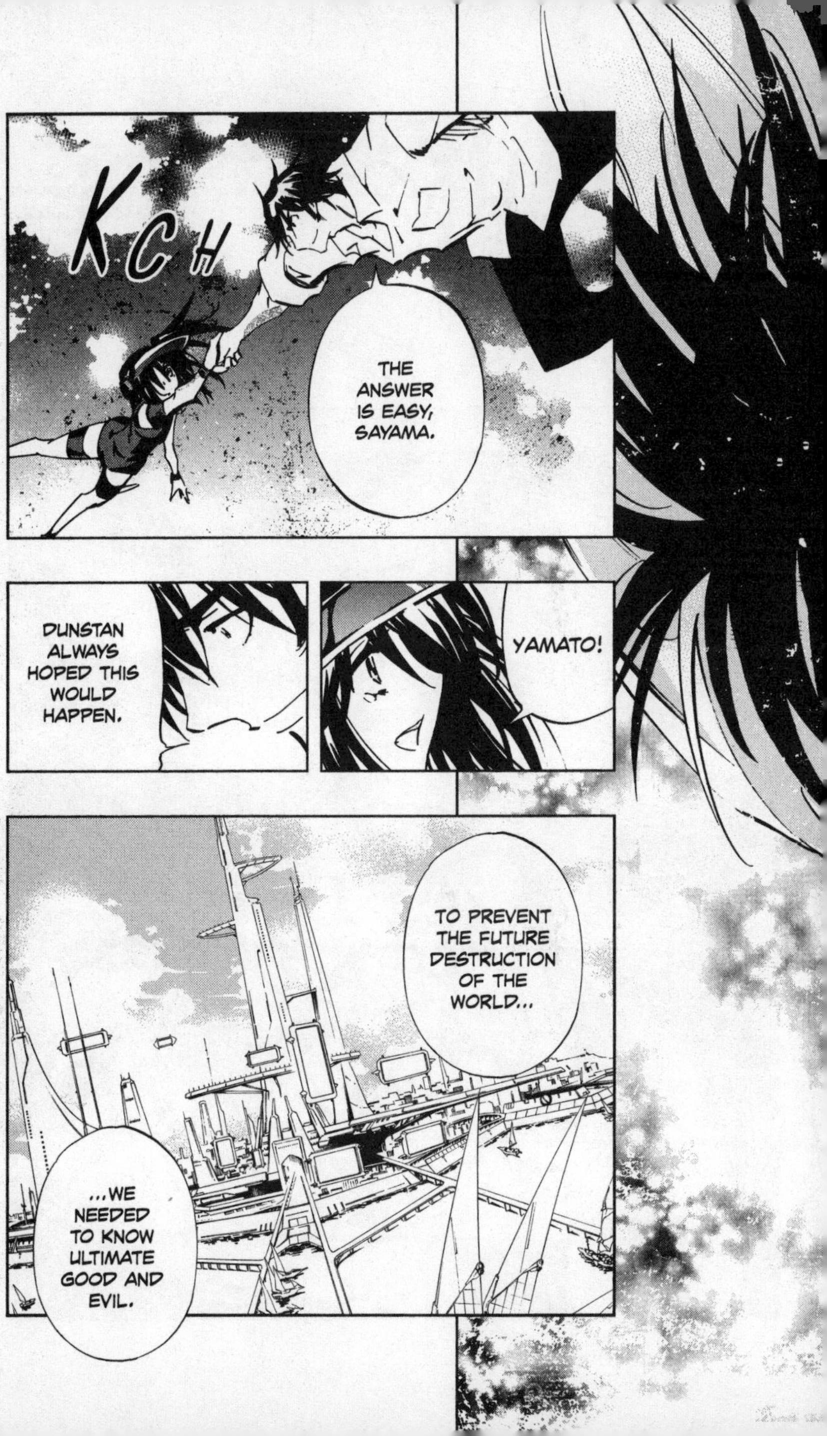
KCH
THE ANSWER IS EASY, SAYAMA.
YAMATO!
DUNSTAN ALWAYS HOPED THIS WOULD HAPPEN.
TO PREVENT THE FUTURE DESTRUCTION OF THE WORLD...
...WE NEEDED TO KNOW ULTIMATE GOOD AND EVIL.

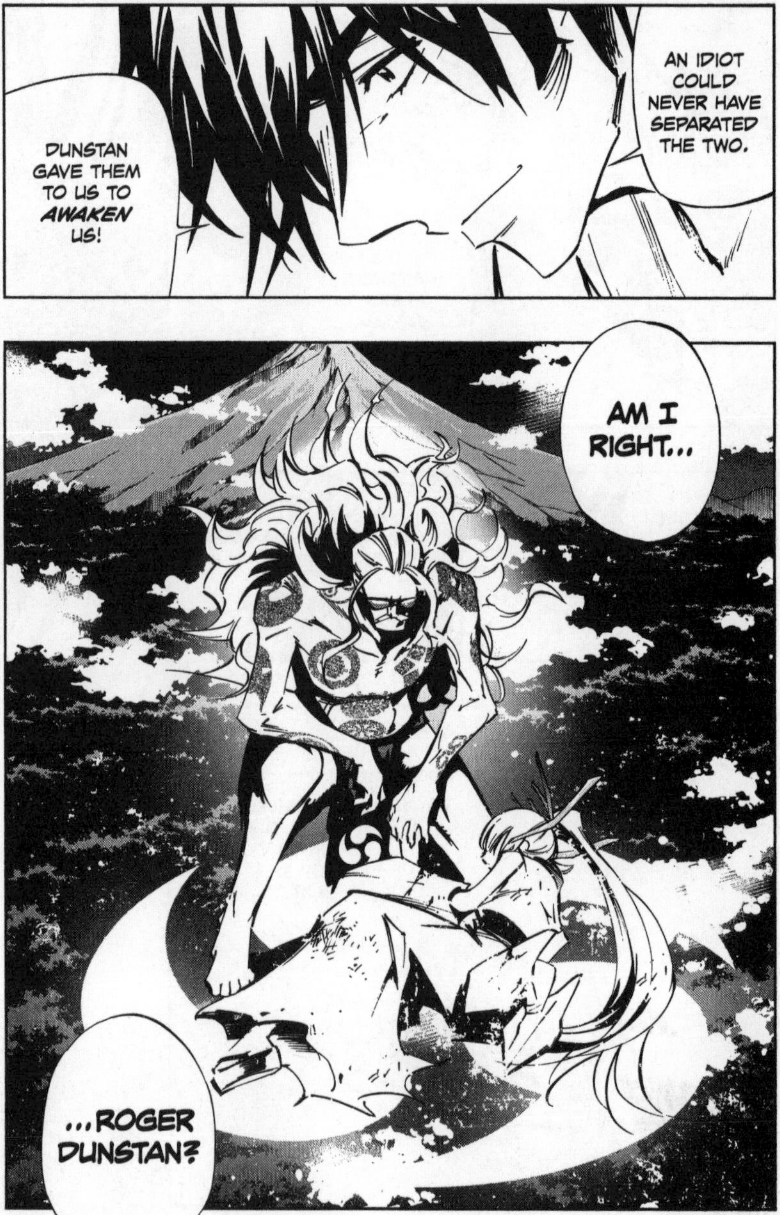
AN IDIOT COULD NEVER HAVE SEPARATED THE TWO.
DUNSTAN GAVE THEM TO US TO *AWAKEN* US!
AM I RIGHT...
...ROGER DUNSTAN?

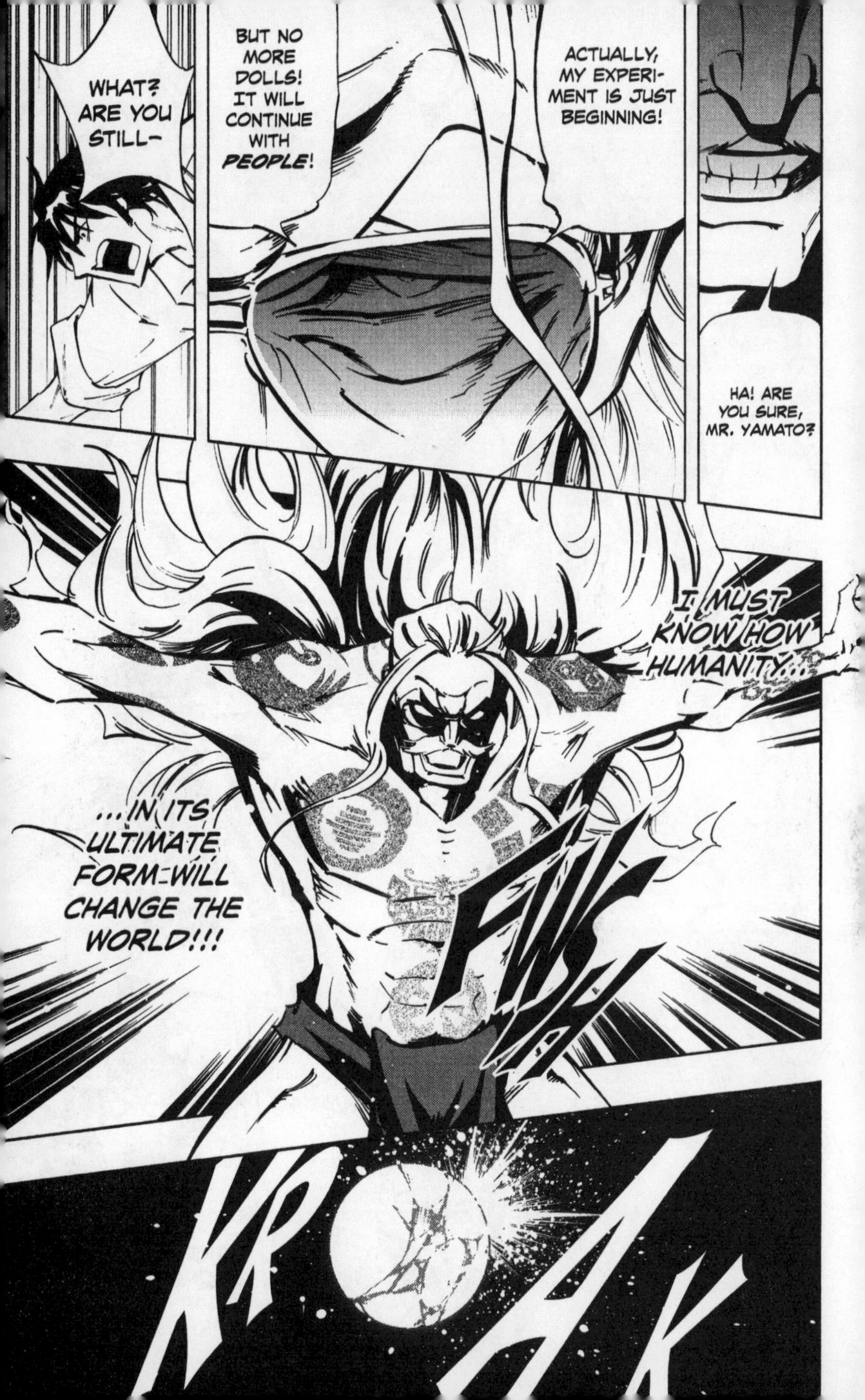
HA! ARE YOU SURE, MR. YAMATO?
ACTUALLY, MY EXPERIMENT IS JUST BEGINNING!
BUT NO MORE DOLLS! IT WILL CONTINUE WITH PEOPLE!
WHAT? ARE YOU STILL-
I MUST KNOW HOW HUMANITY...
...IN ITS ULTIMATE FORM...WILL CHANGE THE WORLD!!!
KRAK

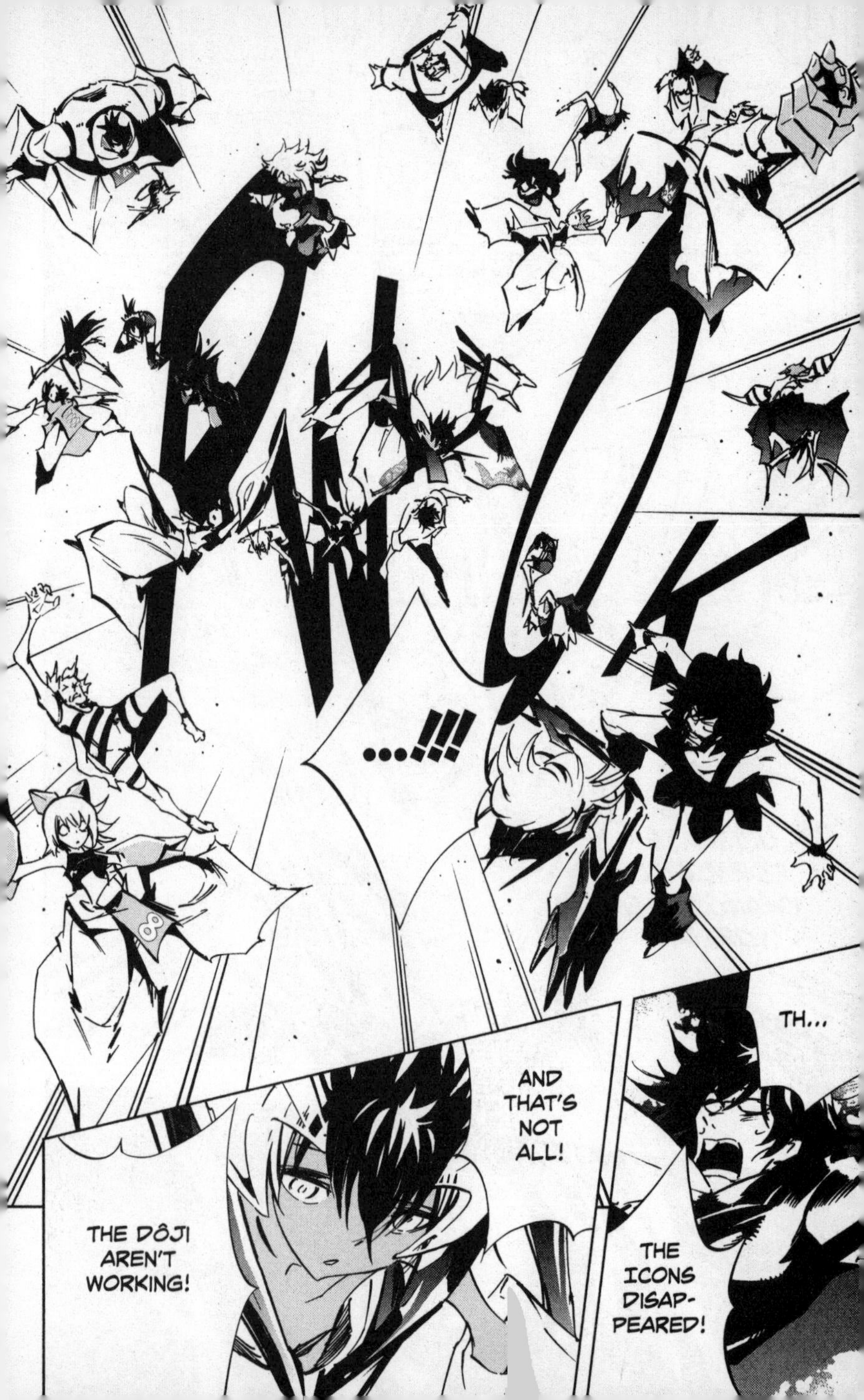
...!!!
TH...
THE ICONS DISAP-PEARED!
AND THAT'S NOT ALL!
THE DÔJI AREN'T WORKING!

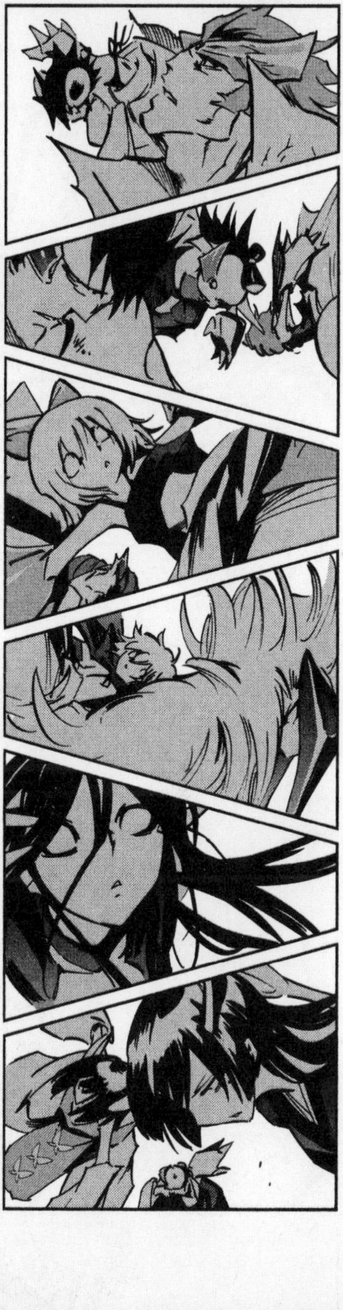

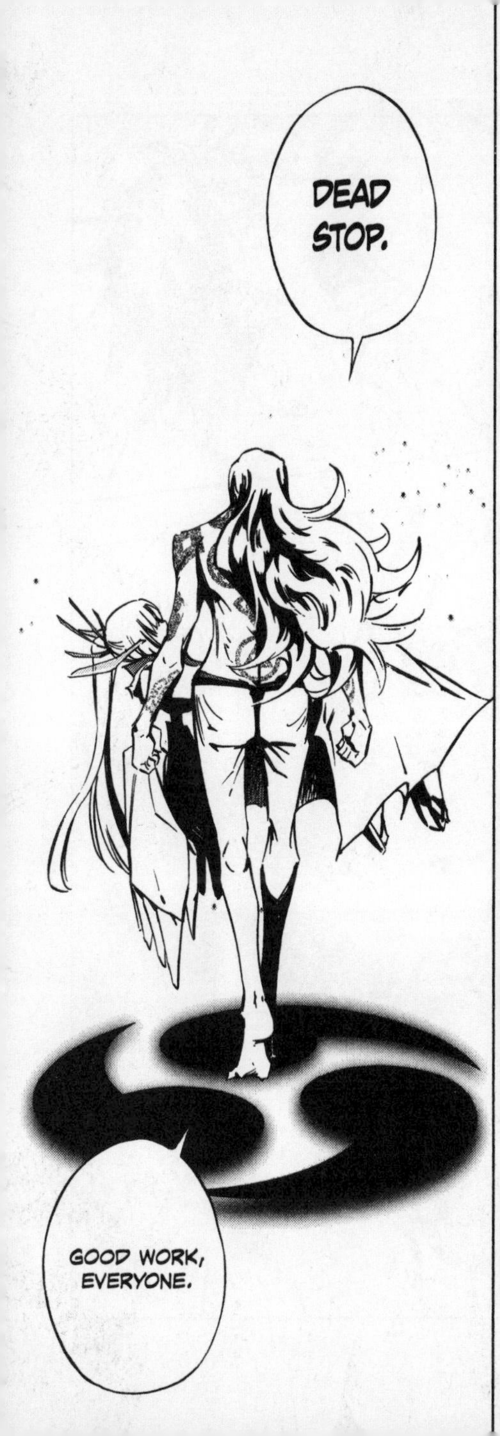
DEAD STOP.
GOOD WORK, EVERYONE.

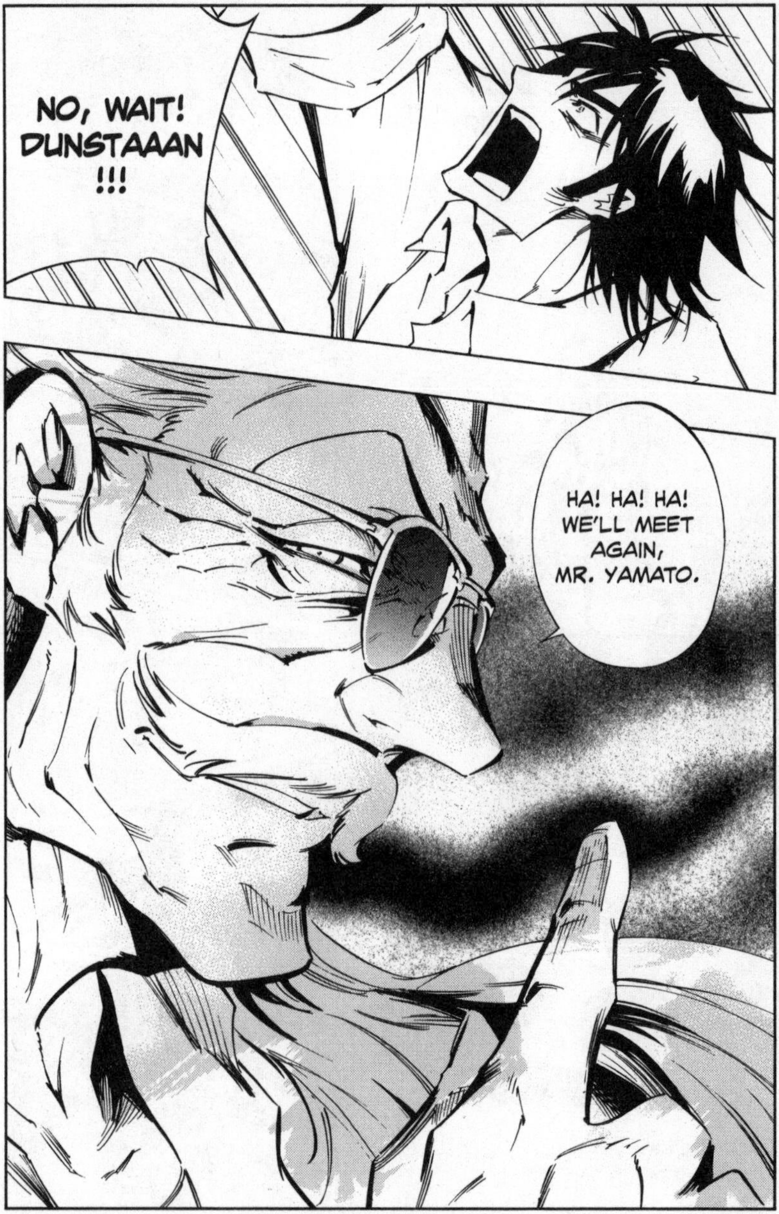
NO, WAIT! DUNSTAAAN !!!
HA! HA! HA! WE'LL MEET AGAIN, MR. YAMATO.

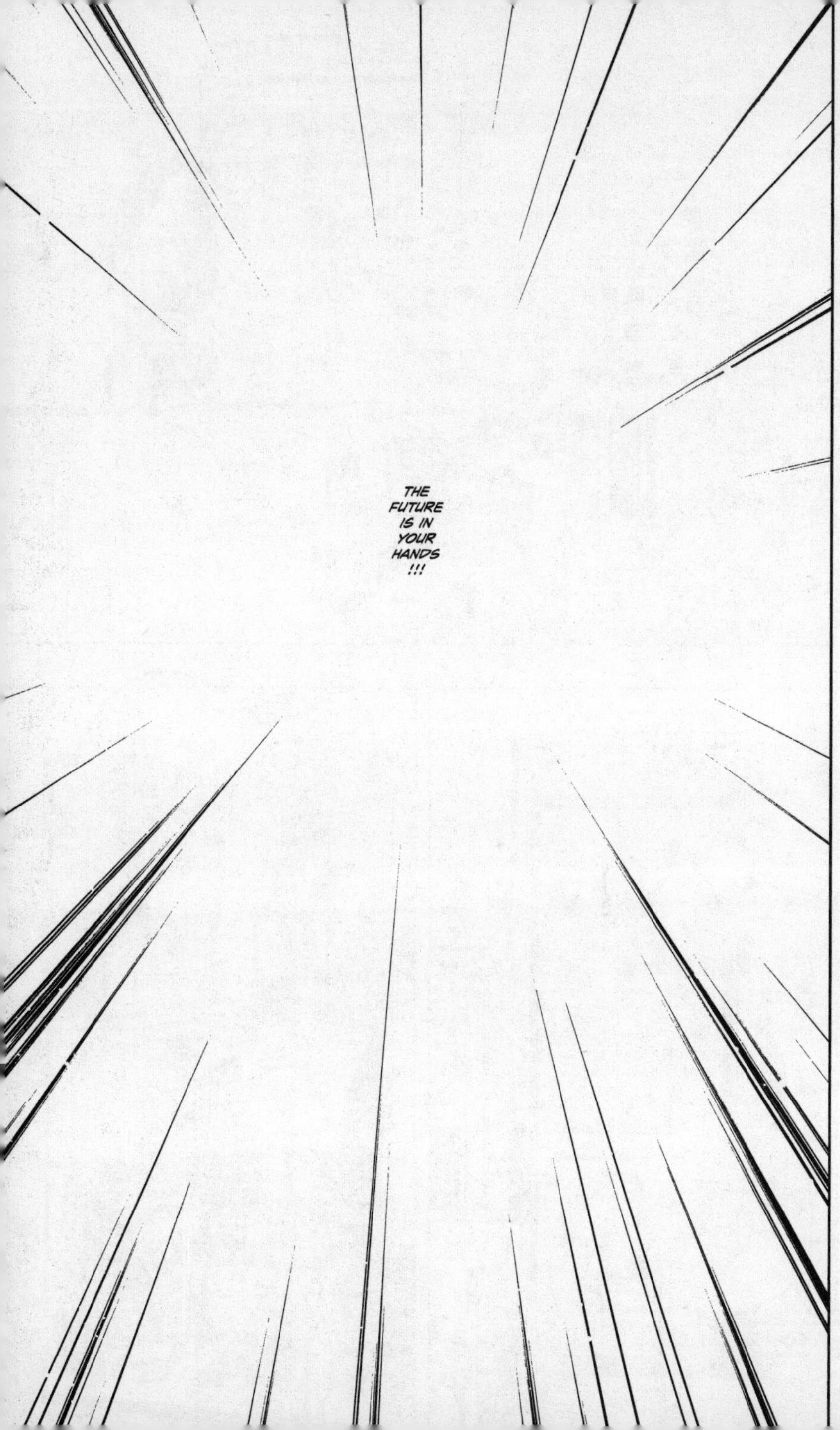
THE FUTURE IS IN YOUR HANDS!!!

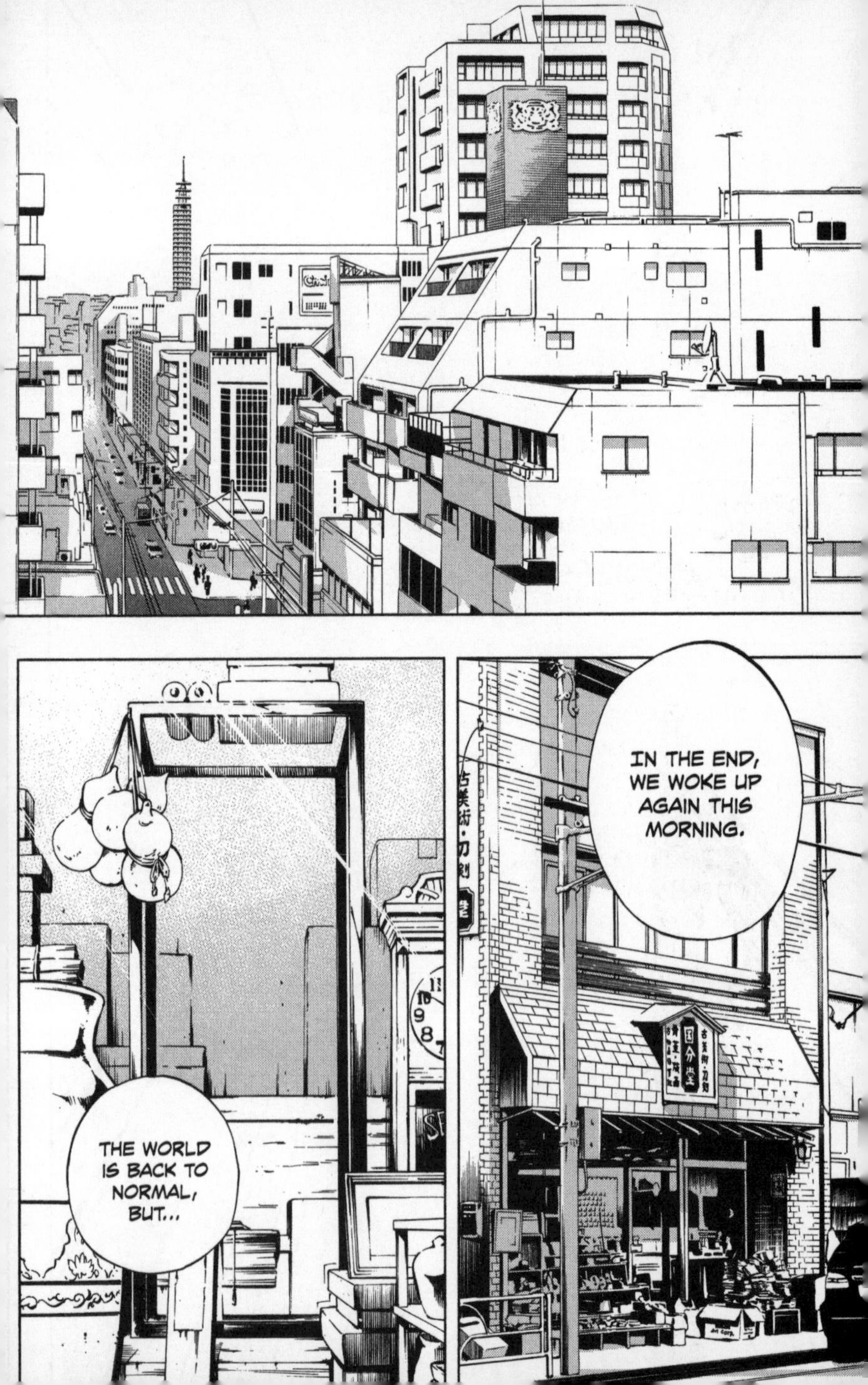
古美術・刀剣
IN THE END, WE WOKE UP AGAIN THIS MORNING.
THE WORLD IS BACK TO NORMAL, BUT...

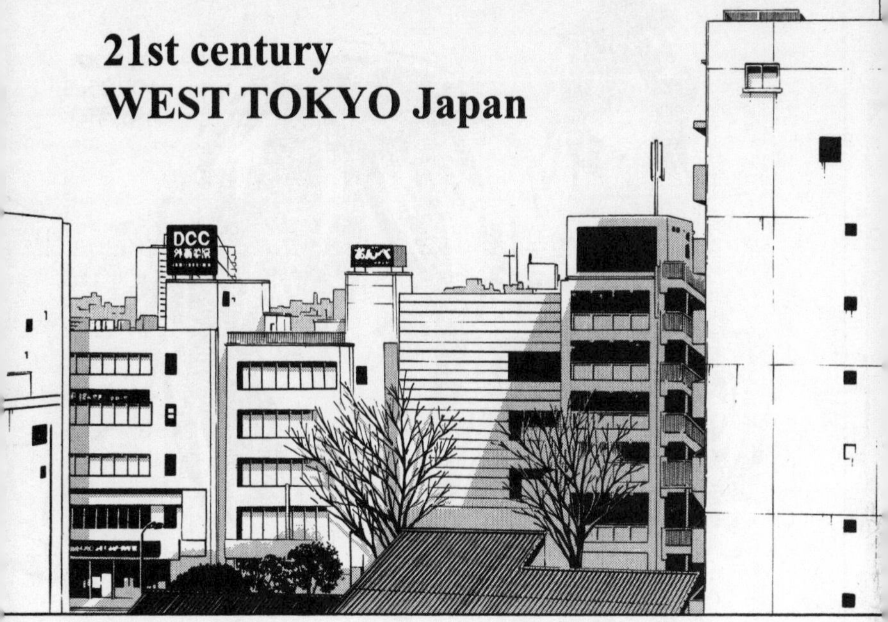
21st century
WEST TOKYO Japan
DCC

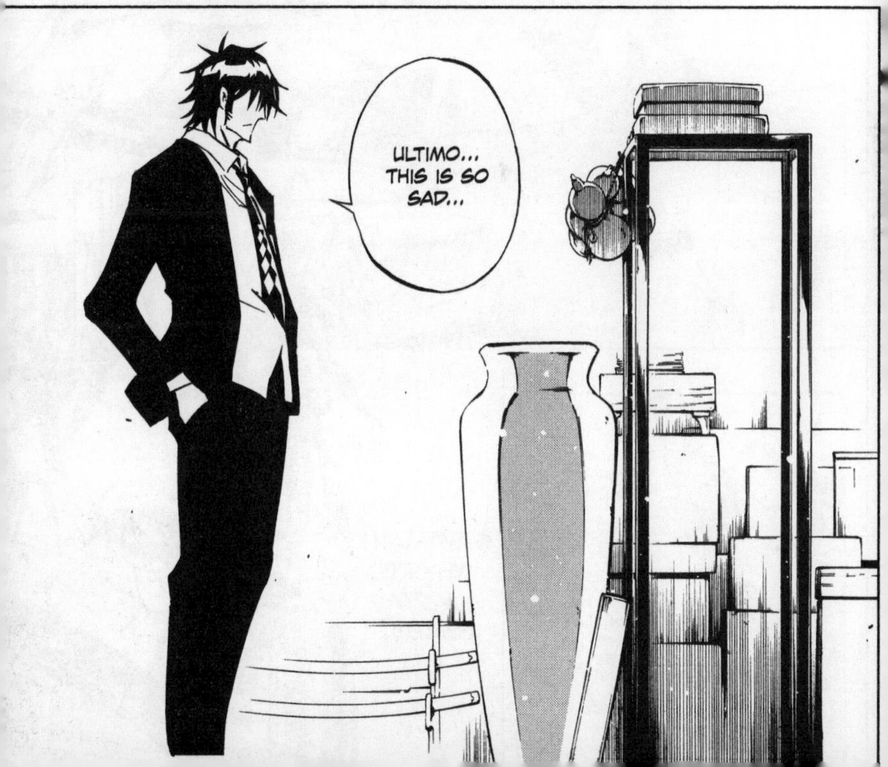
ULTIMO... THIS IS SO SAD...

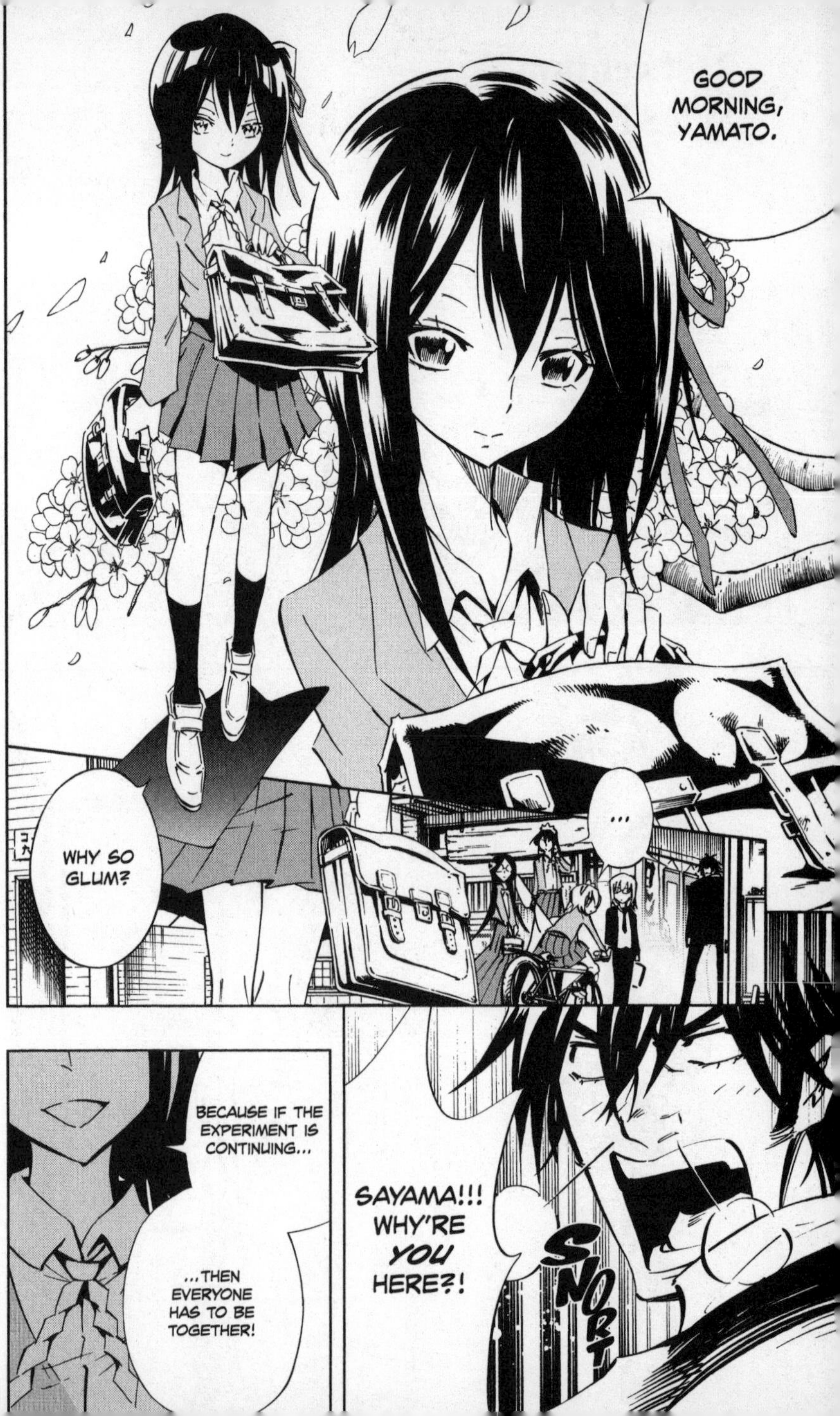
GOOD MORNING, YAMATO.
...
WHY SO GLUM?
SAYAMA!!! WHY'RE YOU HERE?!
SNORT
BECAUSE IF THE EXPERIMENT IS CONTINUING...
...THEN EVERYONE HAS TO BE TOGETHER!

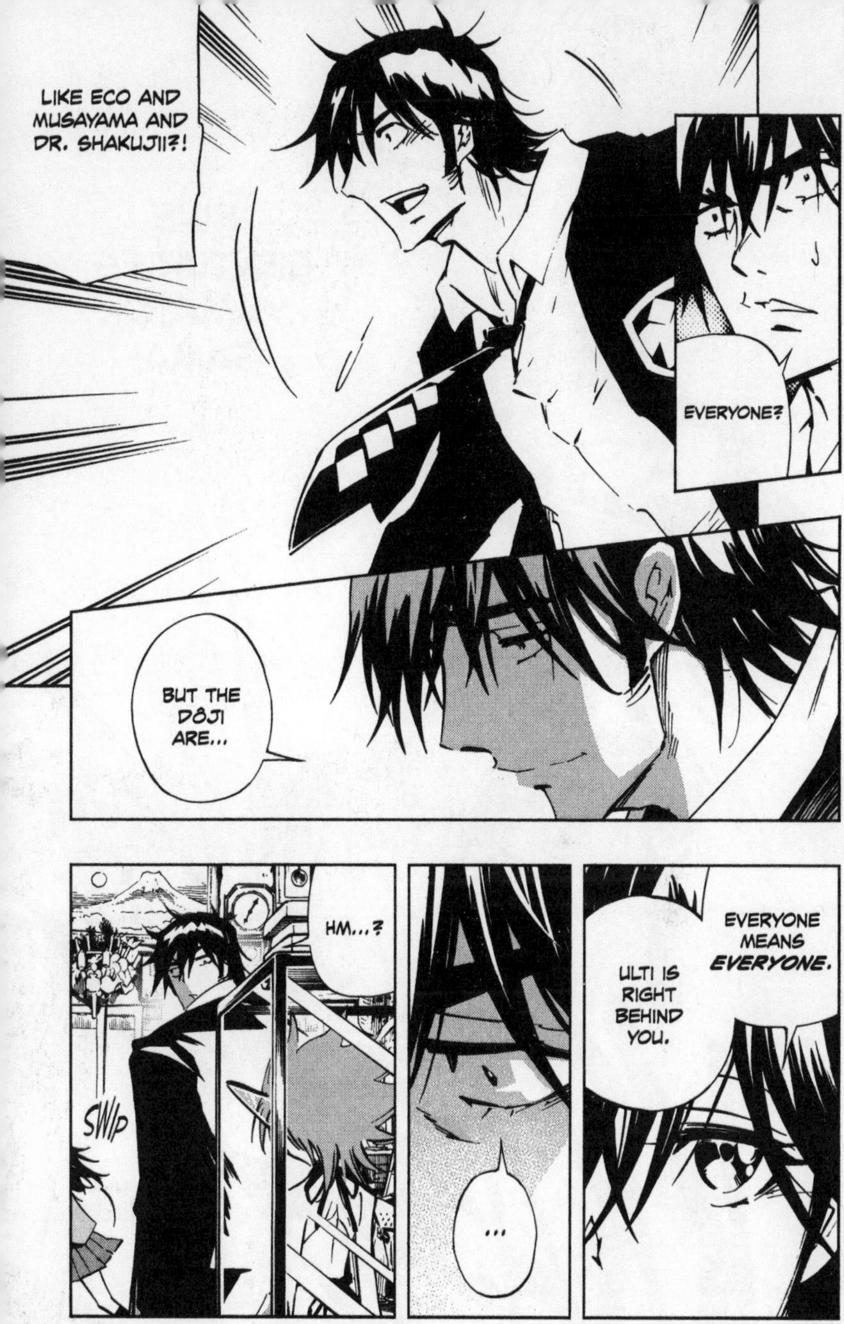
LIKE ECO AND MUSAYAMA AND DR. SHAKUJII?!
EVERYONE?
BUT THE DÔJI ARE...
EVERYONE MEANS *EVERYONE*.
ULTI IS RIGHT BEHIND YOU.
...
HM...?
SWIP

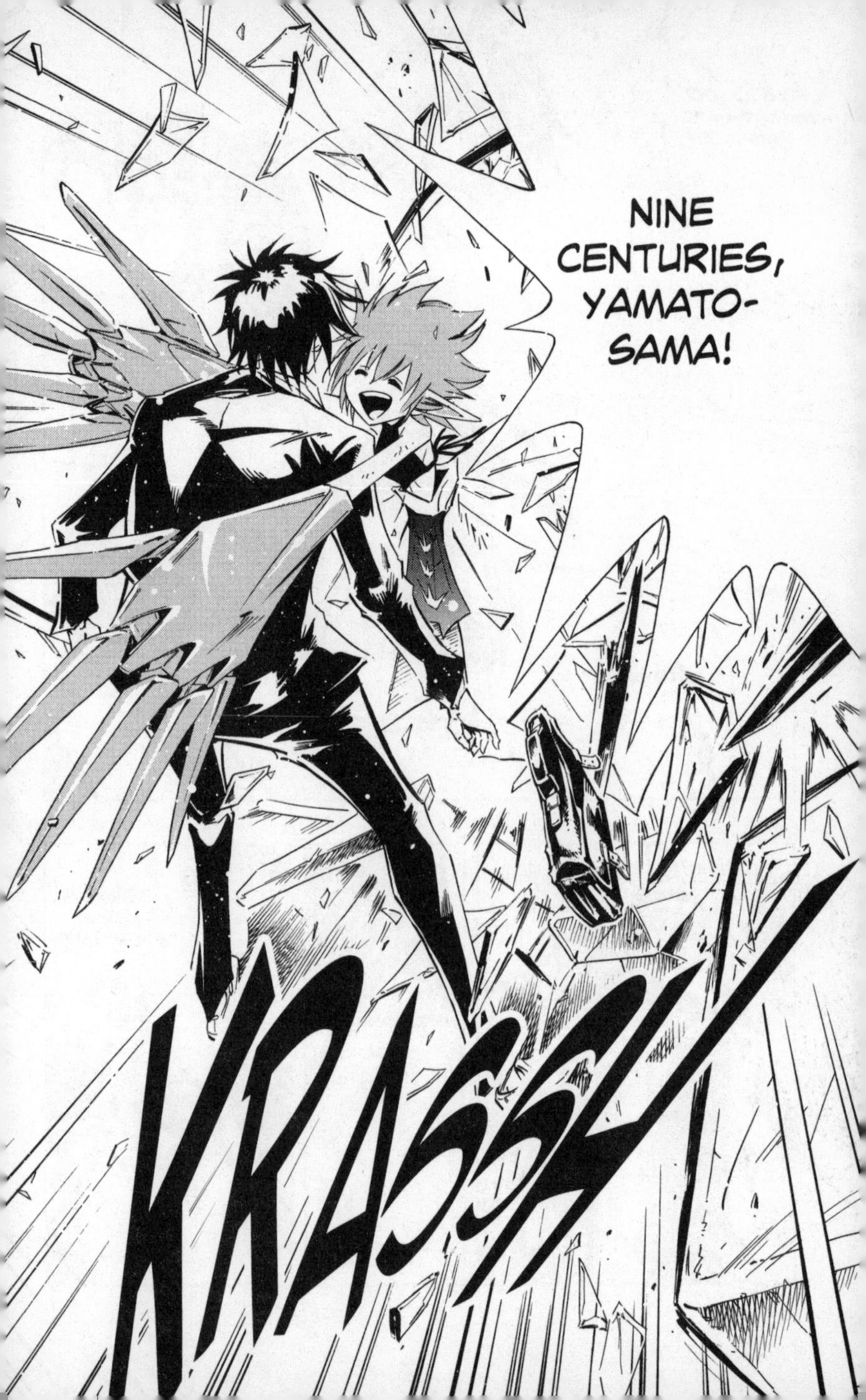
NINE CENTURIES, YAMATO-SAMA!
KRASSH

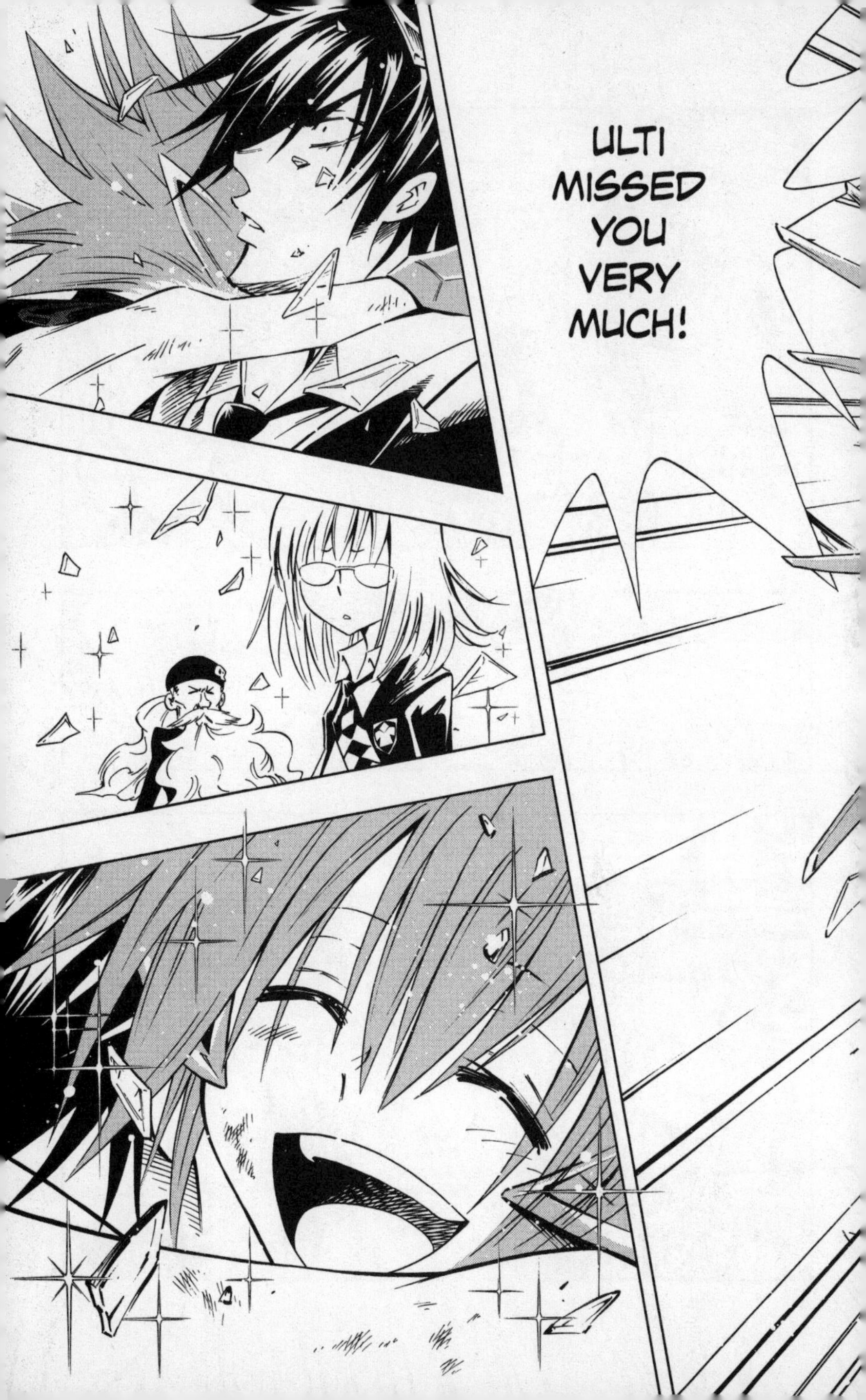
ULTI MISSED YOU VERY MUCH!

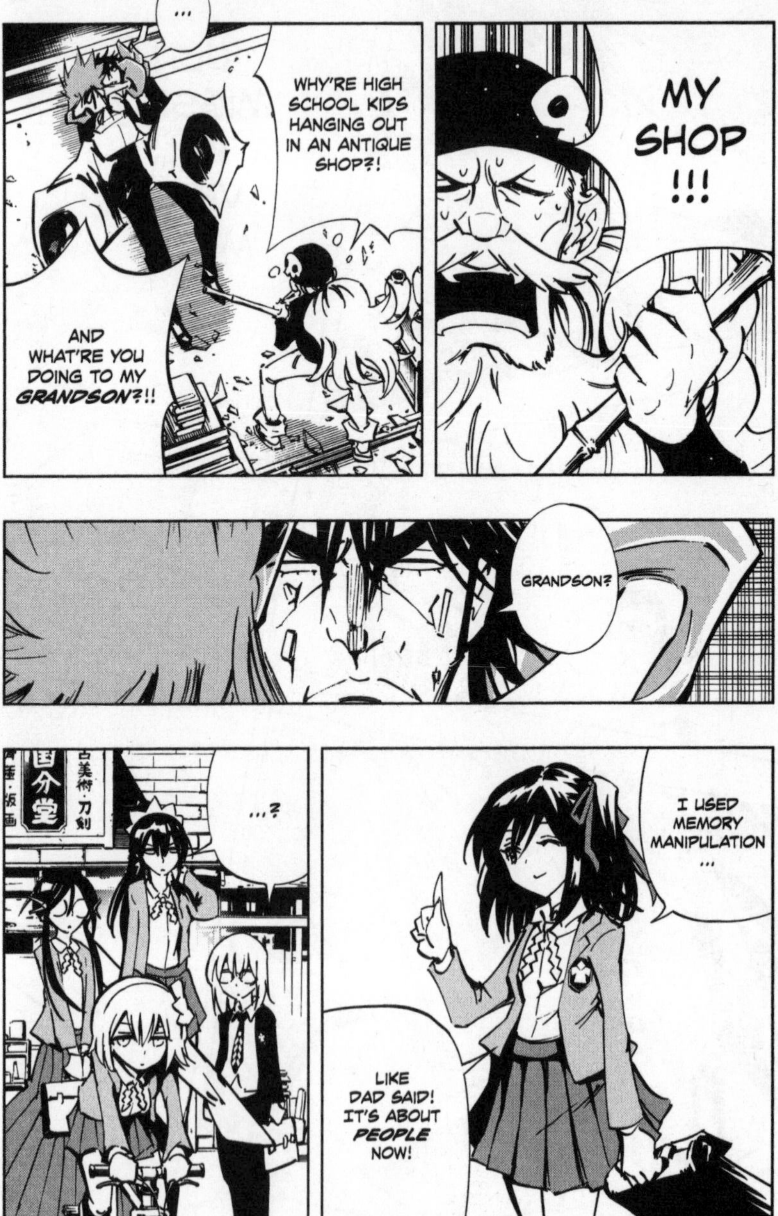
MY SHOP !!!
...
WHY'RE HIGH SCHOOL KIDS HANGING OUT IN AN ANTIQUE SHOP?!
AND WHAT'RE YOU DOING TO MY *GRANDSON*?!!
GRANDSON?
I USED MEMORY MANIPULATION ...
LIKE DAD SAID! IT'S ABOUT *PEOPLE* NOW!
古美術・刀剣
国分堂
...?

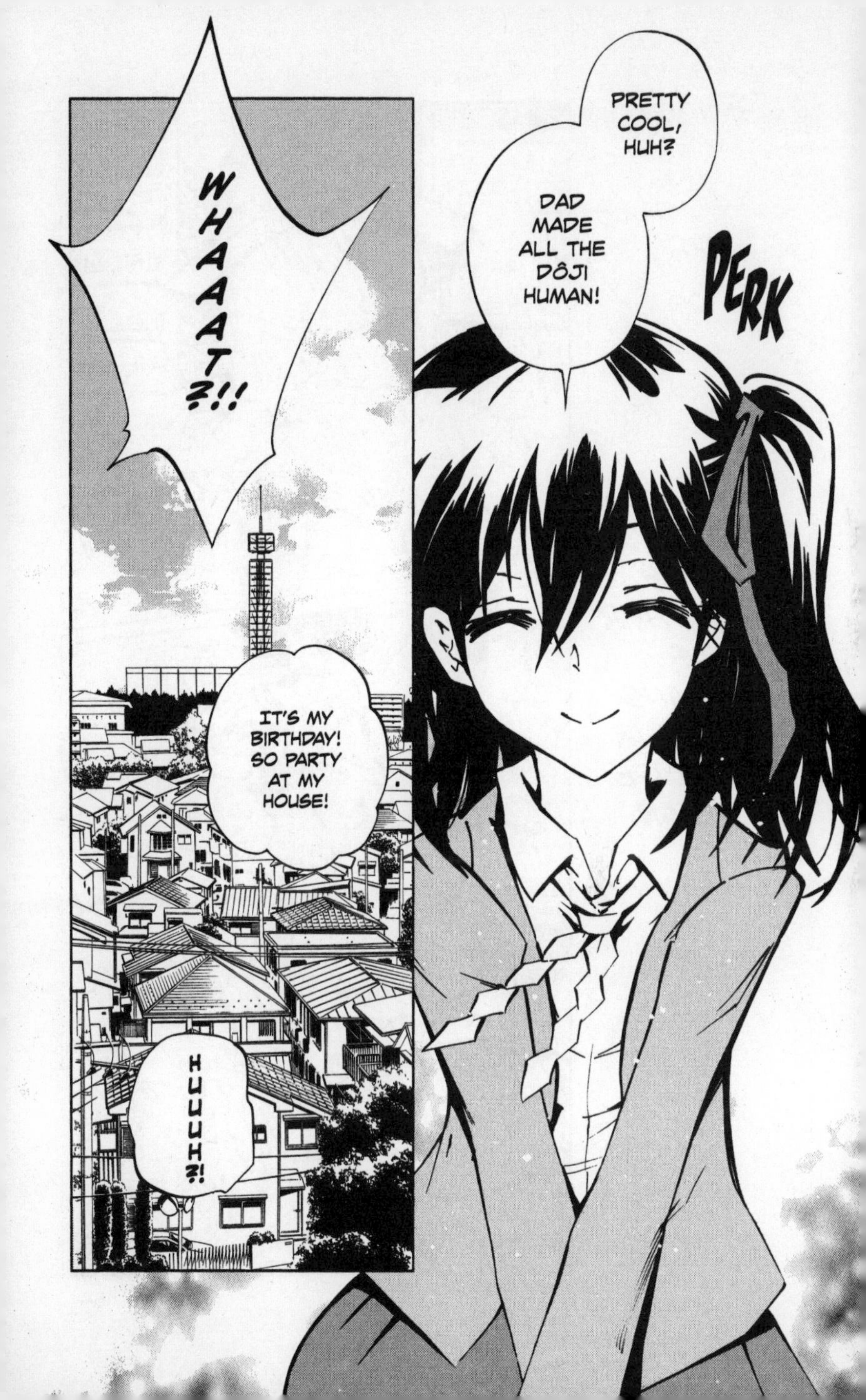
PRETTY COOL, HUH?
DAD MADE ALL THE DÔJI HUMAN!
PERK
WHAAAAT?!!
IT'S MY BIRTHDAY! SO PARTY AT MY HOUSE!
HUUUH?!

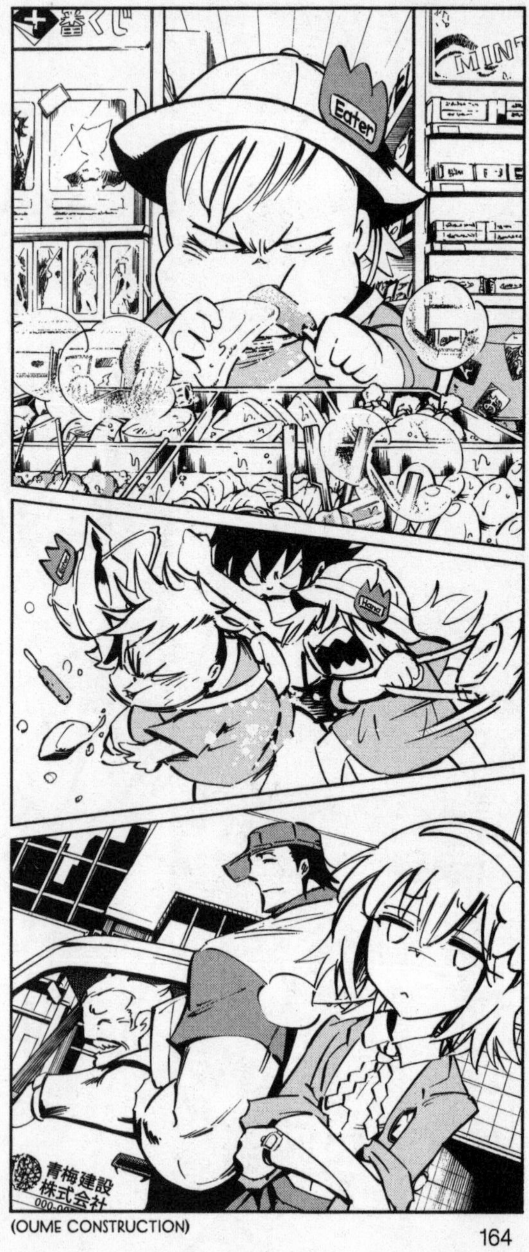
一番くじ
MINT
Eater
Hana
青梅建設
株式会社

THE DÔJI CAME TOGETHER AS HUMANS AND OUR NEW LIFE BEGAN.

(OUME CONSTRUCTION)

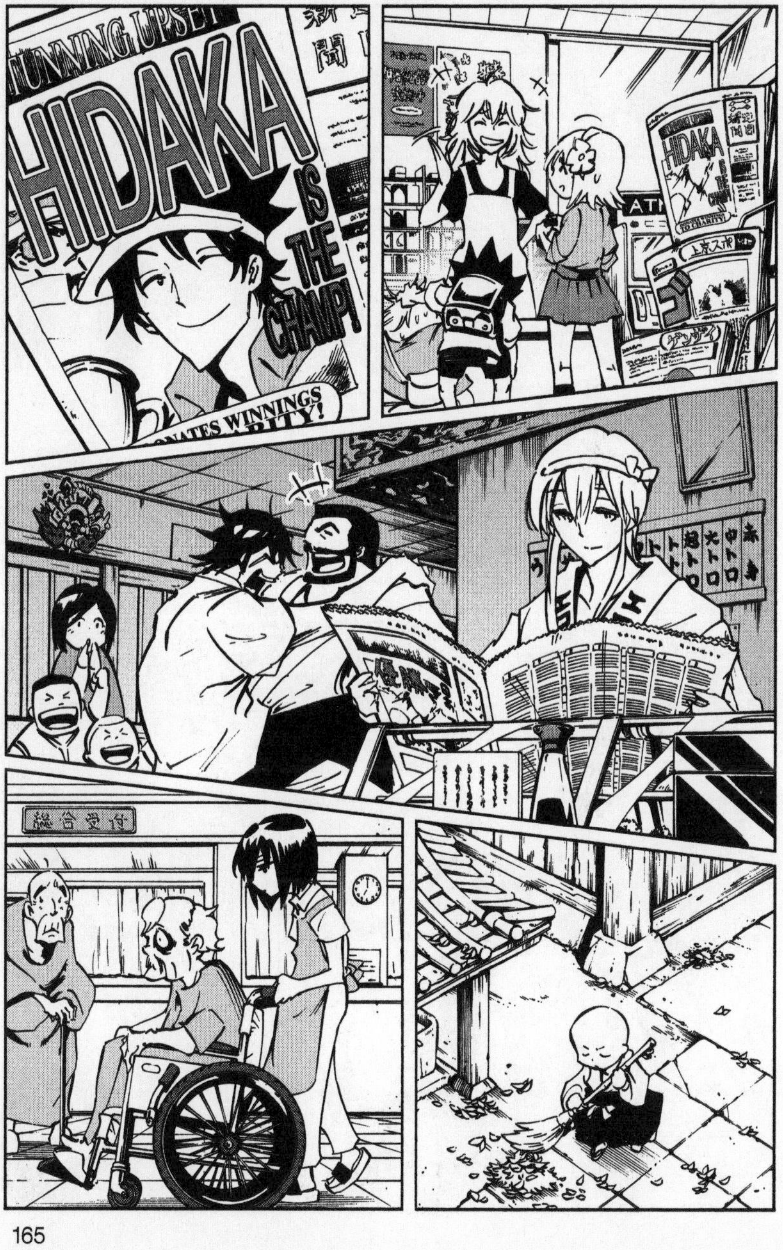

HIDAKA
IS THE CHAMP!
ATM
TUNNING UPSET
HIDAKA
IS THE CHAMP!
ONATES WINNINGS
RITY!
赤身
中トロ
大トロ
超トロ
総合受付

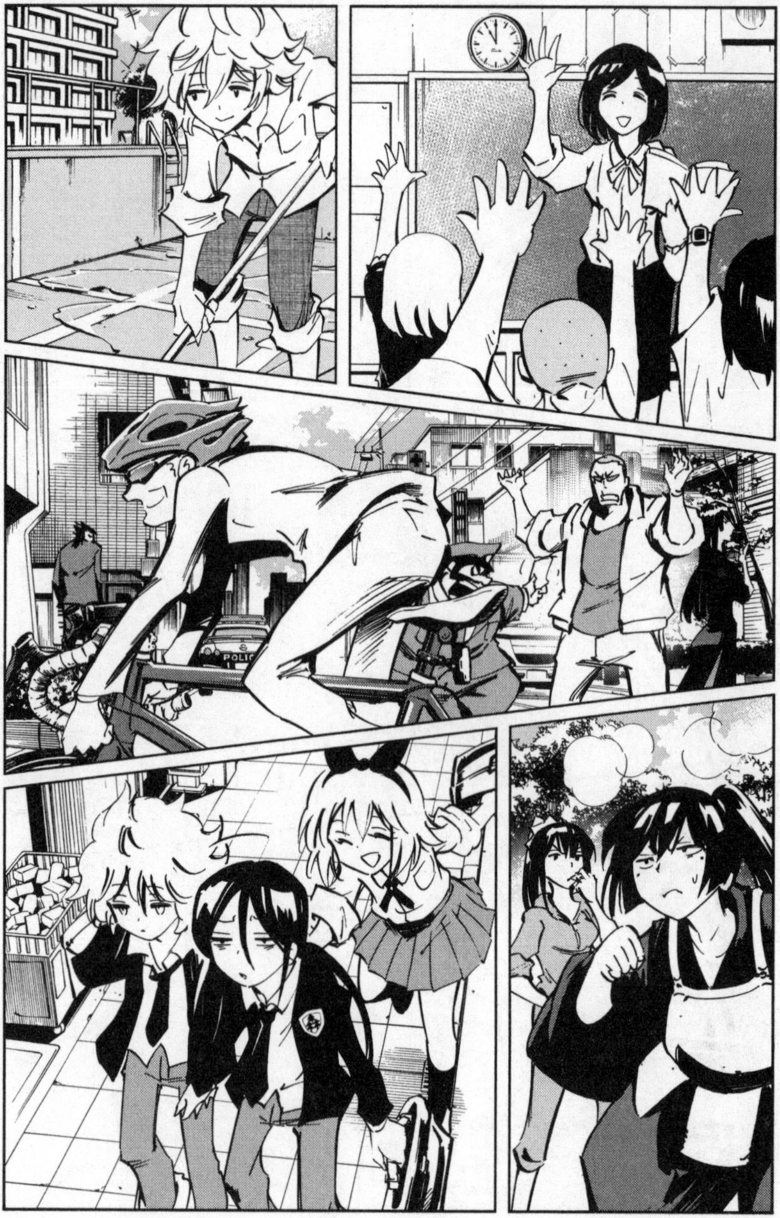

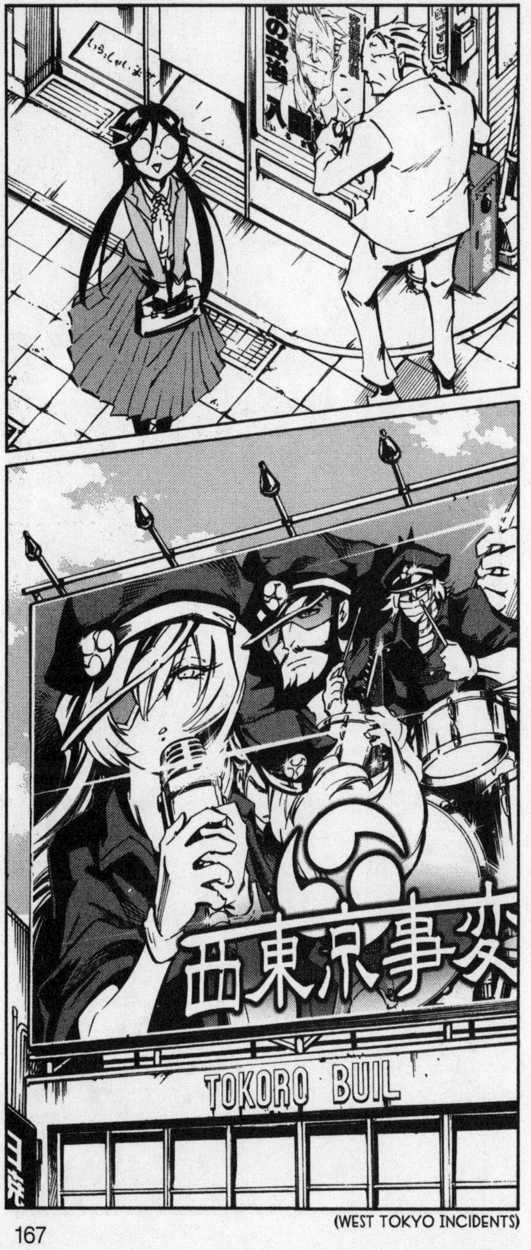
西東京事変
TOKORO BUIL

SOME OF US CHANGED A LITTLE, AND SOME CHANGED A LOT.

(WEST TOKYO INCIDENTS)

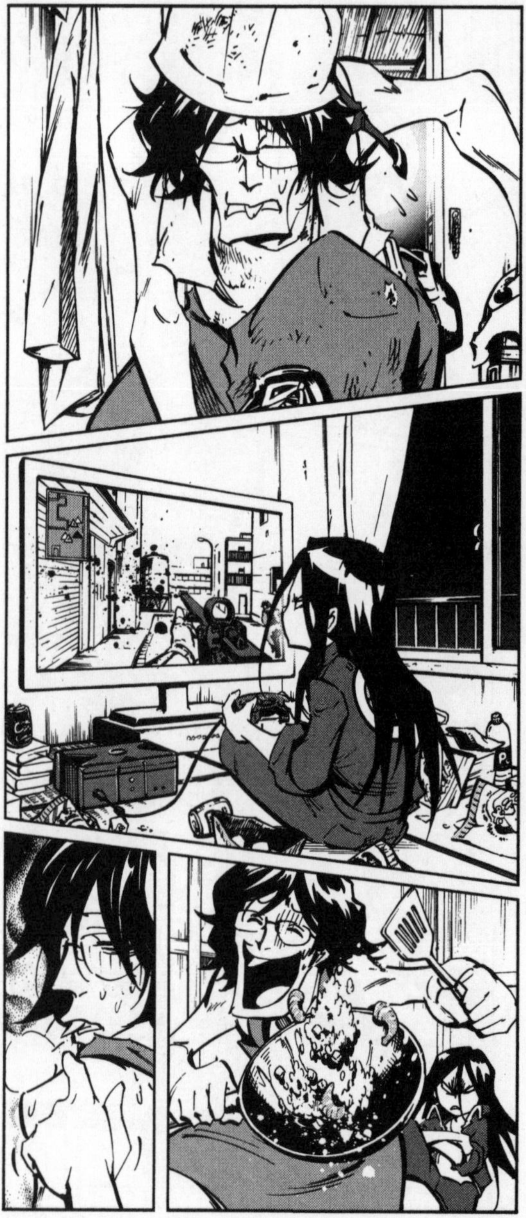

SOME DIDN'T MEAN TO CHANGE AT ALL BUT APPEAR TO BE CHANGING LITTLE BY LITTLE.

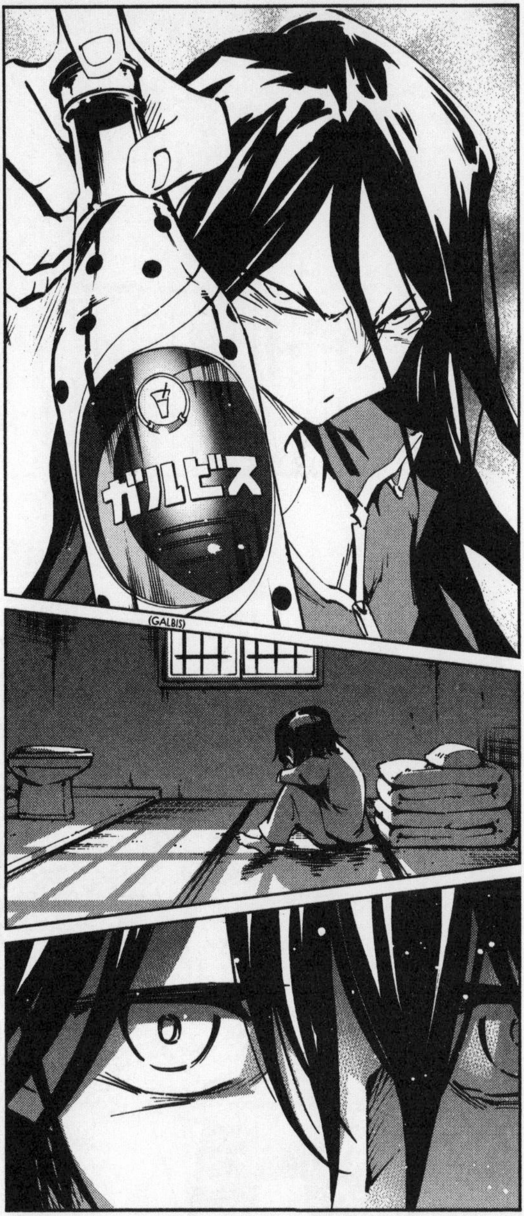
ガルビス
(GALBIS)

AND OTHERS WILL TAKE SOME TIME.

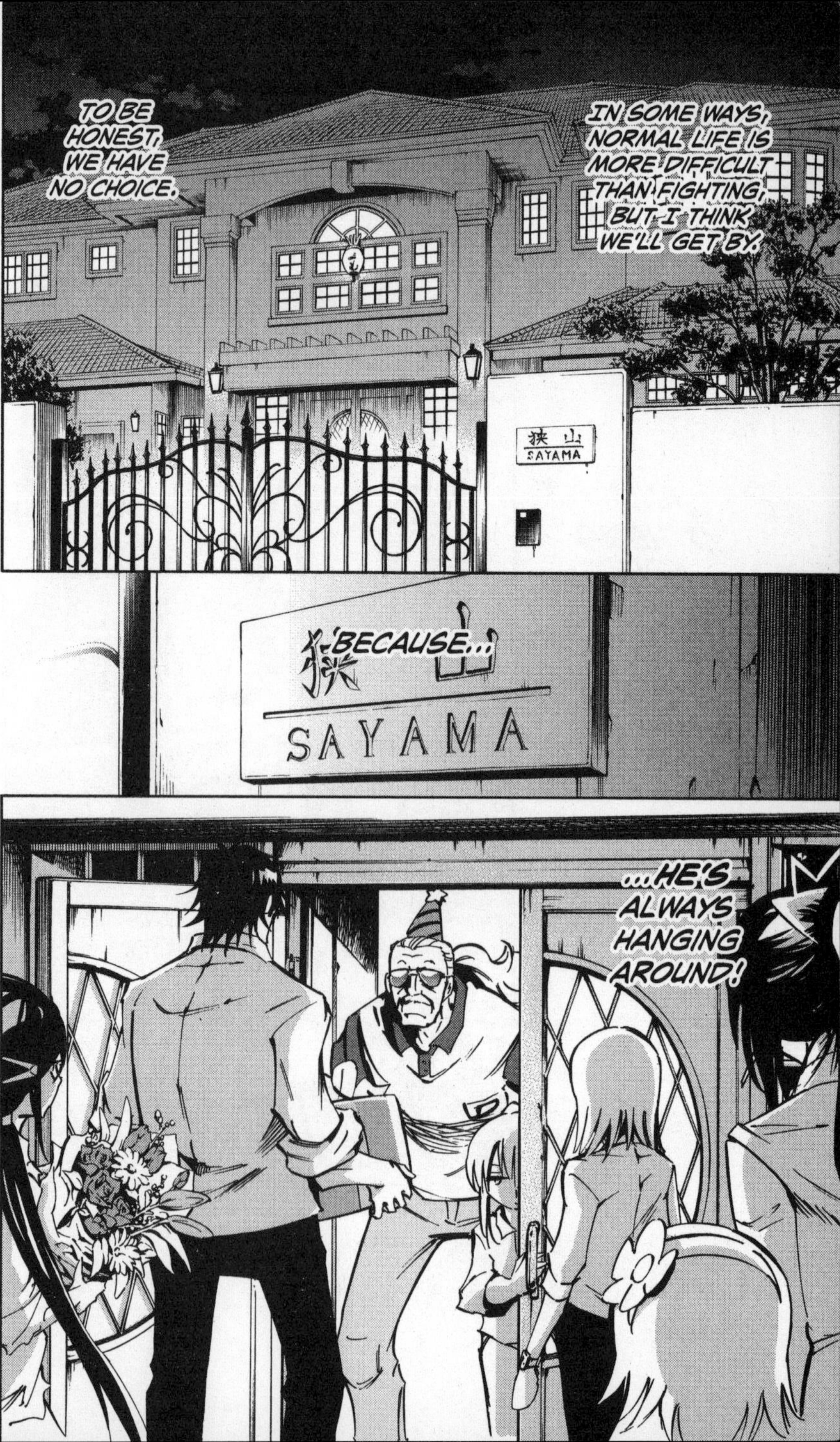
IN SOME WAYS, NORMAL LIFE IS MORE DIFFICULT THAN FIGHTING, BUT I THINK WE'LL GET BY.
TO BE HONEST, WE HAVE NO CHOICE.
狭山
SAYAMA
BECAUSE...
狭山
SAYAMA
...HE'S ALWAYS HANGING AROUND!

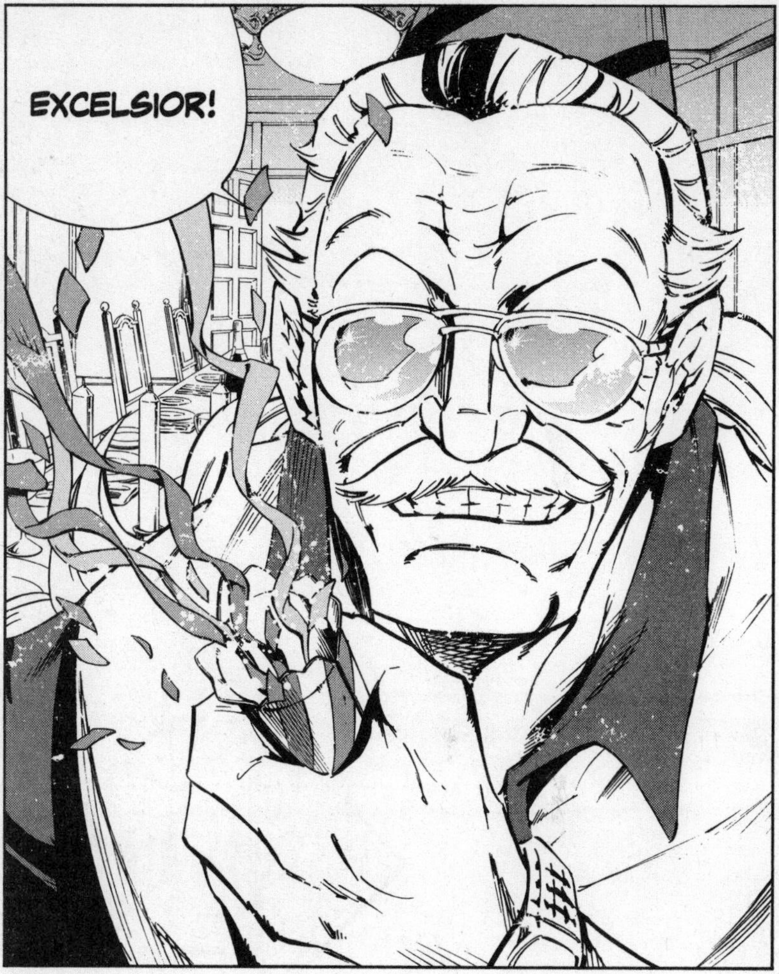
EXCELSIOR!

THE END

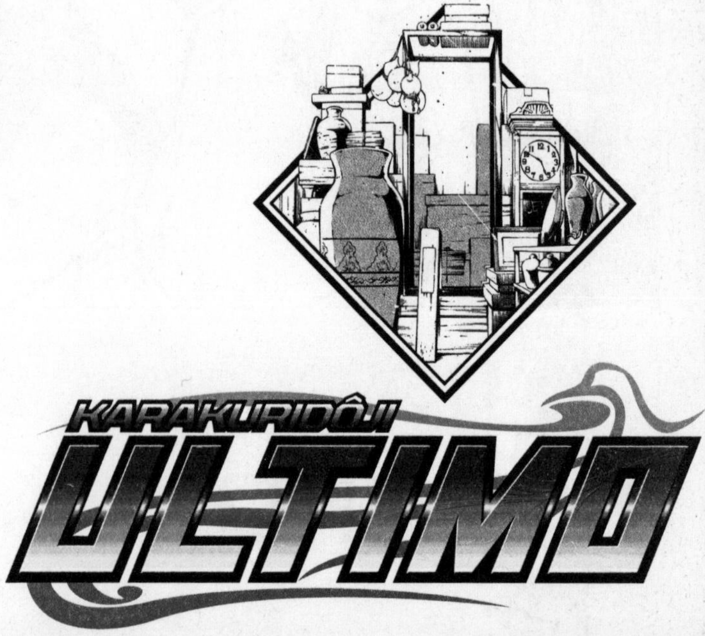

KARAKURIDÔJI

ULTIMO

CHARACTER DATA COMPILATION

KARAKURI ILLUSTRATED PROFILES

5

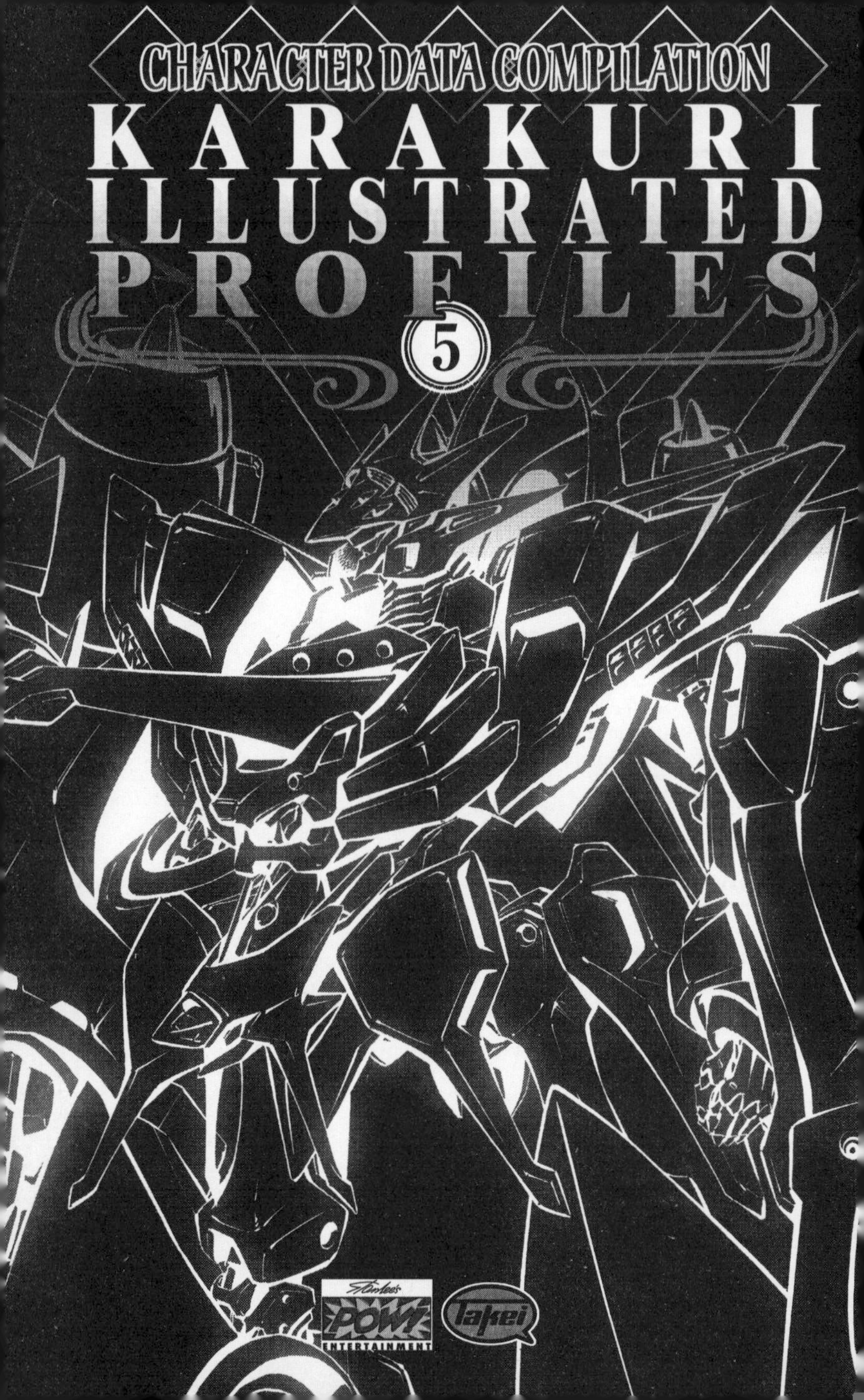

機巧童子とは…その4

あなたの中にある『善』と『悪』が堂々めぐりに
感じられることはないだろうか?
一周してはじめに戻りうんざりするような。

だが決してそんなことはない。
『善』と『悪』は螺旋階段のように交互に訪れる。
フロアの作りが似ているためそう感じるだけで、
確実にステージは一階ずつあがっている。

もちろん休んだっていい。
大切なのはあきらめてそこに留まらないことだ。
最上階を目指して一段ずつ歩み続けることだ。

What is a KARAKURIDÔJI?　Part 4

Do you ever feel the "good" and "evil" within you going back and
forth? Round and round, seemingly ending up exactly where
they began. What's the point of it all?

But they're not just swirling about aimlessly. Good and evil
work in tandem like a spiral staircase—and while each floor
may look similar, there is no doubt that you are going up, one
floor at a time.

Of course, it's all right to take a breather along the way. What's
important is to never let yourself get stuck in a rut.
Keep on moving, one floor at a time, until you reach the top.

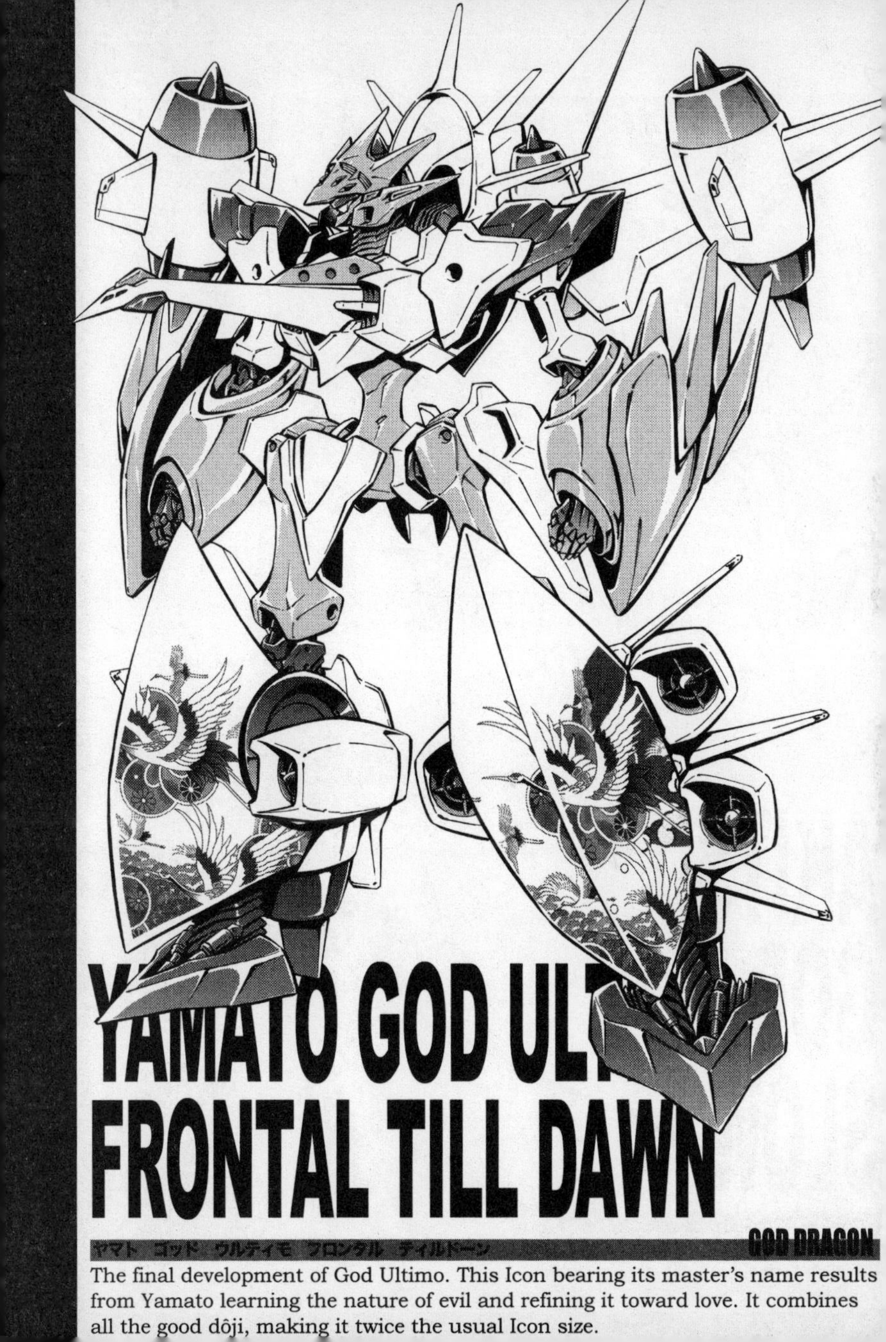

YAMATO GOD ULT
FRONTAL TILL DAWN

ヤマト ゴッド ウルティモ フロンタル ティルドーン **GOD DRAGON**

The final development of God Ultimo. This Icon bearing its master's name results from Yamato learning the nature of evil and refining it toward love. It combines all the good dôji, making it twice the usual Icon size.

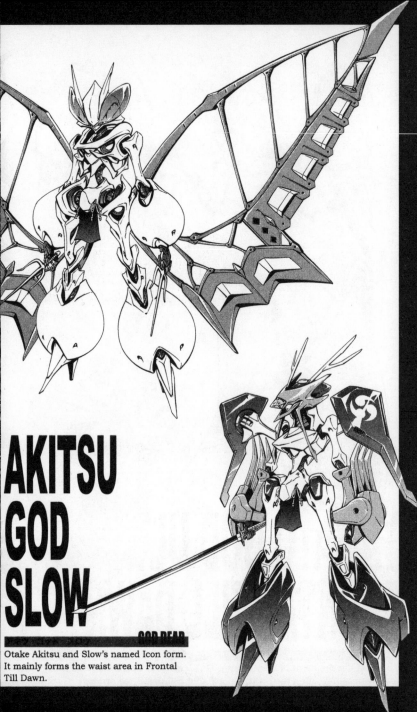

AKITSU GOD SLOW

GOD REAR

Otake Akitsu and Slow's named Icon form. It mainly forms the waist area in Frontal Till Dawn.

In Buddhist terminology, the Six Perfections designate good actions. They are the strength to give, create and oppose evil intent. In Sanskrit they are known as the *paramitas*, which signify something complete and ultimate.

KIYOSE GOD PARDONNER

GOD BUTTERFLY

キヨセ ゴッド パルドネ

Matsumoto Kiyose and Pardonner's named Icon form. It forms the wings in Frontal Till Dawn.
The Icons of Matsu, Take and Ume have boar, deer and butterfly motifs.

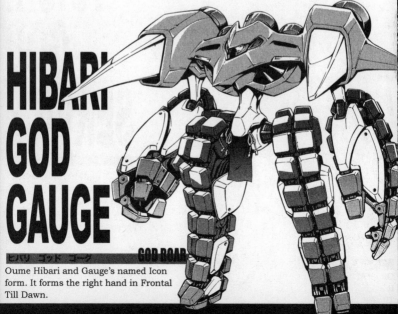

HIBARI GOD GAUGE

GOD BOAR

ヒバリ ゴッド ゴーグ

Oume Hibari and Gauge's named Icon form. It forms the right hand in Frontal Till Dawn.

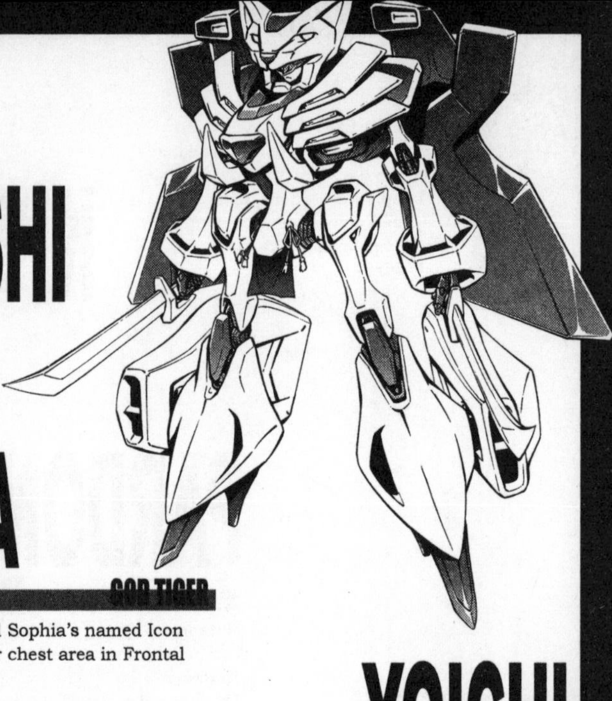

MUSASHI GOD SOPHIA

ムサシ ゴッド ソピア GOD TIGER

Murayama Musashi and Sophia's named Icon form. It forms the center chest area in Frontal Till Dawn.

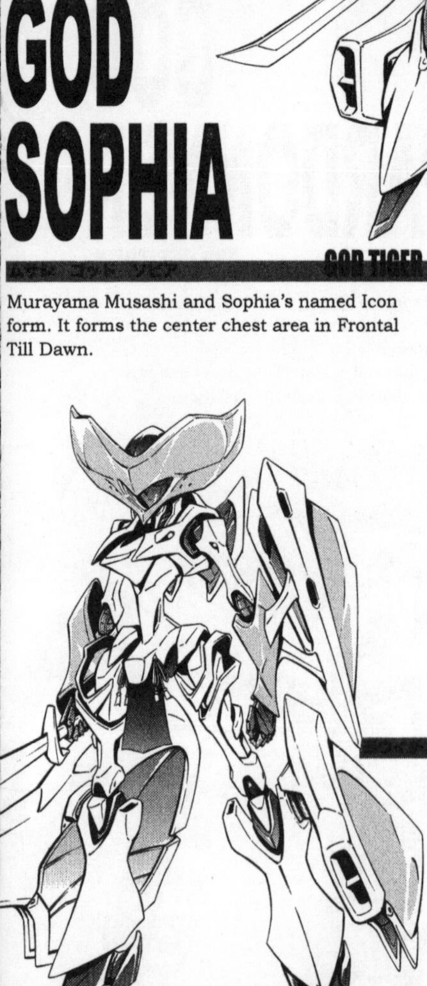

YOICHI GOD SERVICE

GOD SPARROW

Oizumi Yoichi and Service's named Icon form. It forms the left arm's shield in Frontal Till Dawn.

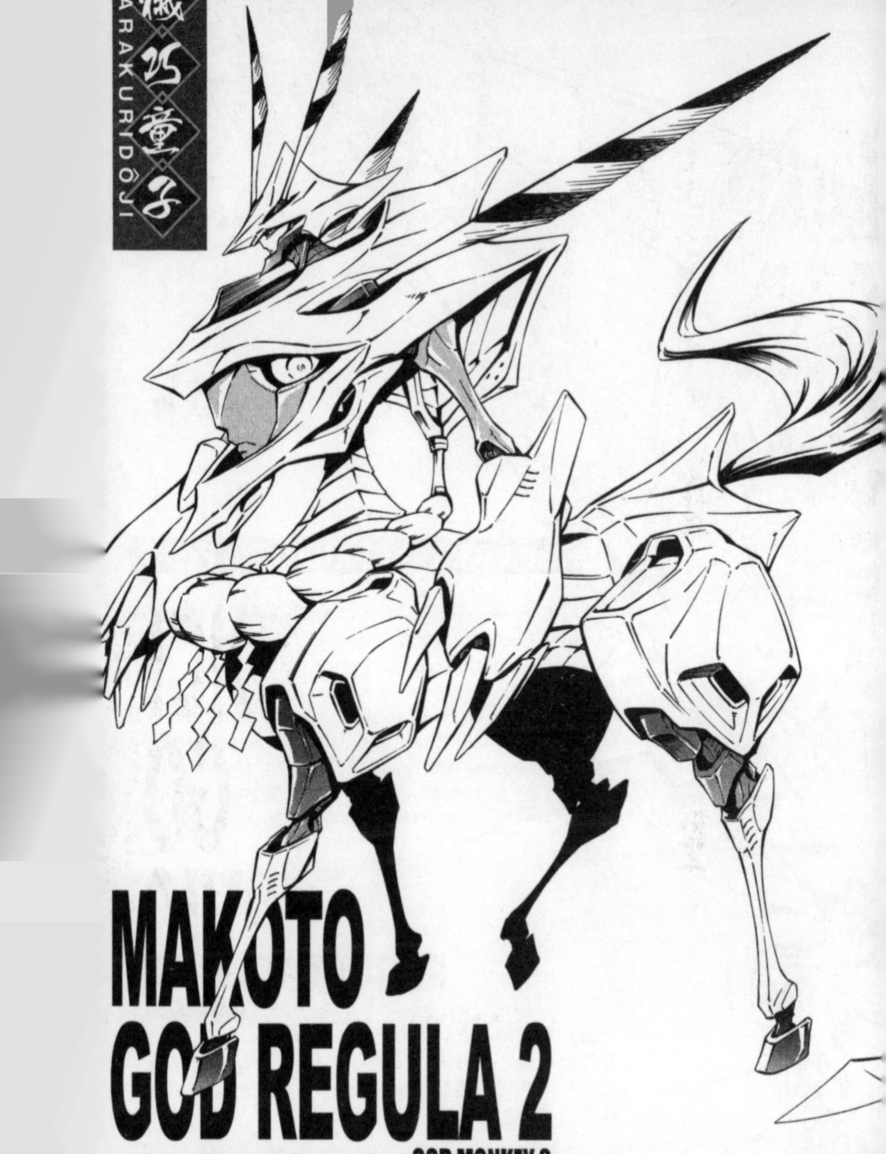

MAKOTO GOD REGULA 2

マコト ゴッド レグラ 2 **GOD MONKEY 2**

Sayama Makoto and Regula's named Icon form. This is the second model, which evolved after Dunstan captured them and their evil increased. The influence of Dunstan's blood is visible in the two faces, as with Universal Milieu. While it didn't appear in the manga, it forms the upper chest area and leg armor in Frontal Till Dawn.

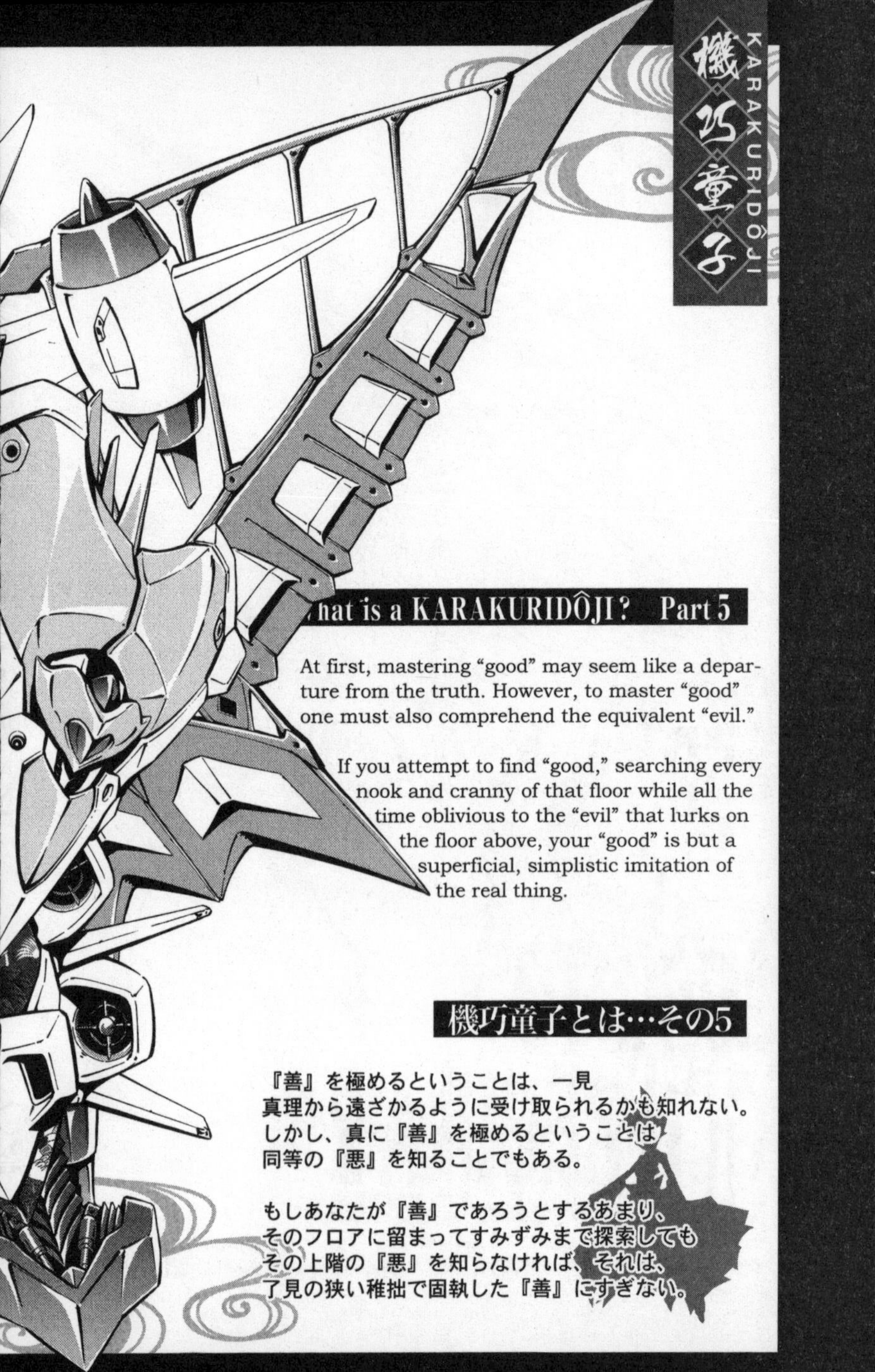

What is a KARAKURIDÔJI? Part 5

At first, mastering "good" may seem like a departure from the truth. However, to master "good" one must also comprehend the equivalent "evil."

If you attempt to find "good," searching every nook and cranny of that floor while all the time oblivious to the "evil" that lurks on the floor above, your "good" is but a superficial, simplistic imitation of the real thing.

機巧童子とは…その5

『善』を極めるということは、一見
真理から遠ざかるように受け取られるかも知れない。
しかし、真に『善』を極めるということは
同等の『悪』を知ることでもある。

もしあなたが『善』であろうとするあまり、
そのフロアに留まってすみずみまで探索しても
その上階の『悪』を知らなければ、それは、
了見の狭い稚拙で固執した『善』にすぎない。

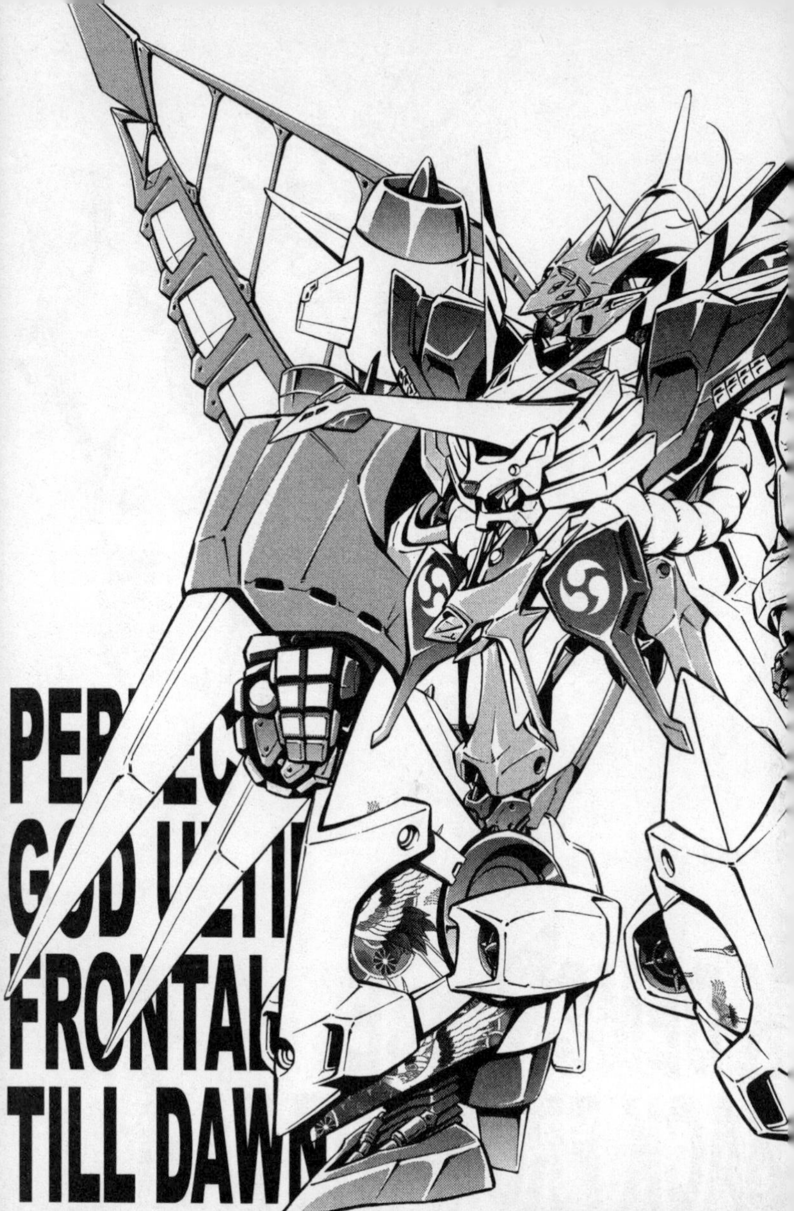
FRONTAL
TILL DAWN

カンゼンタイ ゴッド ウルティモ フロンタルティルドーン

PERFECT FORM GOD DRAGON

The ultimate good Icon formed by the combination of all good dôji.
This is the version including Regula that didn't appear in the manga.

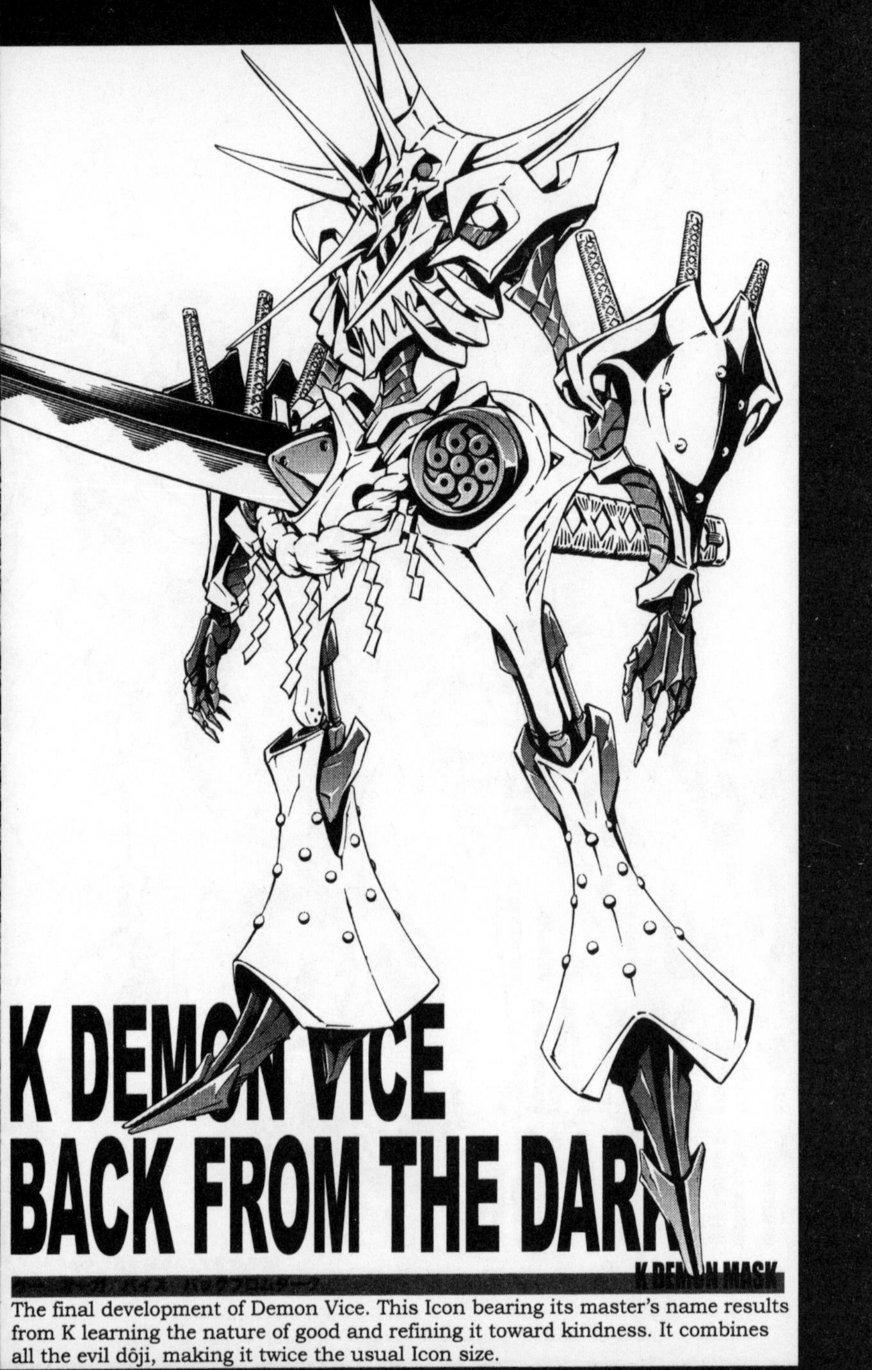

K DEMON VICE BACK FROM THE DARK

K DEMON MASK

The final development of Demon Vice. This Icon bearing its master's name results from K learning the nature of good and refining it toward kindness. It combines all the evil dôji, making it twice the usual Icon size.

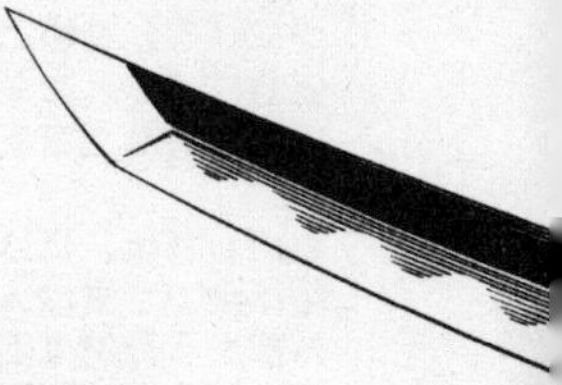

機巧童子とは…その6

『悪』を知るとはその故を知ることである。
何故そうなったのかがわからなければ対処すらできず、
理解できない者としてその世界から排除するだろう。

子供のうちは『仲間はずれ』であり、
大人になると『社会的制裁』である。

そうしておいつめられた『悪』はその感情を
暴力に変え、争いが発生する。
争いをのぞまないのが『善』とするならば
やはり『悪』を知る必要があるということだ。

What is a KARAKURIDÔJI?　Part 6

Understanding evil means understanding the logic behind it.
You cannot take on evil without understanding why it took shape.
Those who cannot comprehend that are destined to be eliminated
from this world.

As children we may find ourselves ostracized by our peers, and that
will not change as we step into more complicated social structures
as adults.

When we are pushed into a corner, evil takes hold of those feelings
of resentment and turns them into violence, breeding conflict. If we
define good as the evasion of conflict, the need arises to
comprehend evil.

機巧童子とは…その7

逆に『悪』を極めし者は『善』もよく知っている。
彼らは『善』を装い
巧みにあなたを支配しようとするだろう。

しかし『善』には愛という最上の武器がある。
愛は全てを受け入れ内包する。
外部から見ればどんなに苦しい状況にあっても
愛を持つ者は苦しみも悲しみもなく、
そこには喜びすら存在する。

『悪』は『善』に苦しみを与えられないどころか
愛を知ることになるだろう。
愛を知った『悪』はその手をゆるめずには
いられないのだ。

What is a KARAKURIDÔJI? Part 7

Those who have mastered evil also know good. They will surely attempt to control you under the guise of good.

However, good has the greatest weapon of them all—love. Love can encapsulate anything. No matter how horrible things may look from afar, he who has love feels no pain, nor sadness, but instead, happiness.

Evil will learn of love when it cannot inflict pain on good, and evil will have no choice but to lower its hands.

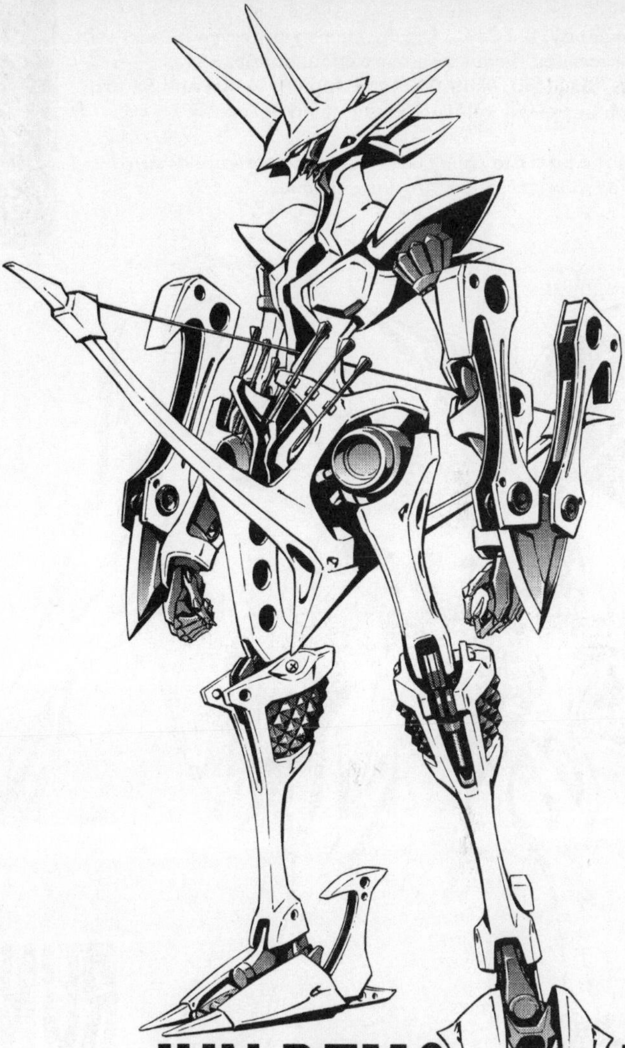

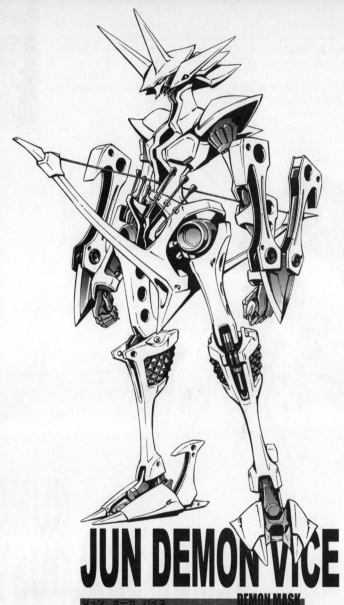

JUN DEMON VICE

ジュン オーガ バイス **DEMON MASK**

Master Jun and Vice's Icon form. As already explained, an Icon's form reflects the characteristics of the master. The way everything about this one suggests a knife shows the current state of Jun's heart.

In Christianity, the Seven Deadly Sins signify seven human evils.
I also associated them with the seven luminaries—
the Sun, the Moon, Mars, Mercury, Jupiter, Venus and Saturn—
and their supposed influence over human beings.

Good is the power to create, and evil is the power to destroy,
as well as to protect from attacking enemies.

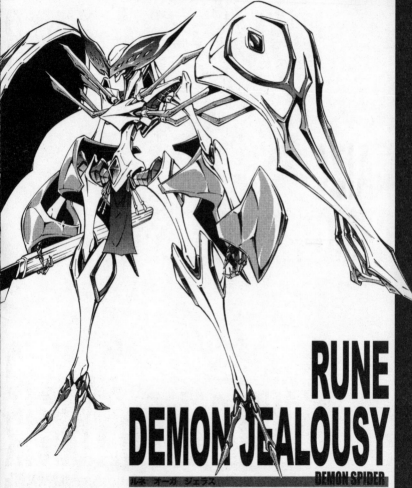

RUNE
DEMON JEALOUSY
DEMON SPIDER

ルネ　オーガ　ジェラズ

Good is the power to create, and evil is the power to
destroy, as well as to protect from attacking enemies.

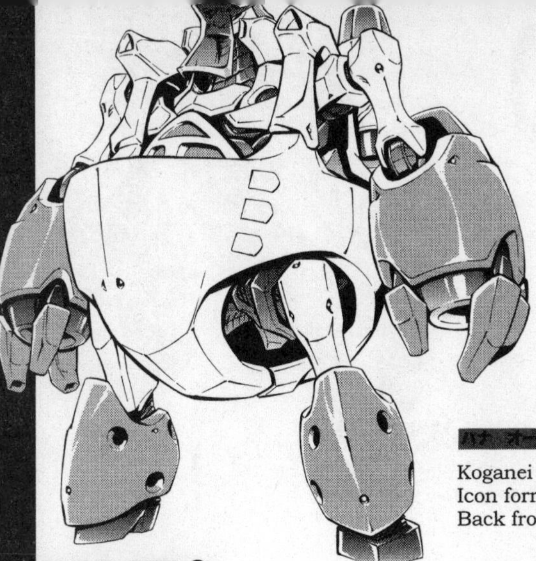

HANA DEMON EATER

ハナ オーガ エテレ **DEMON BEAR**

Koganei Hana and Eater's named Icon form. It forms the left hand in Back from the Dark.

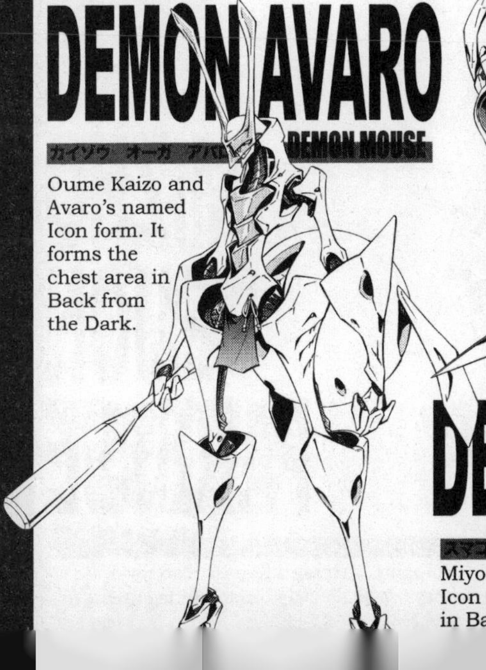

KAIZO DEMON AVARO

カイソウ オーガ アバロ **DEMON MOUSE**

Oume Kaizo and Avaro's named Icon form. It forms the chest area in Back from the Dark.

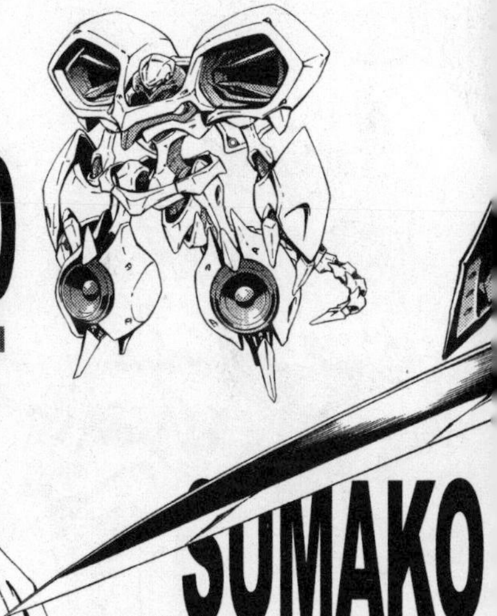

SUMAKO DEMON DÉSIR

スマコ オーガ デシル **DEMON RABBIT**

Miyoshi Sumako and Désir's named Icon form. It forms the lower back area in Back from the Dark.

FUSATARO DEMON RAGE

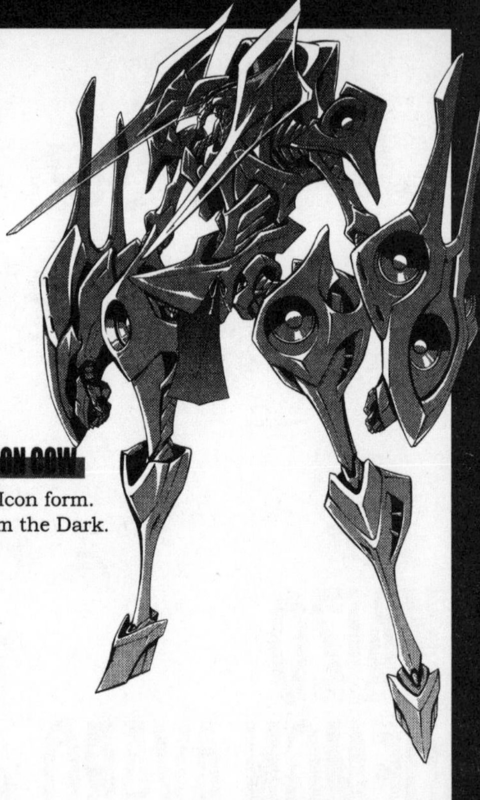

フサタロウ オーガ レイジ **DEMON COW**

Fussa Fusataro and Rage's named Icon form. It forms the right claws in Back from the Dark.

MIZHO DEMON PARESSE

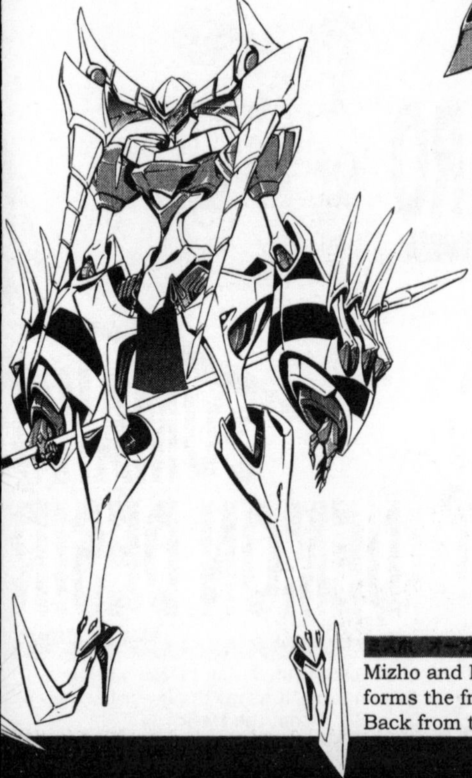

ミズホ オーガ パレス **DEMON SNAKE**

Mizho and Paresse's named Icon form. It forms the front waist area and leg armor in Back from the Dark.

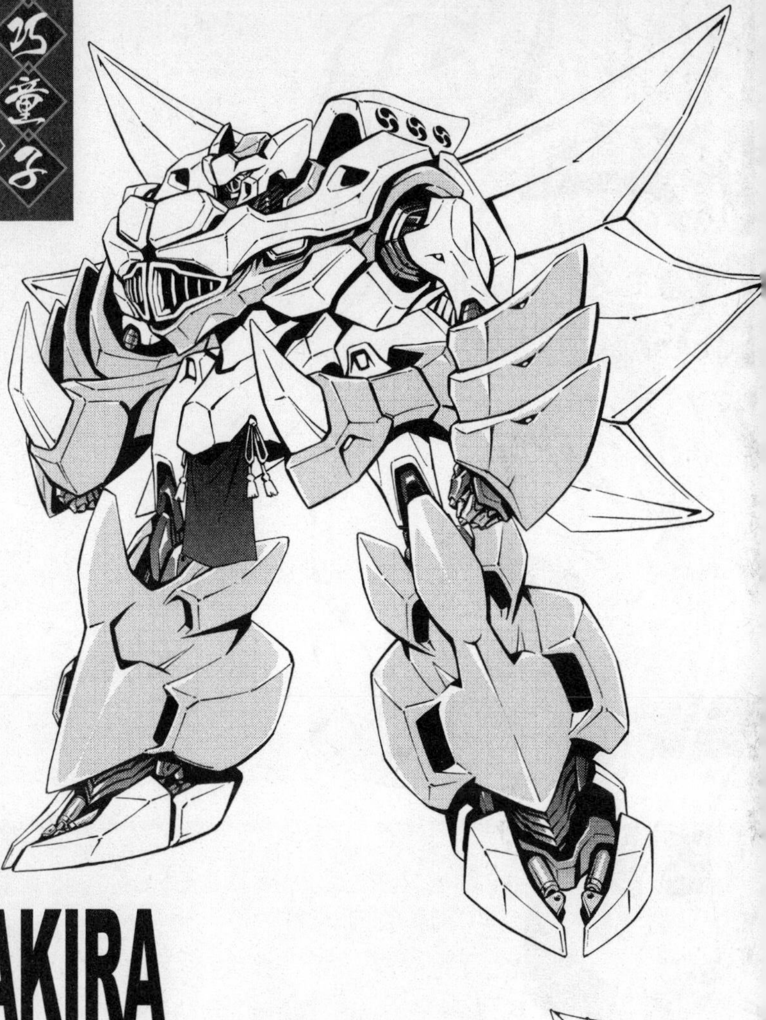

AKIRA DEMON ORGULLO

DEMON DOG

アキラ　オーガ　オルグレオ

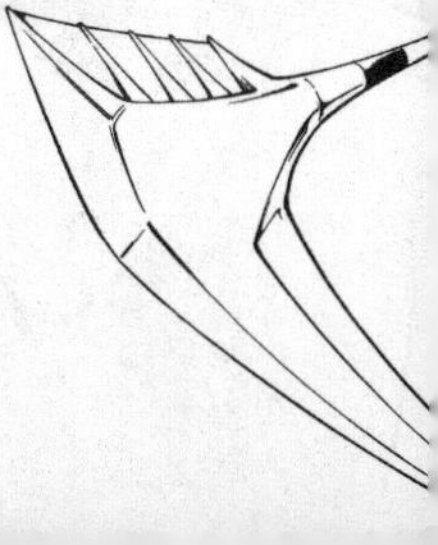

Hidaka Akira and Orgullo’s named Icon form. It forms the back area in Back from the Dark.

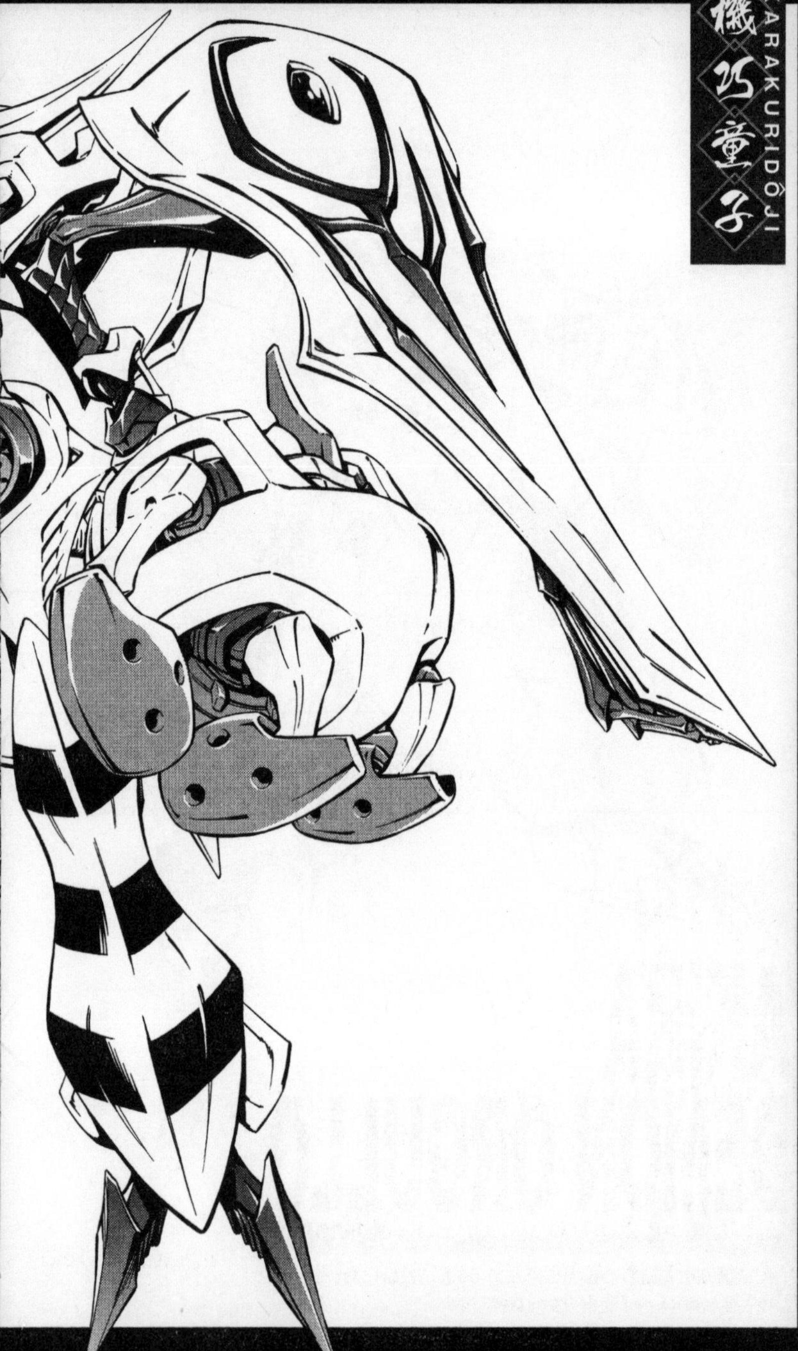

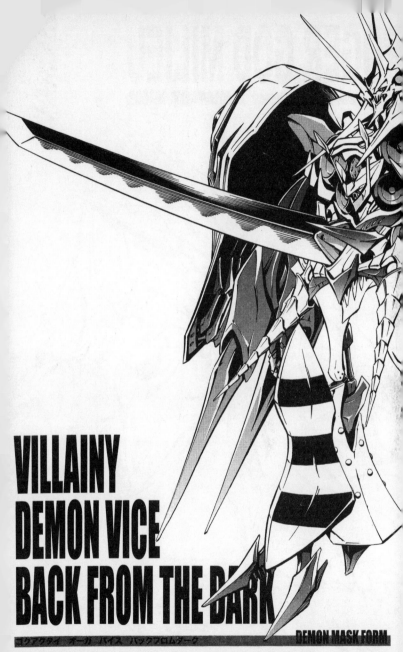

VILLAINY
DEMON VICE
BACK FROM THE DARK

コクアクタイ　オーガ　バイス　バックフロムダーク

DEMON MASK FORM

The ultimate evil Icon formed by the combination of all evil dôji.

ROGER GOD MILIEU

ロジャー・ゴッド・ミリュー

ROGER HEAVEN DRAGON

Roger Dunstan and Milieu's named Icon form. This is its basic form that didn't appear in the manga. When people ask a question, they already have an answer and merely seek confirmation. Milieu's existence shows that Dunstan knew the answer from the start.

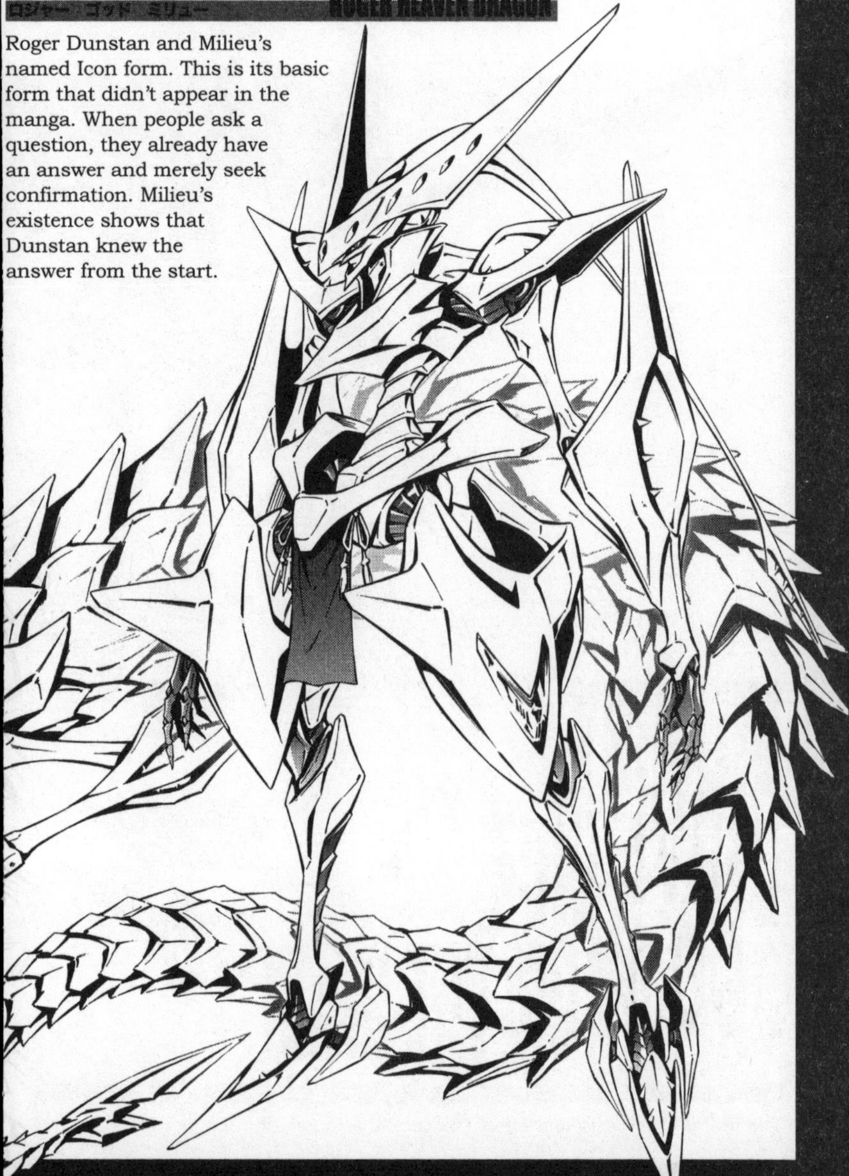

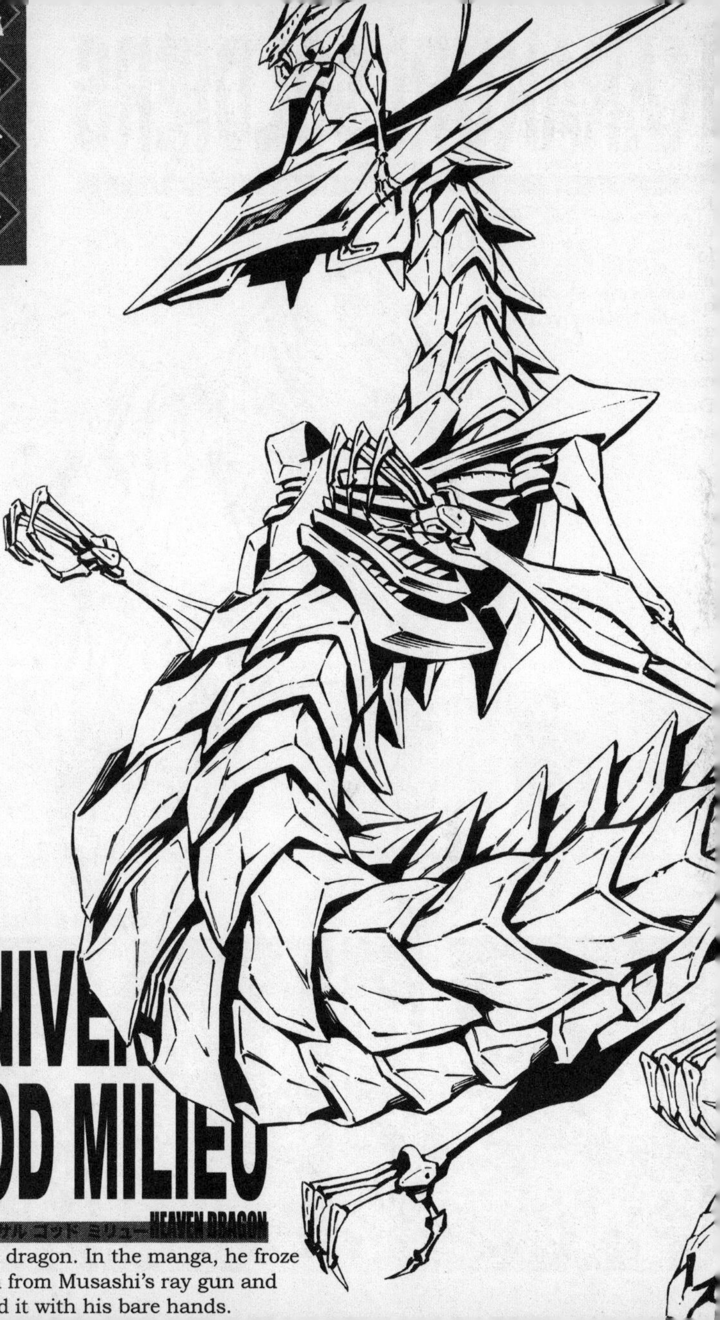

UNIVERSAL GOD MILIEU

ユニバーサル ゴッド ミリュー **HEAVEN DRAGON**

A giant dragon. In the manga, he froze a beam from Musashi's ray gun and grabbed it with his bare hands.

KARAKURI SOLDIERS

These automata defend Dunstan's castle, the One-Hundred Level Tower. There are female and male forms: Megata and Ogata, respectively.

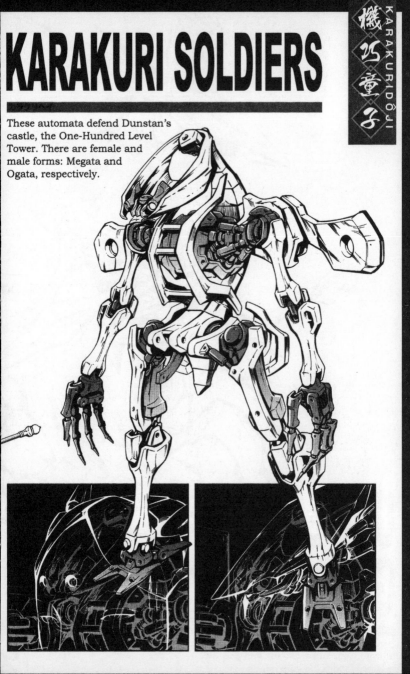

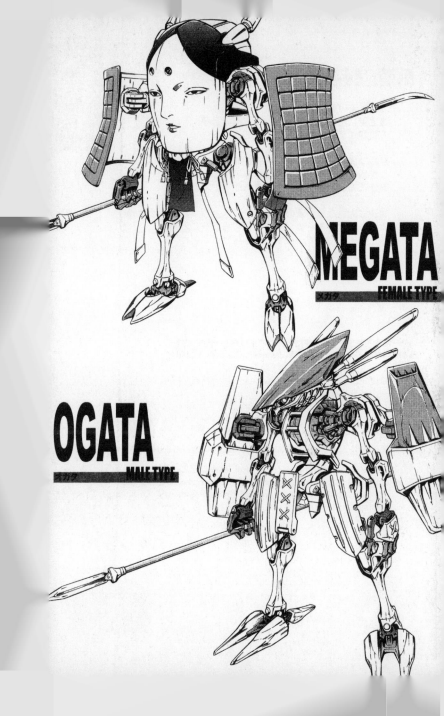

MEGATA
メガタ FEMALE TYPE

OGATA
オガタ MALE TYPE

機巧童子とは…その8

『善』と『悪』の螺旋の果てに
最上階にたどり着き融合した究極の童子、
それがイデオスウルティモである。

無垢な赤子が学習の中で汚れを知り、
しかし究極に至れば真っ白な無垢材が
磨きこまれた柱のような輝きを放ち出す。

螺旋は大いなる一周の果て、赤子へとつながってゆく。
大切なのはあきらめてそこに留まらないことだ。
最上階を目指して一段ずつ歩み続けることだ。

What is a KARAKURIDÔJI?　Part 8

The ultimate dôji fused atop the spiral of good and evil
—that is *Ideos Ultimo*.

What was once an innocent baby learned of the filth of this
world, yet its innocence still shines brightly atop that
ultimate point.

The spiral results in a great loop, one that both begins and
ends at birth. What is most important is to never let yourself
get stuck in a rut. Keep on moving, one floor at a time, until
you reach the top.

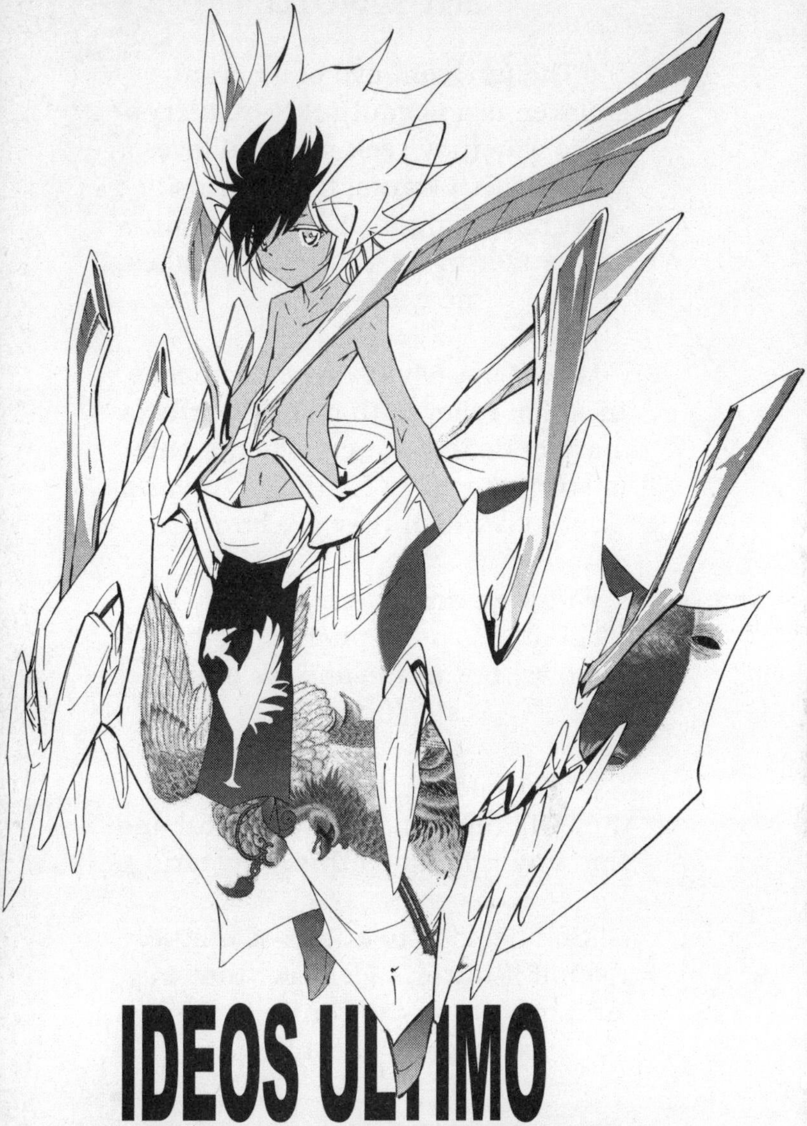

IDEOS ULTIMO

イデオス ウルティモ 究極超越善悪結・神童

This karakuri dôji form has a phoenix motif. The phoenix is a symbol of immortality and reincarnation. However, as a representation of the spiral of good and evil, it is also the answer to everything. There is no Icon form because at this level there is no more reason to fight.

Afterword

The innocent evil of ignorant children is so beautiful I could cry—the way they seek parental love, their selfish wants, their curiosity. Just imagining their lost innocence and suffering as adults also makes me want to cry.

I don't usually cry when someone dies (I'm relieved that their burdens have ended), but I cry when a baby is born. I'm sorry for the dirty world into which they are born.

But even adults are basically like children. Their sphere of activity grows, but in the end it's of little significance.

I suppose if they get strong, they will find anything beautiful and find any ridiculous thing endearing.

So I decided to cut loose a little. Even if it hurts, I feel freer that way, and my journey to continue getting stronger will continue.

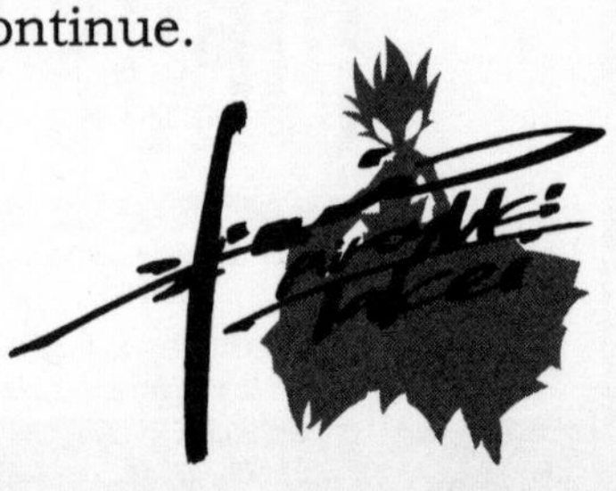

KARAKURIDÔJI
ULTIMO

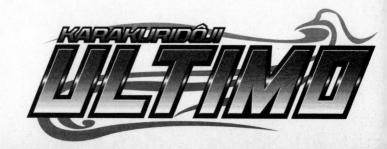

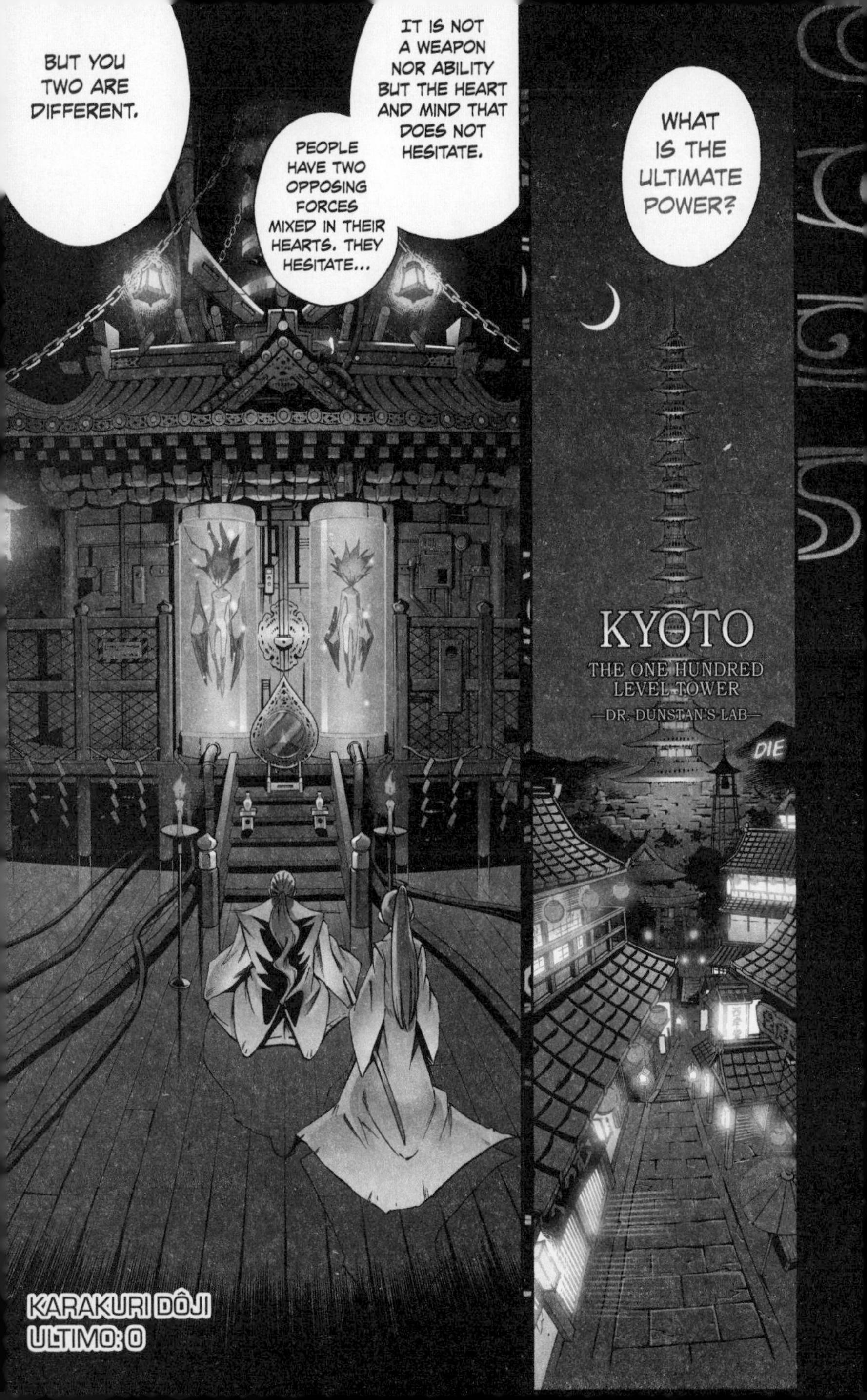
WHAT IS THE ULTIMATE POWER?
KYOTO
THE ONE HUNDRED LEVEL TOWER
—DR. DUNSTAN'S LAB—
DIE
IT IS NOT A WEAPON NOR ABILITY BUT THE HEART AND MIND THAT DOES NOT HESITATE.
PEOPLE HAVE TWO OPPOSING FORCES MIXED IN THEIR HEARTS. THEY HESITATE...
BUT YOU TWO ARE DIFFERENT.
KARAKURI DÔJI ULTIMO: 0

PERFECT GOOD...
MECHANICAL BOY ULTIMO
MECHANICAL BOY VICE
...AND PERFECT EVIL.

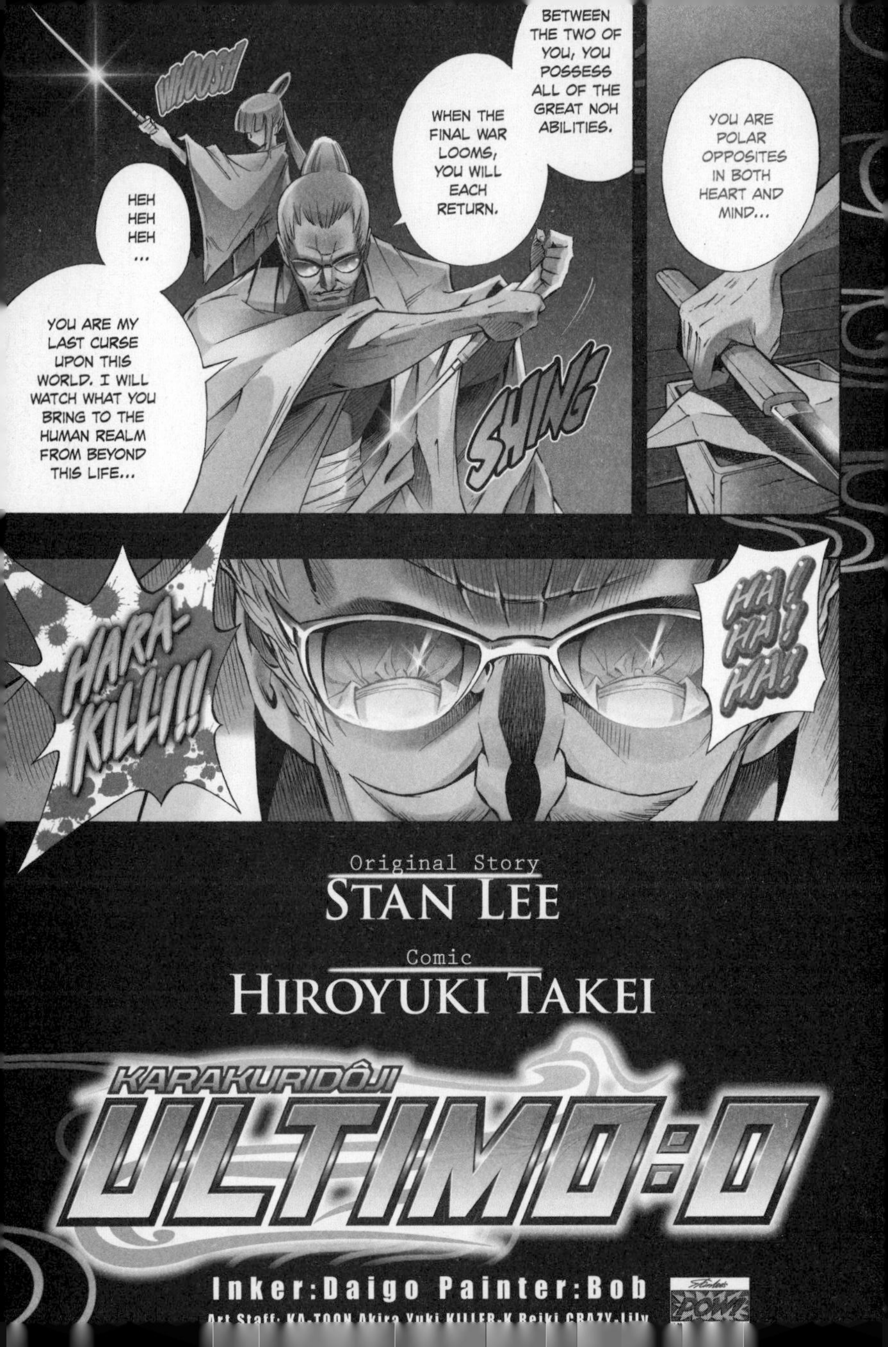
YOU ARE POLAR OPPOSITES IN BOTH HEART AND MIND...
BETWEEN THE TWO OF YOU, YOU POSSESS ALL OF THE GREAT NOH ABILITIES.
WHEN THE FINAL WAR LOOMS, YOU WILL EACH RETURN.
WHOOSH!!
HEH HEH HEH ...
YOU ARE MY LAST CURSE UPON THIS WORLD. I WILL WATCH WHAT YOU BRING TO THE HUMAN REALM FROM BEYOND THIS LIFE...
SHING
HA! HA! HA!
HARA-KILL!!!
Original Story
STAN LEE
Comic
HIROYUKI TAKEI
KARAKURIDÔJI
ULTIMO:0
Inker:Daigo Painter:Bob
Art Staff: KA-TOON Akira Yuki KILLER-K Reiki CRAZY-Lily

KARAKURIDÔJI
ULTIMO

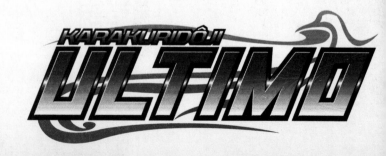

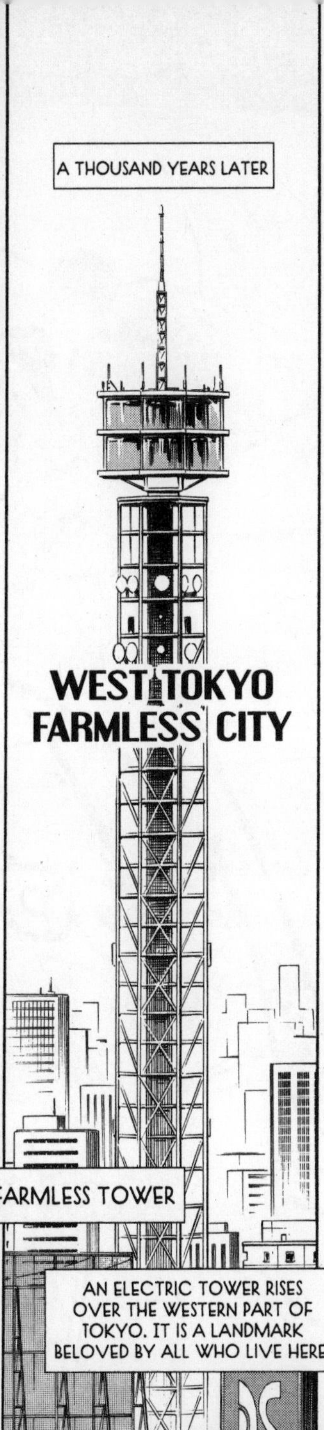
A THOUSAND YEARS LATER
WEST TOKYO FARMLESS CITY
FARMLESS TOWER
AN ELECTRIC TOWER RISES OVER THE WESTERN PART OF TOKYO. IT IS A LANDMARK BELOVED BY ALL WHO LIVE HERE.

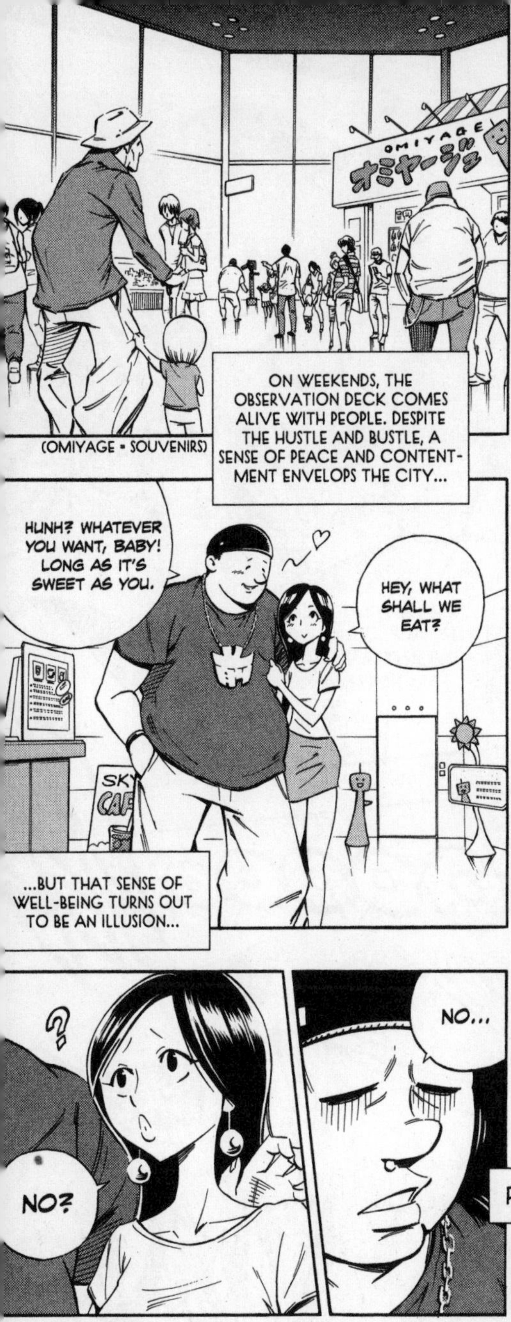
OMIYAGE
オミヤージュ
ON WEEKENDS, THE OBSERVATION DECK COMES ALIVE WITH PEOPLE. DESPITE THE HUSTLE AND BUSTLE, A SENSE OF PEACE AND CONTENT-MENT ENVELOPS THE CITY...
(OMIYAGE = SOUVENIRS)
HEY, WHAT SHALL WE EAT?
HUNH? WHATEVER YOU WANT, BABY! LONG AS IT'S SWEET AS YOU.
...BUT THAT SENSE OF WELL-BEING TURNS OUT TO BE AN ILLUSION...
NO...
NO?

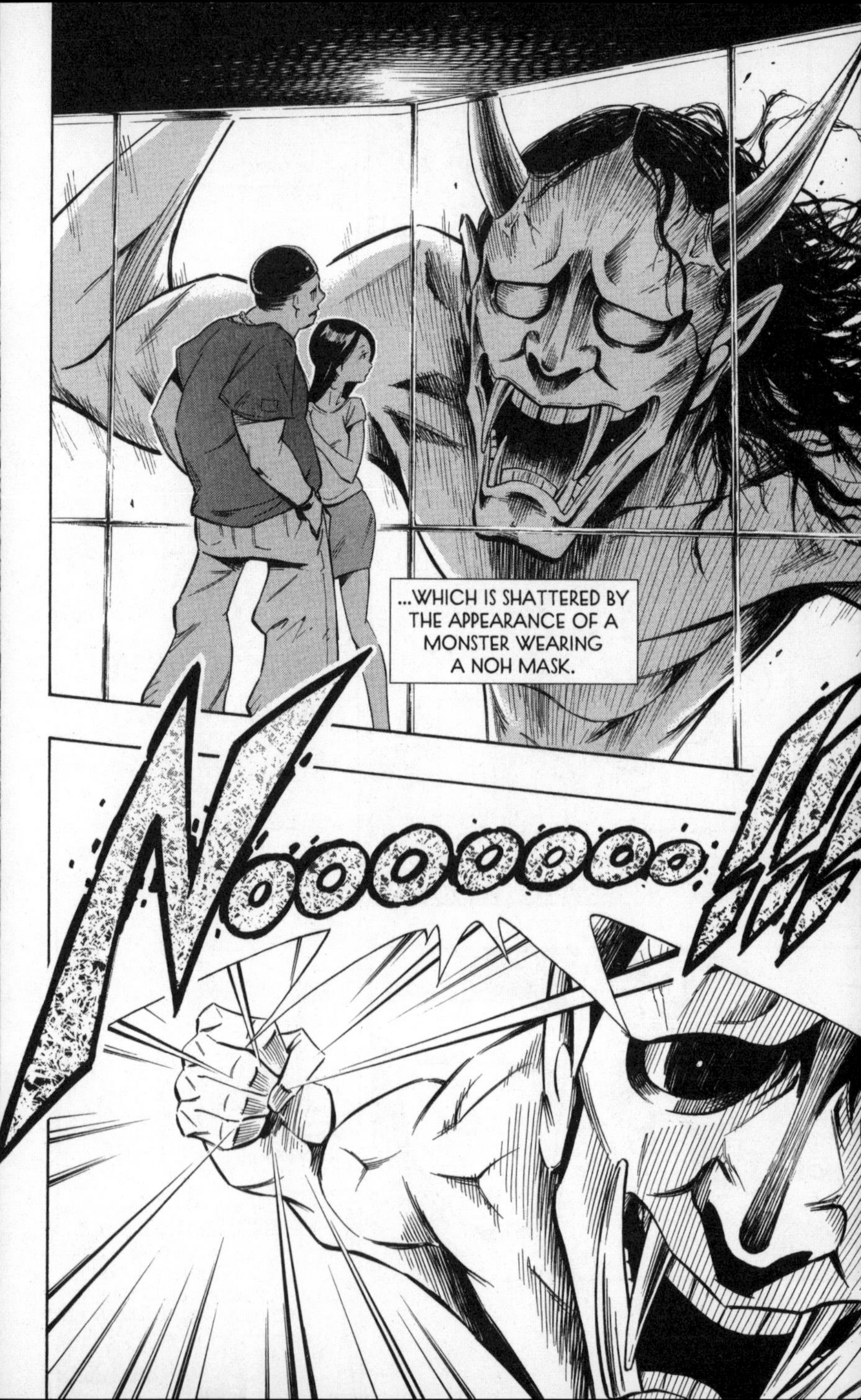
...WHICH IS SHATTERED BY THE APPEARANCE OF A MONSTER WEARING A NOH MASK.
NOOOOOOOO...!!

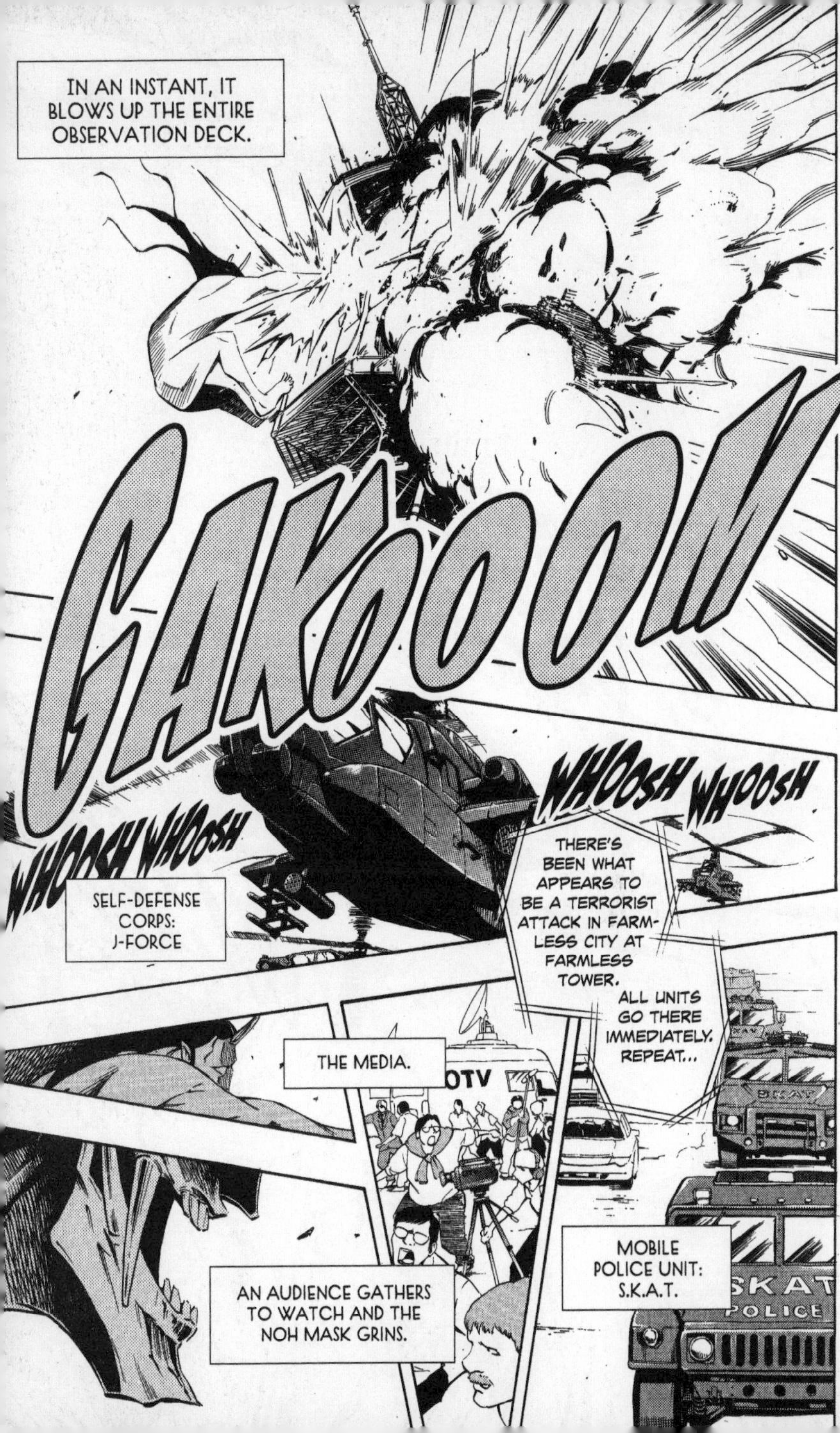
IN AN INSTANT, IT BLOWS UP THE ENTIRE OBSERVATION DECK.
GAKOOM
WHOOSH WHOOSH
THERE'S BEEN WHAT APPEARS TO BE A TERRORIST ATTACK IN FARM-LESS CITY AT FARMLESS TOWER.
WHOOSH WHOOSH
SELF-DEFENSE CORPS: J-FORCE
ALL UNITS GO THERE IMMEDIATELY. REPEAT...
SKAT
MOBILE POLICE UNIT: S.K.A.T.
SKAT
POLICE
THE MEDIA.
OTV
AN AUDIENCE GATHERS TO WATCH AND THE NOH MASK GRINS.

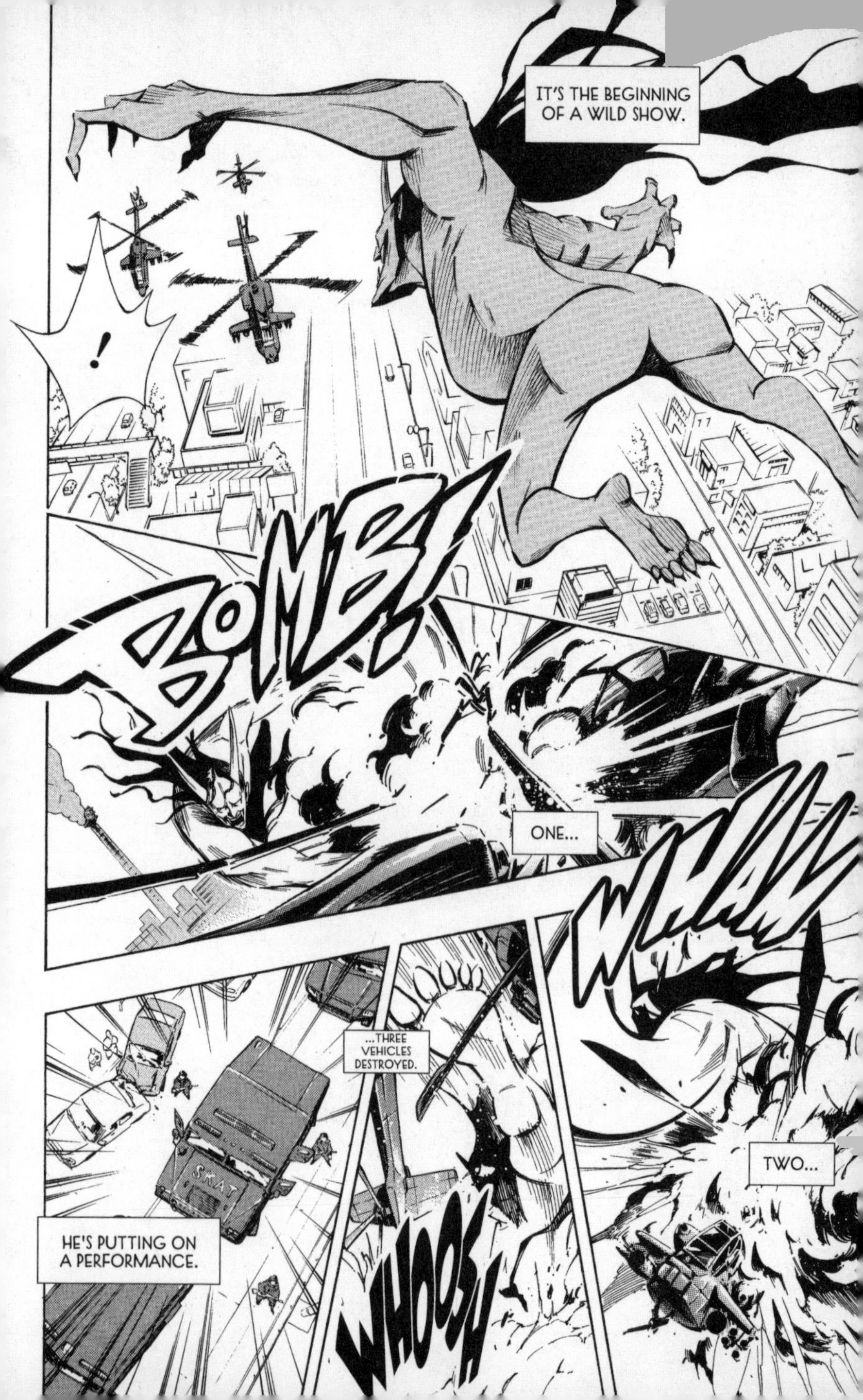
IT'S THE BEGINNING OF A WILD SHOW.
!
BOMB
ONE...
WHAM
TWO...
...THREE VEHICLES DESTROYED.
WHOOSH
HE'S PUTTING ON A PERFORMANCE.

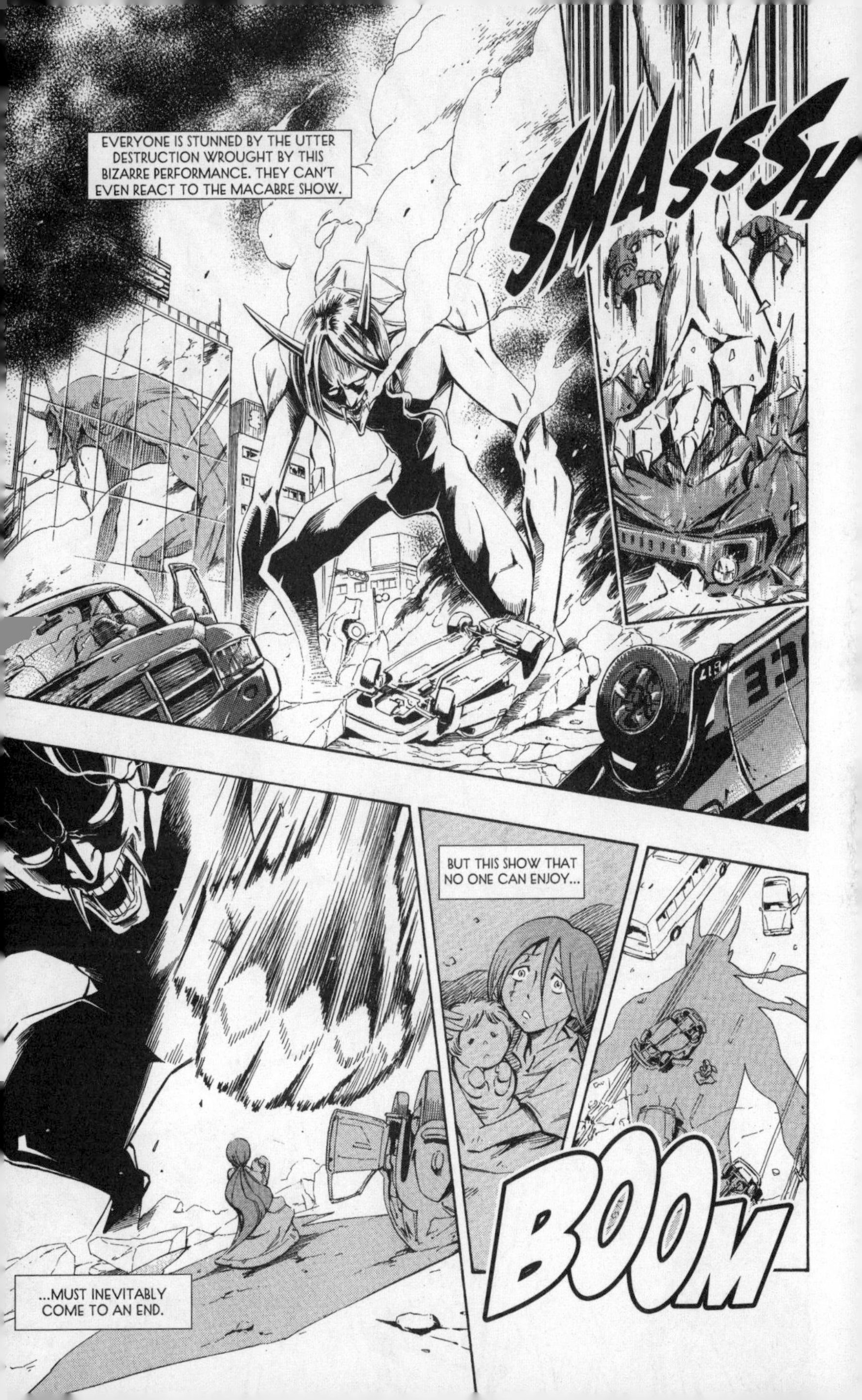
SMASSSH
EVERYONE IS STUNNED BY THE UTTER DESTRUCTION WROUGHT BY THIS BIZARRE PERFORMANCE. THEY CAN'T EVEN REACT TO THE MACABRE SHOW.
BOOM
BUT THIS SHOW THAT NO ONE CAN ENJOY...
...MUST INEVITABLY COME TO AN END.

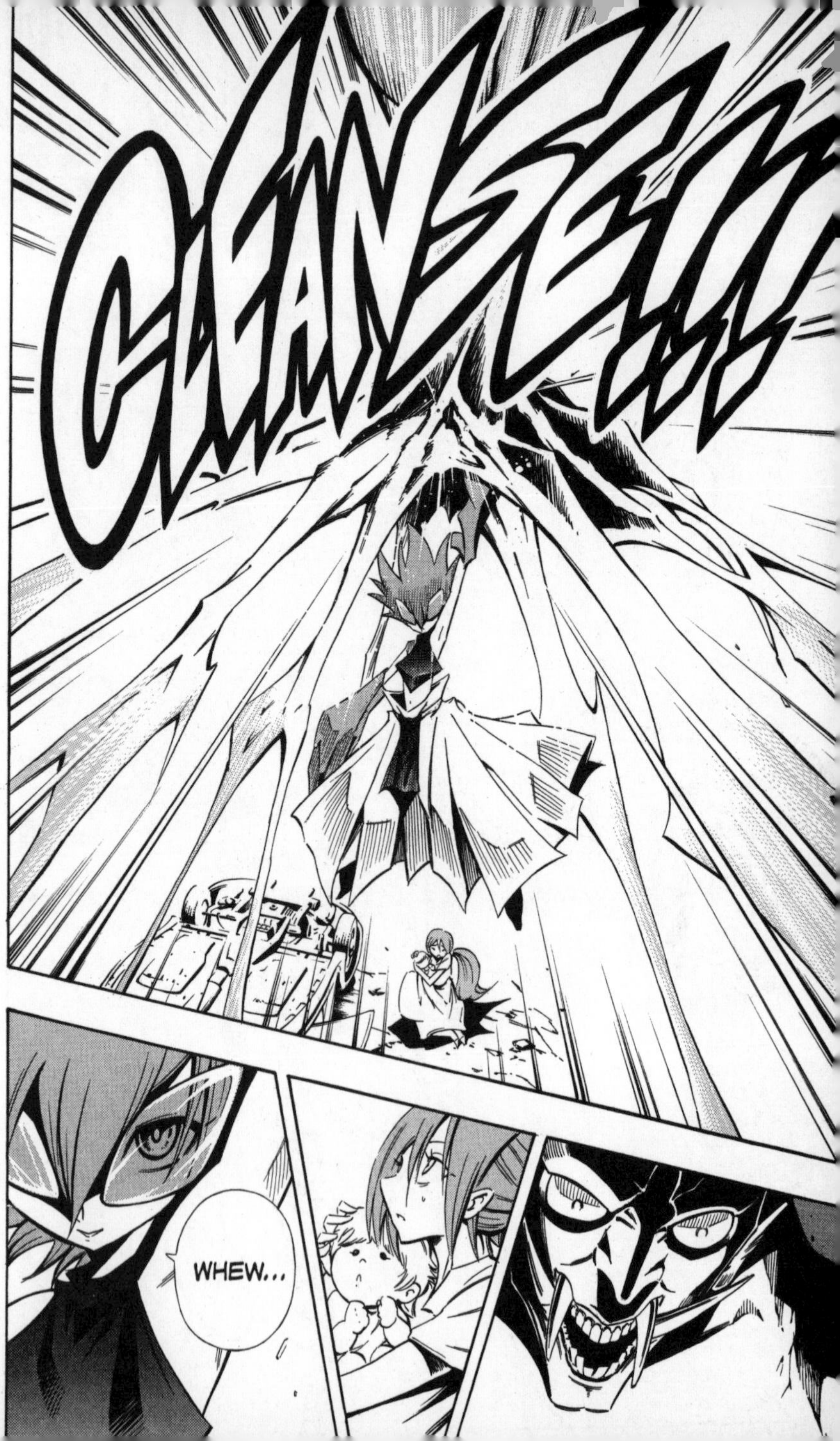
WHEW...

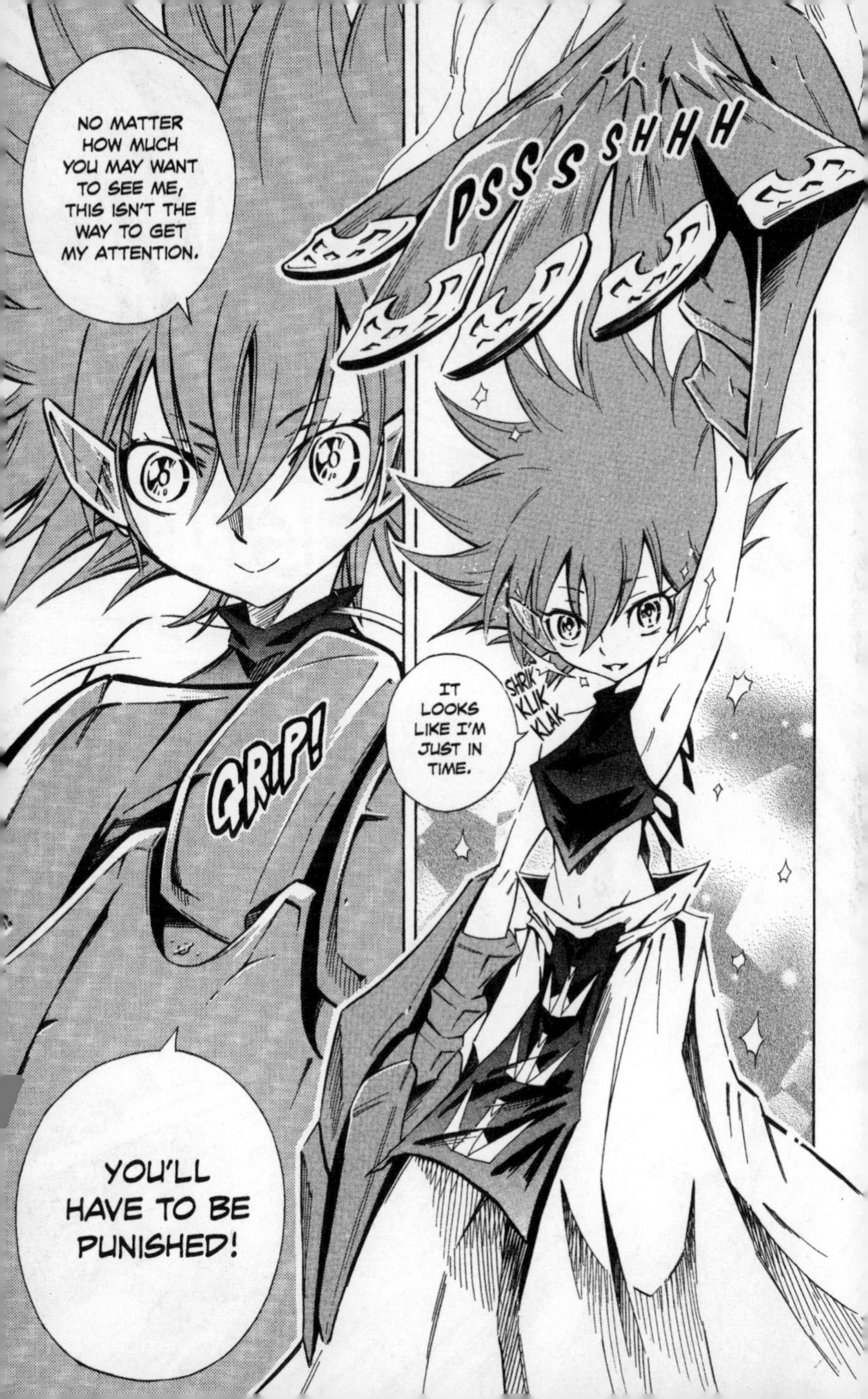
PSSSSHHH
NO MATTER HOW MUCH YOU MAY WANT TO SEE ME, THIS ISN'T THE WAY TO GET MY ATTENTION.
SHRIK KLIK KLAK
IT LOOKS LIKE I'M JUST IN TIME.
GRIP!
YOU'LL HAVE TO BE PUNISHED!

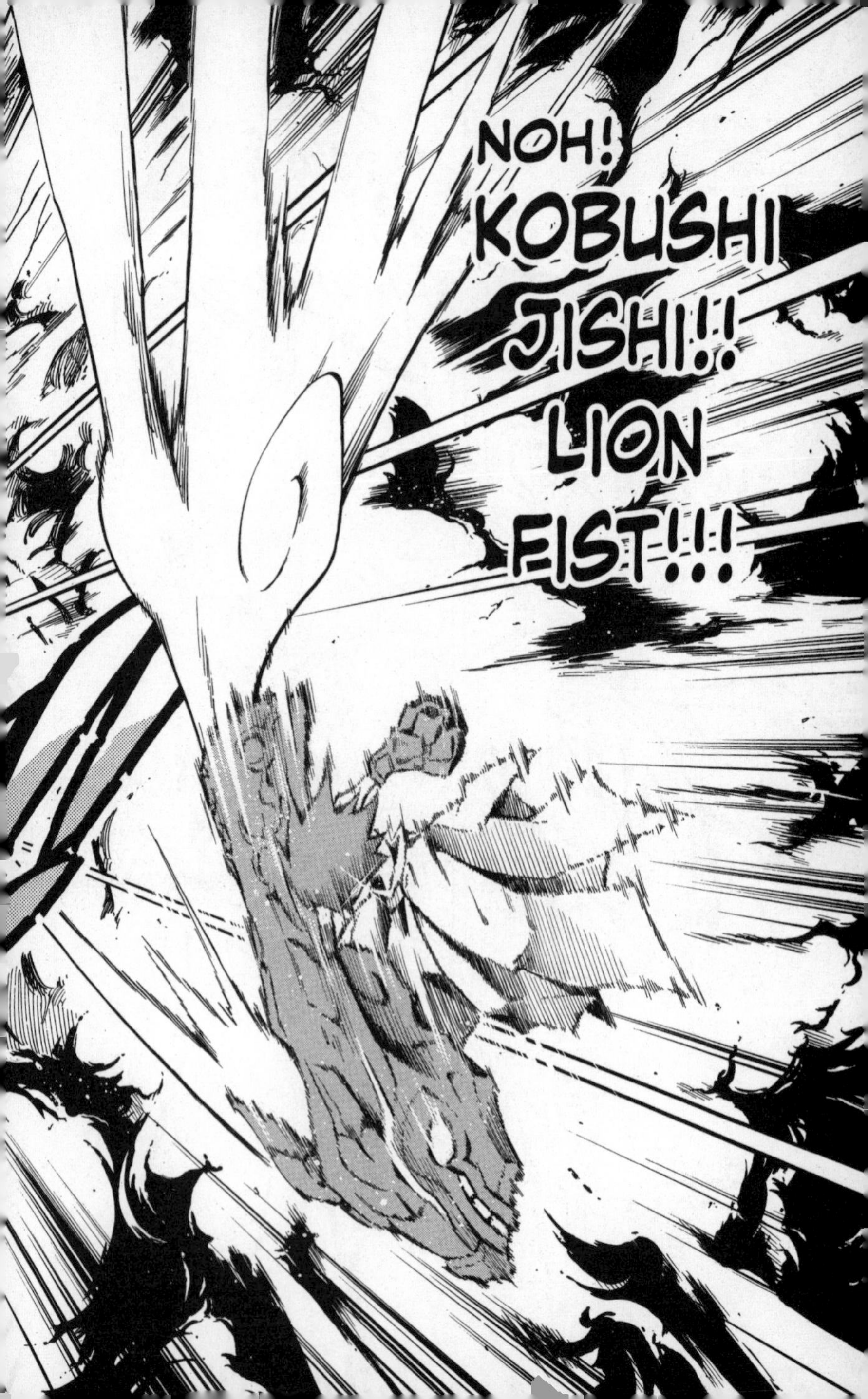
NOH! KOBUSHI JISHI!!! LION FIST!!!

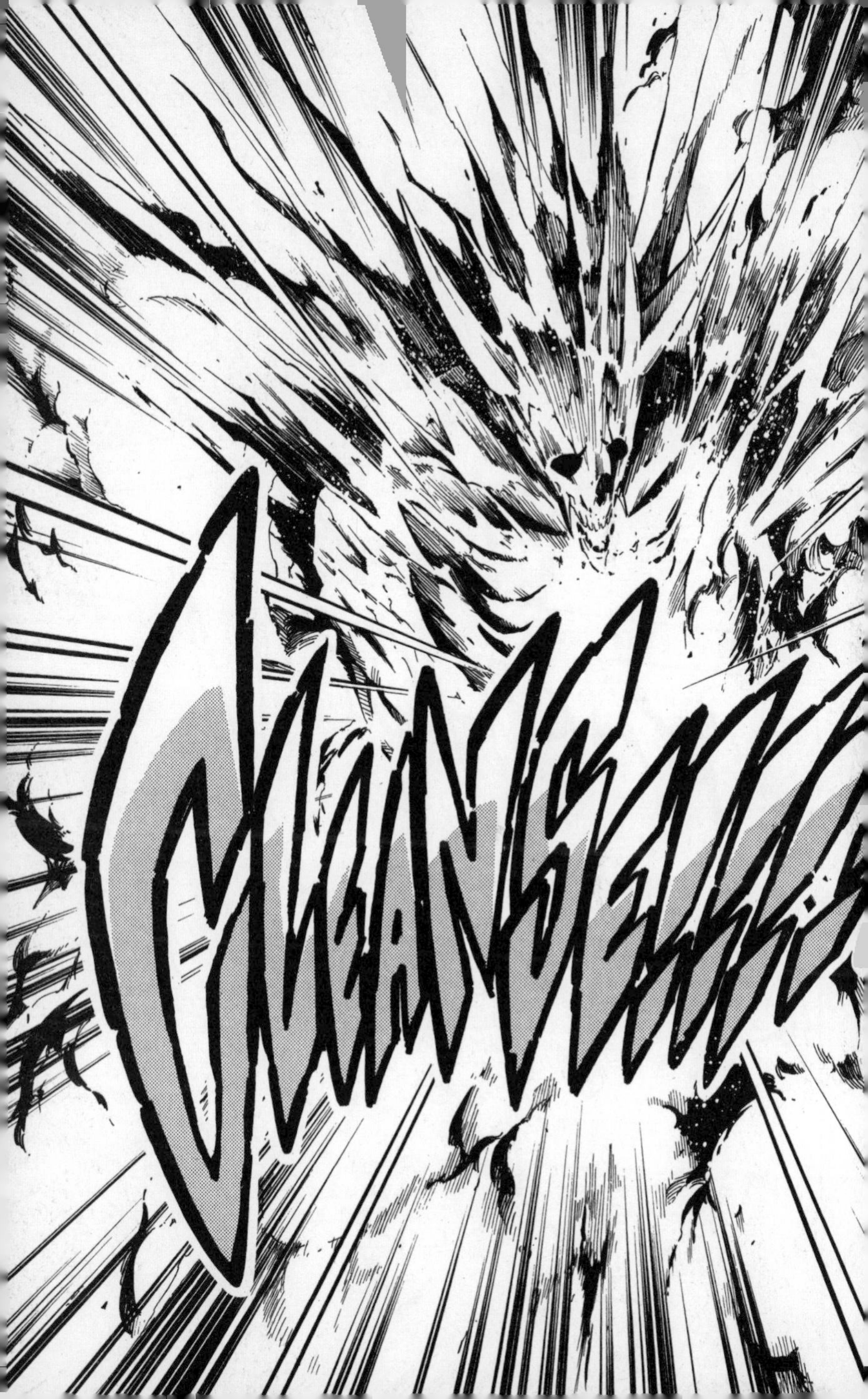

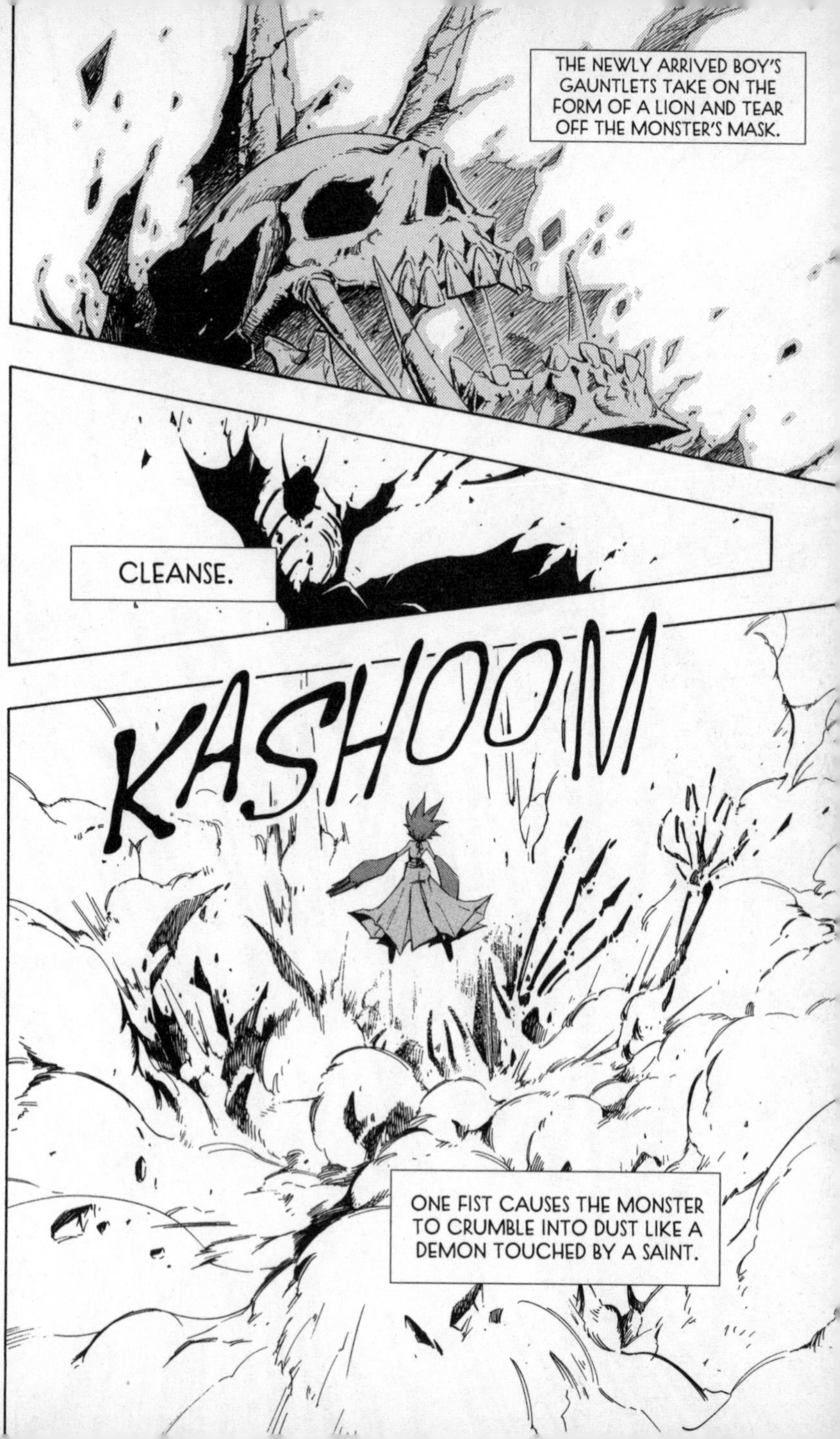
THE NEWLY ARRIVED BOY'S GAUNTLETS TAKE ON THE FORM OF A LION AND TEAR OFF THE MONSTER'S MASK.
CLEANSE.
KASHOOM
ONE FIST CAUSES THE MONSTER TO CRUMBLE INTO DUST LIKE A DEMON TOUCHED BY A SAINT.

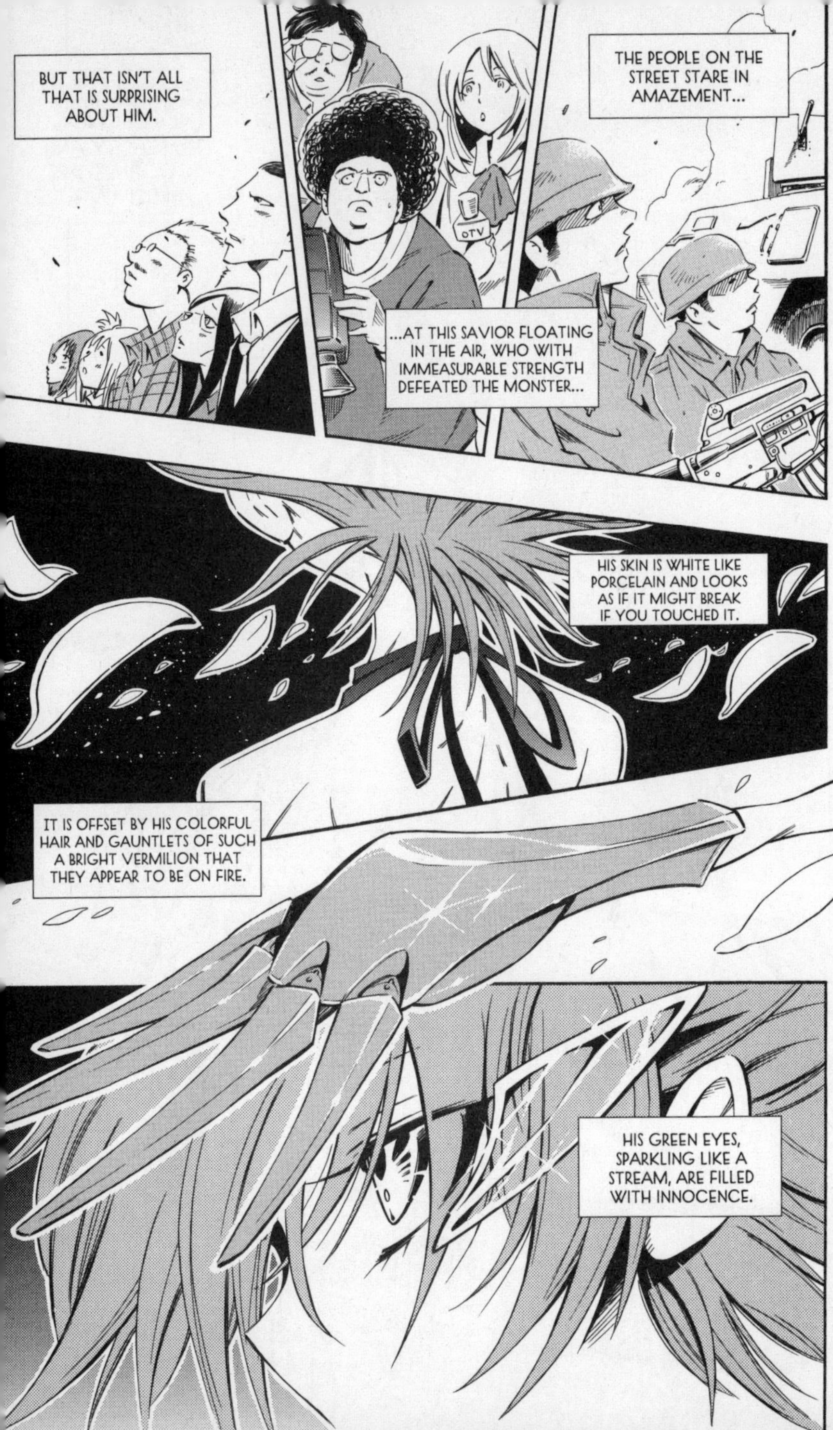
THE PEOPLE ON THE STREET STARE IN AMAZEMENT...
...AT THIS SAVIOR FLOATING IN THE AIR, WHO WITH IMMEASURABLE STRENGTH DEFEATED THE MONSTER...
BUT THAT ISN'T ALL THAT IS SURPRISING ABOUT HIM.
HIS SKIN IS WHITE LIKE PORCELAIN AND LOOKS AS IF IT MIGHT BREAK IF YOU TOUCHED IT.
IT IS OFFSET BY HIS COLORFUL HAIR AND GAUNTLETS OF SUCH A BRIGHT VERMILION THAT THEY APPEAR TO BE ON FIRE.
HIS GREEN EYES, SPARKLING LIKE A STREAM, ARE FILLED WITH INNOCENCE.

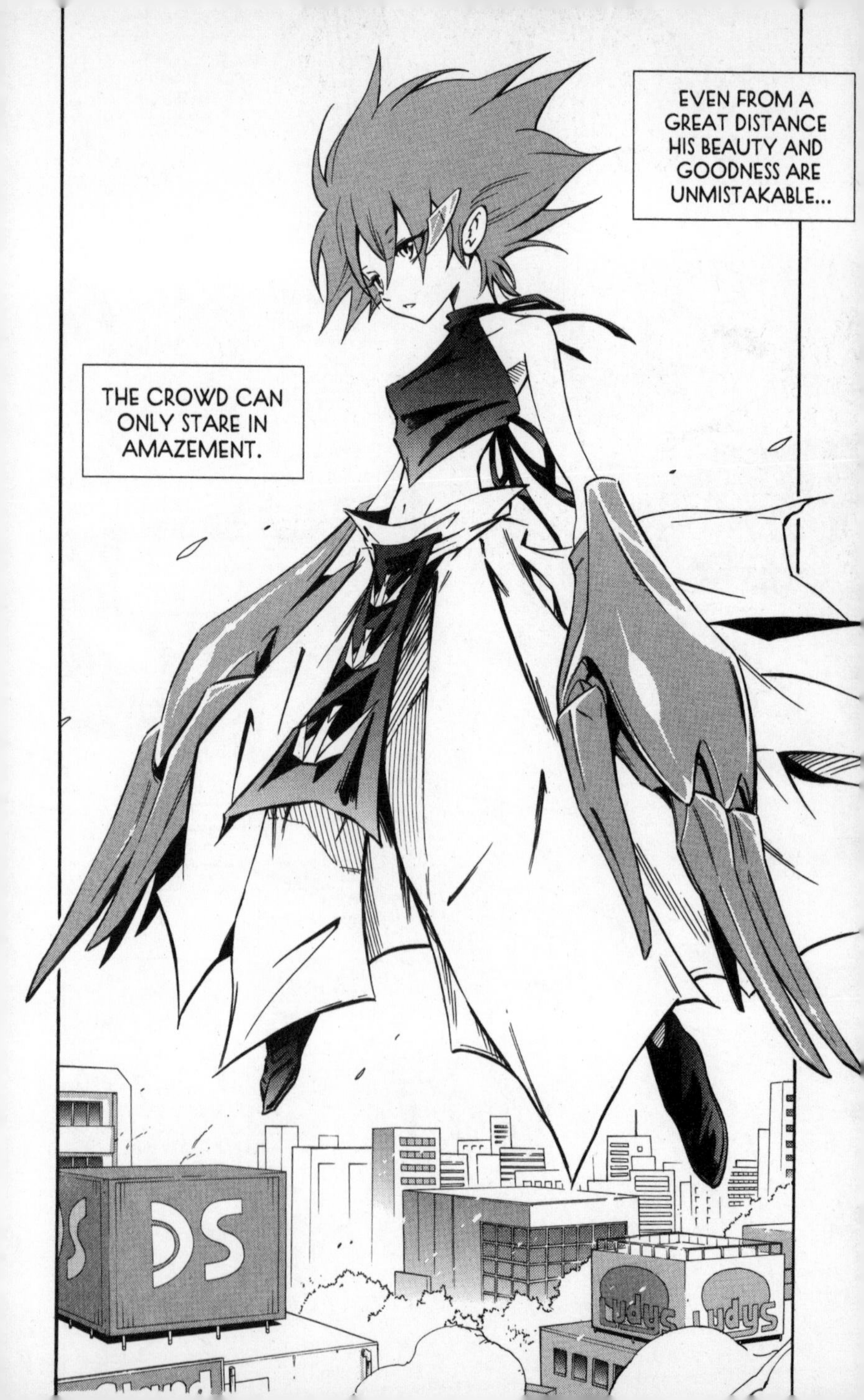
EVEN FROM A GREAT DISTANCE HIS BEAUTY AND GOODNESS ARE UNMISTAKABLE...
THE CROWD CAN ONLY STARE IN AMAZEMENT.

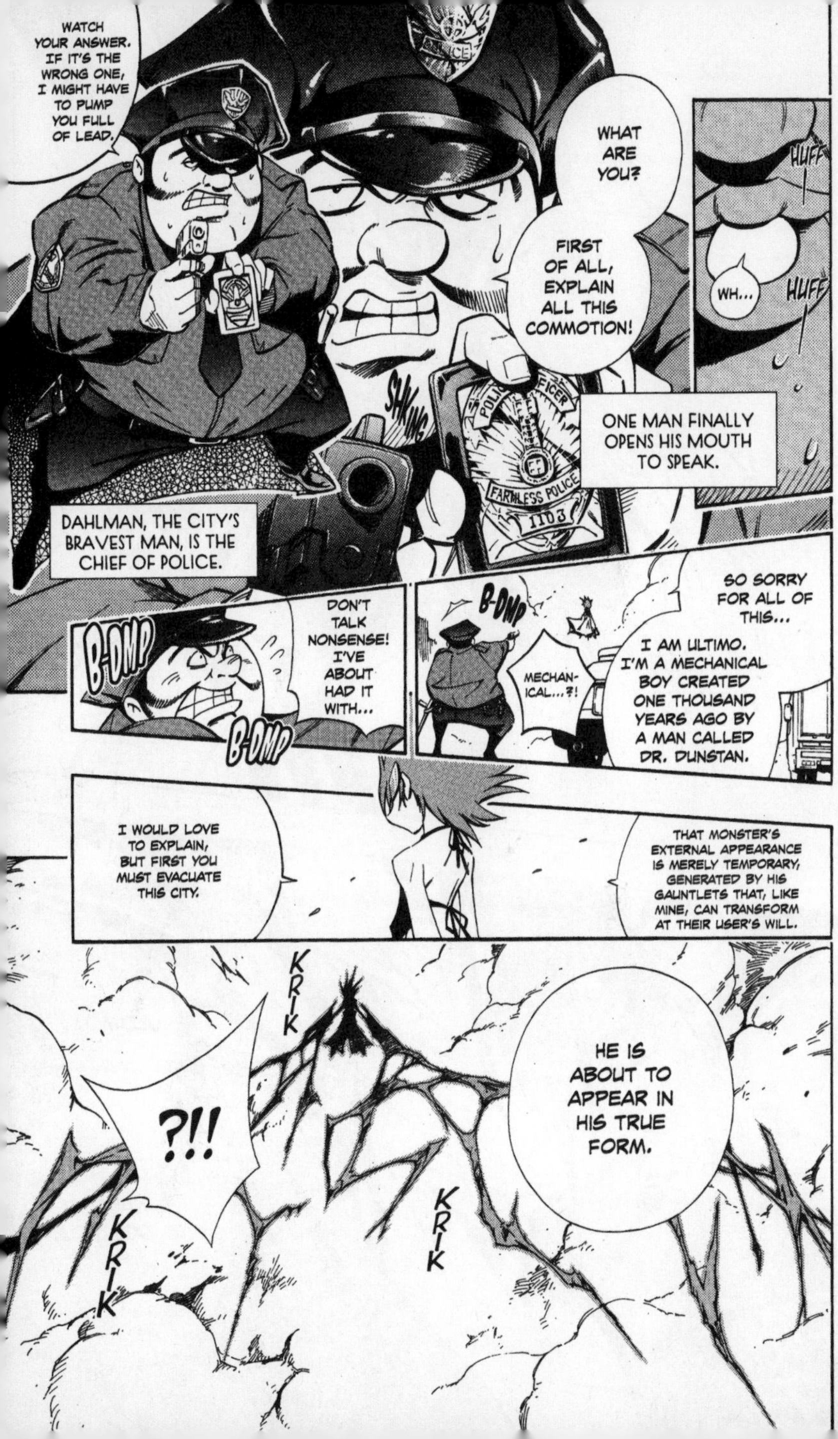
HUFF
WH...
HUFF
WHAT ARE YOU?
FIRST OF ALL, EXPLAIN ALL THIS COMMOTION!
ONE MAN FINALLY OPENS HIS MOUTH TO SPEAK.
WATCH YOUR ANSWER. IF IT'S THE WRONG ONE, I MIGHT HAVE TO PUMP YOU FULL OF LEAD.
SHKING
DAHLMAN, THE CITY'S BRAVEST MAN, IS THE CHIEF OF POLICE.
SO SORRY FOR ALL OF THIS...
I AM ULTIMO. I'M A MECHANICAL BOY CREATED ONE THOUSAND YEARS AGO BY A MAN CALLED DR. DUNSTAN.
B-DMP
MECHANICAL...?!
DON'T TALK NONSENSE! I'VE ABOUT HAD IT WITH...
B-DMP
B-DMP
THAT MONSTER'S EXTERNAL APPEARANCE IS MERELY TEMPORARY, GENERATED BY HIS GAUNTLETS THAT, LIKE MINE, CAN TRANSFORM AT THEIR USER'S WILL.
I WOULD LOVE TO EXPLAIN, BUT FIRST YOU MUST EVACUATE THIS CITY.
HE IS ABOUT TO APPEAR IN HIS TRUE FORM.
KRIK
KRIK
?!!
KRIK

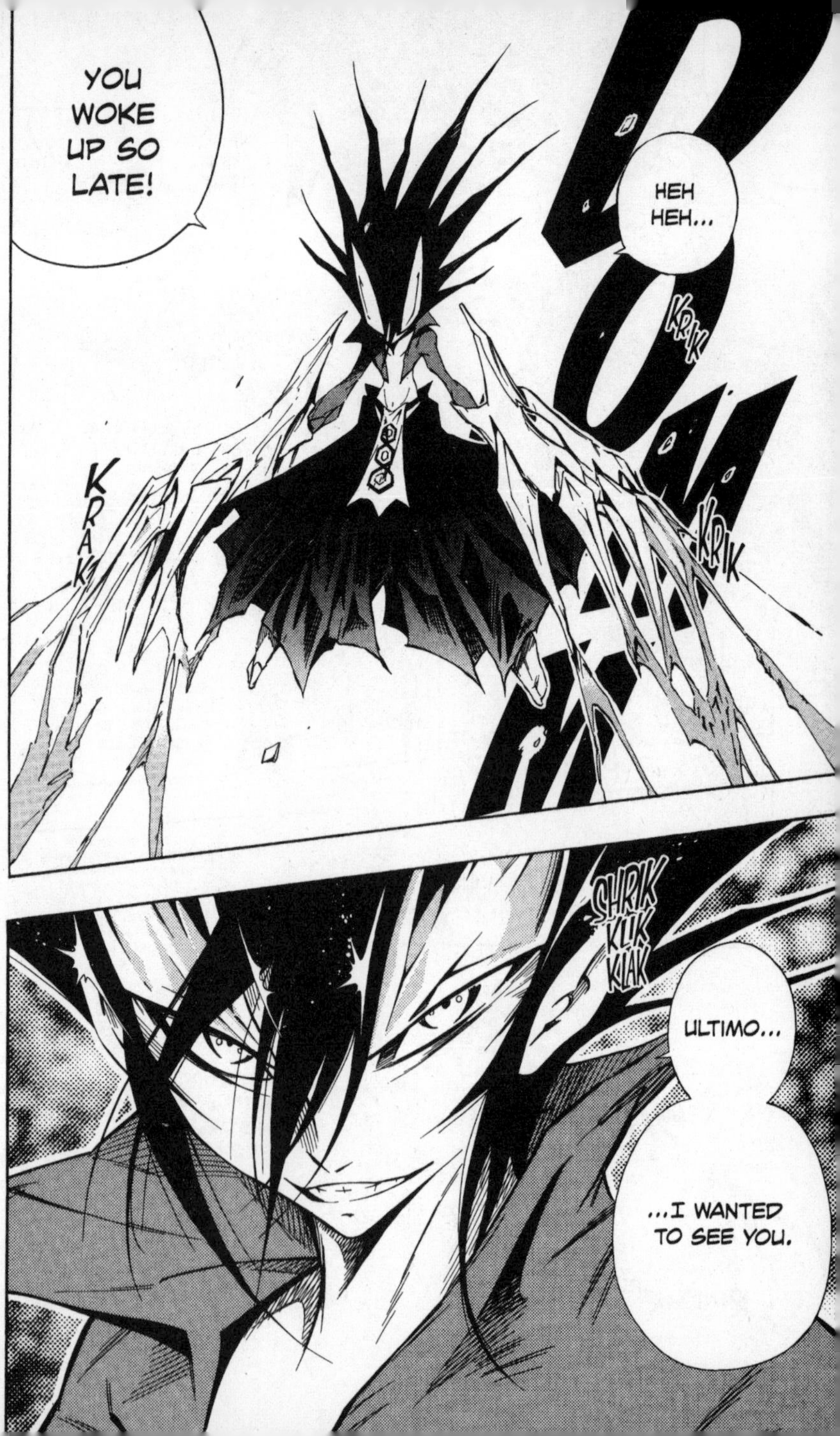
HEH HEH...
YOU WOKE UP SO LATE!
KRIK
KRIK
KRAK
SHRIK KLIK KLAK
ULTIMO...
...I WANTED TO SEE YOU.

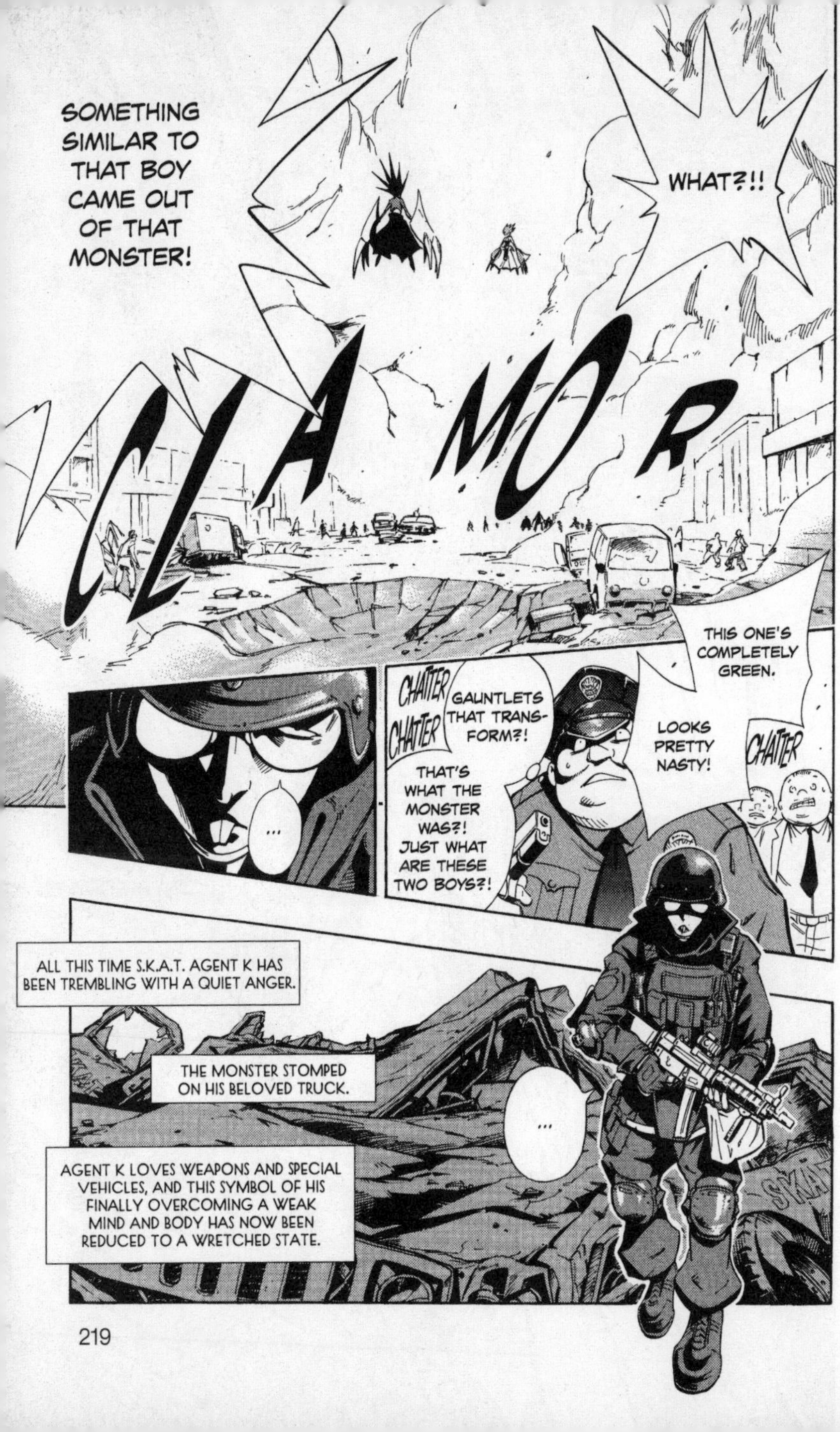
WHAT?!!
SOMETHING SIMILAR TO THAT BOY CAME OUT OF THAT MONSTER!
CLAMOR
THIS ONE'S COMPLETELY GREEN.
CHATTER
LOOKS PRETTY NASTY!
GAUNTLETS THAT TRANSFORM?!
CHATTER CHATTER
THAT'S WHAT THE MONSTER WAS?! JUST WHAT ARE THESE TWO BOYS?!
...
ALL THIS TIME S.K.A.T. AGENT K HAS BEEN TREMBLING WITH A QUIET ANGER.
...
THE MONSTER STOMPED ON HIS BELOVED TRUCK.
AGENT K LOVES WEAPONS AND SPECIAL VEHICLES, AND THIS SYMBOL OF HIS FINALLY OVERCOMING A WEAK MIND AND BODY HAS NOW BEEN REDUCED TO A WRETCHED STATE.

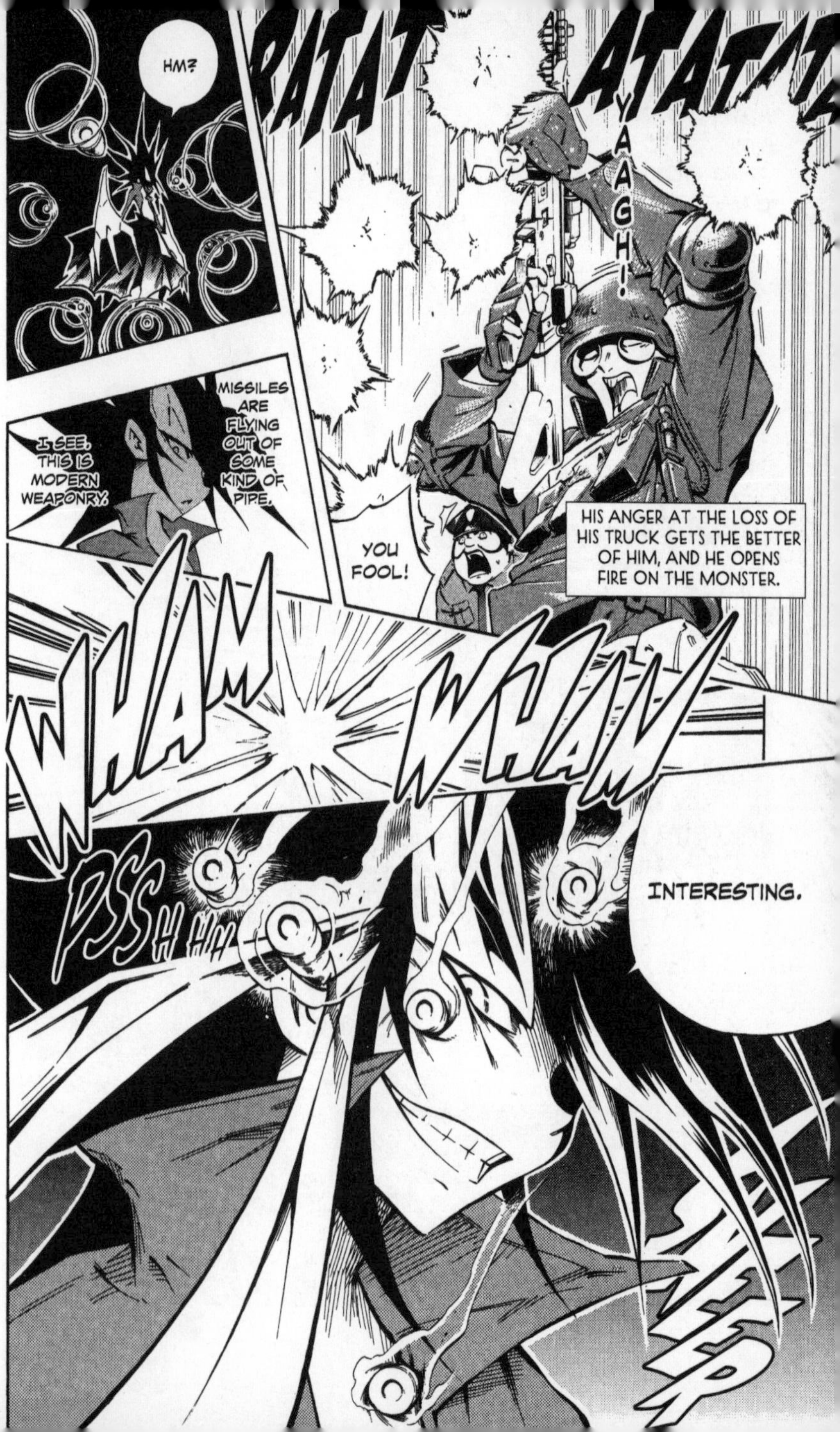
RATAT ATATAT
YAAGH!
HIS ANGER AT THE LOSS OF HIS TRUCK GETS THE BETTER OF HIM, AND HE OPENS FIRE ON THE MONSTER.
YOU FOOL!
HM?
MISSILES ARE FLYING OUT OF SOME KIND OF PIPE.
I SEE. THIS IS MODERN WEAPONRY.
WHAM
WHAM
INTERESTING.
PSSHHH

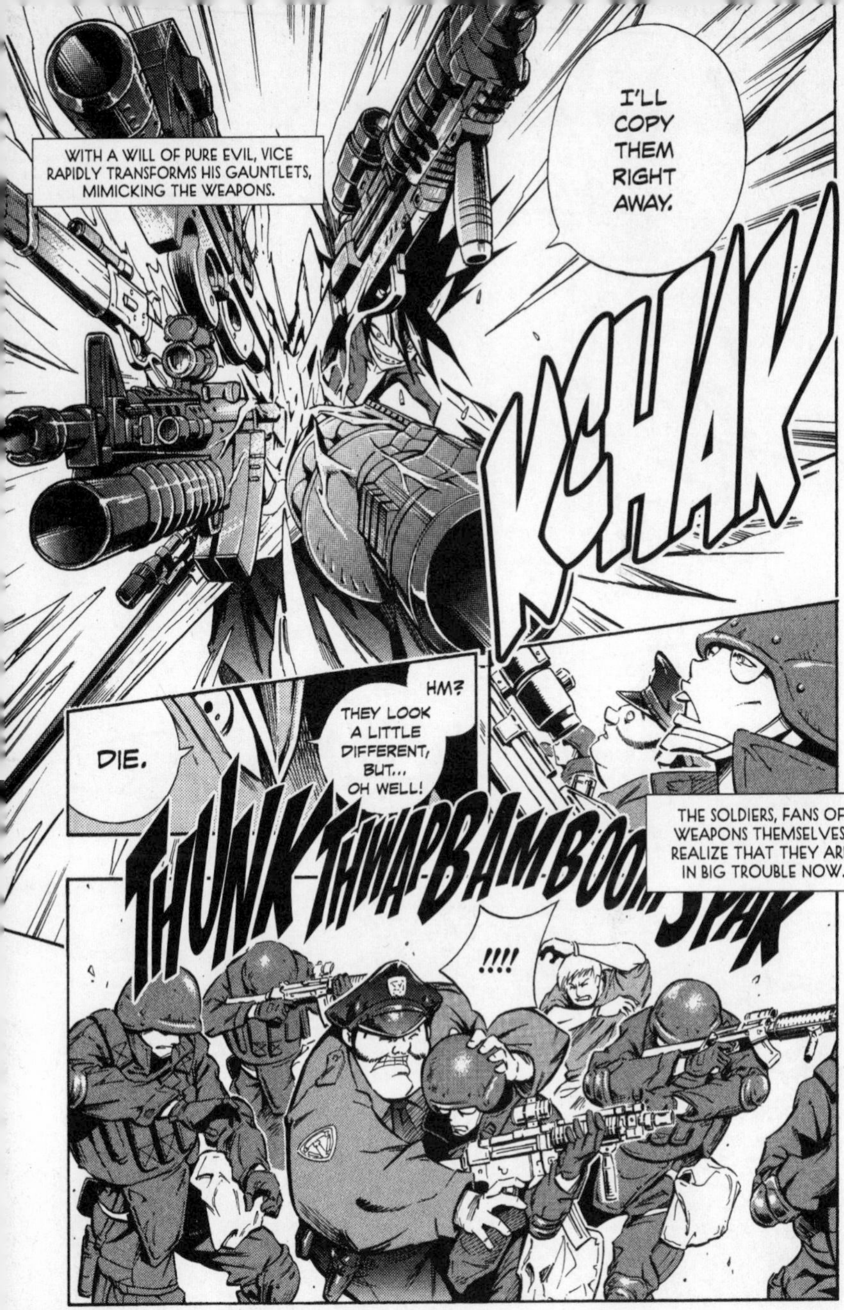
I'LL COPY THEM RIGHT AWAY.
WITH A WILL OF PURE EVIL, VICE RAPIDLY TRANSFORMS HIS GAUNTLETS, MIMICKING THE WEAPONS.
KCHAK
THE SOLDIERS, FANS OF WEAPONS THEMSELVES, REALIZE THAT THEY ARE IN BIG TROUBLE NOW.
HM? THEY LOOK A LITTLE DIFFERENT, BUT... OH WELL!
DIE.
THUNK THWAP BAM BOOM SPAK
!!!!

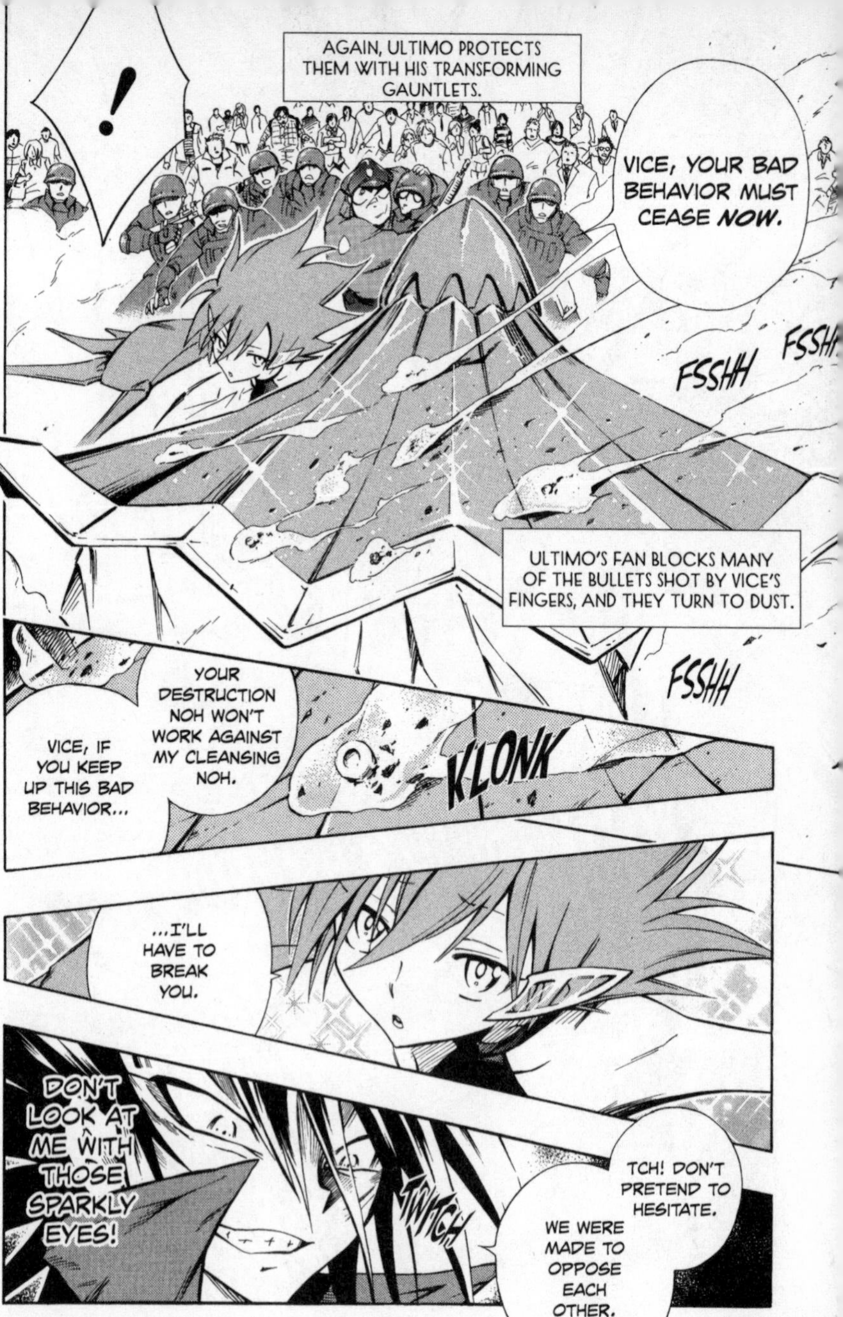
AGAIN, ULTIMO PROTECTS THEM WITH HIS TRANSFORMING GAUNTLETS.
VICE, YOUR BAD BEHAVIOR MUST CEASE *NOW.*
!
FSSHH
FSSHH
ULTIMO'S FAN BLOCKS MANY OF THE BULLETS SHOT BY VICE'S FINGERS, AND THEY TURN TO DUST.
FSSHH
KLONK
YOUR DESTRUCTION NOH WON'T WORK AGAINST MY CLEANSING NOH.
VICE, IF YOU KEEP UP THIS BAD BEHAVIOR...
...I'LL HAVE TO BREAK YOU.
TCH! DON'T PRETEND TO HESITATE.
WE WERE MADE TO OPPOSE EACH OTHER.
TWITCH
DON'T LOOK AT ME WITH THOSE SPARKLY EYES!

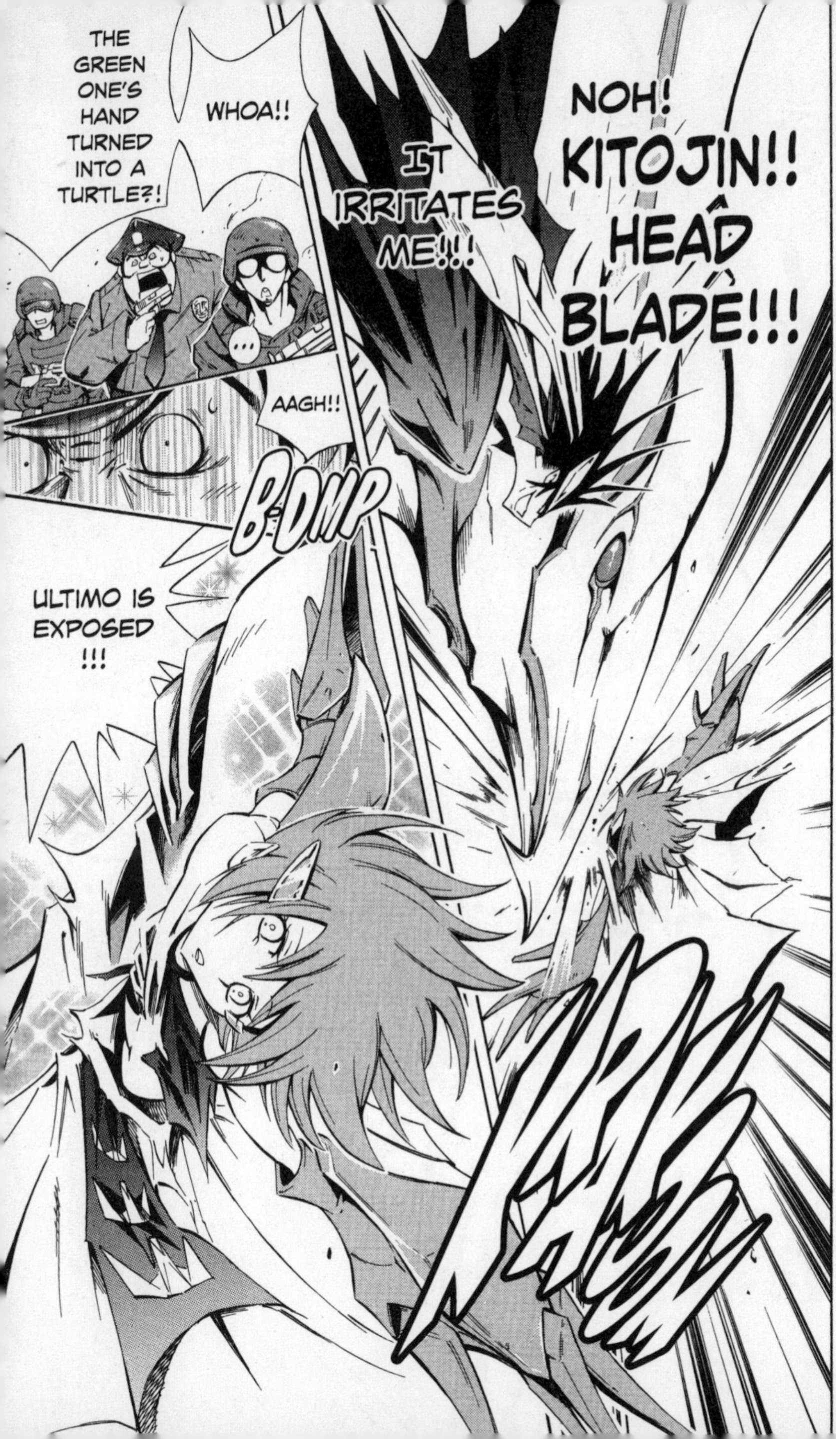
NOH! KITOJIN!! HEAD BLADE!!!
IT IRRITATES ME!!!
WHOA!!
THE GREEN ONE'S HAND TURNED INTO A TURTLE?!
...
AAGH!!
B-DMP
ULTIMO IS EXPOSED!!!

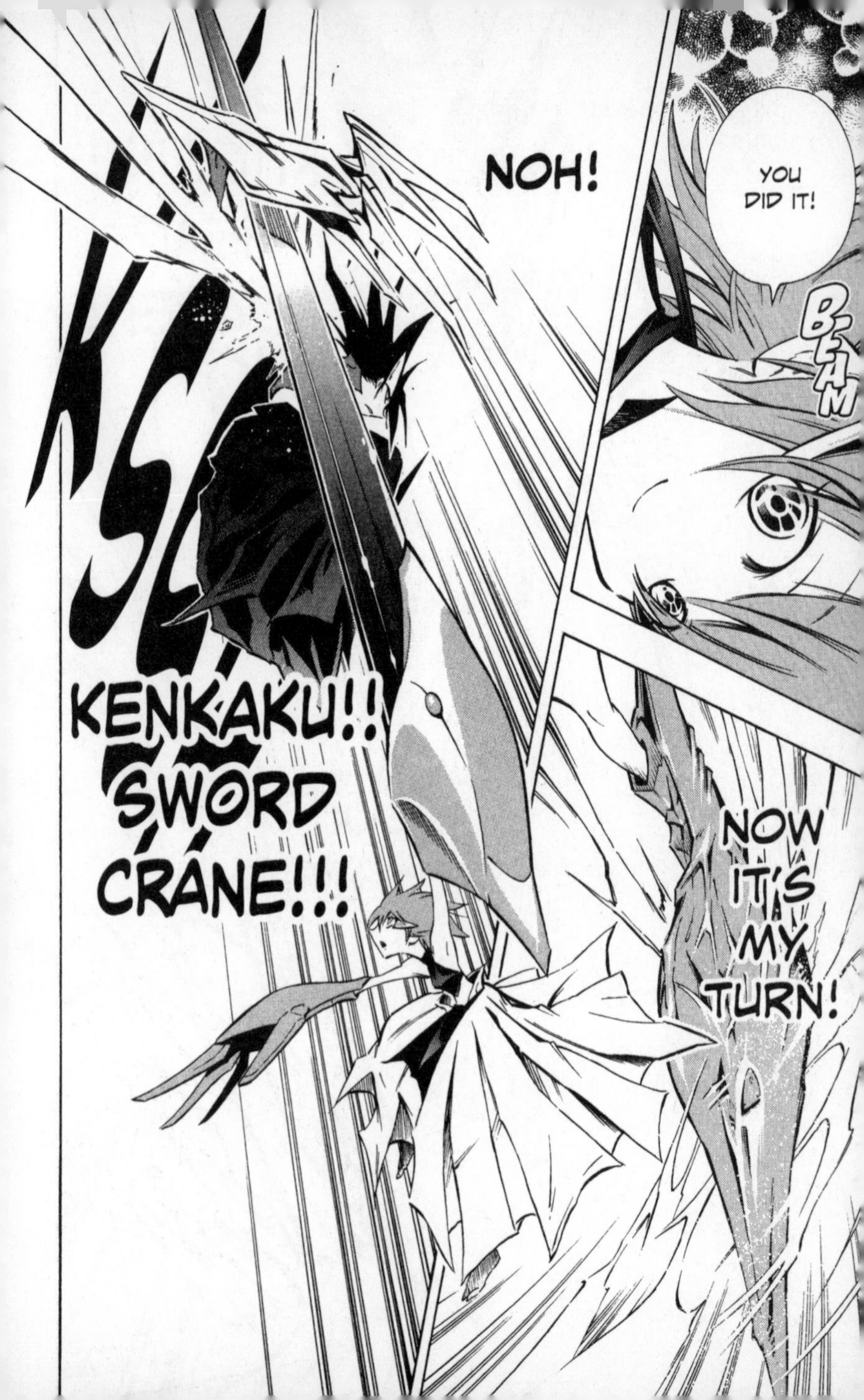
YOU DID IT!
BEAM
NOW IT'S MY TURN!
NOH!
KENKAKU!! SWORD CRANE!!!

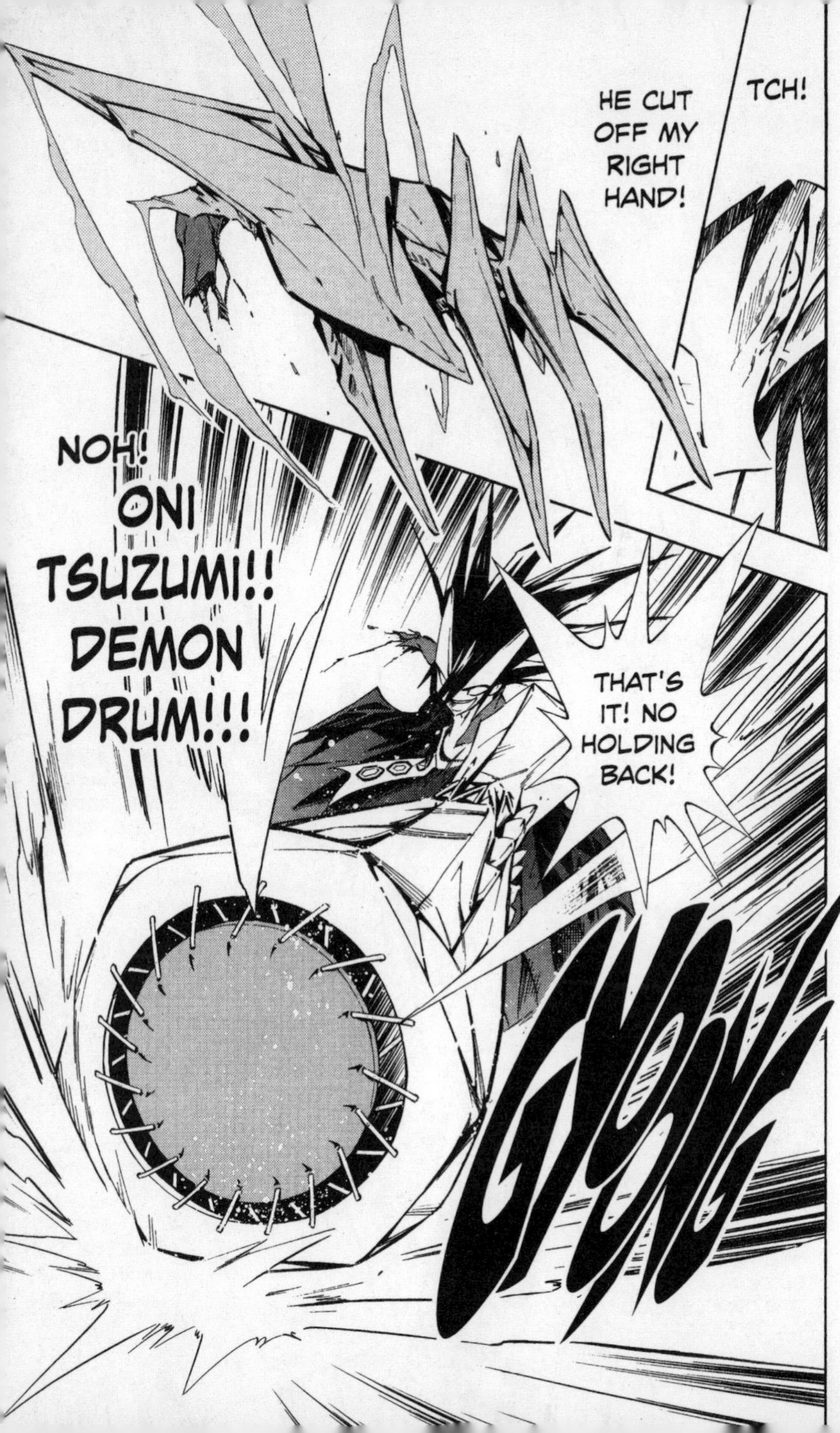
TCH!
HE CUT OFF MY RIGHT HAND!
THAT'S IT! NO HOLDING BACK!
NOH! ONI TSUZUMI!! DEMON DRUM!!!

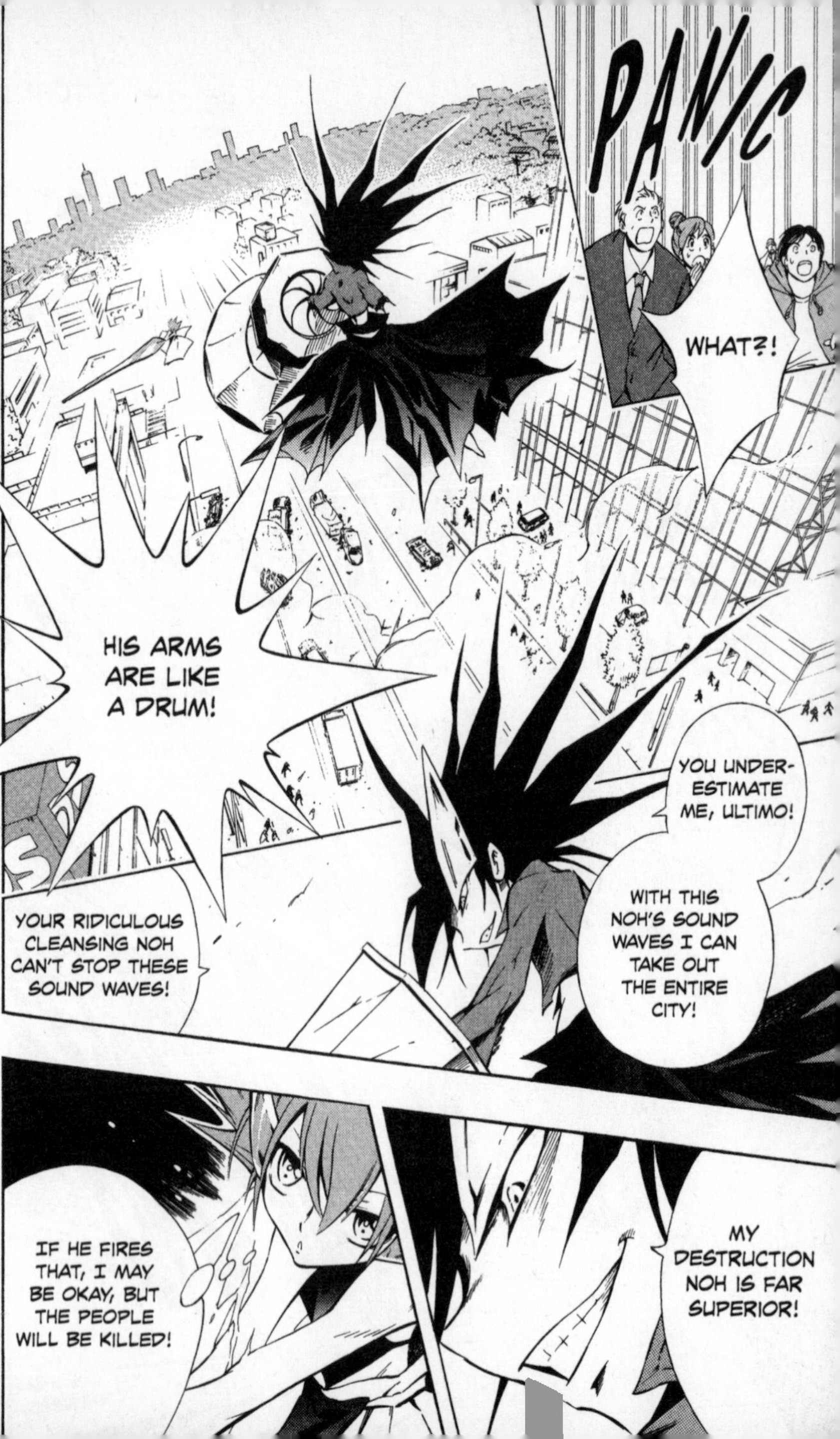
PANIC
WHAT?!
HIS ARMS ARE LIKE A DRUM!
YOU UNDER-ESTIMATE ME, ULTIMO!
WITH THIS NOH'S SOUND WAVES I CAN TAKE OUT THE ENTIRE CITY!
YOUR RIDICULOUS CLEANSING NOH CAN'T STOP THESE SOUND WAVES!
MY DESTRUCTION NOH IS FAR SUPERIOR!
IF HE FIRES THAT, I MAY BE OKAY, BUT THE PEOPLE WILL BE KILLED!

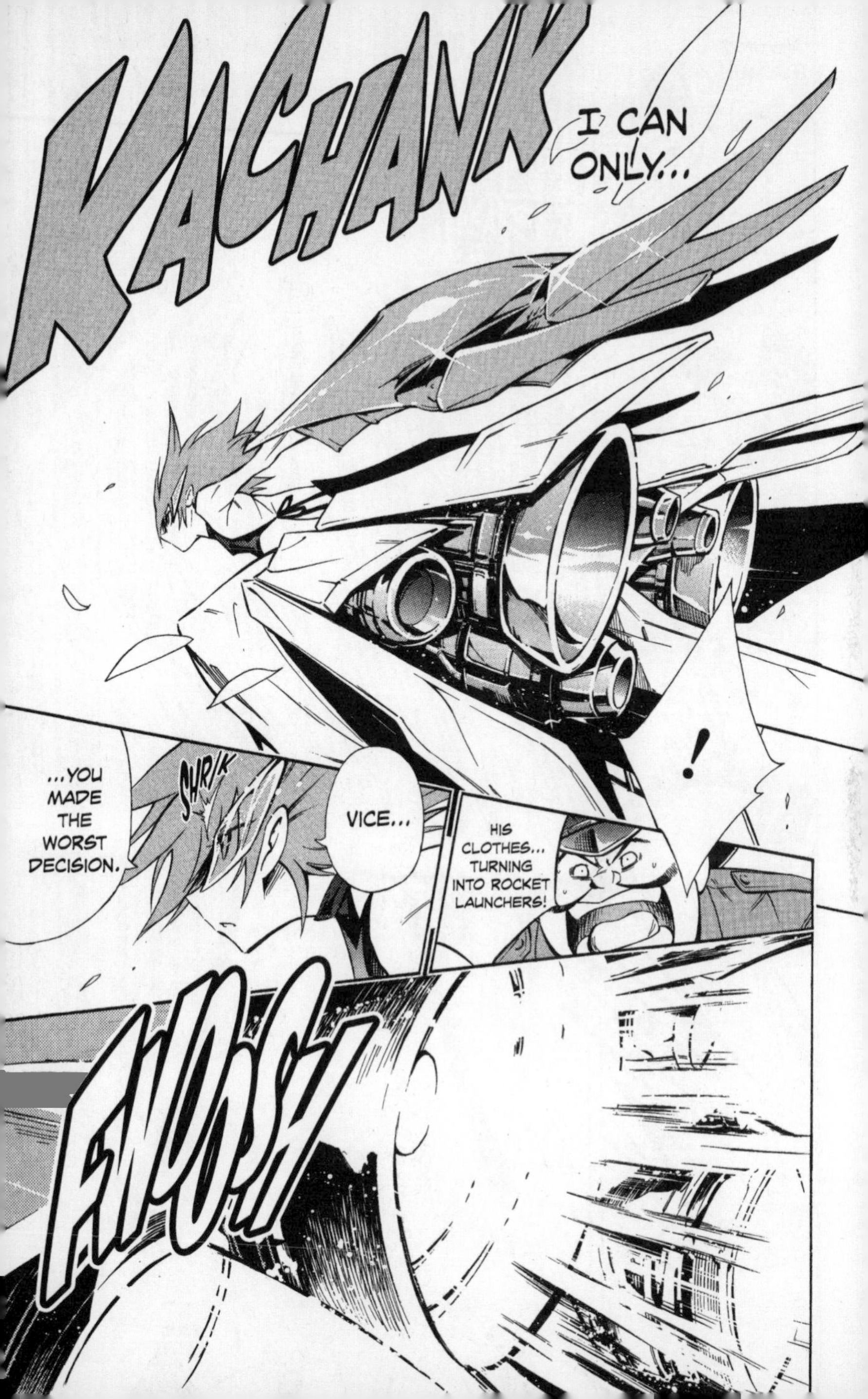
KACHANK
I CAN ONLY...
!
HIS CLOTHES... TURNING INTO ROCKET LAUNCHERS!
VICE...
SHRIK
...YOU MADE THE WORST DECISION.
FWOSH

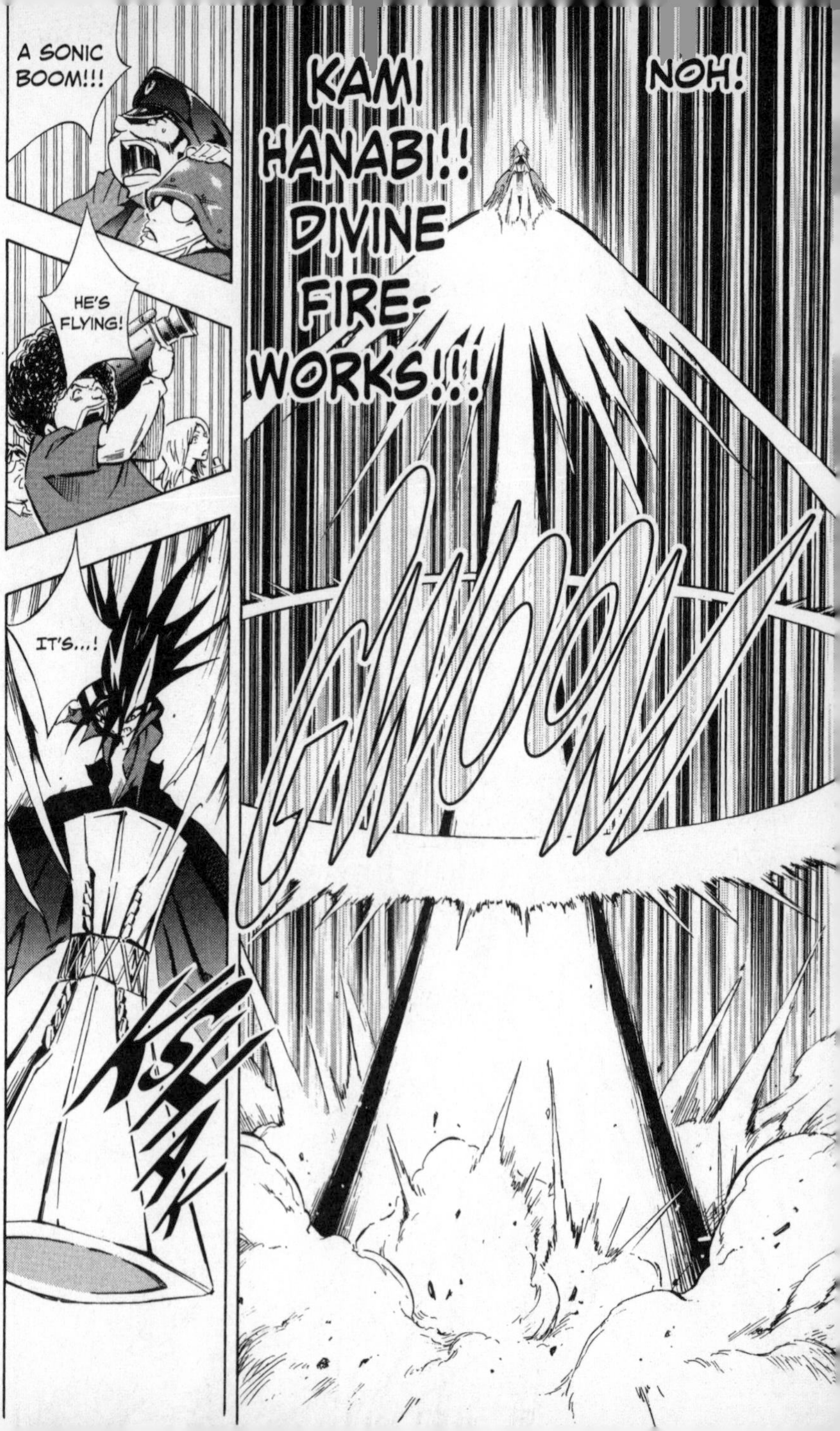
NOH!
KAMI HANABI!! DIVINE FIRE-WORKS!!!
A SONIC BOOM!!!
HE'S FLYING!
IT'S...!

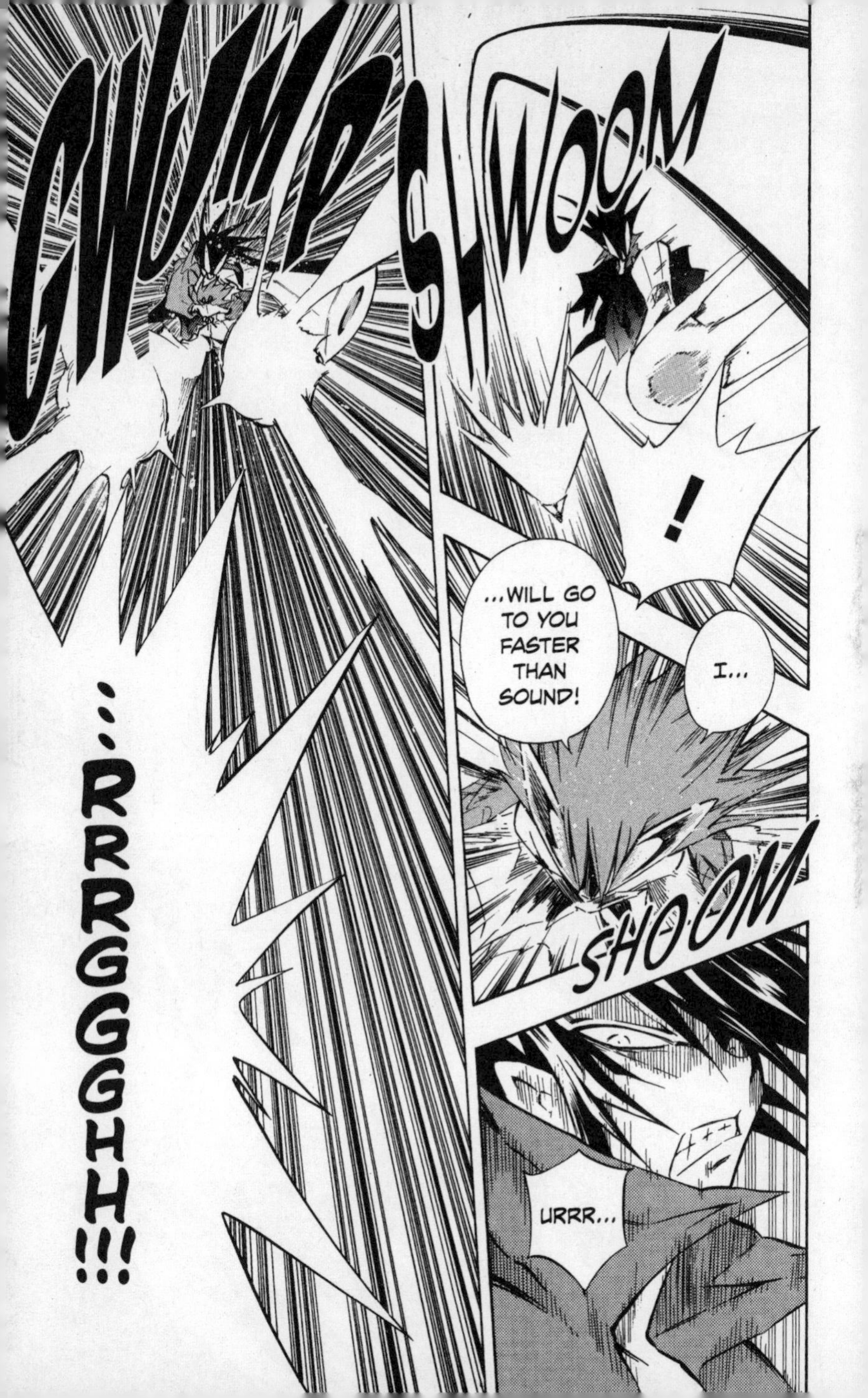
SHWOOM
!
I...
...WILL GO TO YOU FASTER THAN SOUND!
SHOOM
URRR...
GWUMP
...RRRGGGGHH!!!

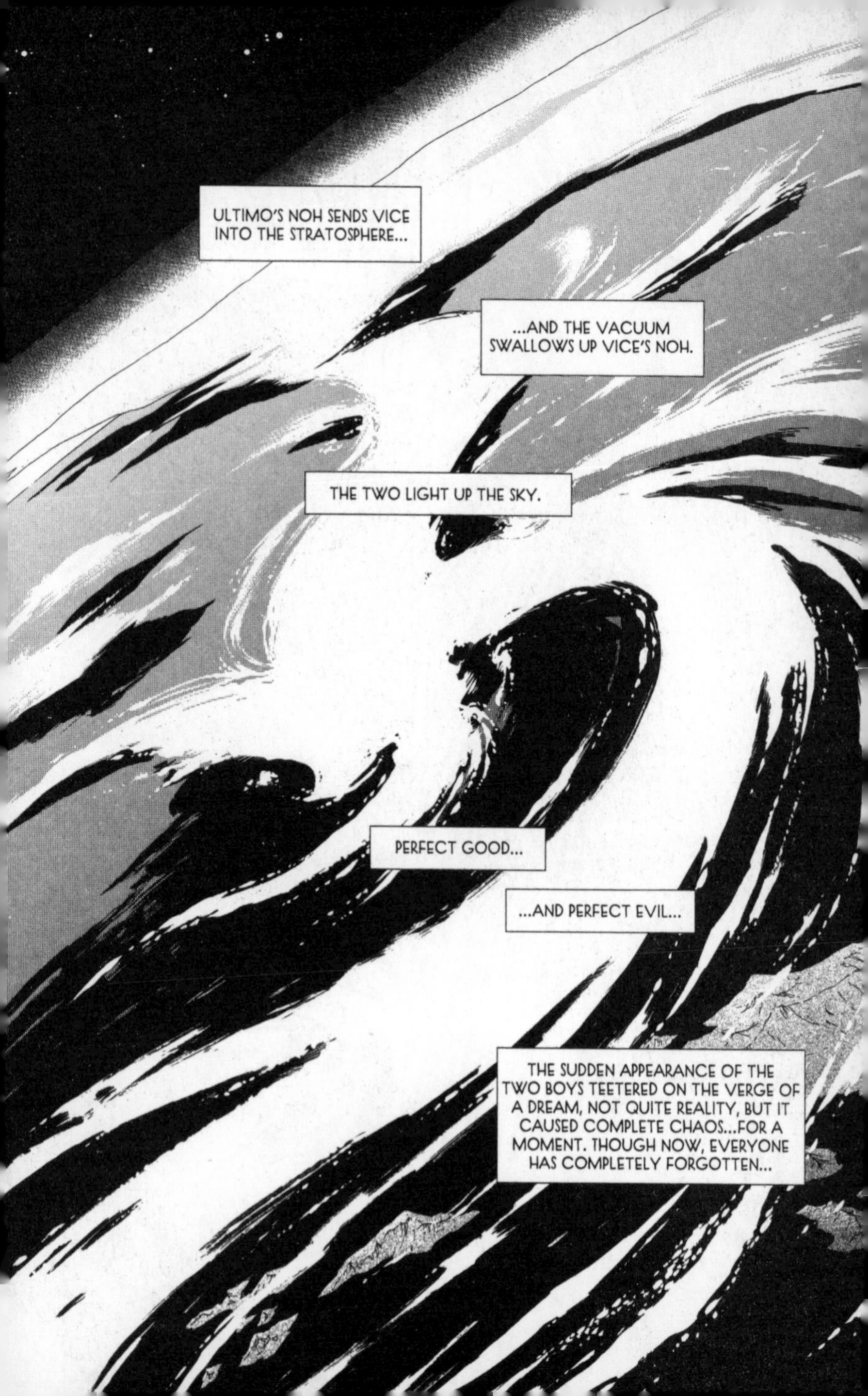
ULTIMO'S NOH SENDS VICE INTO THE STRATOSPHERE...
...AND THE VACUUM SWALLOWS UP VICE'S NOH.
THE TWO LIGHT UP THE SKY.
PERFECT GOOD...
...AND PERFECT EVIL...
THE SUDDEN APPEARANCE OF THE TWO BOYS TEETERED ON THE VERGE OF A DREAM, NOT QUITE REALITY, BUT IT CAUSED COMPLETE CHAOS...FOR A MOMENT. THOUGH NOW, EVERYONE HAS COMPLETELY FORGOTTEN...

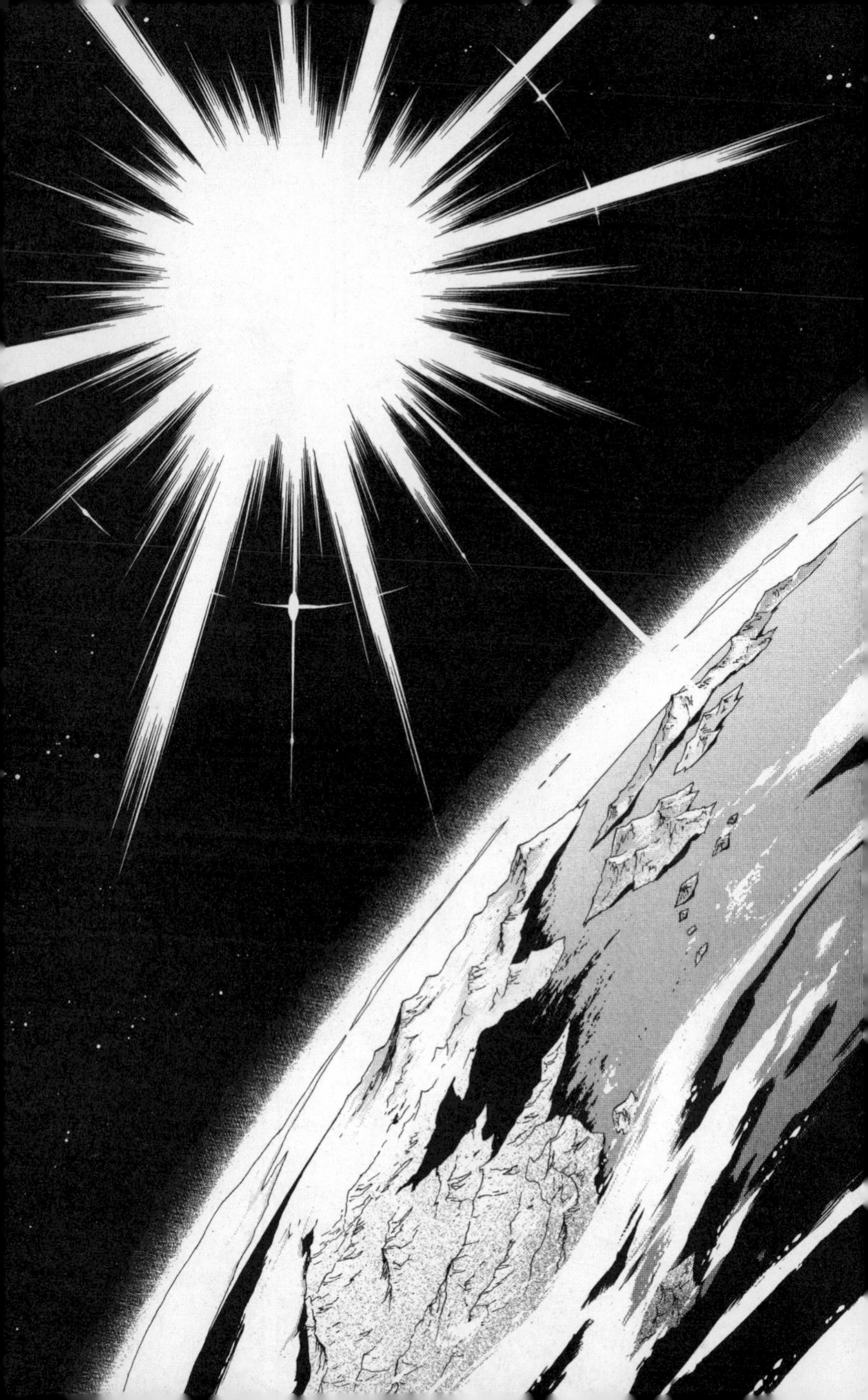

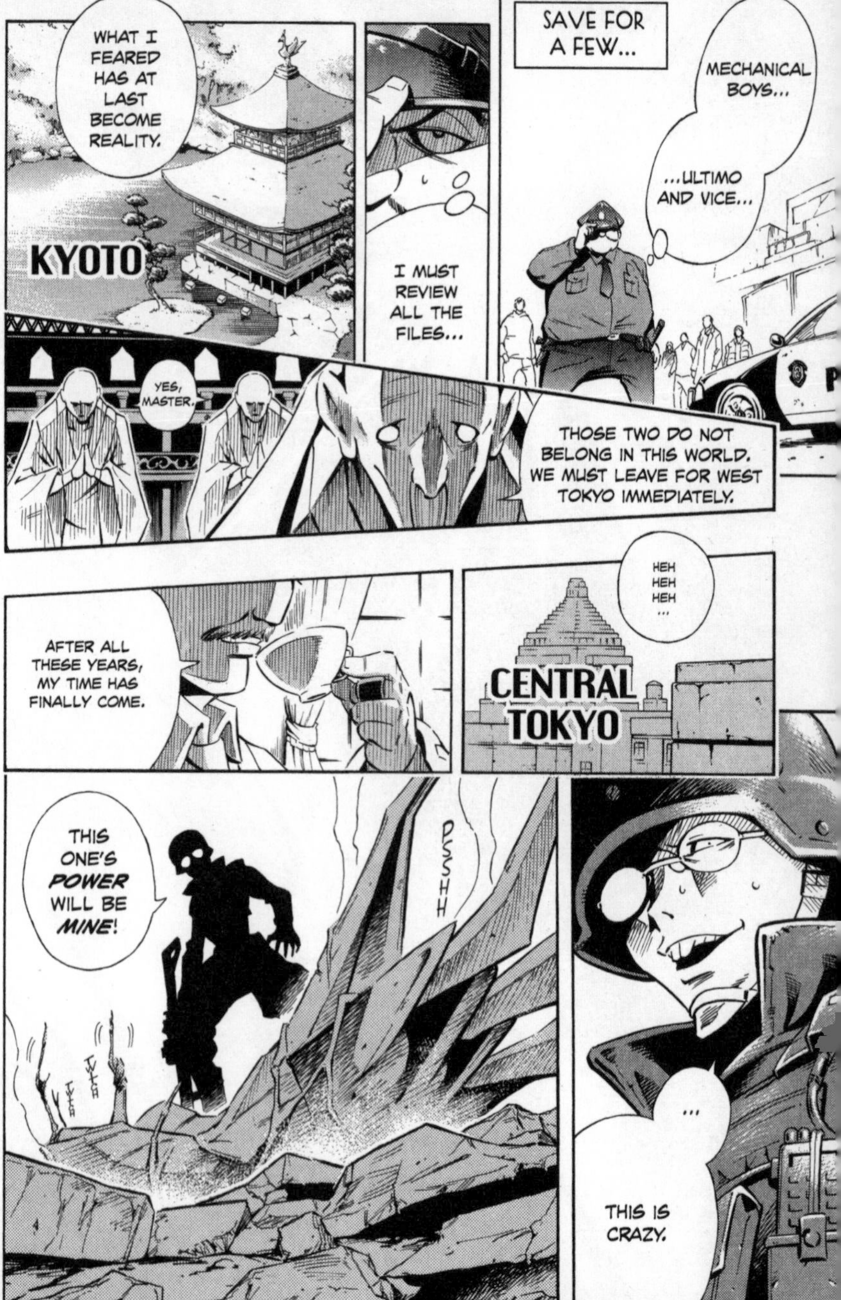
SAVE FOR A FEW...
MECHANICAL BOYS...
...ULTIMO AND VICE...
I MUST REVIEW ALL THE FILES...
WHAT I FEARED HAS AT LAST BECOME REALITY.
KYOTO
THOSE TWO DO NOT BELONG IN THIS WORLD. WE MUST LEAVE FOR WEST TOKYO IMMEDIATELY.
YES, MASTER.
HEH HEH HEH...
CENTRAL TOKYO
AFTER ALL THESE YEARS, MY TIME HAS FINALLY COME.
...
THIS IS CRAZY.
THIS ONE'S *POWER* WILL BE *MINE*!
PSSHH
TWITCH
TWITCH

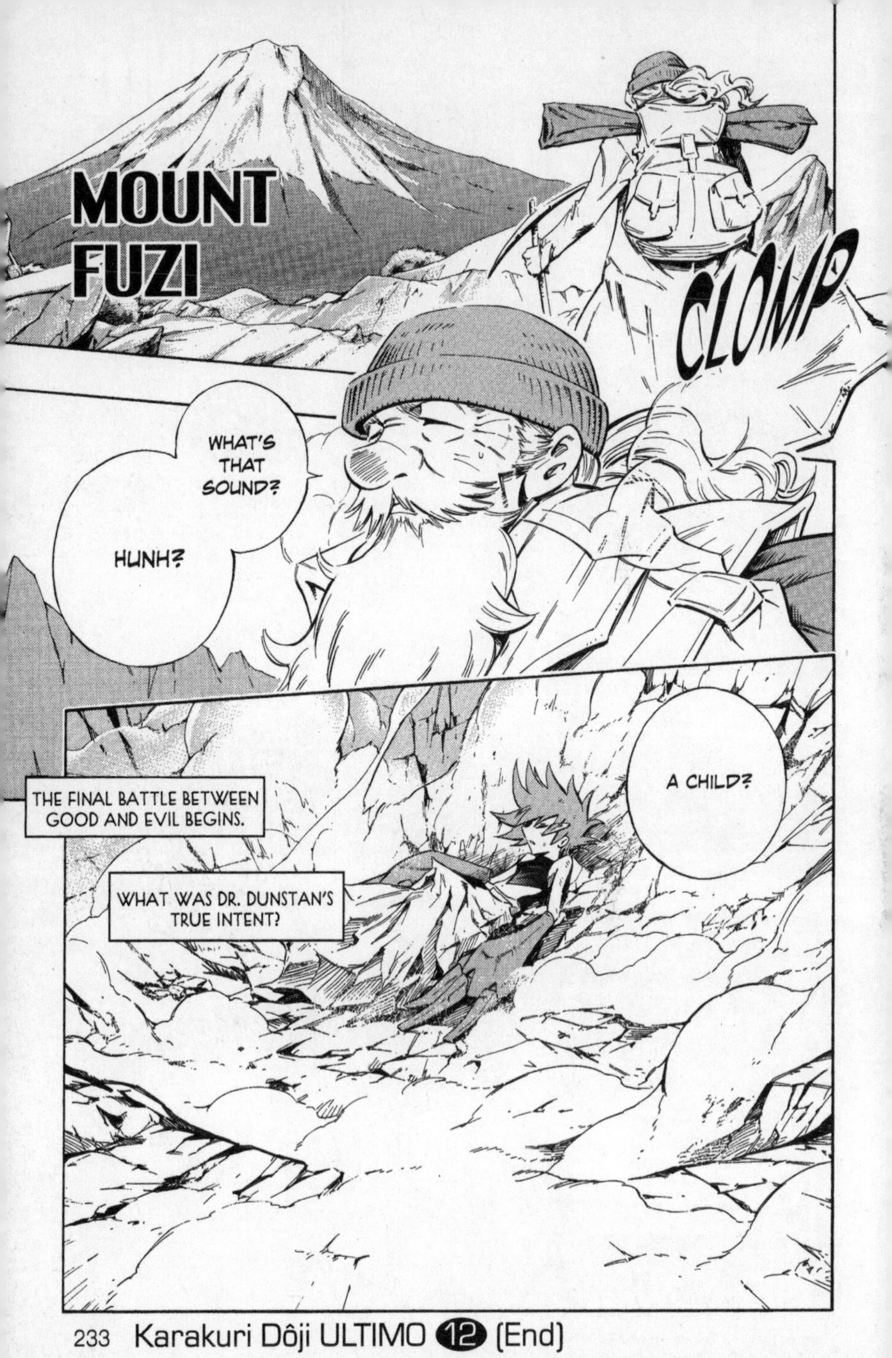
MOUNT FUZI
CLOMP
WHAT'S THAT SOUND?
HUNH?
A CHILD?
THE FINAL BATTLE BETWEEN GOOD AND EVIL BEGINS.
WHAT WAS DR. DUNSTAN'S TRUE INTENT?

ULTIMO

Volume 12

Original Concept: Stan Lee
Story and Art by: Hiroyuki Takei

SHONEN JUMP ADVANCED Manga Edition

Translation | John Werry
Series Touch-up Art & Lettering | James Gaubatz
Design | Fawn Lau
Editor | Megan Bates

Printed in the U.S.A.

Published by VIZ Media, LLC
P.O. Box 77010
San Francisco, CA 94107

10 9 8 7 6 5 4 3 2 1
First printing, December 2016

www.viz.com   www.shonenjump.com

STAN LEE

As a kid, Stanley Martin Lieber spent a lot of time dreaming up wild adventures. By the time he got to high school, he was putting his imagination to work writing stories at Timely, a publishing company that went on to become the legendary Marvel Comics. Starting with the *Fantastic Four*, Lee and his partner Jack Kirby created just about every superhero you can think of, including *Spider-Man*, the *X-Men*, the *Hulk*, *Iron Man*, *Daredevil* and *Thor*. Along the way, he wrote under many pen names, but the one that stuck was Stan Lee.

HIROYUKI TAKEI

Unconventional author/artist Hiroyuki Takei began his career by winning the coveted Hop Step Award (for new manga artists) and the Osamu Tezuka Cultural Prize (named after the famous artist of the same name). After working as an assistant to famed artist Nobuhiro Watsuki, Takei debuted in *Weekly Shonen Jump* in 1997 with *Butsu Zone*, an action series based on Buddhist mythology. His multicultural adventure manga *Shaman King*, which debuted in 1998, became a hit and was adapted into an anime TV series. Takei lists Osamu Tezuka, American comics and robot anime among his many influences.

STAN LEE

I'm delighted that *Ultimo* has been so popular for so long. He's one of my favorite characters, and it's good to know that our Japanese friends feel the same way about him as I do.

Excelsior!
Stan Lee

ORIGINALLY PUBLISHED IN JUMP SQUARE, NO. 19, VOLS. 17–18, 2015.

THE ACTION-PACKED SUPERHERO COMEDY ABOUT ONE MAN'S AMBITION TO BE A HERO FOR FUN!
ONE-PUNCH MAN
STORY BY ONE
ART BY YUSUKE MURATA
ONE-PUNCH MAN
01
YUSUKE MURATA
SHONEN JUMP MANGA
Nothing about Saitama passes the eyeball test when it comes to superheroes, from his lifeless expression to his bald head to his unimpressive physique. However, this average-looking guy has a not-so-average problem—he just can't seem to find an opponent strong enough to take on!
Can he finally find an opponent who can go toe-to-toe with him and give his life some meaning? Or is he doomed to a life of superpowered boredom?
ONE-PUNCH MAN © 2012 by ONE, Yusuke Murata/SHUEISHA Inc.
SHONEN JUMP
VIZ media
www.viz.com

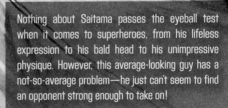

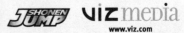

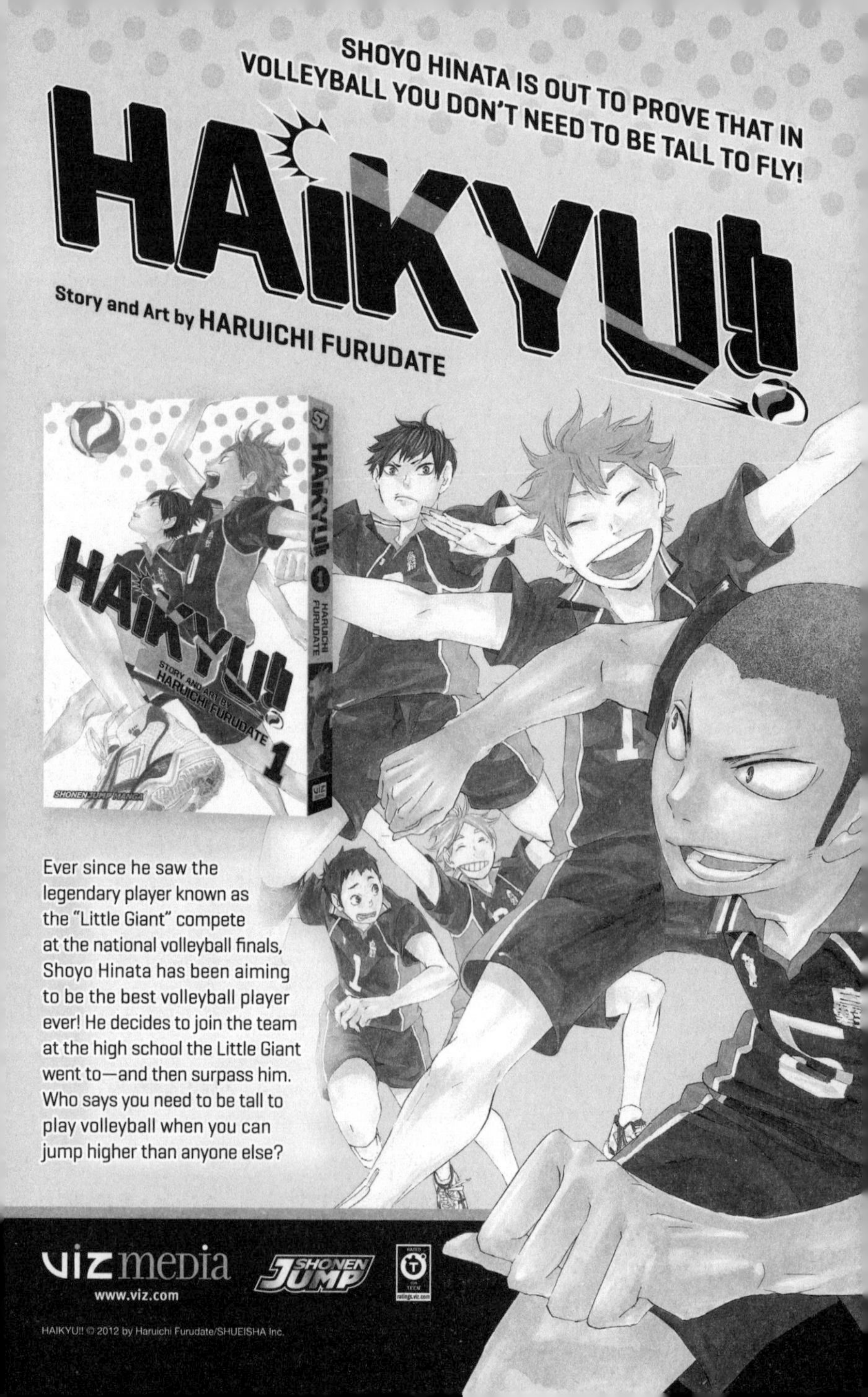

SHOYO HINATA IS OUT TO PROVE THAT IN VOLLEYBALL YOU DON'T NEED TO BE TALL TO FLY!
HAIKYU!!
Story and Art by HARUICHI FURUDATE
HAIKYU!! 1
STORY AND ART BY HARUICHI FURUDATE
SHONEN JUMP MANGA
Ever since he saw the legendary player known as the "Little Giant" compete at the national volleyball finals, Shoyo Hinata has been aiming to be the best volleyball player ever! He decides to join the team at the high school the Little Giant went to—and then surpass him. Who says you need to be tall to play volleyball when you can jump higher than anyone else?
viz media
www.viz.com
SHONEN JUMP
HAIKYU!! © 2012 by Haruichi Furudate/SHUEISHA Inc.

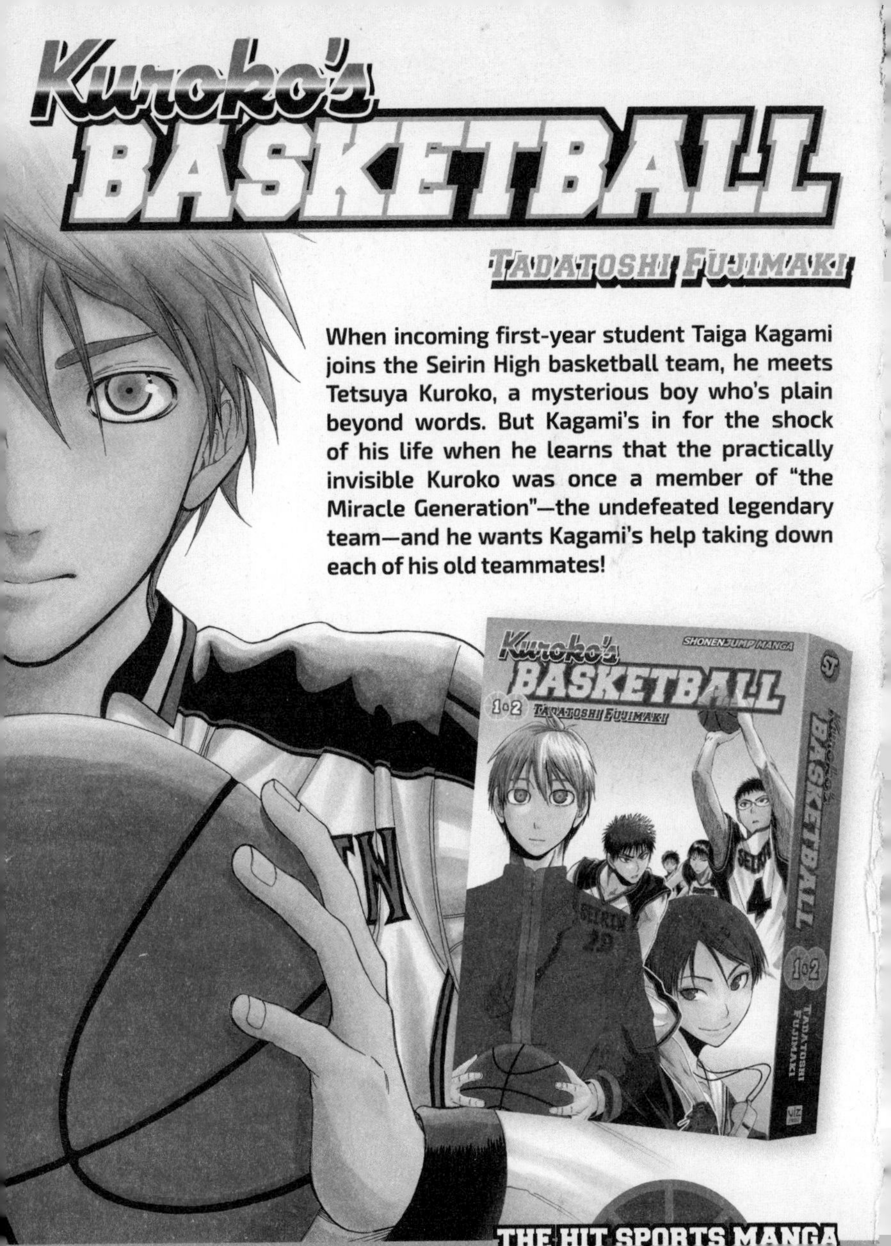
Kuroko's BASKETBALL
TADATOSHI FUJIMAKI
When incoming first-year student Taiga Kagami joins the Seirin High basketball team, he meets Tetsuya Kuroko, a mysterious boy who's plain beyond words. But Kagami's in for the shock of his life when he learns that the practically invisible Kuroko was once a member of "the Miracle Generation"—the undefeated legendary team—and he wants Kagami's help taking down each of his old teammates!
SHONENJUMP MANGA
Kuroko's BASKETBALL
1•2
TADATOSHI FUJIMAKI
SEIRIN
THE HIT SPORTS MANGA

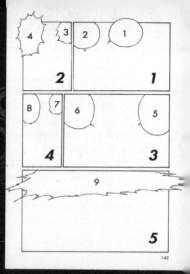

← Follow the action this way

THIS IS THE LAST PAGE

ULTIMO has been printed in th
original Japanese format in order t
preserve the orientation of the origina
artwork.

Please turn it around and begi
reading from right to left. Unlik
English, Japanese is read right to left
so Japanese comics are read in revers
order from the way English comic
are typically read. Have fun with it!